BARBARY LEGEND

Algiers from the sea in the late seventeenth century

BARBARY LEGEND

WAR, TRADE AND PIRACY
IN NORTH AFRICA
1415–1830

BY

SIR GODFREY FISHER

GREENWOOD PRESS, PUBLISHERS
WESTPORT, CONNECTICUT

Library of Congress Cataloging in Publication Data

Fisher, Sir Godfrey, 1885-
    Barbary legend; war, trade, and piracy in North
Africa, 1415-1830.

    Reprint of the ed. published by Clarendon Press,
Oxford.
    Bibliography: p.
    1. Africa, North--History--1517-1882. 2. Great
Britain--Foreign relations--Africa, North. 3. Africa,
North--Foreign relations--Great Britain. 4. Pirates.
I. Title.
DT201.F5 1974   961'.02   74-9166
ISBN 0-8371-7617-4

PREFACE

SOME personal explanation might be expected of the temerity of a writer, without any recognized qualifications of academic training or specialized knowledge, presuming to put forward views radically different from those believed to be sanctioned by long usage. Indulgence might, however, be claimed for the fact that, so far from having been influenced by personal prepossession for any geographical, racial, or religious issues that might be involved, my interest was at first aroused by pure accident and pursued with some reluctance. It was only when I received encouragement from far better judges to undertake a study, described as long overdue, that I ventured to embark on such an unpromising task.

Denigration or iconoclasm for its own sake offers no attraction. My object has been to carry on this study as conscientiously as possible through the medium of eye-witnesses or other contemporary evidence. What may appear to be its fanciful title was, in fact, suggested to me, perhaps quite unconsciously, by one of our most eminent historians. A tendency towards advocacy or selectivity may be excusable, and indeed inevitable, in an attempt to portray a singular type of community which has long vanished and, through no fault of its own, has left little record behind, except such as can be extracted from alien archives or narratives. A brief sketch of an institution, which practically spanned the gulf between the Middle Ages and the Victorian era, and was noted alike for its originality and its continuity, must obviously present great difficulties and, in the special circumstances, leave much room for speculation. I greatly regret that considerations of space have not permitted fuller discussion of many questions that are necessarily intricate in themselves and controversial in their application, or anything more than passing glances at those other states of Barbary, whose history and institutions differed from it in so many essentials.

The longer I have studied the subject the more conscious I have become of the great complexity of Mediterranean history and the fascinating vistas that still lie open to a student with the requisite qualifications and facilities. Three difficulties with which I have found myself constantly faced seem to be specially worthy of note.

In the first place, the very elaborate bibliographies annexed to well-known French works appear to attach surprisingly little importance to our own—often ampler—sources of information.

Secondly, I have failed to find any clear or consistent guide to the principles of public law or naval and diplomatic practices, by which international issues were supposed to be interpreted and regulated. The fundamental questions involved are so complex that little more can be attempted in a work of this nature than to emphasize their obscurities and apparent contradictions.

The third difficulty is the more obvious because it appears to result from the other two. It renders untenable the common assumption that there does actually exist a definite, agreed view about that area which it would be idle, and even unwarrantable, to disturb at this late date. We are, in fact, confronted with at least four incompatible presentations of the subject, which are still recognized.

The first represents a strongly anglophobe tendency, which lays the blame for French difficulties with Algiers less on the local rulers and inhabitants than on the *éternelles convoitises* of England. In the view of de Grammont, 'the long battle of intrigue, which Great Britain maintained from the seventeenth century to assume its predominance over the *Odjeac*, all those dark manœuvres which entailed the expenditure of so much gold and the effusion of all that innocent blood', culminated after all in the accomplishment of the natural destiny and altruistic mission of France. Similarly, in his naval histories of the eighteenth century, Lacour-Gayet depicts Britain as the 'Monster' beside whose violence and illegalities the acts of Algiers ships were mere trivialities.

The second picture represents the Christian powers meekly submitting to incessant insults and depredations from the pirates, or states, of Barbary during a period of three centuries, until the 'conscience of Europe' was unexpectedly awoken from beyond the Atlantic.

According to a third view, which emanates mainly from biographical material, our naval commanders periodically policed the Mediterranean, exercised superintendence over its southern shore, and administered to the Barbary corsairs or pirates 'severe beatings', whenever their patience was exhausted.

A fourth concept suggests plainly that if Britain had any relations with Barbary at all they were of insufficient interest to warrant any mention. Some support for such a view can be found in the remarkable omission from so many serious works, English and foreign, contemporary and modern, of concrete information about maritime activities by the Barbaresques or antagonism to them from other people of the Mediterranean seaboard. The contrast between the flourishing shores of southern Europe and their neglected and often lawless hinterland is no less significant than the singular silence in general histories about those ports which were so closely connected with North Africa and Turkey. Travellers tended to specialize in archaeological research.

The destruction, during the Napoleonic Wars, of the records and traditions of historic consulates and factories, while British enterprise continued the process of expanding commercial and imperial interests elsewhere, was responsible for an almost complete breach with the past. Continuity with the Middle Ages was ended by the final elimination of the famous city-states. Victorian preference for escape into a world of facile romance is illustrated by the popularity of Prescott's picturesque presentation of the Mediterranean scene and the neglect of contemporaneous British and French publications, which might have served to provide a more factual and continuous picture of events and conditions in North Africa. Accuracy of fact or phrase was of decreasing importance.

The purpose of this study can, in my view, best be served by restricting its scope within narrow and clearly defined limits, through concentration, as far as possible, on examination of our relations with the Mediterranean, or Turkish, part of Barbary in the light of contemporary evidence, especially from English sources. Its most natural starting-point would appear to be that early period of modern history which witnessed the initial clashes of Mediterranean and Atlantic forces in the struggle for maritime supremacy and the first permanent establishment of Christian power in North Africa. Even in the year of Agincourt the English were far from indifferent to such issues in Barbary or in their own waters. Similarly, a logical termination of a vitally important period of historical evolution may be found in the peace of Utrecht, with Britain at last firmly established as a maritime power in the Mediterranean and a recognized ally of the Turkish regencies.

In the absence of any apparent uniformity in regard to Turkish and Arab titles I have thought it advisable to refer to statesmen and admirals by their best-known titles, whether chronologically correct or not. The use of the word 'English' seems more appropriate as a rule than 'British', since our consular organization, factories, merchant marine, and navy were all essentially English up to the Union. The first Scot of note only arrived at Algiers after that date, perhaps as the master of a Swedish vessel.

The Barbary States consist of the three Turkish regencies of Algiers, Tunis, and Tripoli, together with the empire of Morocco, and the word 'Barbaresques' is normally used, for convenience rather than strict accuracy, to comprise all the inhabitants of that area. For the purpose of this book the Mediterranean is the sea which lies between Gibraltar and Sicily; the Levant extends from Malta and the Adriatic to the Turkish seaboard; and the expression 'Mediterranean area' is used to include Italian, Spanish, and Portuguese territory from Zante, Corfu, and Ragusa to Madeira, the Canaries, and the Azores. In regard to dates the modern chronological year is employed. In quotations italics are mine unless otherwise stated.

My special thanks are due to Mr. John Walter and Mr. C. R. Edgeley for their kind assistance and advice in regard to the preparation and publication of this book; to Professor D. B. Horn, whose sympathetic interest and generous help first enabled me to embark on the pleasures of historical research; to Sir George Clark and Mr. David Ogg for the very welcome encouragement that they have given me; to Mr. John Ehrman, Mr. J. N. Blakiston, and Mr. Christopher Lloyd for their kindness in reading and advising me about my early script; and to the staffs of the Reading Rooms at the British Museum and Public Record Office; and of the London Library and Folkestone Public Library, particularly their reference sections, for their constant co-operation and patience. It is a source of keen regret that I have not had greater opportunities of availing myself of the facilities and courtesy of the Department of Western Manuscripts at the Bodleian Library.

G. F.

CONTENTS

CONTENTS

'There is scarce a doubt . . . the Algerines are more friendly to the English than to any other nation. . . . The English consul, if a man of judgment and supported by his Government may accomplish more than the agent of any other nation. . . . The privileges and independence of the English consul always excite the jealousy of other agents.'

Official memorandum of CONSUL FALCON, 9 Dec. 1803, from Additional MS. 34921 in the British Museum

ABBREVIATIONS

Add. MSS.	Additional Manuscripts in the British Museum.
A.P.C.	Acts of the Privy Council.
A.P.C. (Col.)	Acts of the Privy Council, Colonial Series.
A.R.	*Annual Register.*
B.M.	British Museum.
Cal. H.O.	Calendar of Home Office Papers.
Cal. S.P. Col.	Calendar of State Papers Colonial.
Cal. S.P.D.	„ „ „ „ Domestic.
Cal. S.P.F.	„ „ „ „ Foreign.
Cal. S.P. Ireland	„ „ „ „ Ireland.
Cal. S.P. Spanish	„ „ „ „ Spanish.
C.M.H.	*Cambridge Modern History.*
Cotton MSS.	Cotton Manuscripts in the British Museum.
D.N.B.	*Dictionary of National Biography.*
E.B.	*Encyclopaedia Britannica,* 11th edition.
F.O.	Foreign Office.
G.M.	*Gentleman's Magazine.*
H.H.W.	*The Historian's History of the World.*
H.M.C.	Historical Manuscripts Commission.
IND.	Public Record Office, Index Series.
N.R.S.	Navy Records Society.
P.C.	Privy Council.
Pol. Hist.	*Political History of England,* ed. W. Hunt and R. Poole.
P.R.O.	Public Record Office.
Sloane MSS.	Sloane Manuscripts in the British Museum.
S.P.	State Papers at the Public Record Office.
V.S.P.	Venetian State Papers.

INTRODUCTION

A STUDENT of external relations with the units of Turkish Barbary, variously described as kingdoms, regencies, military republics, and piratical states, finds himself faced with a bewildering array of difficulties. Our official connexion with those places began only a few years before the Armada, though their waters and, perhaps, their ports had long been familiar to English ships and merchants. It was the direct outcome of antagonism to Spain, for which it is often the fashion to express sympathy in its struggle with our Moslem allies. At the same time it is customary to describe Turkish naval power as non-existent after the battle of Lepanto, and the subsequent career of the Barbary regencies, reduced to the role of 'petty pirates', as one of progressive decline, from 'fall to fall', until the French conquest of Algiers in 1830 freed the Mediterranean from the scourge which had terrorized it for three centuries, and laid under contribution the maritime powers of Europe and America.

Despite important interests, naval and commercial, in the Mediterranean and Levant English histories normally make no allusion to relations with the regencies, apart from references to Blake's activities on the Barbary coast[1]—usually in terms which would have greatly surprised the admiral himself, his immediate successors in the Mediterranean, or his superiors at home—and to Exmouth's operations in 1816,[2] of which there are still so many vague and conflicting versions. Even these events, though illustrating important developments in Mediterranean policy, may be entirely ignored. The attitude of the Levant Company towards North Africa is often very obscure. Little or no mention is made of the Barbary Company, which resulted from our first permanent commercial and political connexion with a Mohammedan country.[3]

[1] Ch. XII and App. K.

[2] Three variants are in *E.B.* i. 650, iii. 384, and x. 73. The 'imbecillity' and 'folly' of the expedition were condemned by St. Vincent, J. S. Tucker, *Memoirs of the Earl of St. Vincent*, 2 vols., London, 1844, ii. 412, and by Lord Holland, H.M.C. Dropmore Papers, x. 414. De Grammont, *Histoire d'Alger sous la domination turque* (*1516–1830*), pp. 376–80, &c.

[3] App. I. The absence of any reference to Barbary in Conyers Read, *Mr.*

Naval histories, too, not only omit much of the factual information that would normally be regarded as essential to the study of such operations, but generally ignore our first naval expedition to the Levant,[1] as well as the most important, best-documented, and least gratifying of England's wars with any of the Barbary States. As this war was stated by the king himself to have arisen through 'a certain misunderstanding' on both sides and to have been ended by a 'very honourable peace', which actually lasted for over 130 years, this field of our relations must be approached with a certain amount of misgiving.[2] It is not lessened by difficulty in reconciling rival versions, from various countries, of naval activities in those waters. This, together with constant recriminations between Christian powers, cannot fail to engender considerable suspicion about the accuracy of the picture which is usually presented to us.

A student will ordinarily search in vain for the normal ingredients of history, those specific details which enable us to assess the character of a country, its geography, economy, and administration, its attitude towards foreign relations and commerce, and the characteristics of its inhabitants. Above all, he is unlikely to find any precise information about what constituted 'Barbary' or our particular interest in that area and the methods that we employed to secure it. What, for instance, were the character, functions, and status of our consuls in the different states of Barbary? Are we prepared to accept either of the diametrically contradictory views on the subject enunciated by Lane-Poole and Plantet?[3] What were the text and purpose of our treaties? How were they negotiated and observed? Little satisfaction or enlightenment can be derived from sweeping generalizations, which are all too often improbable, inconsistent, or even contradictory.

If we admit that there is 'very little reliable record' of affairs in those states, while under Turkish rule, or that large portions

Secretary Walsingham and the Policy of Queen Elizabeth, 3 vols., Oxford, 1925, contrasts strangely with its political and commercial importance at that time.

[1] Sir Kenelm Digby's squadron, *Journal of a Voyage into the Mediterranean, 1628*, Camden Society, London, 1869—'not Pirates but Men of War belonging to Great Britain'.

[2] Rawlinson MS. A. 257, f. 67; Cal. S.P.D. 1682, p. 196; Hertslet's *Treaties*, i.

[3] Lane-Poole, *The Barbary Corsairs*, p. 260; Plantet, *Correspondance des deys d'Alger avec la cour de France, 1579–1830* (Paris, 1889), i, p. lxiv.

of their history are 'very obscure', or that their institutions are of no interest to us, what confidence can be placed in categorical assertions that during three centuries not a day passed without the arrival of at least one prize at Algiers, whose inhabitants down to the 'humblest fellah' lived by the fruits of piracy alone, or that it had the 'most execrable government that ever existed in the basin of the Mediterranean', or that its interior was the scene of 'the most horrible perpetual anarchy'?[1]

If, on the other hand, it is correct that 'an abundant literature survives from which every detail of life in the pirate towns is known',[2] how do we account for our almost exclusive reliance upon writers whose acquaintance with Barbary was extremely slender, such as Jovius, Dan, and Rycaut, and for the existence of so much inconsistency and contradiction? Why is there so little reference in the histories of Playfair and de Grammont, for example, to the actual experiences of the many men who knew those countries and their inhabitants well, and have recorded them in an objective and, at times, appreciative manner?

To a large extent the regencies have been the victims of history in a singularly unscientific form. It is customary for accounts of them to cease abruptly with the capitulation of the city of Algiers and a conventional happy ending,[3] consisting in this case of the deliverance of the Mediterranean from a scourge which had lasted, according to various historians, for three, or six, centuries or even from the days of the Carthaginians.

Had, however, the regency of Algiers come to an equally abrupt end before it was involuntarily involved in the devastating sequel to the French Revolution, we might have been disposed to view it in a totally different light. The description of conditions there by the very experienced Venture de Paradis[4] compares very favourably with Young's contemporary account of France or with Britain as revealed in the *Gentleman's Magazine* and *Annual Register* of that period or later depicted by Halévy

---

[1] Soames, *The Coast of Barbary*, p. 153; de Grammont, pp. i and ii.

[2] Soames, p. 146.

[3] De Grammont, Playfair, *Scourge of Christendom*, *Annals of British Relations with Algiers prior to the French Conquest*, and E. Le Marchand, *L'Europe et la conquête d'Alger*, Paris, 1913. Compare *G.M.* 1830, ii. 70, with *A.R.* 1830, p. 234.

[4] Later adviser to Bonaparte in Egypt.

or Mantoux. The merchants of Marseilles were nervous about its increasing competition, even in their home market, and Pitt may have felt surprise and envy at a consular report on its mode of government.[1] At the same time another consul held up Tunis as a model of administration, and a Scottish merchant has left us an enthusiastic picture of its maritime and inland commerce.[2] Even Tripoli was cited as a pleasant consular post, especially on account of the great respect shown to Christians.[3] Though Algerine forces had just attracted public attention by helping to restore the sultan's fortunes in Egypt, Syria, and Greece,[4] the regencies had practically ceased to be maritime states and 'Christian slavery', as we termed it, hardly existed.

Or, again, our attitude might have been very different before the fateful assembly of the Congress of Vienna, at a time when the three regencies could still be regarded as our oldest and best-conducted allies, and their so-called piracies consisted mainly in the questionable or definitely illegal acts committed by the Christian powers against each other in their waters.[5] While Algiers and Tunis had suffered severely from the long Anglo-French struggle, the inhabitants of the 'piratical port' of Tripoli, which was curiously destitute of ships and seamen, were described as 'truly blest' in the possession of judicial, administrative, economic, and social advantages unequalled in Europe.[6]

By 1830 all this had been forgotten. It was throughout Europe an extremely critical year, which for Metternich pre-saged the ending of the old era, and, as so often during the previous three centuries, Christian relations with Barbary and 'les pauvres diables de Turcs', as the Prince de Ligne had called them, were determined largely by the necessities and

[1] Masson, *Établissements français dans l'Afrique barbaresque*, pp. 584-5; F.O. 3/7, 13 July 1791; Venture, *Alger au XVIIIe siècle*, p. 257, pp. 96-99.

[2] F.O. 77/3, 16 Feb. 1792; MacGill, *An Account of Tunis, its Government, &c.*; Poiret, *Voyage en Barbarie*; Plantet's Introduction to *Correspondances des beys de Tunis*.

[3] Tully, *Narrative of Ten Years Residence at Tripoli in Africa*, pp. 38 and 218.

[4] For Ghazi Hassan, 'the Algerine', see Finlay, *History of Greece*, v. 258-68; Creasey, *History of the Ottoman Turks*, p. 392, &c.; *H.H.W.* xxiv. 420-1. For Greek war, Le Marchand, p. 150, and *G.M.* 1827, ii. 552.

[5] *A.R.* 1816, p. 328, quoting *Quarterly Review*, and criticisms by St. Vincent, Nelson, &c.

[6] Blaquiere, *Letters from the Mediterranean*, ii. 80; F.O. 76/9; *G.M.* 1820, i. 74.

rivalries of the Christian powers themselves.[1] The French government, which less than fifty years before had regarded the dissolution of the Ottoman empire as a 'nightmare', now saw in it the opportunity for escaping from its internal difficulties.[2] The occupation of Algiers was regarded as only one of several alternatives, which included compensating the King of Holland for the rape of Belgium with the throne of Constantinople and inciting Egypt to rebel against the sultan and seize his possessions in Barbary. Apart from very pertinent financial considerations, the Algerine adventure possessed the advantage that no other country, especially Britain, was in a position to interfere. Indeed, relief was actually felt at finding a 'safety-valve' for the restless ambitions of France in such a remote and unpromising field.[3] The chief architect of the adventure later described it as a blunder. The ideals of benefiting the Mediterranean area by introducing into North Africa a higher civilization and Christian principles appear to have been a development, rather than a cause, of the occupation.[4]

The amazing ignorance of conditions in north-west Africa at that time is indicative of contemporary apathy towards it. At the beginning of the century our consul in Morocco complained that more books had been written about Barbary and that less was known about it than anywhere in the world, and an intelligent British merchant thought the best work on the subject was still that of Leo, written in the reign of Henry VIII. In France Algeria had become *un immense inconnu*. The newly appointed minister, who presented the case for the expedition

[1] Compare Nelson's attitude with proposal in 1802, Sir J. Marriott, *Castlereagh*, London, 1936, pp. 97–98. Also our 'paramount' policy of 'political expedience' at Constantinople and Egypt, *A.R.* 1807, pp. 293 and 345, and *G.M.* 1807, i. 472.

[2] Charles-Roux, *France et Afrique du Nord avant 1830*, pp. 360–1. 'Cauchemar traditionnel de notre diplomatie à la fin du 18ᵉ et au commencement du 19ᵉ siècle', partly as facilitating penetration of Barbary by rivals; and, earlier, p. 307, 'la Cour de Versailles tenait l'intérêt pour satisfait et même bien servi par l'existence des États barbaresques', a view held by France and Britain in 1826.

[3] G. Esquer, *La Prise d'Alger*, Paris, 1923, pp. 122–5. Polignac adopted the project as offering France 'une diversion à leurs tristesses nationales, une satisfaction à leur besoin d'activité militaire et de gloire, enfin un avantage politique'. He also relied on French 'nostalgie de l'épopée napoléonienne', Charles-Roux, p. 500. It proved a 'victoire lucrative': Esquer, p. 387; Lord, *Algiers with Notices of the Neighbouring States of Barbary*, i. 121–2.

[4] A French deputy mentioned such ideals in June 1830, and suggested using Algiers for preying on British ships, Charles-Roux, p. 705, a revival in principle of Monson's project of 1620.

of 1830, evidently knew little about it, and a harassed general staff even sought enlightenment in Robertson's *Charles the Fifth*.[1]

Pellissier de Reynaud, the studious and sympathetic official who has left us such an informative account of Algeria in the early days of its occupation, had only a vague knowledge of the causes of the dispute. His sole information regarding the economy of the regency was derived from a very misleading report by an American consul in 1822. He believed that it had always prohibited the export of grain, though that had in fact been called 'the sole and constant' support of France during the critical years of the Directory and the primary cause of the Franco-Algerine rupture.

Such ignorance was by no means exceptional. Esquer has commented on the strange failure of the opposition speakers to make any allusion to 'l'importance politique et économique d'Alger ou au rôle qu'avaient joué les concessions d'Afrique dans le ravitaillement de la France', and their example has been only too faithfully followed. The unlucky consular report has been frequently used as the sole basis for important deductions, in spite of the fact that in this century a writer has unwittingly quoted on one page the now consecrated figure for Algerine foreign trade of £175,000 a year and on another, apparently from our own archives, of £7,000,000.[2]

The resulting failure to appreciate the essential economic interdependence of North Africa and southern Europe, of which the incorporation of Algeria in France was only a logical and mutually beneficial development, has had a profound and lasting effect on our historical treatment of that area. It has helped to foster the illusion of the Mediterranean as a peculiar hot-bed of piracy, which was brought more or less under control from the time of Blake by Christian warships, and of its southern shore as the abode of fanatics and outlaws, whose only

---

[1] J. G. Jackson, *The Empire of Morocco*, 3rd ed., London, 1814, p. vii; Nettement, *Histoire de la conquête d'Alger*, pp. 513–14; Charles-Roux, pp. 684–5. For speech and debate see Nettement, pp. 211–15, and 'Manifeste du Ministère'; Garrot, *Histoire générale d'Algérie*, pp. 665–8. Pananti, *Narrative of a Residence in Algiers*, p. 99, mentions 'extreme want of information about the interior of Tunis, Tripoli and Algiers'. Literature available is in J. Alézard, *Histoire et historiens de l'Algérie* (Collection du Centenaire de l'Algérie), Paris, 1931, pp. 161–2.

[2] G. B. Laurie, *French Conquest*, London, 1909, pp. 20 and 55.

resource, in the absence of trade, industry, and agriculture, lay in constant ruthless depredation on Christian commerce. Such a picture, however convenient to the tortuous politics of the age or gratifying to the chauvinism of more modern times, finds little support in contemporary records. They leave no room for doubt that our commerce suffered chiefly from the violence of Christian corsairs or pirates, especially in English and Aegean waters, and that its difficulties were intensified by the rivalries of regular naval units in the Mediterranean.[1]

It obscures, moreover, the whole basis of our relations with the Barbary coast, which were concerned with the essential value of its port facilities and supplies, not only for our merchant vessels but for the maintenance of warships, naval bases, and military operations in the Mediterranean. This fact was realized continuously from the time of the Armada to the Peninsular War, and a principal object of our strategy throughout that period was to ensure these facilities for our own needs and prevent their enjoyment by the enemy. Corbett's inexplicable omission of all reference to so clearly recognized a fact has resulted in much misunderstanding.[2]

While the French conquerors quickly found, as Christian visitors had so often done in the past, that conditions were very different from what they had been led to believe, the citizens of Paris received the triumphant news with indifference, and the last of the Deys, who appears to have been more respected and regretted in his country than George IV and Charles X in theirs, received a cordial welcome at Naples and Leghorn. Aberdeen, unlike Castlereagh, attached great importance to the strategic position of Algiers and continued to regard it as an integral part of the Ottoman empire.[3] In this he followed Wellington's instructions. Our consul is described in 1841 as holding his *exequatur* from the sultan.[4]

British interest in the maintenance of the *status quo* in that area was not, however, accompanied by any precise information about the Barbary States themselves, which it had become

[1] Ch. VI, X, and XII. [2] Ch. XV.

[3] He told the French Algiers was always considered most important because of its geographical position, Charles-Roux, p. 669. Wellington thought the French were mad, Esquer, p. 175. So did Talleyrand, p. 306, n. 2.

[4] *Diary and Correspondence of Henry Wellesley, First Lord Cowley*, ed. Hon. F. A. Wellesley, London, 1928, p. 212.

the official practice—despite the existence of four separate governments and four distinct sets of treaties—to regard as a single unit. The future Lord Cowley in 1830 spoke of the 'Barbary States' as under the suzerainty of the sultan, and long afterwards his grandson explained that Algiers was 'the capital of the Barbary States and a centre of piracy'. Even so authoritative a writer as Fulton is almost equally vague,[1] and it has become a common practice to use the adjective in a sense that is really meaningless and consequently misleading. A definition by our courts of the early nineteenth century to determine the correct meaning of the term 'Barbary' in a charter-party or insurance policy would be most instructive.[2]

The creation of a legend to satisfy the racial and religious prejudices, the chauvinism, conscious rectitude, and imperialistic impulse of the late nineteenth century was only natural and perhaps inevitable. In a new age of steam and electricity and power politics the existence of small independent Mediterranean states, however historic, of piracy and privateering and legalized slavery must have seemed strangely remote. Even writers of expert works on our Eastern possessions and policy spoke of 'Asiatics' as a single unit and the working of the 'oriental mind' as a uniform phenomenon. The connotation of the term 'Moslem' primarily included despotic government, fanatical intolerance, and almost sadistic cruelty. 'Turk' was an epithet of opprobrium used in our nurseries.[3]

In course of time Mohammedan and pirate seem to have become synonymous terms. Even Lepanto, usually regarded as one of the greatest and most decisive battles of all time, the culmination of the long series of Crusades, has been described as a united effort to crush 'Moslem piracy'.[4] Its immediate sequel, the obsequious courtship of the vanquished by Christian rulers and merchants, is apt to be strangely ignored.[5]

The picture of a stern and ultimately triumphant struggle in the Levant and Mediterranean seas by a united Christendom

---

[1] Ibid., p. 177 and n.; T. W. Fulton, *The Sovereignty of the Sea*, Edinburgh, 1911, p. 527.

[2] App. B.

[3] See, however, *H.H.W.* xxiv. 228; Nelson's letters; Jurien de la Gravière, *Doria et Barberousse*, Paris, 1886, p. 28.

[4] Beazley, *Voyages and Travels*, ii, p. xiv.

[5] Charrière, *Négociations de la France dans le Levant*, iii. 572; Finlay, v. 84–87.

against the relentless aggression of barbarous or semi-barbarous Turks is clearly a fallacious one, which owes much to Prescott's avowed endeavour to prove that Italian charges of Spanish barbarism were unfounded. It ignores some very pertinent facts —the failure at any time of the Christians of the Mediterranean basin to unite whole-heartedly against Islam and the constant dependence of even the principal champions of the Faith on Moslem aid. Christian peoples not only regarded the Turks as more civilized than the Spaniards and French, but even sought to place themselves under their protection and government,[1] while the Spaniards themselves appear to have regarded the Turks as honourable foes.[2] Kheir-ed-din Barbarossa, who has, by some curious process, come to be depicted in our latest histories as an 'infamous character' and 'professional pirate', was in his own age reputed by Christians generally to be a wise statesman, an able administrator, and a great soldier, noted for his orderly and civilized conduct of war and courted in turn or simultaneously by the greatest princes, spiritual and temporal, of the Mediterranean. His career was the subject of intensive propaganda for political purposes, not only in his own lifetime but nearly three centuries later.[3]

Among the surprises that emerge from a perusal of Christian records and narratives of the sixteenth and seventeenth centuries are testimonials to the Turks as a highly civilized people, from both a moral and practical standpoint. Modern military science owes much to Turkish practices of those days, particularly in regard to engineering and the conduct of field operations, and also, perhaps, in connexion with the discipline, training, and welfare of troops. The Turks may not have been a maritime people, but the performances of Kheir-ed-din and Ochiali, both Algerines by training, in respect of naval organization and equipment, especially at great crises, must remain even today objects of profound admiration. It would be interesting to know whether in the course of three centuries practices

---

[1] *H.H.W.* xxiv. 362; p. 154, n. 3.

[2] Note sympathy with loss of Dragut's son; tribute to gallant end of Kheir-ed-din's grandson, Duro, *Armada Española*, ii. 183–4; eulogies of Aruj and Dragut, Lane-Poole, pp. 52–53 and 149; almost simultaneous romances of Cicala and Kheir-ed-din with Turkish and Italian captives.

[3] See Chs. II and III. Jurien classed him with Nelson, St. Vincent, and Alexander and above Blake, also praising his colonial administration.

for the control of neutral shipping have improved radically on
that at Algiers, which has been denounced as 'preposterous'
and 'so degrading' by Lane-Poole and Playfair.

The unquestionable ability of the Turks to maintain law and
order is the more unexpected in view of prevalent impressions
of anarchy and bloodshed. In the eighteenth century Constantinople was said to be not only the largest city in Europe
but the best policed. At the beginning of both the seventeenth
and nineteenth centuries the standard of law and order throughout most of Barbary was reputed to be higher than in Europe,
and at the time of its surrender Algiers was described as perhaps
the best regulated city in the world.[1] The absence of histories
and literature generally has been the subject of criticism,
especially in the case of the regencies, but today the general
standard of living might be regarded as a sounder criterion.
Apart from more material advantages, it is noticeable that
one of the French conquerors found that the majority of the
Algerines were better educated than the majority of Frenchmen, and Campbell added that they were also 'generally
courteous and intelligent'.[2]

The essential fact from the international point of view was
the liberality of Mohammedans in matters of trade and conscience towards peoples of other races and creeds, to which
we have striking testimonials in regard to Turkey and Zanzibar
in Victorian times,[3] and the strict observance of treaty obligations, which has been so grossly misrepresented in defiance of
the most positive evidence of our own records.[4] The 'word of
a Mussulman' was still proverbial in the nineteenth century,
and the Christian practice of 'undeclared war', so prevalent
in the Mediterranean, which taxed even the terminological
ingenuity of Carlyle, was abhorrent to the Barbaresques. Not
only did the Christian powers indulge in a state of 'general
reprisal' during a large part of the seventeenth century, but
early in it 'an expedition against the Barbary corsairs had

[1] Pellissier, *Annales algériennes*, i. 77, and rapid decline, iii. 276–7. Its good
regulation amazed the French, Rotalier, *Histoire d'Alger et de la piraterie des Turcs
dans la Méditerranée*, ii. 475; Esquer, pp. 377–455, etc.

[2] Campbell, *Letters from the South*, i. 259–60.

[3] *H.H.W.* xxiv. 363; Creasy, pp. 108–9; (Lord) Kitchener in Sir P. Mitchell,
African Afterthoughts, London, 1954, p. 59.

[4] p. 197; Morgan, *Piratical States*, pp. 189–90; *A.R.* 1816, pp. 325–9.

become the stock diplomatic formula for covering some ulterior and sinister design' on an unsuspecting Christian power.[1] In 1509 Spanish preparations aroused alarm in various parts of Italy, and in 1830 it was feared that the Algiers plan was really a pretext to mask attack upon the liberties of the citizens of Paris. The contempt of the Turk for Christians, which is referred to frequently during the period of our earlier relations, was attributed to their cruelty and treachery towards each other. Gardiner's statement that the ships of Algiers and Tunis fell upon all Christian commerce as a matter of religious obligation, and Yonge's picture of them as 'enemies of all countries alike; plunder was their livelihood, torture and massacre their amusement' are reflections, not of commercial and other records of the time, but of periodical political propaganda, reinforced by appeal to religious prejudice, of which our own history in the first half of the seventeenth century contains ample evidence.[2]

A few suggestions based on examination of our records may serve as a criterion of Barbaresque aggression and depredation. The small Turkish raids in our waters took place in time of *war* following continuous depredations during fifty years by English ships on the coasts of Barbary and Turkey. The total loss inflicted on English shipping and commerce by the three regencies was probably less than that we suffered from the single port of Dunkirk. The total number of Britons captured or enslaved—all apparently in accordance with the recognized practice of the time—was only a fraction of the number alleged to have been sold into slavery by Cromwell alone.[3] Apart from the period 1620 to 1682, during which there are various references to the goodwill, good faith, patience, and forbearance of their rulers and the 'civility' of their ships, the regencies were at peace with us up to 1816. I have found no evidence that

[1] Corbett, *England in the Mediterranean, 1603–1713*, i. 52; Esquer, p. 208 n. Compare W. H. Prescott, *Ferdinand and Isabella*, 2 vols., ed. Foster Kirk, ii. 458; *Pol. Hist.* v. 248; and about French preparations against Algiers 1681: 'Who shall be voted pyrates next is another question', *Letters to and from Henry Savile, envoy at Paris*, ed. W. Cooper (Camden Society), London, 1857, pp. 237–8.

[2] C. D. Yonge, *The Naval History of Great Britain*, 2 vols., London, 1863, i. 75. Compare T. Carlyle, *Letters and Speeches of Oliver Cromwell*, 5 vols., London, 1871–87, iv. 231, peace with all Moslem states, 17 Sept. 1656.

[3] *Petty–Southwell Correspondence 1676–87*, London, 1928, p. 215; Lord E. Fitzmaurice, *Life of Sir William Petty*, London, 1895, p. 32.

between 1682 and 1830 any other country maintained relations with us so consistently correctly as the three regencies.[1]

One or two misleading impressions, unfortunately still prevalent, might be mentioned here. The statement that 'very little has been written about Barbary, after the expulsion of the Moors from Spain until the nineteenth century, because very little happened'[2] is perhaps a fair example of the present method of approach to its history. It is probably accurate to the extent that Christians' relations with it were determined less by its actions than by their own peculiar needs and ambitions, but it ignores the evidence of well-known published works that momentous events in Barbary in the sixteenth century were largely responsible for delivering Christendom from the nightmare of 'world domination' by Spain, which already showed signs of exhaustion before it embarked on its war with England. Not only had the question whether North Africa was to be a Spanish dominion and the Mediterranean a Spanish lake been decisively determined by 1574, but the way had been opened for the development of English, French, and Dutch commerce and influence in the Levant, Atlantic, and East Indies. Queen Elizabeth and her ministers were not slow to realize the importance of Morocco or the new Algerine state in Western affairs.

Another conventional misconception, that the period of Turkish rule in Barbary was one of sterile stagnation, can be counteracted to some extent by the evidence of contemporary testimonials to the steady, and at one time startlingly rapid, development of the city of Algiers during nearly three centuries from an obscure tributary of Spain to the capital of a strategically important state and even, for a brief moment, the centre of commerce in the Mediterranean, from which the French republican armies were in part fed and financed.[3] As an outpost of empire it passed through the cycle of evolution so familiar to us in later years, from a proprietary province to a colony and then to a self-governing dominion.[4] The business of the Turks, who as colonists have been compared to the Romans, was

---

[1] Not even Portugal, *G.M.* 1830, ii. 169, and 1831, i. 454.
[2] Soames, pp. 133–5.
[3] De Grammont, p. 348; Plantet, ii. 439–52; Add. MS. 34932, &c.
[4] The sultan approved constitutional changes of 1626, 1659, 1671, and 1710.

government and especially the maintenance of law and order. The position and problems of the Turks in Algeria seem to have been somewhat analogous to our own at one time in India. Their retention of the traditions and characteristics of the old Ottoman empire, their strong advocacy of *laissez faire*,[1] not unmixed with fatalism, and the remarkable continuity of their administration over three centuries created a marked contrast with the course of events in contemporary Europe.

During that period Tunis, often written off as 'an essentially pirate state', entirely dependent on plunder, was to an increasing extent a 'granary' for southern Europe, and the repercussions of a severe drought there about the time of the Restoration appear to have extended to London and Archangel.[2] When, very belatedly, Tripoli came within the orbit of our political interest, its social and diplomatic standards were not shown to be inferior to our own.[3]

Discussion of English relations with the regencies appears to have been conducted in a vacuum of prejudice and legend, without reference to reliable statistical data, the contents of treaties, the status and functions of consuls, or Mediterranean economy. Over long periods, indeed, it is doubtful if many of our statesmen or naval commanders, or even, at times, consuls were better informed. It was during a study of obscure consular and economic relations with the Mediterranean that my attention was first attracted to the unfamiliar area of Barbary.

I could, for instance, only regard with surprise and some suspicion historical representations of the piratical career of Algiers, which began with attacks on 'our natural enemy . . . the dark Empire of bloody anti-Christian Spain'[4] at the urgent and even obsequious request of English and French allies, and culminated, apparently, in the declaration of war on the United States in 1812.[5] I was no less impressed by our persistence in

---

[1] i.e. for local administration.

[2] Dudley North's ship to Smyrna loaded grain at Archangel for Leghorn. In 1801 'the preservation of Malta' depended on corn from Tunis, F.O. 77/4, 3 Jan. 1801. For 1830 see Esquer, p. 270.

[3] De la Faye, *État des régences de Barbarie, Tripoly, Tunis et Alger*, pp. 46–100; *Piratical States*, p. 316.

[4] Carlyle, iv. 160 and 208 in 1656. Similar invective was common after 1570 and in 1739–40, &c.

[5] For treaty of 1795 see *American State Papers, Foreign Nations*, i. 28, 30, &c. Peace of June 1815 was partly frustrated by Britain. In Apr. 1816 Captain

dating the open rebellion against the sultan by Algiers and
Tunis from the very occasion which the sultan himself extolled
as a signal example of loyalty and patriotism,[1] or their 'traditional' bad faith from a treaty which all the contemporary
evidence shows to have been faithfully observed by Algiers
and consistently violated by ourselves, or the 'hopelessness'—
alternatively described as the inhuman avarice—of Algiers
slavery from the very period when that same treaty proved the
exact opposite.[2]

With such a 'topsy-turvy' background it is not illogical that
writers should single out, for special commendation of national
figures, such as Chatham, St. Vincent, Nelson,[3] and Exmouth,
the very points which, on closer examination of the facts, reveal
their ignorance of the regencies and our treaties with them,
coupled with disregard for international law or the dictates of
humanity or even, perhaps, the national interest. The omission
of evidence that their utterances or actions may have been in
conflict not only with foreign criticisms, but possibly with the
views of our officials or their own afterthoughts, is aggravated
by the almost complete failure to record the attitude of statesmen, seamen, and travellers, who, though perhaps less eminent,
may have been more judicious, and the experiences of those
consuls whose relations with the regencies were harmonious
and fruitful. When in addition it is considered that even in
authoritative works there is a singular confusion of dates, the
sequence of events, and the titles of rulers; that no discrimination is made between Moor and Turk, pirate and corsair,
captive and slave; and that even Turin is mistaken for Tunis
and Barbary for Bombay,[4] considerable doubt is inevitable
about the realism or equity of our presentation of the Barbary
picture.

(? Commodore) Shaw thanked 'His Highness the Dey for the frank and honourable
manner' in which further representations had been received, describing the 'treaty
as honourable and advantageous to both nations'. His (Shaw's) country was
entirely satisfied and not guilty of bad faith, as supposed, F.O. 3/16, 30 June 1815
and 3/18 of 12–16 Apr. 1816.   [1] p. 144.
    [2] p. 199, n. 1. Compare 'mala fede tradizionale dei governi barbareschi',
Micacchi, p. 103, with evidence that Tripoli observed treaties, 'never failing to
punish severely any who dare violate them', *Piratical States*, p. 316.
    [3] p. 304, n. 4.
    [4] Due to old misprints. St. Vincent's 'traders in human flesh' existed at Turin
and Genoa, not Tunis.

The object of the present book is to suggest some rectification of that picture by reference primarily to the evidence of our own archives and the actual experiences of travellers, as distinct from their moralizations or gossip, and by presenting the Barbaresque point of view as far as it is reasonably ascertainable. It does not pretend to be a history, but aims rather at following the maxims formulated, but not consistently observed, by two of the best-known French writers on this subject.

Masson[1] stresses the necessity for exercising very great caution in accepting statistics of piratical depredations, since they are strangely contradictory. Reasonably reliable estimates may, however, usually be obtained from varied evidence in contemporary records, as well as by comparison with the course of oversea trade. The same qualification applies equally to the, usually irresponsible, figures for captives or slaves and to the often quite irreconcilable claims to naval triumphs and the dictation of treaties.

A salutary elaboration of this theme comes from de Grammont, who, after pointing out that, however barbarous the alleged operations of the great Algerine admirals and Maltese knights might seem, they were in conformity with the standards of the time, poses the tentative, but not unwarranted, question whether modern inventions might not have in store for humanity horrors which would make massacres of the past seem the merest child's play. In any case, a spirit of candour and fair play would certainly suggest that no possibility should exist of the adoption of two separate standards of judgement, that actions or customs should not be considered barbarous or inhuman in the case of the Barbaresques and natural or salutary in our own,[2] and that we should not gloss over or deliberately whitewash or invest with romantic glamour the activities of our own countrymen or coreligionists in a bygone age, while condemning those of the infidel, often without examination, by criteria which would scarcely be realistic even today.

Such considerations have entailed a radical alteration in the scope of this book, which I had originally envisaged as a short

---

[1] Masson, *Histoire du commerce français dans le Levant au 17ᵉ siècle.*, p. 35 n.

[2] Fireships and bombs were barbarous when used between Christians, at Fontarabia in 1640 or Havre and Dieppe in 1694. The 'fiendish torture' of the bastinado became 'much virtue in a Turkish drubbing' at our embassy or in occupied Algeria. For shooting from cannon see p. 275, n. 1.

and simple outline of our relations with the Barbary States over about 250 years, as portrayed in our archives and contemporary literature. A different method of approach has been necessitated by the increasing tendency, following apparently that policy of 'systematic denigration' of which Pellissier complained a century ago, to indulge in wholesale denunciation of the Barbaresques, without the support of any specific charges or citation of reliable authority. This has been further complicated by the common use of such expressions as 'essentially', 'traditionally', 'notoriously', or 'inevitably' over a period dating back, not infrequently, to remote days before the coming of the Turk. The value of the relatively few works of a more specialized nature suffers materially from the habitual assumption that the character and past history of the Barbaresques are already too well known to require elaboration,[1] and that they compare very unfavourably with most, if not all, of their neighbours and contemporaries.

Objectivity, moreover, has not been assisted by the tendency of some historians to concentrate on the woes and heroism of other countries, for which in different connexions they show little concern or appreciation. The Barbaresques have, it seems, all too often been reduced to the role of defendants, who are offered no opportunity of replying to a variety of charges which are neither clearly defined nor supported by specific proof. Even today these are often reinforced by the citation of admissions, proverbs, and anecdotes, alleged, without evidence or even reasonable probability, to emanate from themselves.[2]

It is not unlikely, in such circumstances, that more extensive exploration of this phase of our history, through careful study and collation of appropriate archives and similar contemporary records, will produce a picture that is both coherent and convincing. It might also lead to some reassessment of national policies and administrative methods or revaluation of the protagonists in our Mediterranean struggles. My principal aim, within a necessarily circumscribed framework, has been to indicate some of the difficulties, inconsistencies, and contradictions likely to be encountered.

[1] French documentary evidence is very meagre before 1637, Plantet, p. viii, and Spanish after that date.
[2] Admissions that Algiers had no resource but piracy were patently absurd.

I

BARBARY BEFORE THE COMING OF THE TURKS

THE very uncertainty of what constituted 'Barbary' during the sixteenth, seventeenth, and eighteenth centuries, illustrates the danger of making sweeping generalizations about the character or problems of its inhabitants. For Leo Africanus, writing about 1526, it was the coastal area of northern Africa, extending roughly from Tripoli in the east through the Straits of Gibraltar and along the Moroccan shore to Cape Bojador, and representing, in his opinion, the richest and most civilized portion of the whole continent.[1] To an Englishman, however, at about the same time and for long afterwards, even in official documents or a treaty of George III, Barbary usually meant the empire, or kingdoms, of Morocco. Thus, the Barbary Company had no connexion with Turkish Africa, or in practice with the Mediterranean, and the so-called Barbary pirates were Christian adventurers operating from the Atlantic ports of Morocco.[2]

In the same way, the Barbary coast could mean the southern shore of the Mediterranean from Ceuta eastwards to Cape Bon and then southwards along Lower Barbary to Tripoli (or later to Benghazi and Bomba), or it might be merely the eastern shore of the Atlantic between Cape Spartel and the tropics. The occasional use of the term 'Barbary coasts' may have represented an attempt to combine the two.

The area, which, according to the Scottish traveller William Lithgow in the reign of James I, was termed Barbary 'by ignorant Seamen and ruvide Moors who cannot distinguish ports and provinces',[3] is now usually taken to include the future

---

[1] Leo, *Historie of Africa*, pp. 123, 182, and 184; Gramaye (1622), *Africae illustratae*, p. 1; Barbot (1732); Churchill, *A Collection of Voyages and Travels*, v. 2.

[2] John Smith, *True Travels*, 2 vols., London, 1630, ch. xxviii; Cal. S.P.D. 1611–18, p. 55; Monson's *Naval Tracts*, iii. 70–74; Duro, iii. 327–32; de Castries (Pays-Bas), *Les Sources inédites de l'histoire du Maroc de 1530 à 1845*, i.

[3] W. Lithgow, *Rare Adventures and Painful Peregrinations* (1632), Glasgow, 1906, p. 319.

Turkish regencies, i.e. the 'cities and kingdoms' of Algiers, Tunis, and Tripoli respectively, and the three kingdoms of Fez, Morocco, and Sus, which were united under the Sherif (or Emperor) of Morocco, whenever he was strong enough to control them, together with the semi-independent territories or marine provinces of Tetuan and Sallee. Added complications existed, at varying times, in the shape of Spanish and Portuguese settlements on the coasts, such as Oran, Ceuta, Mamora, and Tangier, kingdoms of native tribes round Constantine and Tlemcen, in the east and west of Algeria; and a large area to the south-east of the kingdom of Sus, over which the Emperor of Morocco at times claimed suzerainty.

The variegated picture was completed by two Naboth's Vineyards, foreign and almost autonomous establishments, dating definitely from the sixteenth century—the *Bastion de France* between Bona and La Calle,[1] which was leased by the merchants of Provence, and the island of Tabarca, slightly to the east, which was occupied, under authority from the rulers of Spain, Tunis, and Algiers, by the great Genoese family of Lomellini. The inhabitants of the island of Jerba, the traditional home of the Lotus-eaters and once noted as the strategic 'navel of Barbary' and the 'cemetery of the soldiery of Spain', appear to have had some peculiar characteristics. They were not incorporated into the kingdom of Tunis until the middle of the seventeenth century, and apparently paid tribute even later to the sultan. Unlike the people of the mainland, they engaged in maritime transport—along the coast of North Africa in small vessels. To the west, roughly opposite Malaga, another small island, the Peñon de Velez, acquired an almost equal prominence when in 1564 allied forces turned the tide against the great Suleiman.[2]

Up to the beginning of the sixteenth century the Moslem inhabitants of Barbary were generally referred to simply as 'Moors'. Thereafter they were usually divided, very roughly and unscientifically, into five main categories—Turks; Moorish refugees from Spain, known as Tagarins and Moriscos; Moors, the usual and very vague name for other city-dwellers; Arabs,

[1] About 1568, Charrière, iii. 929. Leased to Britain 1807–17.
[2] Gomara, *Annales del Emperador Carlos Quinto*, p. 24; Duro, ii. 57; T. H. Weir, *The Shaiks of Morocco*, Edinburgh, 1904, pp. 263–4.

who formed the rural population; and wild or desert Moors, who came from the Sahara to traffic or reside in the main seaports. The native inhabitants were also popularly divided into 'white' or 'tawny' Moors, who lived in the Mediterranean coastal strip, and the 'black' Moors, who were separated from them by a range of sterile mountains.

The word 'Barbaresque' appears to have been applied originally to the Berber tribesmen, who were unacquainted with maritime or urban life. Lithgow referred to the villagers between Tunis and Algiers as 'uncivill' in the sense of uncouth or primitive. Unfortunately, for want of a suitable equivalent, it has become the custom to apply the term to all the varied peoples of the Barbary coastal area. The use of an expression which had no recognized official basis has not unnaturally led to much confusion.[1]

The inhabitants of this region, who had little in common except that they were Mohammedan by religion and generally non-maritime by inclination, found their destinies inextricably intermingled with those of Western Christendom. Unlike Turkey and Egypt, they formed part of the West. The 'Barbary galleys' of Venice called regularly at ports between Tunis and One in western Algeria on their way to England and Flanders in the fifteenth century.[2] Similar traffic was carried on, to a varying extent, by the Genoese, Florentines, Ragusans, and Catalans.[3] Algeria was more accessible to Southampton than to Constantinople or Smyrna.

When in 1509 Spain embarked on the invasion of Algeria, and the combined forces of Venice and Egypt were resisting Portuguese aggression in the Red Sea, it is highly improbable that the Porte had any definite ambitions in Barbary or other parts of the Mediterranean. In fact, the sultan was at the time more interested in combining with Egypt and the Venetians of Cyprus to suppress the Knights of St. John at Rhodes.[4] The historic position of Venice as a meeting-place of East and West

[1] App. B.
[2] Starting from Alexandria they careened at Tunis and normally visited Bougie, Oran, and One, V.S.P. 1202–1509, p. 7, &c.
[3] G. Rambert, *Histoire du commerce de Marseille*, 2 vols., Paris, 1949, ii. 360 sqq.
[4] V.S.P. 1202–1509, p. 115; Doge to Edward IV, 9 Sept. 1465. Edward granted the knights protection against 'unspeakable Turks' and 'any pirates on the Christian side', ? Venetians and Florentines, *Patent Rolls*, 1476–85, p. 193.

seems to have been actually reinforced during the sixteenth century. Events which might have seemed untoward—the fall of Constantinople, the closing of the Black Sea to Christian navigation, the Turkish conquest of Egypt and Syria—tended rather to its advantage. Genoese, Florentine, and Catalan competition declined rapidly. The development of reliable land-routes from Constantinople to the Adriatic gave Venice a new importance as a centre of international politics and cosmopolitan life, which directly affected political and commercial relations with Barbary. From about 1535 Tunis ceased to be a port of call for Venetian ships, which, in an effort to avoid provocation to either pope or sultan, carefully followed a route eastward from the Adriatic, at a safe distance from Malta and Tripoli, the new strongholds of the knights.[1]

Neither Turk nor Moor would seem to have had any natural aptitude for marine activities. They knew very little about navigation. Their shipping terms were nearly all Italian. According to Christian accounts they lost their heads during storms at sea. Duro records that the African Moors had no other craft than small open boats, with at best one short mast. According to Chénier those of Sallee were little better equipped in the eighteenth century. The maritime successes of the Turks were due in the first place to the necessities of war and in the second to their military qualities, tactics, and organization. Their galleys, or 'military rowboats' as they are not inaptly termed, formed only a minor and strictly subordinate part of the land establishments of the Turkish regencies. Christian vessels were used almost entirely for the transportation of Barbary produce, troops, or embassies.[2]

A principal feature of North Africa was the great caravan route, which ran almost parallel with the coast from Marrakesh and Fez to Cairo, Medina, and Mecca, and communicated at intervals with the principal ports. It was connected with the hinterland by subsidiary caravans, the most famous of which brought a variety of valuable commodities to Fez from the area round Timbuctoo. The close connexion between parts of the

[1] Charrière, iv. 405; H.H.W. ix. 323. For English trade with Ragusa see L. Villari, The Republic of Ragusa, London, 1904, pp. 264 and 275.

[2] T. Sherley, Discours of the Turkes, ?1607, ed. E. Denison Ross (Camden Series), London, 1936, pp. 5, 8, and 10–11. Sherley reckoned 7 galleys in Algiers, and Knight in 1638 only 8. In 1660 Winchelsea was very contemptuous of its navy.

Sahara and the new Turkish port of Algiers[1] was soon demonstrated by the supplies of gold, ostrich-feathers, camels, and various drugs, as well as by the presence in the city of desert tribesmen engaged in special trades.

Besides Cairo and Fez, which ranked high among the cities of the world, even in the seventeenth century, less well-known inland centres played a considerable part in Mediterranean affairs. Oran owed its importance to being the port of Tlemcen until, after its capture by Spain, it was superseded by Algiers. In the same way Bona displaced Bougie as the outlet for the produce of Constantine, which, however, seems always to have had a close connexion, political and economic, with Tunis. In the Atlantic Sallee, despite its natural disadvantages, was primarily the harbour of Fez and Mequinez, though at one time tributary to Marrakesh.

The guarding and, to a limited extent, the maintenance of the main land-routes came to be a consideration of the first importance and a reliable indication of the stability of the western area. Security for travellers tended to diminish as they proceeded eastward from Tunis. For the worst section of the caravan—from Cairo to Mecca—it became customary for the Pasha of Damascus, on behalf of the sultan, to provide an escort of field-guns.[2] Wheeled traffic of any other character was impracticable before the middle of the eighteenth century. The application by Christians of this Persian word to maritime practices is very curious and at times confusing.

I have found no justification in contemporary records for either of the conflicting assertions that the arrival of the Turks was a wanton irruption into a scene of Mediterranean tranquillity, or that the inhabitants of Barbary up to that time had been mere savages and pirates. Finlay's statement that the Turks drove out 'the fierce African corsairs' has clearly no basis in fact. The allegation of another Victorian author,[3] evidently influenced by Prescott and frequently repeated by other writers, that 'until the commencement of the sixteenth century, those petty kingdoms interfered but seldom in the politics of Europe and their very existence was but little known and as

[1] Braudel, *La Méditerranée et le monde méditerranéen à l'époque de Philippe II*, p. 178.
[2] Lucas, *La Turquie*, i. 367-83; Churchill, v. 537.
[3] Whitworth Porter, *History of the Knights of Malta*, 2 vols., London, 1853, ii. 35.

little cared for' represents a fundamental distortion of well-authenticated fact. It is definitely contradicted by the evidence of municipal, consular, and commercial records, which might easily have been studied in the well-known works of Capmany, Pardessus, Depping, Mas-Latrie, and others.

In 1465 the doge and senate, applying to Edward IV for assistance against the violence of the Knights of Rhodes and 'the incredible obstinacy and avarice of the Grand Master', point out that 'it is the ancient custom of the State to send annually some of its galleys on trading voyages to Barbary'. In 1485, at a critical time of the Granada war, detailed instructions are sent regarding the return of the Venetian galleys along the Barbary coast, with special reference to One, Oran, and Tunis, and prohibiting the landing there of English copper and tin.[1] Soon afterwards, Henry VII displays keen interest at one end of the North African coast[2] and James IV at the other.[3] There cannot be any doubt that English merchants of the fifteenth century were well acquainted with certain aspects of Barbary trade. Since specific mention is made of Morocco, Algiers, and Tunis as the most important of the petty kingdoms, it may suffice to point out that Ceuta[4] was captured in 1415 largely with the assistance of English ships. In 1485 the kingdom of Fez made a treaty of peace and friendship with the Spanish monarchs, and became in 1494 the subject of two partition treaties between Portugal and Spain.[5]

Tunis comes in for special mention as a port of call for Venetian vessels. It certainly had Genoese and Sicilian ambassadors or consuls.[6] In 1470 it formed an alliance with the King of Naples. In 1482 Louis XI, on his inheritance of the princely

---

[1] V.S.P. 1202–1509, pp. 7 and 149.

[2] *Pol. Hist.* v. 120–1 and *Memorials of Henry VII* (ed. J. Gairdner, 1858), p. 263, both in 1505.

[3] James IV to Cardinal d'Amboise, 14 Oct. 1507, and to 'magnifico viro domino Philippo de Prates Cathalorum Alexandriae civitatis consuli sagacissimo', same date, *Letters and Papers, Richard III and Henry VII* (ed. J. Gairdner, 1861–3), ii. 252.

[4] Hakluyt, vi. 121. Planet, p. lv, attributes it to events of 1492! *H.H.W.* x. 455–8 depicts horrors of this wanton act, drawn partly from Portuguese histories. For earlier Christian aggressions see Froissart's *Chronicles* in 1390, and in about 1404 *The Unconquered Knight* (Don Pero Niño), ed. and tr. Joan Evans, London, 1928, pp. 51–98.

[5] De Castries (Spain), pp. i and iv.

[6] Vitale records Genoese consuls, &c., between 1492 and 1517. For Sicily see Rambert, ii. 402, and Naples in 1470, ibid.

county of Provence, wrote to the King of Tunis, Bona, and Bougie, expressing his desire to maintain the commercial relations which had so long existed between their countries.[1] Bougie, for obvious reasons, had a specially close connexion with France, but the commercial and political importance of Algiers, which was not then an independent unit, seems to have been very small until after 1509, when its representatives made a treaty with King Ferdinand. It is interesting to note that in 1830 the French government based its claim to intervention in Algeria on the continuity of privileged commercial relations with that area during four hundred years.[2]

While Barbary is described as a flourishing and highly civilized area before the Norman Conquest, Leo, who in his youth had been a sort of medical registrar in the 'strangers' hospital' at Fez, records his personal experience of the country in the early sixteenth century. He testifies to the 'civilitie, humanitie and upright dealing of the Barbarians . . . a civill people (who) prescribe lawes and constitutions unto themselves' and are learned in the arts and sciences. Even when resident in Rome he speaks somewhat wistfully of the pleasant life in central Algeria and may have returned to end his days in Tunis, which in 1534 was called by our agent to the Holy See 'a city as big as Rome'. Lane-Poole, on the strength of contemporary documentary evidence, describes the rulers of Barbary in the later Middle Ages as 'mild and just' and their relations with 'the trading nations of Christendom' as 'amicable and just'. That view was evidently endorsed by the agent of Henry VII and VIII at the court of Aragon.[3]

The alleged addiction of the peoples of North Africa to piratical attacks on southern Europe and the inclusion of them in the term 'Barbary pirates' appear to be merely a corollary to the nineteenth-century concept of a rigid dividing-line in the Mediterranean between Christians and Moslems, or between Western civilization and oriental or African barbarism. The history of the area over a period of more than 2,000 years is

---

[1] Plantet, *Tunis*, i. 7.

[2] Nettement, p. 211; Garrot, p. 596. There was, however, no continuity, ibid., p. 595.

[3] Leo, pp. 123, 182, and 184; Lane-Poole, pp. 7 and 22–26. Stile wrote Henry VIII, 26 Apr. 1509, that, if he had been sent to 'the Turk or any king of Barbary', he would have been as well treated as in Spain, *Memorials of Henry VII*, p. 445.

clearly incompatible with such theses. Quite apart from any religious considerations, the difficulty of distinguishing between war, trade, and piracy was periodically manifested through attempts to create political divisions or frontiers which were economically, and at times ethnically, artificial and unreal. The example of Roman aggression against an inoffensive or unsuspecting neighbour in Cyprus before the Christian era on the specious plea of piracy was imitated by the Portuguese on the great city of Ceuta in 1415 and, according to Leo, on the English trading post of Anfa forty years later.[1] Similar justification is still offered for Spanish attacks on Mers-el-Kebir and Oran early in the next century. It would be interesting to know what construction should be placed on the King of Aragon's destruction of the *nid de Corsaires*, into which Marseilles is said to have developed in 1431.[2]

The possibility that Tunis was a flourishing commercial centre before the foundation of Rome; the assertion that Carthage was second only to Rome in the western part of the empire as a centre of business and 'Latin culture and letters'; or the claim that Africa played a more important part than Italy in the early development of Latin Christianity would be matters of purely academic interest to the student of modern history but for constant insistence on the theory that inhabitants of the North African coast were essentially and inevitably pirates and enemies of Europe.

There can be no question but that the principal cities played a prominent part in the expansion of Mediterranean commerce, culture, and international relations. It has been said that Frenchmen traded and travelled in Syria in the time of Haroun-al-Raschid in almost precisely the same way as a thousand years later in the reign of Charles X. The connexion between Tunisia and the peoples of Italy was even older and at times much closer. The practice of the Christian religion was at least tolerated in the former area from very early times. Suspicions that the peoples of Sicily and Calabria might be more sympathetic to Moslem rule troubled the Spaniards throughout their occupation.[3]

The capitulations granted to Christian traders in North

---

[1] *E.B.* vii. 699; Leo, p. 397.   [2] Rambert, ii. 519.
[3] *C.M.H.* i. 286–7; Reinach, p. xxxviii; see p. 154, n. 3.

Africa apparently date from the Abbasid occupation of Egypt. They evidently helped to form the basis of Mediterranean intercourse long before the first Crusade, as the history and maritime regulations of Amalfi indicate. It was then the great cosmopolitan port of south Europe, which drew its prosperity very largely from its Tunisian neighbours of Palermo and Bougie, until it was crushed by the Norman crusaders and supplanted by the less strictly commercial ports of Venice, Pisa, and Genoa.

A very significant feature of the Mediterranean was the existence of potential bridges across the Straits of Sicily[1] and Gibraltar. These might be said to have existed in a physical sense in the former case during part of the Roman empire and again in the tenth and eleventh centuries, when Sicily was governed by officials from Mahdia. A reversal of the relationship during the following period, and the exaction by the Angevin and Aragonese rulers from the African princes of tribute as the price of peace, evidently did not prevent the development of prosperity on both sides of the strait or peaceful passage through it.

The western strait was at first even more happily situated. Some two centuries prior to its capture by the Portuguese, Ceuta was the headquarters of the Genoese consulate-general for the kingdoms of both Fez and Granada,[2] and, even after Spain's conquest of the latter, the Moors continued to represent an important element in Valencia, Aragon, and Catalonia. Barcelona, judging from Prescott's description, more nearly resembled a Moorish city than a Spanish one. The great maritime code compiled there in the fourteenth and fifteenth centuries—the Book of the Consulate of the Sea or the Good Customs of the Sea, seems to suggest that, for practical purposes of sea-traffic, the rest of Spain and Barbary, both within and without the straits, were treated as a single unit.[3]

Though Castile was regarded as safeguarding the frontier between Christendom and Islam, its inhabitants were not averse to migration into Moorish territory. Prescott attributes the peculiar system of concubinage among the Castilian clergy

---

[1] V.S.P. 1592–1603, p. 194.
[2] Capmany, Cal. Dip. xiv. 34, 1267.
[3] Twiss, *Black Book of the Admiralty*, iii. 107 n. and 531.

to 'the contagious example of their Mahometan neighbours'. According to a Spanish historian Granada swarmed with immigrants or visitors from Europe, Africa, and the Levant until it became 'the common city of all nations'. In 1313 only a very small proportion of the population were said to be true believers. In the years to come it was not uncommon for Spanish nobles to seek asylum there and even serve 'under the Moslem banner'.[1]

The contrast between Prescott's unbounded admiration for the character and achievements of the 'sprightly intellectual' Spanish Arab and his contempt for the piratical savages of Barbary or the superstitious 'slaves of Eastern despotism' or the 'degrading political and religious institutions' of the 'sensual and sluggish' Turk reveals an outlook that is steadfastly and uncompromisingly Western. Like Duro, he appears to have little knowledge of events in Italy. His overriding interest there was to emphasize the military prowess of the Castilian Gonzalo de Cordova even at the expense of the 'Old Catalan', King Ferdinand. He did not realize that the Sultan Bajazet, of whom he speaks so contemptuously as a 'barbarian monarch', was probably a more liberal theologian[2] and almost certainly a more influential political personage in Italy than Queen Isabella or the 'consummate statesman' Cardinal Ximenes. The result of Castilian policy on the western Mediterranean was, as Duro suggests, quickly apparent.

The relatively peaceful and clearly prosperous interval between the varied operations of St. Louis and his brother in Syria, Tunis, and Sicily, and the outburst of aggressive nationalism and religious discord which closed the fifteenth century, coincided with the pre-eminence of Barcelona as a mercantile centre, first for the Mediterranean and soon afterwards for the Levant as well. Aided by the Aragonese acquisitions of the Balearic Islands, Sardinia, Naples, and Sicily, and by the favour that it enjoyed with the rulers of Barbary, it quickly developed, despite a late start, a commercial and consular organization that was unrivalled in southern Europe—at all events when, after the fall of Constantinople, the famous mercantile republics

---

[1] Prescott, i. 317. Compare Tlemcen, *E.B.* xxvi. 1035.

[2] He had sermons of Savonarola translated: P. Villari, *Life and Times of Girolamo Savonarola*, tr. Linda Villari, Florence, 1888, p. 439. See also pp. 354 and 358.

of Genoa and Venice had been shorn of some of their colonial magnificence. Its network of consulates and factories facilitated peaceful and regular intercourse throughout southern waters from Seville on the Atlantic to Alexandria and the 'dry port' of Damascus, the gateways to the Orient. For its contact with the Turkish mainland it apparently became indebted to the good offices of the Venetians in Crete and the Genoese in Chios.

The cosmopolitan and liberal attitude of the time towards maritime affairs is indicated in a number of ways. Most striking of all, perhaps, was the general adoption of the principles and practices collected, from experience of other well-known codes and sea-manuals, in the Book of the Consulate of the Sea. Its remarkable continuity and universality are illustrated by the text of a celebrated judgement in an American court of justice.[1] As it is shown to cover all practices normally known to modern maritime law, it is surprising to find how little reference to illegal violence at sea is contained in this or earlier codes and manuals of instructions. An interesting sidelight on regard for international law is found in the dying years of Saracen rule at Alexandria. The Turkish flagship, on a mission to the Sultan of Egypt, was rammed, perhaps on purpose, by a Venetian vessel, but the admiral took no action out of fear, or respect, for 'the Laws and Privileges of the Harbour'.[2] Such concern for local or international requirements appears all too infrequently in the Levant and Mediterranean during the next three centuries.

The functions and status of consuls are to be found less in legislation than in treaties and concessions. Depping's claim of absolute inviolability for consuls in Moslem countries is controverted by the very explicit evidence of the treaty between Pisa and Tunis of 1398 and of incidents to Venetian and Catalan representatives at Alexandria. Such agents were clearly held responsible not only for the misconduct of their officials but even in certain cases for the acts of a third party. A curious parallel comes from Tunis over a period of two centuries. In 1465 the Venetians explained to Edward IV the serious responsibility their ships had incurred through damage inflicted by the

[1] Twiss, iii, p. lxxiv, de Lovio *v*. Boit, 1815.
[2] Baumgarten, 1507: Churchill, i. 436.

Knights of St. John on Moorish passengers and goods. In 1658, after several years of controversy, England formally recognized the same principle in its treaty with Tunis, and subsequently extended it to the other Barbary States.[1]

On the other hand, consuls enjoyed, under normal conditions, official status and personal privileges which left their imprint long afterwards in France and Spain, but were only gradually recognized in England and northern Europe. Administrative grades were distinguished along practical and logical lines, very similar to modern usage. The 'overseas' or 'maritime' consuls of Venice and Florence destined for Moslem posts were directed, financed, and trained in a manner perhaps not inferior to that of French diplomats in the eighteenth century. Other consular arrangements were not exclusively national. Foreigners of noble birth were proud to act as Catalan consuls. Even a Doria or a Cosimo de' Medici was willing to join the merchants' ranks in order to qualify. Our own earliest consuls, appointed to Pisa by royal patents of Richard III and Henry VII, were such famous financiers as Lorenzo Strozzi or the Buonvisi.[2]

The spirit of reciprocity and co-operation survived for a time even the test of nationalism and fanaticism. The Provençals would appear to have benefited by the use of Catalan consuls, ships, and safe-conducts. The first mention of a French consulate, over a long period prior to 1548, comes from a Barcelona record which shows that in 1498, during the brief French occupation of Naples, a merchant, apparently a Catalan, was appointed 'French and Neapolitan' consul at Alexandria.[3] The fact that Charles V continued, as late as 1525 and 1539, to make appointments to this important Catalan-French consulate, following Turkish confirmation of the ancient Egyptian capitulations, is an interesting instance of Ottoman policy.

Of the many ominous signs which portended the deterioration of law and order in the Mediterranean consequent upon the recent unifications of the kingdoms of Spain (1479) and France (1482), the most significant were those schemes for territorial expansion which took the specious form of crusades.

[1] Cal. S.P.D. 1657-8, p. 309.

[2] Rymer, Foedera, xii. 270, 314, and 553.

[3] Philip de Parets. He and his sailor brother were Catalans, not French. See Capmany, Memorias históricas sobre la marina, commercio y artes de la antigua ciudad de Barcelona, ii., 307-10 and App.; and p. 22, n. 3.

They were, not unnaturally, regarded with suspicion and antagonism by the 'petty states', including Aragon, which had for so long contributed to the stability of the area. A system, under which the comity of nations and the sovereign rights of civilized countries were subordinated to the pretences or convictions of religious organizations, cut at the roots of international law and the sanctity of treaties.

In the year 1485, when, as a result of protests against the lawless attacks by Spanish cruisers, the rulers of Fez and Spain concluded a treaty of peace and friendship, the tranquillity of the Mediterranean seemed reasonably assured. The western states of Italy were on good terms with the Turks, whose soldiers were actually co-operating with the Neapolitan army. War seems to have been taken very lightly. In Italy, Barbary, and even Granada, foreign mercenaries had formed the principal force. In the Mediterranean armed merchantmen may have constituted the nearest approach to naval strength. Apart from Naples, perhaps, galley-slaves were unknown,[1] and slavery as an institution is said to have become obsolete.[2] For Italy, Barbary, and eastern Spain it was a golden age of luxury and culture.

Two years later the civilized practices of war and the laws of humanity were severely shaken when the entire population of Malaga, an enemy city which had surrendered at discretion, was condemned to slavery and distributed to other places at home and abroad. The same year witnessed the introduction of the Inquisition into Catalonia, a great stronghold of Western liberty and progress. Prescott points to the subsequent operations 'as affording the best data for estimating the extent of Spanish perfidy in later times'.[3]

Somewhat inconsistently, he also stresses the importance of 'those maxims of public law universally recognized as settling the intercourse of civilized nations, a science imperfectly developed in the sixteenth century, but in its general principles the same as now, founded, as these are, on the immutable basis of morality and justice'. So far as the Mediterranean was con-

[1] The introduction of galley-slaves was condemned by Ferdinand, Isabella, and the friars, as creating a 'new hell', Gomara, *Crónica de los muy nombrados Omiche y Haradin Barbarroja*, pp. 357–8.

[2] For piracy and slavery, see Rambert, ii. 413; L. Villari, p. 215; *H.H.W.* ix. 319–23.

[3] Prescott, i. 478.

cerned Prescott's 'new dawn', or his 'new era in modern political history', may be said to have begun with that curious defensive treaty which aimed at the expulsion of the French barbarians from Italy with the aid of various potentates, including the sultan and his pensioner the pope.[1]

The French project for a private crusade against the Turks, or against Islam as it was also very loosely designated, may have been unwelcome and disturbing to Ferdinand, who from the first year of his reign had endeavoured to prevent the introduction of maritime lawlessness from the Atlantic, and in 1489 had taken the drastic step of prohibiting the use of privateers.[2] When Charles VIII unexpectedly included in his pretensions to the imperial throne of Constantinople claims to the kingdoms of Naples and Jerusalem, the problem of maritime warfare arose in a new form. He could only form his marine expedition by the indiscriminate begging of ships, and one March morning in 1494 Toulon woke to find itself unexpectedly a great naval port. Its local squadron was described as 'un tas de brigans et mauvais garsons', who had only been kept in order by the employment of all available land forces.[3] It is not at all clear why the same author should be so indignant at the Venetians for hanging the officers of the French scouting-vessels who some time previously were found operating in the then peaceful and carefully preserved waters of the Adriatic.

In defiance of Ferdinand's strict prohibition Spanish privateers flocked to the scene. While corsairs of Biscay and Pisa intercepted the rich booty which King Charles was carrying off from Naples, a noble Valencian actually joined the French, and was eventually executed by the Turks at Constantinople. Venice, which alone seems to have maintained a regular navy and done its best to observe its obligations to both pope and sultan, found itself exposed to awkward questions of neutrality. The unaccustomed spectacle of a Guipuscoan at Ostia blockading Rome and blackmailing the pope,[4] who should at least have been recognized as an ally, may well have led to the organization of the papal galleys, which appear to have been regarded as a novelty.

[1] P. Villari, p. 354.   [2] Duro, i. 347–8.
[3] 'On en mendia partout', de la Roncière, *Histoire de la marine française*, iii. 3, 6, and 13.   [4] Duro, i. 18; Prescott, ii. 63–65.

By 1498 Ferdinand had found it necessary to authorize the unrestricted use of privateers in the Mediterranean apart from the imposition, on moral and practical grounds, of a strict veto on raids in Barbary waters. The swarm of Spanish and French corsairs in the Straits of Sicily and Gibraltar was presumably diminished by the temporary reconciliation of France and Spain through the partition of Italian territory. This must have roughly coincided with rival French and Spanish negotiations in Egypt and Syria, with the establishment of Turkish commercial relations at Venetian ports[1] and Tripoli,[2] and with the appearance of Aruj Barbarossa at Tunis.

At that time the historic kingdoms of Tunis, Tlemcen, and Fez appear to have been threatened with disintegration, partly from internal dissensions, of which the Spaniards found evidence at Algiers, Bougie, Jerba, and Melilla, and partly from Portuguese and Spanish inroads. These last are characteristically attributed by Robertson to the attitude of the Moors, whether natives or recent expatriates from Spain, 'all zealous professors of the Mahometan religion and inflamed against Christianity with a bigoted hatred proportional to their ignorance and barbarous manners'. Playfair likewise throws the responsibility on increasing ravages by Moorish 'pirates' in revenge for the conquest of Granada, and more especially by the refugees 'whose fury naturally fell upon the Spaniards nearest the Mediterranean'. He adds, moreover, that 'it was not confined to these alone. English traders were great sufferers;[3] indeed the Moors openly avowed themselves the common enemies of Christendom. Ferdinand was seriously alarmed.'

The king's anxiety, however, probably arose from a different cause. After the tragedy of Malaga he made increasingly liberal concessions as further conquests took place. The final one, ratified by both sides on 25 November 1491, after the capitulation of Granada, provided for the free use by its inhabitants of their own religion, laws, customs, and property. They were to have the right to migrate where they wished and were to be furnished with ships for conveyance to Africa during the next

---

[1] Finlay, v. 22 and n.   [2] Duro, i. 82.
[3] Only two losses are recorded—one ship captured by a Spanish corsair and the *Christe* taken near Minorca by Aruj ?1513, Gomara, p. 360; *Letters and Papers, Henry VIII*, 1515-18, p. 215.

three years.[1] One of Prescott's statements suggests that the Spanish Arabs may not have had any strong desire to remove to Africa or any assurance of a warm welcome there. While Boabdil retired to Fez, his wife Fatima and children settled in Madrid and became Christians.[2]

In some quarters, however, the fall of Granada was looked on as merely the prelude to a 'second conquest' across the straits. Already in 1492 the royal secretary was reporting hopefully on the subject.[3] In 1493 Ferdinand was receiving from agents in different parts of Barbary reports about events there, including minor raids on its inhabitants. In 1494 the pope fixed the line of demarcation between the Spanish and Portuguese spheres in Morocco. In 1497 advantage was taken of a favourable moment to occupy without opposition the port of Melilla, either because it was situated opposite a potential danger spot at Almeria, or because Ferdinand was nervous about increasing inroads by the Portuguese who were already in 'possession of the best ports of Morocco and were gradually extending their outposts into the interior'. It is noteworthy that, instead of using privateers for Melilla, ships prepared for a West Indian expedition were sent there in spite of the protests of Columbus. To him, as to the Victorian editor of Leo's work, the affairs of 'petty Barbary princes' seemed strangely insignificant beside the great adventure in the West. Ferdinand and Charles V, however, both realized that security along the Barbary coast was an essential preliminary to Spanish expansion. In the same year the Viceroy of Sicily availed himself of a favourable opportunity to occupy the stronghold of Jerba.[4]

In the face of increasing persecution and denial of rights the 'marvellous patience' of the Granada Moors gave way, and in 1500 a formidable rising took place. Since the Soldan of Egypt was regarded as a protector of the Spanish Arabs, Peter Martyr's mission[5] there in the following year may well have been intended for a measure of appeasement. If so, it was frustrated by the bigotry of the Church and the cupidity of private interests to the manifest advantage of Venice.

[1] Prescott, i. 477–8.
[2] *Vida del Cardenale, Gonzalez de Mendoza*, in Gomara, pp. 275–7 and 289–91.
[3] De Castries, p. iii; Duro, i. 63–64.
[4] Ibid., pp. 46–47.
[5] Prescott, ii. 126 and 138.

Forces set free from the Italian war experienced no difficulty during 1505 in occupying Cazaza and also Mers-el-Kebir, which is variously described as a wealthy commercial city and a 'formidable nest of pirates'.[1] The enthusiastic slogan of the soldiers 'Africa for King Ferdinand', the dying instructions of Queen Isabella for the extirpation of the Mohammedan religion in North Africa, alarm at the situation in Andalusia and Valencia, and evidence of increasing aid, native and Christian, from Barbary, all tended to promote the 'African ideal' advocated by Cardinal Ximenes. Two bald facts are cited from the records of 1506, presumably on account of their novelty. One mentions the capture of three Moorish galliots and 195 prisoners. The other refers to the destruction by the Sicilian galleys of an expedition of Turks who were about to 'try out their fortunes in those seas'.[2]

A memorial, addressed to Ferdinand and referred to Ximenes at some date prior to the Mers-el-Kebir expedition, presents an extremely interesting picture of conditions and events on the Barbary coast. It describes the practice of Spanish privateers, particularly those from Jerez and the Bay of Cadiz, cruising along the shore from Bougie to Cape Aguer on the Atlantic, not only in light single vessels but in squadrons sufficiently powerful to occupy temporarily fortified towns and carry off from 400 to 800 captives at a time. It adds that, under the freebooting system, the whole coast of Africa was kept in a state of panic, and that, even though the would-be adversaries of Spain were reduced to seeking shelter as best they could, they were carried off in droves like animals.

An official report shows that a raid involving considerable loss of persons and cattle took place opposite Gibraltar as early as 1493. It also relates that the Moriscos fled from Tlemcen, Bougie, and Tunis, and made for Bokhara and Mecca without pausing at Alexandria or Damascus. Panic and despair are said to have reigned. The occupation of Melilla, Cazaza, and Mers-el-Kebir led to large-scale raids in the interior. In 1507 one of these resulted in the capture of 1,500 Moors, 4,000 head of cattle, and other booty before being interrupted by a large

---

[1] Ibid., p. 430. Previous complaint was by Moors against Spanish cruisers, de Castries, p. iii. The city was noted for wealth and civilized life. The expedition was suggested by a treacherous Venetian, Rotalier, ii. 53.   [2] Duro, i. 53.

force from Tlemcen, which killed 2,000 Spaniards and carried off 400 prisoners. The chronicler Zurita describes the Moorish corsairs as springing up like crabs owing to the negligence and cupidity of the Spanish privateers, which were more accustomed to rob the king than his enemies.[1]

There does not, however, seem to be any evidence in Duro's documents, or other researches, of any large departures of refugees from Spain after the initial exodus. No mention is made of the capture of armed vessels at previous ports or at Oran and Bougie. The number of captives at Oran[2] hardly seems excessive in view of the scale of land operations. No details are quoted of the help given by the Genoese to Barbary.

After the completion of preliminary operations,[3] which included the capture near Melilla of the Peñón de Velez and joint action with the Portuguese on the Atlantic coast of Morocco, the celebrated Pedro Navarro was sent in 1509 with an expeditionary force of 10 galleys and 80 ships, 8,000 foot and 3,000 horse, against Oran, which Prescott describes as the 'principal port of the trade of the Levant'. The undertaking was an unofficial one, conducted at the risk and expense of Ximenes and various shipowners. Though its avowed purpose was the extension of Christianity, the size of the force aroused suspicion that some more important place, possibly Rome, might be the real objective.[4] It was not long before Ferdinand's French ally expressed his conviction that the 'infidel' against whom the Spanish operations were directed was not in Africa but the dominions of France.

Though no formidable opposition was anticipated, the result of the Oran expedition must have surpassed the most sanguine expectations. Late on the 16th of May the fleet sailed from Cartagena, followed by a large number of lesser craft, and arrived at Mers-el-Kebir the following night. By the evening of the 18th Oran had been captured at a cost of 30 Spanish lives; 4,000 inhabitants were slaughtered in cold blood and 5,000 were carried off to Spain, together with booty valued at half a million gold ducats.

[1] Duro, pp. 62–67.

[2] 300 (later quoted as 20,000, Dapper, *Africa*, p. 217).

[3] Duro, i. 68–89, gives more reliable details of Navarro's operations, 1507–11, than Prescott, ii. 430–42, and Lane-Poole, pp. 12–13.

[4] *Letters and Papers*, 1509–13, p. 3.

Dissensions between Navarro and Ximenes resulted in the return of the latter to Spain, and further operations were continued under Ferdinand's direction. These proved so successful that by 1510 Navarro had captured Bougie and Tripoli with few casualties and great spoil. Ambitions were developed and temporarily encouraged by papal exhortation of extending Spanish dominion into the Holy Land. This may have seemed no idle dream, as Egypt was ripe for conquest, and the islands of the Aegean were still mainly in Christian hands.

Whether this amazing result was the outcome of Castilian valour, Navarro's exceptional skill in handling this heterogeneous force, typically Aragonese diplomacy in dealing with native rulers, the defenceless condition of a crumbling civilization, or, as seems most probable, a combination of all four, is a matter for conjecture. The most extraordinary feature, undoubtedly, is the sharp contrast between Spanish accounts of the strength of these places, probably much exaggerated in accordance with the practice of the time, and the exceptional ease with which they were taken.

The actual fighting, which resulted in the capture of Oran, Bougie, and Tripoli, apparently occupied less than two whole days and involved the death of about 350 Spaniards, or a fraction of the loss sustained previously in a single irregular raid from Mers-el-Kebir. Indeed, in the highly profitable operations at Bougie the only Spanish casualty is said to have been the victim of his own archers. Prescott's account of 'two pitched battles' and Duro's picture of assailants being greeted by the erratic fire of over a hundred cannon may be contrasted with the report of our agent in Spain that the inhabitants of this wealthy city were 'nakyd people fearing sore the gunschot'.[1] Even in Jerba and the surrounding islands, which had for some time been a Turkish stronghold, the natives were found to be very ignorant of fire-arms. The bow was evidently regarded as the sovereign weapon in Barbary if employed by Turks or Englishmen.[2] Even later the walls of fortified towns like Algiers and Tripoli are described as very weak.

[1] Ibid., p. 124, 23 Jan. 1510. Bougie was wealthier and gayer than Oran, Rotalier, i. 66.

[2] The Spanish ambassador reported, London, 1505: 'it is believed in England that the English bowmen could in a few years conquer the whole of Africa', *Pol. Hist.* v. 121.

It was at Jerba that the 'facile conquest' was brought to an unexpected and disastrous halt. Duro merely mentions the island at the time as a refuge for corsairs after raids on Sicily, Naples, and Sardinia. He evidently failed to realize that it had for some years been occupied by Turks, and was perhaps already regarded as an advanced base of the Ottoman empire. Aruj Barbarossa, who with his fellow Turks had apparently been invited to Tunis for protection against the Spaniards of Sicily, was installed in the government of Jerba soon after its evacuation. His successes over the Spaniards are said to have led to recognition by the sultan, who sent him two galleys and the *caftan* or official robe of authority.[1]

Although the Spaniards attributed the failure of the costly operations in 1510 and 1511 to such fortuitous causes as bad weather and lack of fresh water, the magnitude of their preparations for the second attempt, which included an appeal to Henry VIII for 1,000 archers,[2] may have determined the final rupture by France. The prestige of Spain suffered a severe blow from the disaster of Jerba, which long continued to be a thorn in its Italian dominions.[3]

Soon afterwards a fanatical sheikh of the Zouave people, alarmed at Spanish encroachments in Algeria, appealed for help to the Turks 'as being the most formidable nation of the period, and the most warlike people of that time'. This appeal was answered by the arrival of a small body of Turks under their 'bey' Aruj,[4] whose slight force of three vessels was reinforced by the loan of two foists from the King of Tunis. That monarch apparently hoped to be rewarded by the re-incorporation in his dominions of Bougie, which, after being long 'turmoiled' by the rival claims of Tunis and Tlemcen, had during the previous century developed into an independent and flourishing commonwealth.

Neither Duro nor Prescott appears to have had any know-

[1] Rotalier, i. 85; *H.H.W.* xxiv. 352.

[2] Duro, i. 95. Lord D'Arcy, as 'admiral in the war of Ferdinand against the Moors', brought to Cadiz 1,500 archers who 'did not agree' with the Spaniards, *Letters and Papers*, 1509–13, pp. 227, 420, 497, and 967; *D.N.B.* xiv. 50; *The Times* leading article 'Red Caps', 23 May 1955.

[3] Only Duro mentions two campaigns, i. 355–61. For the earlier, see Prescott, ii. 441, and Rotalier, i. 71–73.

[4] Weir, pp. 48 and 52.

ledge of Turkish activities, political, naval, or commercial, in the West. Neither took any interest in the foreign relations of the various Barbary States, their institutions, their internal affairs, or their economic interdependence.

Even on this inadequate basis the immediate results of the new 'Castilian policy' were assessed in very different terms by the two historians. Duro, whose outlook is more critical and factual, foresaw its dangerous implications even in the lifetime of Ferdinand and Ximenes. Prescott's romantic optimism could see nothing but its triumphant success and the complete vindication of the careers of the cardinal and Navarro regardless of historical facts and his own inconsistencies. The discomfiture at Jerba was only a slight check in the 'brilliant career' of the disciple of Gonzalo, who is first described as a 'celebrated engineer' and later as a 'rude unlettered soldier'.

It is hard to acquiesce in Prescott's final estimate of Ximenes —at least in relation to the Moors and Jews. He was a principal promoter of the 'religious bigotry' which is, with very dubious accuracy, said to have 'belonged to the age'. His exhortation to his forces before the attack on Oran was not based on principles of either truth or morality and was calculated to evoke the very excesses which Prescott deplored.[1] The tribute to the 'courage and vigour' of the regent's activities against 'the Barbary corsairs' omits all reference to the final humiliation of his forces at Algiers, which was more spectacular than that at Jerba.

Equally remarkable is the account of the acquisition by Ximenes and Navarro of 'some of the most opulent marts of the Barbary coast' and the consolidation of 'security for commerce by sweeping the Mediterranean of the pestilential hordes of marauders which had so long infested it'. More recent historians will be surprised to learn that, though Navarro's conquests were subsequently lost to the Spanish crown 'through the imbecility or indolence of Ferdinand's successors', those of Ximenes were so solidly organized 'as to resist every attempt for their recovery by the enemy and to remain permanently incorporated with the Spanish empire'.[2]

---

[1] Prescott, ii. 432–3.
[2] Ibid., pp. 441–2. Captured by Algiers in 1708 and recovered in 1732, they passed finally to Algiers in 1791.

The revolutionary effect upon the Mediterranean system was as little expected as it was unwelcome. The old flourishing trade of the Catalans, Genoese, and Venetians was gradually strangled, mainly to the disadvantage of Spain's economy. The immediate beneficiaries were the English commercially, the French politically, and the Turks territorially. While we hear little of Moorish refugees from Spain, Jews exiled from the peninsula appear to have achieved an extraordinary pre-eminence in Morocco[1] during the century. The startling rise of the new port of Algiers was also largely due to the influx of Aragon Jews.[2]

The concentration of Christian writers on the purely maritime aspects of Barbary and their indifference to its internal history and characteristics have led to the assumption that the countryside, which represented the life-blood not only of its coastal fringe but to a large extent of Mediterranean economy, was a scene of stagnant misery or of anarchy and bloodshed. It is curious that the one picture which has come down to us over nearly two centuries is one of peace and prosperity at the very time that the ferment in Algeria, the struggle between the rival claims of 'Africa for King Ferdinand' and 'Africa for the Arabs', led to the intervention of the Turks and the consolidation of an alien regency.

However imperfect and superficial Leo's description may seem, one cannot but be impressed by the evidence of continuity as manifested by Jackson's verdict on Morocco three centuries later, or by such items as the fragrant rose-gardens of Tunis,[3] the dyers of Dellys, or the savage mountaineers of Tenez. In principle, the trend of commerce remained little altered over perhaps a thousand years—the exchange of the necessities of life and articles of luxury for the so-called 'contraband' of northern metals and timber. Eighteenth-century travellers like Shaw, while appreciating the quality of local products, emphasized the close resemblance between the methods and customs of rural Algeria and Tunisia and those of the Old Testament. In Victorian days Pellissier, who admired the virtues of their people and regarded them as the

---

[1] H. de Castries, *Une Description du Maroc sous le règne du Moulay Ahmed el Mansour, 1596*, Paris, 1909, pp. 119–20. [2] Established by Kheir-ed-din.
[3] Blaquiere, ii. 166.

potential backbone of North Africa, regretted the dangers of external contacts on their 'patriarchal innocence'.[1]

Reports of one new phenomenon, however, reached Leo at Rome, the development of a small tributary of a larger native tribe into the 'great and princely estate' of a Turkish ruler. The new departure had a special significance in that it took place, not through pressure by a maritime power but in the teeth of the one that was then regarded as omnipotent. It seems to have been derived primarily from an expression of the popular will and from the peculiar character of the region. The only mention of this singular little community during the reign of Ferdinand arose from the fact that 'those of Algiers', unlike the more powerful overlords, insisted on negotiating a formal treaty at the Aragon court[2] instead of accepting terms imposed by Navarro. As we also learn from Arab sources that a peculiar 'fifth rite' had its origin in the neighbourhood, and practised at Algiers the revolutionary doctrine that the watchword for Islam should be efficiency and not descent, we are perhaps justified in assuming that the special role played by that city during three centuries of Turkish dominion was by no means accidental.[3]

The social questions with which religious law was mainly concerned in Barbary were probably as familiar to the Turks at that time as to Western legislatures today: 'a living wage, employment of children, cruelty to animals, rabies, the drink question, gambling, speculating, combines, corners, retaliation'.[4] Segregated trades and organized guilds for merchants and craftsmen existed in very much the same way as in an Italian city like Florence. New problems connected with tobacco and drugs, forgery and counterfeit money, plague epidemics and the social diseases, appear to have been introduced from outside at later dates. Christian views about slavery and the rights of women in Barbary were evidently very defective.

Victorian advocates of *laissez-faire* smiled indulgently at a

[1] *Revue des Deux Mondes*, iii. 139, 1856.

[2] Signed at Saragossa, 24 Apr. 1510, on same terms as old Granada treaties, Prescott, ii. 440; Duro, i. 80.

[3] Weir, p. xlii. 'One of the most original towns in the Mediterranean world under the Turks', *Encyclopaedia of Islam*, 5 vols., Leyden and London, 1913, i. 259.

[4] Weir, p. xxiii.

social order in Turkey and other Moslem countries based on
the regulation of prices and the rationing of foodstuffs, but paid
tribute to the liberal attitude towards foreigners, not only in
religious matters but in freedom of trade.[1] Up to late in the
fifteenth century the right of asylum seems to have been freely
recognized by Spaniard and Moor, and no reproach attached
to the word 'renegade'.[2] It was the radical change in the Spanish
attitude that induced Prescott to remark that 'the Mahometans
would seem the better Christians of the two'.[3]

[1] *H.H.W.* xxiv. 363.
[2] Prescott, ii. 123 n.
[3] Ibid., ii. 150 and n.; *H.H.W.* x. 163 and n.; *Piratical States*, p. 170.

II

THE BARBAROSSA BROTHERS AND THE FOUNDATION OF THE TURKISH STATE IN ALGERIA

THE discrepancy between presumably reliable contemporary evidence relating to the history of Turkish rule in Barbary and the customary representation of it in recent times is particularly apparent in the case of the two celebrated brothers who, for some debatable reason, became known to Christians by the name of Barbarossa. Comment is unavoidable on the tendency to ignore completely the sympathetic references or, at times, surprisingly generous tributes from contemporaries, who might have been expected to be hostile to them, alike on religious and political grounds. It is remarkable that Kheir-ed-din should be highly spoken of—not only as a great naval officer but as a statesman—by our diplomatic agents and by our leading chronicler of that portion of history, Richard Knolles.

It is not unlikely that the more impartial and better-informed personages of the century compared the qualities and achievements of the Barbarossas by no means unfavourably with those of the now more famous Conquistadores. We can only regret that they have done so little to explain the process by which a small body of maritime adventurers, discredited aliens, without the aid of ships, war supplies, or foreign allies, acquired, within the space of two or three years and in the teeth of local hostility and the armed might of Spain, a powerful, and durable, state in central Algeria.[1]

Little enlightenment can be obtained from a comparison of well-known works by a great variety of historians. Prescott represents Spanish power as remaining unchallenged on the Barbary coast even after the death of Ferdinand and Ximenes. He is apparently unaware of the presence in the Mediterranean

---

[1] 'An adventurer with a motley following of untrained bandits and nomads', Lane-Poole, p. 50; Plantet, i, pp. lvi–lvii.

of Turks or similar disturbing elements. Duro, ordinarily so factual, cites no concrete record of maritime contributions by Aruj. For contemporary evidence of the latter's career he relies almost entirely on Lopez de Gomara, whose very positive conclusions he completely ignores. De la Roncière rightly refers to the career of Aruj as 'prodigious'.[1] He is first mentioned in that narrative as stationed off Elba with 30 warships, at the very time that other accounts represent him as engaged in activities at Cherchell with 16 vessels or (more probably) at Algiers with 2 simple galliots. Events, dates, and localities at this stage are usually left tantalizingly vague, when they are not involved in hopeless contradiction.

A certain amount of conjecture is unavoidable about occurrences and conditions in an island as remote from the West as Mitylene. It was, however, clearly an important centre of the peaceful commerce carried on by Christian traders—more especially the Venetians and Genoese—during the time that the Barbarossa brothers were growing to manhood. Even if we discount entirely such Turkish and Arabic narratives as have come down to us, a reasonably accurate picture of their character and qualities can surely be obtained from a study of certain Christian accounts, which give evidence of an unusual degree of impartiality and reliability.

From these it is clear that the brothers were not renegades, outcasts, pirates, barbarians, or 'infamous' characters. Kheir-ed-din, for instance, who occupies such a large place in the annals of the day, was not, as often stated, a 'renegade Christian'. He is described, apparently quite correctly, by Gomara as a 'Turk, son of a renegade and grandson of a Christian'. Since Aruj died childless in 1518, he could not possibly have been the father of Kheir-ed-din or his successor to the governorship of Algiers in 1533. If Aruj was born not earlier than 1474, Kheir-ed-din, who was some years younger, could not have been an octogenarian, much less in his ninetieth year, in 1546. The one thing of real importance is that from 1533 he was admiralissimo of the great Sultan Suleiman the Magnificent.

Even the place of birth and early upbringing of the brothers has been adduced as evidence that they were 'born pirates'. It is true that previously, according to Finlay, Mitylene had

[1] iii. 142–3.

been a base for the Catalan, Italian, and Sicilian pirates, who infested the entrance to the Dardanelles, capturing Turkish ships and carrying off inhabitants of the mainland for sale or ransom. It was there that, after its settlement by the Turks, the father of the Barbarossas, a retired janissary, described as *un honnête Musulman*, made his home, married the widow of a Greek priest, and evidently prospered as a potter, since he is said to have owned a vessel for the transportation of his wares and traded sometimes as far as Constantinople. Most of the family must still have been resident there in 1501, when Venetian and French forces attempted to seize the island as a suitable base for operations against the Dardanelles on the strength of a Genoese report that it was *moult riche, fertile et prenable.*[1] Jurien suggests that the sons were still there then as very young men.

Of their mother's first children we hear nothing except that they continued to form part of the family. The two daughters of her second marriage are said to have been brought up as Christians in accordance with the custom which left females in such cases a free choice of their religion. Their four brothers learned to read and write from the Koran, and were all taught to work from an early age. While Elias studied for the priesthood, Isaak became a carpenter. Aruj, who was apparently the eldest and favourite son, worked on his father's boat, and Kheir-ed-din, the youngest, helped in the pottery. References to their virtuous upbringing and happy family life, including maternal affection for the grown sons, is of special interest since they come from a contemporary historian.

Gomara's enthusiastic admiration for Kheir-ed-din, the most famous of the brothers, is the more remarkable in that he was a Spanish priest, evidently a very loyal supporter of Church and State, writing at a time when the admiral had been spreading terror through the dominions of Spain, and because, as Prescott tells us, he was well acquainted with the principal men of his time and enabled, by long residence at court, to form reliable judgements both of current events and of official reactions to them.[2] He was attached to an embassy at Venice during one of Kheir-ed-din's Adriatic campaigns, took part

---

[1] Hubbard, *Day of the Crescent*, p. 141; Finlay, v. 59; de la Roncière, iii. 50.
[2] *Conquest of Mexico*, ed. Foster Kirk, 2 vols., London, undated, ii. 181–2.

in the disastrous expedition of 1541 against Algiers as chaplain to Cortes, and was interested in naval history. Aretino,[1] who must surely have known Gomara at Venice; Brantôme, who wrote at a time when relations between France and Algiers were very strained; and Diego Haedo, a Spanish ecclesiastic who wrote about Algiers soon after the Barbarossa line became extinct, speak of him with almost as much authority and generosity.

It is a striking testimonial to the spirit of free speech and fair-play that these and other writers, such as Maréchal Vieilleville, could openly speak in praise or defence of prominent infidels. Even in England the Duke of Norfolk is recorded as extolling the number and quality of Kheir-ed-din's forces at Algiers.[2] It is quite possible that Andrea Doria had a higher opinion of his great rival than of his Spanish, French, and Italian col-leagues. The people best able to judge about the relative merits of Ottomans and Western Christians were the free states of Italy, and especially the Venetians, whose views are little represented in our histories.

The two brothers, who became famous as the founders of Turkish rule in North Africa, were evidently not ignorant or devoid of culture. It is highly improbable that Aruj found time to indulge, as alleged, in a long and flowery correspondence with a Moorish princess, but Algiers in his time, like other centres of Arabian learning, was evidently a place where books were highly prized. 'The best gifts', said the historian Ibn Askar soon afterwards, 'which a man can give to his sons are books of learning.'[3]

It is possible that Kheir-ed-din, who is said to have devoted most of his wealth to founding a college at Constantinople, was still at Algiers when it became the chosen residence of a learned Moorish writer and diplomat whose hobby was dialectics and the collection of books.[4] His skill in engineering was demon-strated by the construction of the famous mole at Algiers and also apparently of its handsome new city, as well as by the

---

[1] Aretino extolled him as 'King of Algiers' above Suleiman, Pietro Aretino, *Il Secondo Libro delle Lettere*, ed. F. Nicolini, Bari, 1916, ii. 54–55; E. Hutton, *Pietro Aretino, Scourge of Princes*, London, 1922, p. 201 n.

[2] Cal. S.P. Spanish 1531–3, pp. 797–8.

[3] Weir, p. 217.

[4] *H.H.W.* xxiv. 354; Weir, pp. 215–17; Leo, p. 684.

siege-works at Nice, which the Spanish commander del Guasto regarded as superior to anything that he had seen.[1] The experiences of Navarro and the still more celebrated engineer Vianelli suggest that the fortifications of Aruj at Jerba were not inferior to those at better-known places. Members of the Spanish expedition sent against him at Algiers in 1516 may well have shared that view.

It is significant that the brothers were good linguists. Besides, presumably, Turkish, Arabic, and Greek Kheir-ed-din spoke French well enough to create the belief that he was a native, and Spanish fluently in spite of a lisp. He conversed in Italian with prisoners of war and perhaps with his second wife, who was the daughter of the Governor of Reggio and an accomplished musician.[2] Although the poet Pietro Aretino is said to have received a very friendly and laudatory letter from Kheir-ed-din, who clearly corresponded at times with various prominent Christians, only one letter appears to be still extant, and even that may possibly be no more than an extract.[3]

If we exclude one or two incidents which are surely extremely improbable, there does not appear to have been anything particularly irregular about the early career of Aruj. He embarked on an official but disastrous expedition from Constantinople against the Knights of Rhodes who were then operating in Cretan waters, was captured, and ransomed after a period in the galleys. He was later entrusted with a privateer by merchants of Constantinople—'an employ too honourable, advantageous and conformable to his disposition to reject'[4]— and subsequently served in turn under the Mamelukes of Egypt, under the influential Bey of Satalia, and from about 1504, 'while still a young man', under the King of Tunis.

It was about this time that he is recorded as committing his 'first big pirate outrage'.[5] This was the capture of the papal flag-

---

[1] Rang, *Fondation de la régence d'Alger*, pp. 368-83; Charrière, i. 566-7; Ekrem Rechid, *La Vie de Khairredine Barberousse*, Paris, 1931, pp. 222 and 224.

[2] Duro, i. 268.

[3] Gomara, p. 539, ? early 1540 to Federico Gonzaga, Viceroy of Naples, 'Friend of your friends and enemy of your enemies, I will now clear the sea of privateers (corsarios), so that only traders will use it. If now an enemy should attack your navy my galleys will join with yours as far as possible, and I will give you my best help. You will have further details from John', i.e. Juan de Gallego.

[4] Morgan, *A Complete History of Algiers* (2nd ed., London, 1731), p. 221.

[5] S. R. H. Rogers, *The Barbary Pirates*, London and Glasgow, 1939, p. 17.

ship, which was far more powerful than his small craft, was at war with Islam, and presumably had many Turkish prisoners among the galley-slaves, whose treatment, even in those days, aroused the compassion of Italian visitors to Rome.[1] The flagship was the actual aggressor, as the galliot (or brigantine) is described as immobilized at the time. Haedo, who probably understood the respective relations of the pope and the King of Tunis with the various Christian states,[2] speaks of it as a 'noble exploit' which caused Aruj, even in Christendom, to be regarded as 'a most valiant and enterprising commander'.

Some idea of his career may be suggested by a comparison of dates. In the year 1500 King Frederick of Naples turned to the sultan for assistance. In the same year Sicilian forces were withdrawn from Jerba.[3] The suggestion that at about the same date Aruj was installed there under the authority of the King of Tunis would fit in with the description of his age, which might then be twenty-six. He presumably came to Tunis with a ship or ships of Turkish origin. An Arab chronicle mentions that he was given a *zebec* by the governor, who was brother of the future Sultan Selim or closely connected with him.[4]

His capture of a Sicilian ship with 360 Spanish soldiers[5] off Lipari at some vague date is said to have led to his official recognition as *bey* by the sultan. Lane-Poole places the action in 1505, the very date at which Zurita records the unexpected appearance of Turks in Sicilian waters and the (otherwise unmentioned) destruction of their total force. Even more curious is the picture presented by de la Roncière of the pope stabbing his French allies in the back and simultaneously, with tears in his eyes, imploring their aid against the Barbary pirates.[6] This is described as taking place in May 1510, when

Lane-Poole, pp. 35–36, gives Haedo's account. Gomara, Duro, de la Roncière, and Jurien ignore it.

[1] 'Poor fellows! They must envy the dead', Grossino in 1512, *Isabella d'Este*, ed. J. Cartwright, 2 vols., London, 1903, ii. 59.

[2] Haedo, *Topographia e Historia General de Argel*, i. 215–18. Genoese, Tuscans, Venetians, and Catalans normally courted Tunis. Gomara called Julius a 'bad Pope but good man', *Annales*, p. 36, and later cited him with Francis I, Louis XII, and Ferdinand the Catholic as examples of perfidious diplomacy, ibid., p. 132; *H.H.W.* ix. 434.   [3] Prescott, ii. 201 and 209; Duro, i. 31.

[4] Rang, i. 15–22; Hubac, *Les Barbaresques*, pp. 116–17. See Haedo, i. 267.

[5] Gomara, p. 356; Duro, i. 99; Haedo, i. 218–19. The captives were presented to the Sultan and King of Tunis.   [6] iii. 84.

Spain had almost completed its easy conquest of Barbary. The effect of the disaster at Jerba was clearly seen in a massive but ineffectual attack on Tripoli by land and sea forces of the King of Tunis. An equally unsuccessful rising was launched by the King of Tlemcen.[1]

At some time in this period Aruj was joined by Kheir-ed-din. Elias was killed beside Aruj in Egyptian waters, while Isaak remained in Mitylene as a merchant and engaged recruits for Aruj. Either, however, Elias and Isaak had alternative names or they are confused at times with two other brothers or half-brothers.

Aruj appears to have arrived in Algeria with a force of trained soldiers, which must have been very small, if he had only five inconsiderable vessels.[2] He was joined by some 3,000 men of the Zouave tribe, who were preparing to besiege Bougie. The main operation was on land, and his subsequent exploits at sea appear to have been limited to the possible capture of a Genoese galliot in the course of an enforced voyage from Bougie to Tunis. There could in any case have been little time available for marine activities, since the campaigning season both by land and sea was usually limited to the summer months. Out of a maximum period of five years spent in Algeria two were taken up with disastrous assaults on Bougie in the summers of 1514 and 1515.[3] The first cost him an arm and an enforced convalescence. The second, according to Duro, was begun by the deliberate burning of his ships in order to ensure complete concentration on the task in hand.

This suggests, and helps to corroborate, two important factors, viz. that his objective was essentially a military one, and that he was not hampered by the presence of galley-slaves, a most important consideration in combined operations.

It is, indeed, possible that Kheir-ed-din himself began his service as an oarsman. Long afterwards, at the great battle of Prevesa, he had only volunteer Turkish rowers alike in his flagship and reserve galleys. According to Jurien, he never allowed anyone but Turkish oarsmen on his own ships or those

[1] Duro, i. 95.
[2] In previous year he had 3 ships and 2 foists, and for Bougie expedition one galley, one galliot, and 3 foists, Gomara p. 360. Two foists belonged to Tunis.
[3] Duro, i. 100 and n., but see Lane-Poole, pp. 40–44.

of Algiers, and thus doubled their effectiveness as compared with corresponding Christian units. It is noteworthy that in 1596 the less intelligent janissaries were employed as oarsmen in the Turkish navy, and volunteers were used even later in Venetian galleys.[1]

After the unexpected failure of the second siege Aruj settled at Djidjelli.[2] He possessed no ships or money, and could no longer count on any support from Tunis, whose ruler was thenceforward mainly hostile. None the less he is said to have won the goodwill of the 'indomitable mountaineers' of the hinterland. Arab accounts suggest, moreover, that close relations were maintained with the Ottoman Turks. Kheir-ed-din is said to have parted company with Aruj in the autumn of 1514 and settled at Jerba. He may well have taken steps to obtain assistance from the sultan during the Syrian operations. It seems very probable that Aruj did receive some aid and encouragement.[3]

At all events, he had by 1516 been invited to assist in shaking off the Spanish yoke at Algiers. It is improbable that the invitation arose out of a refusal to pay tribute after Ferdinand's death, which only took place in a remote part of Estremadura late in January 1516.[4] By September of that year Cherchell and Algiers had been taken in spite of the Peñón or island fort, which blocked the latter harbour. Still less credible are statements that the invitation came from the Governor of Algiers, Selim Eutemi, who tried to capture the Peñón by force, and that in return he was treacherously murdered by Aruj in his bath, during service at the mosque, or at table.[5]

---

[1] Duro, i. 234; J. B. E. Jurien de la Gravière, *Doria et Barberousse*, p. 269. In Turkey (1596) 'the unaptest Janissaries are set upon the Galleis to learne to row at sea', Cotton MS. Nero B. xi, f. 7. Algiers's small force was successful because 'swift and light as fire' (Cervantes), Duro, i. 323-5 and iii. 434. It left little room for armament, soldiers, refugees, or captives.

[2] Duro, i. 101.

[3] The sultan sent the brothers 14 Ottoman ships, but had to recall them in 1516, Jurien, p. 89; Peysonnel, *Voyages dans les régences de Tunis et d'Alger*, p. 390.

[4] De Vera's expedition, authorized 12 Apr. 1516, landed 30 Sept. unopposed, like de Moncada in 1519. It lost 3,000 killed and 400 prisoners on land, Duro, i. 102-3.

[5] Duro calls Aruj 'horribly cruel', but without evidence, e.g. in Gomara documents, pp. 443-87. *Annales*, pp. 46 and 56, simply report in 1516 'he makes himself King of Algiers', and in 1518 'the Spaniards slay Arudj Barbarossa, who waged war gallantly (*gentilmente*) against Moors and Christians by land and sea'. Prescott

What does seem certain is that dissension arose between the two factions: the country Arabs, who marched against Algiers with a force of some 3,000 (or 5,000) men under the fanatical Sheik Benalcalde, and the partisans of Spain headed by Selim, who is officially described by the Spanish Admiral de Vera as honourable and loyal.[1] While there seems to be no precise information as to how Selim was killed, it is clear that Aruj, whether he arrived at the head of a large army or by sea with only two foists, built by himself at Djidjelli, took complete charge of the city, removed all traces of the King of Spain's arms or other insignia, and proceeded to inflict a crushing defeat on the powerful force which de Vera sent to avenge Selim's family.

It is related that the popularity and prestige of Aruj immediately became so great that the Moors obeyed him more willingly than any previous ruler. His authority was promptly and firmly established throughout the 'kingdom', i.e. central Algeria, and he even extended his triumph momentarily to Tlemcen, the stronghold of extreme nationalism. Though his spectacular defeat of de Vera is said to have caused small boys in the streets of Spain to mock the returning soldiers for having been beaten by a one-armed man,[2] he was unable to expel or starve out the small garrison of the Peñón, which a detailed report of that year shows to have been in a very precarious condition.

United action by Spanish forces and local partisans led to his expulsion from Tlemcen and death during the retreat—in apparently his forty-fourth year and eight years after his first action against Navarro at Jerba. His end was sufficiently notable to be celebrated in Spain by a heroic poem in 1796 and by a tragedy, which in 1827 was played at the court theatres. From the various claimants to the distinction of killing him a Spanish knight was singled out and granted permission to incorporate in his arms the head of Aruj.[3] A portrait, probably

condemns Spanish inventions of Moorish and Jewish cruelty, i. 276 and ii. 153–6 and 509–22. De Tassy said 'Horror and Contempt' of Algiers were mainly due to stories by Spanish monks.

[1] Letter of condolence to Selim's sons, 10 Aug. 1516, Gomara, p. 445.
[2] Rotalier, i. 113 n. Regarded as 'more than a man and king', Duro, i. 103 and n.
[3] Duro, i. 126 and n.

still extant, describes him with unusual correctness as 'Premier Fondateur de la Régence d'Alger'. It has been said that his only comparable contemporary was Hernando Cortes.[1]

Another portrait reproduced early in the next century[2] does not appear at all inconsistent with Lane-Poole's verbal picture of the 'gallant, impulsive, reckless, lovable soldier of fortune' or with Haedo's more detailed description. This continues, in Morgan's English version:

He was a man excessively bold, resolute, daring, magnanimous, enterprizing, profusely liberal and in no way bloodthirsty except in the heat of battle, nor rigorously cruel but when disobeyed. He was highly beloved, feared and respected, by his soldiers and domestics, and when dead was by them in general most bitterly regretted. He left neither son nor daughter. He resided in Barbary fourteen years during which the harms he did to the Christians are inexpressible.[3]

The outstanding feature of the critical period in Algerine history between the death of Aruj, which apparently took place late in 1518, and the definite emergence of Algiers as an important Mediterranean state, after the capture of the Peñón in 1529, is the absence of official or other reliable records. It is most unfortunate that this interval should coincide exactly with a complete blank in the Spanish documents annexed to Gomara's narrative. Indeed, with the exception of one incidental reference to the death of Aruj, no official mention of either brother is cited between 1516 and 1529 in that volume or in the works of Jurien, Duro, and de la Roncière. No less unfortunate is the absence of reliable, or at least documentary, information about the relations of the Barbarossas with the Ottoman empire during the development and maintenance of the new Algerine state. I have seen no convincing evidence for the generally accepted assumption that, on the disastrous death of his brother, Kheir-ed-din resorted to an ingenious or desperate innovation in applying to the sultan for his official protection, and that, by the opportune arrival from Constantinople of a substantial force of Turkish troops and artillery, he was enabled to defeat the powerful expedition directed against

[1] H.H.W. xxiv. 477.

[2] Charles-Roux reproduces the brothers' portraits. Kheir-ed-din's features were as familiar to Christians as Doria's, Jurien, p. 84.

[3] Lane-Poole, pp. 52–53; Morgan, A Complete History of Algiers, p. 257.

Algiers by Hugo de Moncada, the newly appointed Spanish General of the Sea. Indeed, the objections to such a view seem to me insuperable, unless we are to reject entirely this portion of Gomara's narrative.

Among the principal difficulties is the absence of any evidence that any important alteration took place at that time in the relations between the Barbarossas and the Porte, which were evidently of long standing, or that Kheir-ed-din did at that moment stand in urgent need of assistance. Quite apart from the time-factor, which makes it very doubtful if an expedition of this magnitude could have been sent to Algiers at such short notice, there remains the important question whether the sultan was not in a more difficult position in the Levant and eastern Tunisia than Kheir-ed-din at Algiers. If such a large armament had in fact arrived either before or soon after the crushing and profitable victory over de Moncada the prestige and power of the Turks would surely have been greater than it had ever been before in Algeria, and no necessity would have arisen for the humiliating flight to Djidjelli, even if the interior did prove hostile.

The relations between Aruj and other parts of the empire had evidently been continuous and perhaps increasingly close throughout the Algerian adventure, which coincided with Selim's conquest of Syria and Egypt. Nothing could be more natural than for Kheir-ed-din to advise the sultan of the death of the local Ottoman representative and of his own provisional recognition by the Turkish soldiers. Probably he, like various other commanders at Jerba, which was the principal corsair centre, or Turkish outpost, west of the Levant, already held commissions from the Sultan or his recognized deputy. It is not unlikely that, when, at a favourable moment, Kheir-ed-din was dispatched to rejoin his brother at Algiers, either with, or slightly ahead of, some 800 Turkish soldiers,[1] the consolidation of a Turkish province in Algeria, similar to those of Syria and Egypt, was already under consideration. Any such development may have been halted by the unexpected French crusade against Turkish ports in Tunisia and the Levant and the death of Aruj. No date for the recognition of Kheir-ed-din

[1] Gomara, p. 370. One brother in Mitylene recruited soldiers from Turkey, Duro, i. 103.

in his new functions or its implementation by material assistance is quoted. It is very unlikely that any decisive step could even have been contemplated when, early in the year, following a French check at Monastir, de Moncada left Sicily to prepare his Algiers expedition. The one fact that seems to stand out clearly amidst so much that is confusing and contradictory is the strategic importance of that section of African coast which lay between the Spanish strongholds of Bougie and Tripoli, opposite to Sardinia and Sicily.

It is a curious circumstance that our standard naval history of Spain adheres closely to Gomara's narrative for details of this important expedition, while presenting an entirely different picture of its very dubious sequel, and thereby undoubtedly doing much to influence modern concepts of Algerine history. It seems to be agreed that the fleet under de Moncada arrived in mid-August with some eighty vessels, and that its dispatch was due to apprehensions of Turkish aggression, which had repercussions as far apart as Guipúzcoa, Marseilles, Genoa, and Sardinia.[1]

Gomara not only makes no reference to any kind of intervention by the sultan, but intimates that the position in Algiers was by no means unsatisfactory. The election of Kheir-ed-din as king or governor of Algiers and Tenez was recognized by the Turkish soldiers, of whom a considerable body remained from the time of Aruj, and also by the people of Algiers. He also received the powerful support of Benalcalde, at that time his friend and ally. While Gomara stresses the fact that he was very poorly provided with artillery, he makes no suggestion that the Algerines had any ships worth mentioning. Duro, however, attributes the dispatch of de Moncada to a raid which Kheir-ed-din made with forty foists on Bona (!!) to avenge his brother's death. More specific evidence of the position in the Mediterranean comes in a dispatch of 27 May 1519 from the emperor at Barcelona, instructing his Neapolitan galleys to join those of Genoa in pursuit of thirty-two Moorish vessels which had been doing great damage off the coast of Sardinia. A French document suggests that they were corsairs from the Tunis area making

---

[1] Contrast improbable accounts by de la Roncière, Duro, i. 127–30, and Gomara, pp. 379–92. Note absence of documents 1519–28 or further mention of Algiers in *Annales* until 1540.

reprisals in French and Genoese waters for Navarro's aggressions on the 'pirates of the Tunisian coast'. They are described as terminating this *sanglante riposte* by landing two mutilated captives near Marseilles with instructions to 'go and tell your Christian kings: "This is the crusade you have proclaimed" '.[1]

Both Duro and Gomara describe the shipwreck of the great expedition as one of the gravest disasters in African history. While de la Roncière contents himself with the fantastic statement that there were only a thousand survivors, the others give an equally improbable account of the immense and *immediate* advantage which accrued through the salvage of artillery, money, captives for the galleys, and timber for ship-building.

Here the various histories very definitely part company. The French seem to have led an uneasy life with most of their Christian neighbours and on the eve of Pavia were flirting with Tunis and the Porte. Duro tells us that, while de Moncada with the remnant of his fleet took refuge in Ibiza, a cloud of corsairs under Kheir-ed-din and other prominent leaders, whom Gomara, however, describes as residing in Jerba, assailed or desolated Valencia, Catalonia, the Balearics, Sardinia, and Sicily, committing all sorts of atrocities and even bearding the emperor in his own port of Barcelona. The departure of Charles with an imposing fleet for Flanders in May 1520 left Kheir-ed-din complete master of Algiers, Bona, Tunis, and Tlemcen, 'and above all the sea'.[2]

The documents, however, which Duro himself cites, show that early in November 1519 de Moncada with 8 galleys was again in action off the coast of Sardinia with a Turkish fleet of 13 vessels. In May 1520 he launched a successful attack with 100 ships from Sicily, capturing the principal base of the corsairs at Jerba and restoring the native chieftain as the emperor's vassal. No less remarkable is the fact that, despite the ruinous war in Provence and Italy between French and Spanish forces, the Turkish ships seem to have achieved no visible advantage in the notoriously disaffected territories of Spain.

---

[1] De la Roncière, iii. 147–8. At Amalfi in 1528 Barbary slaves aiding Doria hacked de Moncada's corpse, crying 'va maintenant, va dévaster les rivages de l'Afrique', Jurien, p. 169.

[2] Duro, i. 130. However, Venetian traffic with the Channel, and English to the Levant, flourished: de la Roncière, iii. 154 and 183; Duro, i. 201–15; *Pol. Hist.* vi. 305 n.; Hakluyt, v. 62–63.

Gomara paints an entirely irreconcilable picture. Soon after the encounter with de Moncada Kheir-ed-din quarrelled with Benalcalde and had to fly for refuge to Djidjelli with his five ships. Neither Duro nor de la Roncière makes any mention of that port at this stage. Gomara, whose chronology is very erratic, tells us that Kheir-ed-din captured it from Benalcalde and merely used it as an asylum for his family and property. He then proceeded to Jerba, where he joined the group of corsair leaders whom Duro and others represent as operating with him from Algiers.

If, as seems probable, Djidjelli served as his base of operations from 1520 to 1525,[1] he may well have spent the initial period in consolidating his position there with the aid of refugees and adventurers, both Christian and native, and of 'contraband' supplies from the Venetians and Ragusans, as well as, doubtless, from other neighbouring sources. He had brought with him a fair proportion of the Turkish soldiers whom Aruj had retained in garrison at Algiers, but by 1522 it would appear that his remaining force was too weak to occupy Bona, even with the help of local partisans.

If there is no positive evidence to the contrary, I would suggest that concrete assistance of any importance was first sent to Djidjelli after Ottoman forces had been freed for less urgent purposes on the surrender of Rhodes. With such a large body of regular soldiers Kheir-ed-din could have been in a position to embark on his progress overland to Algiers. He would at last be capable of performing his principal function as governor-general of the province of Algeria and hope to complete the task previously envisaged by Aruj.

Whatever the exact course of events may have been, the fact remains that by the year 1525 Kheir-ed-din was installed in Algiers as the administrative centre of a province or state which was to remain Turkish for three centuries, until it was dissolved by external forces. The system adopted closely followed that recently introduced into Egypt, but for a variety of reasons it was to prove more efficient and durable.

The key to the position may be found to some extent in the difference between the functions of Kheir-ed-din and the ill-

[1] Rang, i. 191–2; *Letters and Papers*, iv. 1127, 'King of Gigert', compare Dapper, p. 244.

fated de Moncada during his connexion with Algeria. The latter then held the titles of 'Captain General of the Sea' and 'Captain General of the Maritime Army and conquered territory in Africa'. In other words, he was primarily commander-in-chief in Mediterranean waters, with the added responsibility of the *presidios* or coastal forts in Barbary, a position very similar to that of the Capudan pasha, or Captain General of the Sea, at Constantinople. The principal task of Kheir-ed-din as governor-general and General of the Sea was one of colonial administration and expansion, his functions as admiral, which would include supervision of dockyards and coast defences, being incidental.

As governor-general his office was essentially military. He would not normally set foot on the sea, and his naval duties were performed by a lieutenant, until later in the century they were entrusted to a separate officer who, as the local Captain of the Sea, became directly responsible to the sultan. It seems clear that from 1525, when Algiers was recaptured, the celebrated commander Jayredin, a native Turk who was known to Christians as Cachidiablo, conducted naval operations in the name of Kheir-ed-din.[1] The rather vague evidence suggests that the latter did not, during his stay in Algiers, exercise any control over Turkish naval officers, or corsairs, at ports in Tunisia.

The honourable title of Great Corsair—an unfortunate and misleading term since it is neither Turkish nor English—was less appropriately bestowed in those days on Kheir-ed-din than on his friendly opponent, Andrea Doria, or even, perhaps, on Sir Richard Grenville.[2] Apart from the great triumph at Prevesa, to which his personal contribution is conjectural, I know of no record of his prowess on the high seas. As late as 1537 his naval fame had not apparently reached Venice. Gomara, who had an extravagant admiration for his naval exploits, arrived at the matured judgement that the Algerines achieved nothing at sea until he re-entered the Mediterranean as the sultan's grand admiral and became so essential a factor in the pre-eminence of the Ottoman empire.[3]

[1] Cachidiablo and Sinan 'the Jew' came from Asia Minor.

[2] A. L. Rowse, *Sir Richard Grenville*, London, 1937, pp. 303 and 313. Brantôme called Kheir-ed-din *roi corsaire*.

[3] Gomara, p. 349, confirmed by *Annales*. After Prevesa Harvel reported (Venice, 1538), 'Barbarossa finally sheweth himself a grete captayne', and 'if

In conferring upon him official authority as governor-general in Algeria the sultan is said not only to have granted him licence to enlist recruits from Turkey, a practice which appears to have been sanctioned from the time of Aruj to that of the last Dey, but to have supplied him with 2,000 janissaries, members of a military force already renowned for its discipline, training, and patriotism. They evidently helped to reinforce the tradition which made Algiers a 'military power' for three centuries, and provided an organization which, by retaining many of the old virtues of that famous corps and modifying some of those defects that were in Turkey so seriously to impair its character and usefulness, aroused favourable comment from European observers even in the nineteenth century.[1]

From this time Algiers had a standing army, which provided it with the nucleus of a regular naval establishment. The result of concentrating in that city the administration, army, and marine of the new state was that, in Armstrong's words, it 'became perfect in its military and naval organisation and its power of attack, perhaps the most mobile force that the world has seen'.[2] The careful planning and the strict discipline involved seem entirely inconsistent with the uncontrolled licence of privateering and individual enterprise. It was the infusion of that spirit in his fleet that Duro regarded as Kheir-ed-din's principal contribution to the great victory at Prevesa. It is also seen in the record of the regular troops of Algiers, vouched for by foreign observers from the sixteenth to the nineteenth centuries, who, while engaged in active fighting, did not deign to plunder 'even the value of an asper'. Their Turkish contemporaries struck a Christian ambassador as being in their manners more like 'some Turkish monks or Fellows of some College', and Sir Philip Sidney was among those who thought we had much to learn from them.[3]

The outstanding feature of what may be termed Algerine waters during the period prior to the capture of the Peñón in 1529 is their placidity or, alternatively, the singular ineffective-

soche audacitie be grounded with prudence and good councel Barbarossa is worthye of grete lawde', *State Papers, Henry VIII*, vol. viii. 80 and 83.

[1] App. L.

[2] E. Armstrong, *The Emperor Charles V*, 2 vols., London, 1902, i. 268–9.

[3] Sir W. Stirling Maxwell, *Don John of Austria, 1547–75*, 2 vols., London, 1883, i. 291.

ness of the rival marines. Spain, France, and Turkey were fully engaged in maritime operations far afield—in the Levant, Spanish Main, and English Channel. After the fall of Rhodes, France and Spain were at war with each other and negotiating for Moslem assistance from Fez to Constantinople and Persia. So far as the Mediterranean was concerned, France, which had seen Provence overrun by Spaniards and Toulon sacked, had ceased to have any naval importance. Of the two special heroes of French campaigns at sea Pedro Navarro is last described as commanding 'two little miserable ships' off Genoa in 1528[1] prior to his imprisonment and execution at Naples. Prégent de Bidoux met his death in a triumphant victory near Nice over a Turk galley, or even a mere galliot.[2] Early in 1532 King Francis was appealing—evidently in vain—to the Sacred College in Rouen for maritime aid to save the important bastion of Provence from an alleged Algerine menace.[3] The alliance or *entente* with Kheir-ed-din dates from the following year.

The customary divergence between Spanish and French reports during the period can only be touched on lightly, the more so as in the former Gomara and Duro are apt to disagree with each other, while the accounts of Jurien and de la Roncière have practically nothing in common with either. In 1525, the year that Francis surrendered his fleet to the emperor after Pavia, and Kheir-ed-din had returned to Algiers, we learn from Duro that a Spanish fleet of 60 ships was attacking a port on the Atlantic coast of Morocco, apparently in the Portuguese sphere; that the Spanish galleys at Alicante were in a state of mutiny; and that their commander, Machin de Renteria, whose squadron formerly drove Aruj away from Bougie, had, single-handed, gained a signal victory off Valencia over an Algerine fleet of 18 vessels. Gomara, however, asserts that they never came into contact with each other at all.

Evidently the principal centre of interest was Tlemcen, where Kheir-ed-din succeeded in winning over the local ruler, in spite of the dispatch of 5,000 soldiers from Spain. The ill-provided, waterless rock of the Peñón also suddenly became a focus of interest and anxiety. While Kheir-ed-din is described

---

[1] *Biographie universelle*, xxx. 251–2.   [2] De la Roncière, iii. 163.
[3] De la Roncière, iii. 335 and n. The Algiers ships numbered 26, not 120, Charrière, i. 195.

as surrounding the fort with 45 vessels and 8,000 men and launching a desperate assault upon it, the emperor was confident that the dispatch of two chartered Genoese carracks with 200 soldiers would be sufficient for its relief. It is possible that they approached just in time to witness the surrender.[1]

In view of the absence of any details in the Gomara documents and serious discrepancies in accounts of the number and fate of the survivors it seems not unlikely that the position was quickly surrendered as hopeless. Duro differs from most of the traditional accounts in stating that the commander—instead of being burned alive or otherwise tortured to death—remained a captive until the raid on Cherchell the next year. It is possible that he was one of the seventeen captains who, according to Gomara, were executed on that occasion, with unspeakable tortures, for attempting to rise and join in the Spanish attack. Jurien, however, thinks it most unlikely that Kheir-ed-din would butcher such a valuable officer. Actually the principle of ransoming or exchanging prisoners of war was as well established in Turkey and Barbary as in Spain and Italy. Indeed, special regulations about the ransom of important persons by the King of Tunis are mentioned about this very time. I have not seen any *first-hand* accounts of contemporary events in Algiers or evidence of any immediate interest in the fall of the Peñón.

Cachidiablo appears to have acted at this time with a degree of caution and timidity that suggests his conventional repute may have rested on a very slender basis. If we can trust Gomara's account, which is not inconsistent with official Spanish reports, Cachidiablo hesitated for three months to make any raid on the coast of Valencia in spite of Moorish unrest there and the elaborate preparations of Portuondo's expedition (? at Genoa) for the defence of the Kingdom of Granada. It was only on learning that the Spanish force was at sea that the Algerine finally made his hasty and, as it proved, belated raid on Murla and other villages near Oliva, carrying off a number of Moors and giving encouragement to others. The raid was evidently regarded by both the Viceroy of Valencia and the empress as a distressing novelty, and the defeat of

[1] Duro, i. 158; Gomara, pp. 395–6; Jurien, pp. 188–92. Charles's letters of May and June 1529 are in Gomara, pp. 489–93.

Portuondo's fleet of eight galleys and a brigantine caused consternation. This was reputed 'the most signal and notable victory that Barbarossa has had over Spaniards in a sea-battle' and 'the greatest loss inflicted on a Spanish fleet of galleys'. Even more remarkable are other statements by Gomara that, miraculous as it might seem, less than twenty Turks lost their lives in the action, and that a notable part had been played in its success by the slings of some Moriscos who had been landed on the island of Formentera.[1]

The fame of this exploit spread over a wide area. Sinan, 'the Jew', a native of Smyrna, who seems to have been the sultan's lieutenant in Tunisian waters and later became one of his chief admirals, is said to have arrived, voluntarily or under instructions, at Algiers with 60 ships. Anxiety was even expressed about the possible abandonment of Bougie and Oran and for the safety of Cadiz. An attack was hurriedly directed by the new captain general, Alvaro de Bazan, with 30 galleys—not at Algiers but against Cherchell, a naval supply base which was defended only by a remote citadel. According, apparently, to an official report by Bazan the town was taken without resistance, 8 or 9 abandoned vessels seized, and some 800 Christian galley-slaves liberated. Considerable loss was, however, incurred by the troops while engaged in plunder ashore.[2]

The discrepancies between this account by Duro and the very varied versions of Gomara, de la Roncière, and Jurien are truly remarkable. Some interest might attach to the statement of the last-named that this was the first occasion on which Kheir-ed-din and Andrea Doria met each other. Duro, however, makes no mention of either, and Kheir-ed-din was at that time probably engaged in the interior. It may well be, however, that the two had previously met, as friends or foes, in Tunisia or even at Djidjelli. Of greater interest is the fact that none of the other historians make any allusion to the participation of French galleys, which de la Roncière claims to have numbered thirteen and to have been badly used by Doria. The various accounts of Barbarossa's retaliations or menaces—against Genoa, Napoule,[3] Valencia, or Cadiz—seem to agree only in

[1] Gomara, pp. 397–9.   [2] Duro, i. 161–2; de la Roncière, iii. 241.
[3] Attack on Napoule by Barbarossa with 50 ships was frustrated by 3 Genoese vessels!—de la Roncière, iii. 334.

respect of their complete ineffectiveness. While de la Roncière makes exaggerated and mutually contradictory statements on the subject, it seems clear from Gomara's narrative and subsequent conclusions that Kheir-ed-din was fully occupied ashore with the affairs of Kuko and Tlemcen. Algerine successes at sea appear to have been limited to a very few merchant vessels, of which only one—variously described as captured in Majorca or off Cadiz—is represented as being of great value.

The only authenticated act of belligerence at sea during Kheir-ed-din's subsequent stay in Algeria took the form of an attack, allegedly made in 1532 but more probably soon after his departure. It was again made by Bazan, who, with 10 galleys and 2,000 troops, landed at One, *west* of Oran, to make contact with 'Barbarossa's enemy', the King of Tlemcen. He razed the place after killing and capturing a number of *Moors*, and defeated at sea Axaba Reis, who tried to resist him with 8 galleys and galliots. If the date is correct his action had little effect, since Doria was calling for urgent action in that area from 1533 onwards.[1]

Apart from the defenceless roadsteads of Djidjelli, in uncomfortable proximity to the Spanish port of Bougie, and Cherchell, which was even more dangerously situated, the only harbour available to Kheir-ed-din was Algiers, once the capture of the Peñón had rendered it practicable for cruisers or merchant vessels. From that time France began to realize that raids on Algerines might lead to retaliation, and that their goodwill could be of greater value than alliance with Spain. The emperor, who seems to have been strangely averse to direct attack on the port, showed his appreciation of the new development by instructing his brother's ambassador to bargain with the sultan for the restitution of the Peñón.

His judgement was fully vindicated. In spite of a very modest start the new harbour, even before Kheir-ed-din's departure, offered a welcome to the merchant vessels of Christian nations and witnessed the novel spectacle of two French warships—not to mention their admiral and his mistress—fraternizing with its inhabitants.[2] Little credence can be given to reports of the transportation there by Kheir-ed-din of 70,000 Moors from

[1] Duro, i. 164, but see Gomara, pp. 404 and 507–8.
[2] De la Roncière, iii. 347–8.

Spain in 1529 or 1533 or the employment of 30,000 slaves (or even 7,000) on the construction of the famous mole, which after 1529 connected the Peñón with the mainland, and created a very restricted but relatively secure harbour on that notoriously inhospitable coast.[1] Clear evidence, however, exists that the 'excellent city' of Algiers was becoming a centre of political interest to Christian nations.

The 'truely drawn' plan of Algiers,[2] which the French king had made for himself in 1541 and of which our ambassador happily obtained a copy, shows it still to have been a small place. So, too, does the description in the same year by an eye-witness in Gomara, whose statement that most of the houses were new is a significant indication of that phenomenal development—à l'américaine,[3] as Monsieur Braudel so aptly describes it—of Algiers throughout the next century.

By the time of Charles's abdication Spanish power in North Africa had shrunk to almost negligible proportions, while the Turkish regency of Algiers had become a formidable Western state. Even more alarming must have seemed the economic and social contrast between the two kingdoms. The Spanish outlook is strikingly illustrated by Armstrong, who, after paying an enthusiastic tribute to the military and naval power of Algiers at the time, tells us that the 'élite of the Algerine forces contained no inconsiderable number of Spanish renegades' and that the 'corsair state offered a refuge to the adventurers, the criminals, the renegades of the Mediterranean basin from the Straits of Gibraltar to the mainland of Asia Minor, and acted as a rallying point for the undisciplined fanaticism of North Africa'.[4]

---

[1] Gomara estimated the population in 1541, apart from soldiers, at 3,000. In 1529 Cachidiablo created sensation by bringing away 200 refugees. Before 1559 Algiers had only one *bagnio*. Haedo mentions 700 Christian captives working on the mole in 1531. He knew some of them personally, i. 258.

[2] *State Papers*, viii. 642, ? reproduced by Lane-Poole, p. 115.

[3] Braudel, p. 698. A mutilated report from Peter Vannes, agent at Rome, describing Algiers as *praecipua civitas* and *regio opulenta*, mentions its trade with Christians through a reliable system of safe-conducts. The pope, Norfolk, Vannes, and Kheir-ed-din's envoy were all in Marseilles, negotiating? extension to Turkey of Franco-Algerine *entente* of 1532. See App. G; *Letters and Papers* 1533, p. 593; V.S.P. 1527–33, p. 435; *Letters and Papers*, ix. 357–9.

[4] Armstrong, i. 268–9. The Barbarossas 'brooked no rival', and relied on Turkish soldiers. See App. L. Haedo says Algiers was governed 'in all peace and justice' up to 1541 and that Kheir-ed-din welcomed ships and merchants of all races there.

Neither libertinism nor fanaticism was, however, characteristic of Turkish rule in Algiers, or consonant with the record
of its two rulers at that time, Hassan, the son of Kheir-ed-din,
and Sala, the ablest of his lieutenants. According to Armstrong
himself, and other British historians, anarchy, villainy, and
vice flourished in southern Europe, while Venetian diplomats
regarded England as the worst-governed country in Christendom and conditions in the adjacent waters as a scandal.[1] 'Wise
rule', combined with strict discipline, was recognized as the
secret of the successful administration of Algiers amid great
dangers and difficulties, and the Moslem spirit of toleration was
a source of constant apprehension for Charles and his successors.

An illuminating picture is available from other sources. In
1551 Nicholas de Nicholay,[2] later geographer general to the
King of France and previously, perhaps, English consul in
Crete, accompanied an embassy from the King of France to
the 'King' of Algiers, Hassan Barbarossa. After a very inaccurate historical sketch and a wholesale denunciation of the
Turks of Algiers as merely Christian renegades—apparently
a rehash of Spanish propaganda, since his personal experience
of Christian renegades there was by no means unfavourable—
he gives an interesting picture of conditions in and around that
city, where he roamed about freely and 'in quiet', at Teddell
(Dellys) and at Bona.

He describes Algiers as 'very merchant-like . . . inhabited of
Turkes, Moores and Jewes in great number which with mar-
veilous gaine exercise the Trade of Merchandise'—a populous,
bustling, well-ordered city, with 'very faire houses', a 'great
number of Bathes and Cookes houses', a busy port, numerous
trades and a fertile countryside, separated from the city on the
west by 'many faire and pleasant gardens', i.e. the suburban
villas which, even in the nineteenth century, were such a
celebrated feature of Turkish Algiers. Special mention is made,
as always, of the great abundance and variety of cheap food.
About the same time the Spaniard Marmol speaks of Algiers as
already the richest city in Africa, of its progress at the expense

He compares rush of Turks with that of Spaniards later to America. He and
Marmol describe modernity of its palaces and its 'wealth and delights' in 1545.

[1] V.S.P. 1558–80, pp. 328 and 370.

[2] Nicolas de Nicolay, *Les Négociations, pérégrinations, et voyages faicts en la Turquie*,
Antwerp, 1576, partially reproduced in English in Osborne, i, and Purchas, vi.

of Spain, the great volume of customs receipts, and its agricultural wealth.

The people of Teddell Nicholay describes as 'very merry and pleasant' and mainly engaged in the famous dyeing industry, the secret of which, as we know from Hakluyt and Playfair, was long sought by Christian competitors. Bona, where he found the renegade governor 'very curteous and liberal', was the centre of an extremely rich area, which also supplied Jerba and Tunis, and was soon to become a bone of contention between the merchants of France, England, and Genoa. The coveted coral fisheries were already being exploited by the Genoese, apparently for the benefit of Andrea Doria, as well as by Frenchmen.

When we remember that this represented only the initial stage of economic progress and consider the conditions which existed in Spain and Italy at the accession of Philip II, it would seem not unreasonable or unnatural for the 'starving peasantry' and other oppressed inhabitants to regard the regency as a land of freedom and opportunity, in much the same way as their descendants three centuries later looked to Britain and America.

There seems to be no evidence as to when or how Englishmen first began trading directly to Algiers, but, as the profitable commercial route followed the northern coast of the Mediterranean, it may be that they sold their wares indirectly through European ports, such as Marseilles, Genoa, or Pisa. That the Turks of Barbary did not prey on peaceful traders and that Prescott's picture of the Mediterranean as a scene of desolation, in which an occasional Christian merchant crept fearfully along the shore, is largely fictitious may fairly be inferred from our own records. Hakluyt's statement that from 1511 a regular and 'commodious' trade was developed by our tall ships into the Levant through the 'straits of Marrok' is definitely confirmed by the existence of consulates in Chios and Crete from 1513 and 1522 respectively, while a similar establishment at Venice was at least projected in 1535.[1]

It is surely remarkable that there should be no record of complaint from a trade in which not only eminent merchants

[1] Hakluyt, v. 62–63; *Letters and Papers* 1509–13; Rymer, xiii. 358 and 766; Cotton MS. Nero B. vii, f. 96.

of London but such great personages as Edward VI or a Duke of Norfolk[1] were interested, and which was regarded as a nursery for our seamen. On the surface, at least, it presents a marked contrast to our experiences in Spain, where our ships were liable to be requisitioned or embargoed and our merchants thrown into prison—as, for instance, in 1540 when a petition by the consul and merchants in Andalusia records their imprisonment at San Lucar for 'the Bishop of Rome's mattars' and the loss of 'all theyre goodis to their utter undoing'.[2] Even more startling is a comparison with contemporary conditions in the channel or on the Irish coasts.[3]

At the same time there is evidence of a considerable development of French trade, especially with Syria and Egypt under the protection of the Catalan consul. Early in 1542 the French ambassadors were instructed to inform our government that, as a result of the permission given to the Turks to trade in France, 'an almost incredible profit has accrued to the French nation from that free intercourse of trade, of which the Spiceries of Antwerp, and indeed of the whole of Flanders, have already felt the consequences'. As troubles developed in Provence and adjacent areas it became the practice for important passengers, and even goods, passing between France and Turkey, to be transferred from one vessel to another at Algiers, which Haedo soon after describes as the great entrepôt of Christian trade.[4] In the Adriatic, too, Venice was actively engaged in trying to induce the Turkish merchants to transfer to it their flourishing business with Ancona, and found in Ragusa a competitor for trade between England and the Levant.

It can hardly have been on account of his naval exploits that Kheir-ed-din was summoned to Constantinople in 1533 by the sultan at the instigation of his grand vizier. Indeed, the fleet that he was able to collect at Algiers was so small, though well equipped, that he was afraid of the poor figure he might cut on arrival. His reputation, however, was so great that, in spite of the ill will of some of the ministers, who may have been in the

---

[1] Sir Clements Markham, *Edward VI*, London, 1907, pp. 156–7. For Norfolk, see Hakluyt, v. 69.

[2] Cotton MS. Vespasian C. vii, ff. 91*b* and 102; *State Papers*, viii. 426.

[3] Lediard, *The Naval History of England*, i. 100, 106, and 113; *Carew Papers*, 1515–74, pp. 33–34.

[4] Cal. S.P. Spanish 1542–3, p. 57; *Topographia*, ch. xxiv.

Venetian interest, he was received with *grandísima pompa*, which included much saluting, festivities, and dancing.[1]

Except for one very brief and wholly involuntary visit after his defeat at Tunis in 1535 he never saw Algiers again, and his subsequent connexion with it was probably completely nominal, except in his general capacity as commander-in-chief of the sultan's navy. His actual residence in that city can only have been brief, and it is more than probable that, had he died in the spring of 1533, his name would only survive in some highly specialized work on the internal history of Algeria before it was definitely incorporated in the dominion of France.

It is, however, necessary to follow his fortunes at some length in order to remove misconceptions prejudicial to Algiers, the product of some strange confusion of thought, which tends to represent the official acts of one of the greatest personages of the Ottoman empire as evidence of Algerine piracy and barbarism.

[1] Gomara, pp. 405 and 409. He sailed with 7 galleys and 11 foists.

III

KHEIR-ED-DIN AND THE FRANCO-TURKISH ALLIANCE

THE issues which led to Kheir-ed-din's urgent summons to Constantinople appear to have been threefold—the reorganization of the Turkish fleet, which had fallen into disrepute; the importunity of a claimant to the throne of Tunis, described as the sole survivor of the forty-five brothers of its bloodthirsty ruler,[1] and the opportunity of effecting an arrangement for active co-operation with France in the Mediterranean which had apparently been advocated and, indeed, initiated by Barbarossa himself—perhaps to counteract friendly advances which the emperor was making to the sultan.

The first task was tackled with characteristic energy and thoroughness. By the next spring a fleet of 100 ships and about 20,000 men was ready for a voyage to concert measures with the French at Savona. In accordance with the Turkish custom, under which armies had to pay their way, and in contradistinction to the troops of Charles V, for instance, who twice sacked Rome and were the terror even of friendly countries for lack of pay, and to the French fleets which were later reduced to borrowing large sums from Kheir-ed-din, Dragut, and others to pay for the barest necessities, the expedition started out with 800,000 ducats in cash. This may be compared with the 30,000 livres which the French thought adequate for the maintenance of Kheir-ed-din's larger fleet during a winter at Toulon.[2]

The extent of his new responsibilities may best be gauged by the expedition, consisting of 200 galleys and as many transports, which carried the sultan with his well-equipped army of 200,000 men and 25,000 horses in 1537 to the famous camp at Valona. Unlike a Venetian fleet, which is said to have lost about 40,000 men from disease while lying in the port of Zara, it apparently arrived in good order, and Duro may well have

---

[1] Sir W. Stirling Maxwell, *Don John of Austria, 1547–75*, ii. 11.
[2] Duro, i. 221; de la Roncière, iii. 387 n.

been justified in saying that it was to such operations that Suleiman owed his title of 'Magnificent'.

Kheir-ed-din's last expedition was perhaps the most characteristic and the most maligned. He was given an unexampled welcome at Marseilles in the summer of 1543, and the beautiful spectacle of his fleet at Toulon soon after aroused universal admiration by its gay appearance and superb organization. Its commander, who during the winter preparations at Constantinople had been 'continually in the arsenal, where he did both eat and drink to lose no time', would have appreciated an enthusiastic testimonial from a French ambassador, which in its conclusion somewhat resembled Christian accounts of Turkish encampments: 'There was no noise of drums or trumpets or insolent cries, such as one hears, not only in Christian armies, but even in the congregations of the most reverend Fathers: And this is the result not of any lack of bravery on the part of the Turks, but of the respect which they bear to their captains and superiors.'[1] Perhaps, however, the tributes to the strict discipline and excellent behaviour of 30,000 men during their long stay at Toulon are even more remarkable. They are not easily reconcilable with denunciations of wholesale plundering and wanton atrocities on the voyages which preceded and followed it.

It is not surprising that Duro speaks of Kheir-ed-din as 'the creator of the Turkish navy, its admiral and its soul', and that it was Algiers that came to be recognized, not without justification, as the training-ground for such qualities and the source from which the sultan drew not only his best cruisers and seamen but, at critical times, some of his chief admirals, even in the late seventeenth and eighteenth centuries.

It was Ochiali, for instance, who came with his Algerine squadron, after the crushing disaster of Lepanto, to restore so speedily the naval supremacy of Turkey, and it was his successor at both Algiers and Constantinople, Hassan Veneziano, who issued a stern warning to the negligent officials at the great Turkish arsenals 'certifying them all that from his infancy having been trained up in like affairs, as well under his master Ochiali, as also in Algiers, Tunis and Tripoli in his own government, he knew how to command and what to look for at their

[1] Ibid. iii. 386.

hands'.[1] The principle, so consistently observed at Algiers, that
he alone was fit to command who had first learned to serve,
was illustrated by the fact that the efficient and orderly manner
in which its port and arsenal were administered earned the
commendation of foreigners, including its French conquerors
in 1830.

The inferences drawn from Kheir-ed-din's character and
achievements have, however, been less well founded or favourable to Algiers. This is largely due to the fact that the pact with
France, though only new in one logical and, indeed, inevitable
development, has come to be regarded with peculiar abhorrence,
unlike similar alliances in the time of Nelson or Napoleon III,
and also to the national *amour-propre*, which was wounded by
the secondary role of the French navy,[2] as compared with the
ships of Turkey, or even of Algiers, in the furtherance of
those policies throughout the greater part of the sixteenth
century.

French operations in the Mediterranean appear to have been
almost exclusively military, and French mariners were mainly
employed elsewhere, in English and Scottish waters, in the
Atlantic and even in the Pacific and Indian Oceans. Their
achievements in those areas can only be considered extraordinary, especially in view of the military commitments of
France and its internal difficulties, both political and economic.
The resultant dependence on foreign shipping in the Mediterranean was in evidence long before the great battle of Pavia.
Even prior to that disaster and the subsequent defection of
Andrea Doria it would seem that some sort of combination with
the forces of Turkey and Algiers was contemplated. The claims
put forward by modern writers to the naval achievements of
France and even to its political influence in North Africa and
the Levant during the century appear to call for more careful
study in the light available from not only English and Spanish
sources but French evidence as well.

Francis I, with his erratic conscience and unpredictable
changes of foreign policy, hardly appeared to advantage as a

[1] Cal. S.P.F. 1588, p. 165; for Ochiali, see Finlay, v. 86, and for Kheir-ed-din,
Haedo, i. 268–9.

[2] In 1525 the French Mediterranean navy consisted of foreign ships, de la
Roncière, iii. 200. The 'Débâcle de la Marine Française' began about 1575, ibid.
iv. 206–22.

Paladin or champion of Christendom.[1] He is said to have been the first great political propagandist and his versatility is shown in official panegyrics of Barbarossa and the conduct of his fleets and armies; in representations of the great service rendered by France to Christendom in introducing this new factor under French guidance to counteract the destructive ambitions of the emperor; and in the smear campaign aimed at discrediting the activities carried on in the cause and at the urgent request of Kheir-ed-din's French allies.

It is not surprising that subsequent historians, who, like Jurien de la Gravière, were sincerely convinced that the establishment of French dominion in Algiers constituted the noblest work of the nineteenth century, should unhesitatingly have availed themselves of the material best suited to what Pellissier has criticized as the policy of 'systematic denigration' of Algiers, in order to find a whipping-boy for the deficiencies of France, and obscure its dubious record of political and naval activity in Mediterranean and Levant waters up to late in the seventeenth century. Such an attitude was in fact entirely consonant with the prevailing tendency of the Victorian and Edwardian eras.

The special denunciation of Turkey, and eventually of Algiers, arose out of the existence of the Franco-Turkish alliance, usually assigned to the year 1536,[2] which is represented as essentially wicked and 'unhallowed', the source, it is claimed with a singularly ungrateful lack of realism, of so many of the misfortunes of France.

More logically, perhaps, any sense of shame might have been derived from the discreditable state of affairs created by the duplicity and insatiable ambition of the princes, popes, and republics who showed no hesitation in paying tribute to the sultan for his favour and protection, or invoking his aid against each other. The mutual recrimination and public washing of dirty linen must have been largely responsible for the contempt in which, according to Haedo and later writers, the Turks held the Christians.

---

[1] See *Annales*, pp. 131-4, and comparison with Henry, ibid., pp. 129-30 and 134.

[2] Five small Turk ships, left at Algiers, fought with France against Spain and wintered at Marseilles, 1536-7, de la Roncière, iii. 357 n.

French sympathy with Turkish aggression seems to have dated back to the time of Louis XI,[1] and the inhabitants of Naples are said to have appealed to both the sultan and the pope for aid against the invading forces of Charles VIII.[2] The same unfortunate people were kept in order by Mohammedan forces of Charles V, about the time of the sack of Rome.[3] The irresponsible callousness of French and Spanish rulers regarding the character of the troops or corsairs they employed or the manner of their remuneration contributed to wanton destruction and atrocity in their Italian wars, and produced remarkably favourable comments from Christian observers on Turkish methods of warfare.

The description of Francis as the 'shamefaced but determined' partner in a 'close and lasting alliance' with the Turks is little better founded than Prescott's picture of a Christendom united against the Turkish menace. The 'revirements' and 'vicissitudes' of Francis's policy are severely criticized by de la Roncière, and subsequent claims based by the French on their long-standing and privileged alliance with the sultan (extolled by Charles IX as 'so great a prince') are hard to reconcile with modern condemnation of its first public manifestation.

Henry VIII, who evidently had no intention of joining a Holy League against the Turk except in return for some substantial concession—a papal divorce or the occupation of Boulogne—found an excuse in the unsettled state of Christendom. 'Good faith, charity and true friendship were scarce in the world; for his part he had tried with one side and the other, and in both instances had met with plenty of fine words but no deeds.' His criticism that 'peace is not yet established in Italy' was hardly valid at a moment when his own northern border was described as ravaged by 10,000 'Scottish robbers', when an interval in the destructive warfare on either side of the channel was being occupied with rival claims for piracy, and when Ireland was in its almost perennial state of upheaval. Better founded was the contention that it would be 'a foolish and highly improper thing for King Henry of England to remit money to Your Majesty [Charles V] and help him to keep no

[1] Cal. S.P. Milan 1385–1618, p. 233.
[2] Hubbard, p. 9.
[3] Cal. S.P. Spanish 1527–29, p. xiii.

less than three armies in Italy, which in his opinion ought to be elsewhere'.[1]

As the rest of Christendom appears to have lived in dread of the 'universal domination' of Spain, and the rift between France and Venice was so fundamental that they are said never to have fought side by side officially after 1504, it is not perhaps surprising that not only the inhabitants of Tunis but Catholics, Lutherans, and Greeks in Europe often preferred Turkish protection or rule, that oppressed Christians fled to the more free and enlightened atmosphere of Algiers, just as the Hungarians did to Turkish territory,[2] and that even in distant England there was an element anxious to establish relations with the sultans of Morocco and Turkey and with Kheir-ed-din at Algiers.

In the spring of 1536 the various agreements made by Francis with the infidels in the past were publicly denounced to the pope by Charles in what his partisans describe as a noble fashion but the French, who threw all the blame on the emperor, regarded as an indecent exhibition. No wonder the embarrassed pope did not know what to say and may already have begun to suspect that the Turks were the best of the three.[3] Later, a similar altercation took place at the diet of Augsburg. Each charged the other with violation of the law of nations in regard to the murder of Francis's ambassadors on their way to Constantinople and the French seizure of Marano.[4]

Actually, Charles, like his grandfather, displayed no disinclination to make advantageous agreements with the infidels of North Africa. Two years later he offered Kheir-ed-din himself dominion over Algeria, together with Bona, Bougie, Bizerta, Tunis, and Tripoli (or alternatively La Goletta), in return for his assistance in maintaining order on the high seas and crushing France and Venice.[5] It is even alleged that Kheir-ed-din and Ochiali escaped destruction at the great sea-battles of Prevesa and Lepanto through Spanish connivance.[6]

---

[1] Ibid. 1529–30, pp. 462, 618, 391, and 342.   [2] *H.H.W.* xxiv. 362.
[3] Charrière, i. 295–309, but see Pastor, *The History of the Popes*, xi. 248–50.
[4] Charrière, i. 544–95.
[5] Armstrong, ii. 4–5; Duro, i. 235 n.; Gomara, pp. 530–9. Instructions included 'ménagements à observer à l'égard de Barberousse et ses intérêts à Tunis et Alger'. In 1538 Pole sought a truce between Spain and Turkey, *Pol. Hist.* v. 427.
[6] See accounts in Duro, i and ii.

French, and subsequently Christian, resentment dates with special bitterness from the siege of Nice in 1543.[1] The Turkish fleet had reluctantly arrived at the urgent request of the French, 'famished and exhausted', and found nothing ready as promised —no adequate forces, no plans, and no supplies. Kheir-ed-din rated them furiously—from a prince of the blood downwards— for their incompetence and breach of faith. They had difficulty in dissuading him from returning immediately, and the Spanish garrison of Nice were amazed at the extraordinary deference with which he was treated.

The conventional account of the subsequent proceedings is well expressed by Armstrong:

The gigantic Franco-Turkish fleet laid Nice in ashes. The port of Toulon was throughout the winter the unhallowed market for the sale of the population of Nice, whom Barbarossa had carried off as slaves. In the early spring the corsair sailed homewards, stripping the Italian coasts of their inhabitants. . . . Under the eyes and with the aid of a French admiral of royal blood, the worst of Turkish atrocities were perpetrated upon the harmless prince who was the French king's kinsman. French Catholics in vain strove to wash out the stain of the burnt town with the blood of the neighbouring Provençal heretics.[2]

French accounts go even further in depicting the vain efforts of the French to protect the hapless inhabitants of Nice, which Barbarossa had not wanted to attack and which had recently been subjected to the tender mercies of the Spanish plunderers of Tunis, and the pathetic spectacle of men like Leone Strozzi having to be the helpless witnesses of Turkish barbarities on the Tuscan coast. Similar allegations about the indignation or disgust of Paulin or Saint-Blancard at Kheir-ed-din's asserted atrocities at Aegina, Reggio, and other places should be examined in the light of contemporary evidence, including the dispatches of our own agents or, at times, the correspondence of Charles himself, and of the careers and characters of the French admirals cited.[3]

Knolles, who usually draws from Venetian sources, makes special mention of the 'rare courtesie' and generous behaviour

[1] A 'scandale inouï', Duro, i. 263.
[2] Armstrong, ii. 16.
[3] For Saint-Blancard, see Charrière, i. 373–83, and de la Roncière, iii. 346–7. Succeeded by three 'larrons', ibid., pp. 372–6.

displayed by Kheir-ed-din on the Italian coast in 1534 and 1543,[1] and de la Roncière tells us that French testimony was *unanimous* as to the extraordinarily good behaviour of the Turks at Toulon. 'To see Toulon', wrote one witness, 'one might imagine one's self at Constantinople, everyone pursuing his business with the greatest order and justice', or again, 'Never did an army live in stricter or more orderly fashion than that one.'[2] One instance of Kheir-ed-din's monstrous conduct, cited by the indignant Heinrich, reveals nothing that would not be considered perfectly legitimate and reasonable by modern standards in the same circumstances.[3] It would be interesting to know who were the purchasers at the alleged sales of Christian captives in Toulon.

As regards Nice it would appear from Spanish reports that the *French* burned the town and then ran away. In any case, nothing could be more frank and authoritative than the statement of Maréchal Vieilleville himself:

La ville de Nice fut saccagée contre la capitulation, et puis bruslée, de quoy il ne faut blasmer Barberousse ny tous ses Sarrazins, car ils étaient déjà assez éloignés quand cela advint. . . . *On rejeta cette méchanceté sur le pauvre Barberousse pour soutenir l'honneur et la réputation de France, voire de la Chrétienté.*[4]

The 'stripping of the Italian coasts' is a manifest exaggeration. Kheir-ed-din, who was not a corsair but the sultan's admiral and minister, refrained from molesting the shores of Genoa, Elba, and the papal states, where the pope was said to have been more afraid of the Neapolitan viceroy's levies.[5] He only attacked the Spanish territories of Naples and Sicily and also Tuscany, where Leone Strozzi, the turncoat prior of Capua, is described by Duro as urging on the Turks against his

---

[1] Knolles, *Generall Historie of the Turkes*, pp. 432 and 496.

[2] iii. 386.

[3] Heinrich, p. 58. Municipal accounts show officials were ordered to investigate murder of Turks in suburbs, Charrière, i. 573 n.

[4] Heinrich, *L'Alliance franco-algérienne au XVIᵉ siècle*, p. 55. Harvel and Wotton reported French burned the town, against Turkish wishes, and fled, *State Papers* ix. 516–17 and 519–22, refuting Duro's unsupported charge that Turks violated capitulation by plundering Nice, i. 264. Venice later blamed Turks for its own treachery, L. Villari, p. 287, and by 1578 they had 'learned excellently to imitate Christians in putting out false news', Cal. S.P.F. 1578–9, p. 76.

[5] *State Papers*, x. 6.

own countrymen, while flaunting the Cross of St. John on his breast.[1]

It is unfortunate that such an authority as Armstrong, who gives vivid accounts of the bad behaviour of the imperial forces, even in friendly territory, thereby moving Charles himself to weep for shame, should have overlooked so much evidence in the diplomatic correspondence of the time. Charles's own ambassador Veltwic frequently reports with contemptuous satisfaction Francis's attempts to re-establish his credit at Constantinople, and our own agent at Rome records the preference of Italian statesmen and church dignitaries for the Turks immediately after Kheir-ed-din's last visit. The memoirs of the French ambassador Montluc and his official declaration to the Venetian senate in 1544 are even more enlightening. The latter asserted that no force, Turk or Christian, had previously conducted itself so *modestement* as on Kheir-ed-din's last expedition; that no one could complain of any wrong done by his armament; that it had displayed every courtesy and allowed all whom it met at sea to pass unmolested; and that it had paid for everything it had to take. In the former he records Turkish contempt for French inefficiency and his own verdict on Barbarossa's forces: 'Ils sont plus robustes, obéissans et patiens que nous; ils ont un avantage, qu'ils ne songent à rien qu'à la guerre'[2]—a clear refutation of French charges, then or later, that the Turks 'amused themselves' with plundering and slave raids, instead of attending to the serious business of war.

The active alliance was terminated, while French and Turks still fraternized happily in Constantinople, by the conclusion of a new one between France and Spain, which provided for a partition of Italian territory, highly satisfactory to themselves but less so to some Italian states, which promptly turned to the Turks for protection. Any unhappy recollection of the infidels was probably quickly obliterated by the sack of Siena, of Milan, and, for the second time, of Rome. The contrast

[1] Brussels and Venice reported heavy fighting by Barbarossa against forts at Pozzuoli, Lipari, and Ischia—'lieu grandement fort dedans la mer', *State Papers*, x. 6, 20, 48, &c. Gomara praised his exploit.

[2] Charrière, i. 578–9. While Montluc deplored 'calomnies passionnées', his soldier brother said, whether the alliance was legitimate or not, it was 'utile et commode', since it entailed no obligation, and Suleiman was less exigent than Henry: E. Lavisse, *Histoire de France*, 9 vols., Paris, 1910–11, V². 109.

between these horrors and the peaceful entry of a Turkish army of 30,000 foot and 4,000 horse into the city of Castro 'où ils n'ont fait aucun dommaige ne violence'[1] must have created a favourable impression of the Mussulmans. Paul IV looked to them for aid against his Most Catholic Majesty, and even late in the following century Sicilians were anxious to place themselves under Ottoman rule.[2]

Refutation of the customary charges as to the misconduct of Barbarossa's forces, his neglect of French interests, the consequent uselessness of such an expedition, and the great sacrifices made by France both of treasure and prestige comes not only, as already suggested, from a great deal of contemporary evidence but from the actions of France itself in the years following his death. Francis's successor, after invoking the aid of the Algerines and Turks for the specific purpose of harrying the coasts of Sicily and Naples, became insistent as to the absolute necessity of the Turkish fleet wintering in the Mediterranean, preferably at *Toulon*, since otherwise it would be impossible to preserve the conquests made with its assistance.

To repeated requests of this nature the sultan opposed an inflexible negative, citing the danger to his dominions and other drawbacks of publicly committing almost the whole of his naval force to an absence of twenty months in so distant a sphere, and stressing in particular 'la pauvreté et l'indigence de toutes choses' so characteristic of French fleets and ports and, more especially, the unhappy experiences of Kheir-ed-din during his stay at Toulon. At this final explicit and humiliating reply the ambassador burst into a more than usually violent fit of abuse, suggesting that ways should be found to lower the pride of those barbarous, ungrateful Turks and to chastise 'la canaille d'Alger', whose assistance had previously been so actively solicited.[3]

Even as late as 1591 Kheir-ed-din's famous expedition was cited as an admirable precedent by our ambassador in a formal appeal to the sultan to follow the example of Suleiman 'of

---

[1] Charrière, i. 337. The correspondent, a bishop in Rome, also reported Barbarossa found Saint-Blancard 'ung homme terrible', ibid. 340. See *State Papers*, viii. 188, and, for Neapolitan complicity, Charrière, i. 337 and Haedo, *Topographía e Historia General de Árgel*, i. 269–70.
[2] See p. 154, n. 3.
[3] Charrière, ii. 415 n. and 418 n.

blessed memory', in sending a vast armament to help France against the encroachments of Spain, thereby conferring 'infinite glory' on himself, great benefit to 'the faith', apparently one common to all three allies, and 'inestimable favour upon my mistress and the poor King of France'.[1] As it turned out the necessary aid was furnished to Henri by the galleys of Algiers.

Malicious reports have, however, continued to pursue the great Turkish admiral after his death, which took place in July 1546. According to the *Biographie universelle*[2] he died exhausted by the manifold vices of the harem, while Duro deplores the scandal of an octogenarian caught in the toils of a bewitching young bride. Lane-Poole, who is a generous admirer, suggests that he died in his ninetieth year, which is arithmetically impossible. Actually he seems to have died in the early sixties[3]—no great age for a Turk—and unexpectedly, from natural causes, in the performance of his duties. The French ambassador wrote Francis that it was no matter for sorrow, since he had shown himself ungrateful and inimical to France, though it would be good policy to win the favour of his son before the emperor could do so. It is at least interesting to know that the news that 'the King of the Sea is dead' was conveyed by a French ambassador, travelling on a French ship, to Hassan Barbarossa, who immediately suspended his campaign in western Algeria and returned to Constantinople.

The memory of few men has been held in greater honour or more consistently cherished in their own country. He died loved and lamented by all who served under him, and for generations to come no Turkish ship sailed past his tomb on the banks of the Dardanelles without paying the tribute of a salute and prayer to the great admiral. The naval supremacy, which Turkey owed to him, lasted long enough to see its rule firmly established on the southern shore of the Mediterranean, and the administrative system which he inaugurated in Algiers was admired and regretted three centuries later by its French conquerors.

Duro has briefly sketched the career of this 'extraordinary

---

[1] V.S.P. 1581–91, pp. 514–15.

[2] Or Vertot, Morgan, p. 363. Such accusations are incompatible with Haedo's pleasing picture, i. 275–7.

[3] Lesbos was only occupied in 1462. Haedo says he died of fever aged 63.

man', who rose, entirely by his own unaided efforts, from potter's apprentice and deck-hand to be creator of the Ottoman navy, King of Algiers and Tunis (!),[1] and respected and feared alike by the King of France and the Holy Roman Emperor. Gomara tells us that he was the first to teach the Turks not to fear the Spaniards. In the diplomatic correspondence of the day—unlike the much-quoted writings of Jovius—he is normally spoken of with great respect. Brantôme, who must have been personally acquainted with many of his opponents and colleagues, expressed the opinion that France or any other country would have been proud to claim him as a native son and that neither modern nor ancient history provided his equal as a founder of empire.[2] Even the intolerant Father Dan, writing nearly a century after his death, allowed that he was a great man, 'de cœur et d'esprit'.

Although Kheir-ed-din was an Ottoman subject and had been a Turkish official for at least the greater part of his adult life, it is not unintelligible that Spaniards should have regarded the struggle as a personal one between him and Spain, since they saw in him not only the creator and inspiration of the Ottoman navy but the real founder of the regency and the promoter and champion of the French alliance. It seems incredible, however, that a Turkish admiral, whose 'naval exploits are among the glories of the reign of Suleiman the Magnificent', should in modern times be disparaged as an extraordinary—and, I believe, technically impossible—sort of Jekyll and Hyde personality—a 'pirate-admiral', a combination of Turkish naval officer and 'Algerine pirate', 'Admiral of the Sultan's pirate fleet', 'a pirate and at the same time the representative of a great power', which was, in fact, probably the mightiest and most civilized of its time.[3]

Even less excusable is the attempt to foist upon Algiers the responsibility for his alleged misdeeds as the sultan's com-

[1] Duro, i. 267–8; Gomara, p. 349—in error for Tenez.
[2] Œuvres complètes de Brantôme, Paris, 1864, Grands Capitaines, ch. xxii, 'jamais des Romains ny des Grecz grands conquéreurs de réaumes et de terres il n'y a eu un tel'. An earlier edition, B.M. 12234, bbb 11, says, i. 89 n., Barbarossa was in eighteenth century credited with birth in France to increase French prestige. H.H.W. xxiv. 479 assigns him 'all the qualities of a statesman . . . united to those of a soldier'.
[3] Gomara, p. 349.

mander-in-chief, and so create the legend of not merely a sea-
port, but a powerful state, being entirely dependent for its
recognized, and indeed much envied, prosperity on slave-
trading and plunder. A case in point is the application in 1541
of the term 'Barbarossa's lair' to a place which he had visited
only once involuntarily after he became Capudan pasha. It
was clearly not against a mere piratical den or corsair base
that the emperor so obstinately hazarded his fortunes and reputation in that year. His objective was essentially a political one
of great importance. Equally misleading is the statement that
that action was fought with the 'pirate Barbarossa', who had
not been in the Mediterranean for more than five years.[1]

Before returning to developments in Barbary and its relations
with Christian powers it would seem advisable to try to dispose
of certain other allegations, which are used by partisans of those
powers to discredit the Barbaresques. In all these cases special
stress is laid on plunder and barbarity,

It is frequently stated that the 'Algerian pirate' Kheir-ed-din
seized the kingdom of Tunis from an unoffending neighbour,
made himself king, and delivered up the defenceless city to the
fury of his janissaries.[2] It would, however, appear that he
actually went there on the orders of the sultan to install a more
popular ruler, was received with open arms by its inhabitants,
and accomplished his task without bloodshed. When the
Spaniards made a counter-invasion he refused to take the pre-
caution, which Napoleon later did in similar circumstances, of
killing his captives, and perhaps owed his defeat to that lack
of ruthlessness. The 'merciless loot', to which Charles delivered
up the 'unresisting and unoffending city . . . equalled', according to one of our historians, 'the worst atrocities ever imputed
to the Turks', and involved not only the destruction of works
of art, libraries, and mosques, but the slaughter of many
thousands of men, women, and children and the enslavement
of as many more.[3] This liberation of the country from 'the
pirates' is actually cited today as enhancing the power and
prestige of the emperor and Christendom. Some forty years

See *Annales*, Gomara, Haedo.

[2] Heinrich, p. 19 and Pellegrin, *Histoire de la Tunisie*, p. 129, decisively refuted in
Gomara, p. 518. See Haedo, i. 262–3; Jurien, p. 232; App. D.

[3] Creasey, p. 177.

later Charles's example was followed by his son Don Juan in very similar circumstances.[1]

Kheir-ed-din's surprising counterstroke against Minorca, a strategic centre and, in the eyes of the French over a long period, *un nid de pirates*, was hailed by both Gomara and Brantôme as an exceptionally brilliant and courageous exploit, but has since degenerated, in most French, Spanish, and English works, into a mere 'plundering raid', with a remarkable discrepancy of attendant detail. The emperor himself made the colourless report that it had been taken and abandoned.[2]

Barbarossa is generally credited with the cold-blooded massacre of the gallant defenders of Castelnuovo, but Lane-Poole tells us that they were 'surprised to find themselves chivalrously treated as honourable foes'.[3] An equally unmerited sneer at his alleged refusal to attack Orbitello, because a 'corsair', actually the admiral of a very powerful and highly civilized fleet, did not like attacking fortresses, may be compared with the anger of the same allies some seven years later, when Dragut, instead of harrying the coasts of Sicily and Naples, insisted on trying to reduce the strongholds of Tripoli and Malta.[4] Indeed the terrible losses suffered by the three Barbarossas—Aruj, Kheir-ed-din, and Hassan—through persistent attempts to storm a series of fortresses may be taken as convincing evidence that they were not mere corsairs, devoted to the pursuit of easy plunder. There is no evidence, I believe, that he wantonly plundered Aegina or even visited it,[5] but he did later in those waters take the, for those days, very unusual step of executing some of his captains for piratical acts. Finlay's claim that 'Barbarossa plundered 25 of the Greek islands, reduced 80 towns to ashes and carried off 30,000 Greeks into slavery'[6] is a strange commentary on his normal theme that the

---

[1] Maxwell, ii. 15, describing scenes at Tunis and Bizerta; Rotalier, ii. 266.

[2] Gomara, p. 421, confirmed by Brantôme. Charrière, i. 277–8; Duro, i. 223. Henry rejoiced, Cal. S.P. Spanish 1534–5, p. 584.

[3] p. 105; Armstrong, ii. 5; Charrière, i. 413 n. Like Gomara Brantôme thought it 'un des plus beaux exploitz qu'il fist contre les chrestiens'. For Turk depredations contrast L. Villari, pp. 283–4, with Pastor, xi. 273 n.

[4] Duro, i. 267; de la Roncière, iii. 504.

[5] Finlay, v. 68–69, quoting *Journal de la Croisière du Baron de Saint Blancard*, Charrière, i. 340–53 and 371–83, which does not mention Barbarossa's presence or any landing.

[6] Other accounts disagree, especially M. D. Volonakis, *The Island of Roses and Her Eleven Sisters*, London, 1922. The twelve privileged islands received 'virtual

Christians surpassed the Turks in cruelty to the Greeks and that the Venetians were the worst offenders. It is curious, too, that these last not only paid an indemnity for their own sufferings but appear to have been reckoned among the friends and admirers of the Turks.[1]

The legend of disparagement has, however, not merely persisted but been developed, until Kheir-ed-din is today frequently represented as not merely a 'professional pirate'[2] but the 'infamous' leader of a horde of savages, while we cherish the memory of men who may have been distinguished for better seamanship but hardly for a more honourable career or one of so much constructive achievement. The leaven worked so well that nearly three hundred years later, on the conclusion of the most destructive maritime war then known, in which the Barbary States, according to much better informed British opinion, had played a pacific and lawful part, the vain and unstable Sir Sidney Smith launched the fateful crusade designed to 'secure Europe for ever from the outrages of the African corsairs, and to cause governments favourable to commerce and in peace and amity with all civilized nations, to succeed to states, *radically and necessarily piratical ever since the days of Barbarossa*'.[3]

---

autonomy' in 1540 on voluntary surrender 'in accordance with the sacred Mussulman law', p. 296. They suffered chiefly from Christians' 'exterminating raids', ibid., pp. 304–5.

[1] *State Papers*, ix. 423.

[2] A Mediterranean anachronism before 1600, Duro, iii. 330. 'Turkish naval officer' in Index, *State Papers*.

[3] *A.R.* 1815, pp. [157–60]. Resented Algiers's reluctance to break with France after 1798. Received facilities at Algiers on two voyages. In 1826 requested commercial concession there. Bunbury, who ridiculed him, *D.N.B.* liii. 166, was officially connected with Barbary.

IV

THE REGENCY OF ALGIERS IN THE ELIZABETHAN ERA

THE 'wise administration' of Algeria by the Barbarossas and their immediate successors bore easily discernible fruit in the rapid development of the political and economic importance of Algiers and in the extension of Turkish dominion in Barbary.

After the collapse of the Turco-French alliance in 1544 the struggle in the western Mediterranean resolved itself into a contest between Algiers on the one hand and Spain on the other, aided by the Moslem rulers of Morocco and Tunis. The principal concern of the beglerbeys, somewhat curiously described as the 'Great Corsairs', was with operations on land, where the size of their armies, greater perhaps than any Englishman commanded prior to Waterloo,[1] contrasted with their modest sea-force of some twenty to thirty light but, it was usually pointed out, well-equipped galleys and foists.[2] It was mainly a period of protracted and costly siege-warfare.

The year 1551 was a crucial one. Kheir-ed-din's old lieutenant Dragut, representing the sultan in eastern Barbary, found compensation for his defeat at Malta in the capture of the knights' other stronghold of Tripoli, which the emperor regarded as one of the 'two eyes' of Christendom,[3] in that it helped to ensure the security of Spanish rule in Sicily and of the economic life-line between the Levant and Spain itself. As a result of its loss, according to a report of the Duke of Medina Sidonia, many of the inhabitants of Valencia and Catalonia were soon dying of hunger.[4]

In Algeria, then administered by Hassan Barbarossa, the same year witnessed the inauguration of a series of signal

---

[1] In 1555 Algiers had 7,000 janissaries, 30,000 other foot, 10,000 Arab horse, and 30 field-guns. Hassan Barbarossa soon after had larger forces.

[2] Christian reports distinguish 'big' Turkish ships and 'small' Algiers cruisers. In 1554 Algiers had 8 galleys and 12 foists; in 1581 36 ships, mostly very small.

[3] Armstrong, ii. 239.   [4] Braudel, p. 798.

successes with the crushing defeat of a Spanish army outside Oran, involving, it was said, the loss of 12,000 prisoners.[1] Two years later the important kingdom of Tlemcen was finally incorporated in the regency, and a protégé of the sultan was placed by Algerian troops on the throne of Fez. In 1555 Bougie was captured, and in 1559 an Algiers squadron entered the Atlantic to attack the coasts of Spain and Portugal and sell its prisoners in the port of Cadiz itself.[2]

The dominion of the Turks in Barbary may be said to have been definitely assured by the great naval victory of Dragut and Piale in 1560 over the Spanish fleet near Jerba, and for the first time perhaps a Turkish success was enthusiastically welcomed in England. Our ambassador at Paris reported joyfully that Philip had suffered a greater loss than ever his father had done at Algiers, and, like Gresham, expressed relief at this elimination of the Spanish menace.[3]

There can be no question about the remarkable growth of Algerine power and prestige at that time. Our records speak respectfully of the 'King of Algiers', his army, navy, and ambassadors, and the sultan paid him the compliment of making extensive demands on all three.[4] Thus in 1565 we find Hassan arousing great alarm in Spain by a series of violent assaults on Oran, before playing a prominent part in the siege of Malta. It was reported that Philip's troops, usually regarded as the best soldiers of the day, preferred desertion into France to participation in another expedition to North Africa.[5]

In 1569 one of his successors, Ochiali, was charged with the conquest of Tunis, intervention in the Morisco rising in Spain, and dealing with French violations of the treaties. The following year the Algerine fleet, which only a short time before had been intercepting West Indian galleons in the Atlantic and suffering severely at the siege of La Goletta, was summoned to aid the sultan in the conquest of Cyprus.

[1] Ibid., p. 797; *Topographia*, ch. xxxiv.

[2] Braudel, p. 797.

[3] Cal. S.P.F. 1560–1, p. 105; (Sir) J. E. Neale, *Queen Elizabeth*, London, 1934, p. 103; Duro, ii. 17–47.

[4] Cal. S.P.F. 1559–60, pp. 287, 478, and 506. Osborne, as Lord Mayor, addressed Hassan Veneziano as 'Right high and mightie King', Hakluyt, v. 269.

[5] Cals. S.P.F. 1559–60, p. 340 and 1560–1, p. 433; Duro, ii. 45; V.S.P. 1558–80, p. 213.

Ottoman setbacks, including the crushing defeat of the sultan's navy at Lepanto in 1571, added rather surprisingly to the prestige and independence of Algiers—always, however, within the framework of the Ottoman empire.[1] The Algerine squadron alone of the Turkish forces had emerged with credit from the great battle, and, under its admiral and viceroy Ochiali, became the nucleus of the new fleet, which was to restore, however temporarily, Ottoman naval supremacy. During the intervening period, when Ochiali was forced to resort to Fabian tactics and allow Don Juan of Austria to recover possession of Tunis, the Algerines, under the rising star, Morat Reis, carried the war into enemy territory, landing troops near Ajaccio and harrying the Italian coast.

The year 1574 witnessed a return—this time a permanent one—to the position existing before Lepanto. Venice had made a humiliating peace, and Tunis was reconquered, together with the greatly prized Spanish fortress of La Goletta. In the same year the death of Selim II ended Turkish enterprise for many years to come, and in Morocco the first official step was taken to establish English commerce on a permanent footing. Four years later Spain was glad to conclude a truce with the sultan, which, however, did not, in practice, include Algiers, Tripoli, and Tunis.[2]

The distance from Constantinople, the impossibility of finding a suitable winter base, and increasing dangers in the various waters adjacent to Turkey had precluded any offensive action by the Ottoman fleet in the Mediterranean. As a result the King of Algiers, or bashaw as we now began to call him, became the officially recognized representative of the empire in the West, though his authority was in fact limited by the transfer of many of his functions and responsibilities to the aga, or elected commander-in-chief of the Turkish regular troops, and to the Captain of the Sea, who was appointed by the sultan.

The apparent isolation of Algiers helped to illustrate two

---

[1] Turkish power increased by 1574, having taken Tunis, Cyprus, and La Goletta. It seemed the allies had slunk home, ashamed of their victory, *Memorias del Cautivo en Túnez* (El Alférez Pedro de Aguilar), Madrid, 1575, p. 63; Duro, iii. 151–95; Finlay, v. 103.

[2] Intrigues of Ochiali and France frustrated Mediterranean peace, Charrière, iii. 880 n. and iv. 47 n.–86; Duro, ii. 301 and 302 n. Algiers complained of sudden French hostility in 1580, Masson, *Établissements*, pp. 84–85.

facts that might previously have been obscured. It was regarded by the Spaniards as a bona-fide belligerent in contrast to the 'pirates' of England, France, and Holland, with whom they carried on a ruthless war, and its organized navy, however small, proved, with the assistance of the galleys of Bizerta, more than a match for the heterogeneous contingents of corsairs furnished by Spanish cities and satellite countries.[1] During the next few years it was intercepting galleons and carracks returning from the East and West Indies, raiding the Canaries, playing havoc round Barcelona, and paralysing vital Spanish communications in the Mediterranean.[2]

The Spanish monk Haedo gives a graphic account of Christian complaints, apparently during the years preceding our war with Spain, about the unorthodox procedure of Algiers galleys, roving the Eastern and Western seas, winter and summer, 'devoid of dread' and 'laughing all the while at the Christian galleys (which lie trumpetting, gaming and banqueting in ports of Christendom) neither more nor less than if they went a hunting hares and rabbits, killing here one and there another'.[3] One would be inclined to regard this as a picturesque piece of imaginative writing, were it not substantially confirmed by the mockery of Cervantes and the more sober testimony of English, French, Venetian, and Turkish reports.

It is not difficult to understand why the sultan should have entrusted Algiers and Tunis with full responsibility for the defence of his dominions against attack from the West, or why Elizabeth and Walsingham attached so much importance to the co-operation of the Bashaw of Algiers. Far less comprehensible is our subsequent attitude of sympathizing with Spain over the havoc wrought by our 'piratical' allies, while condemning the failure of the sultan to aid us in ravaging Spanish dominions.

The period immediately following the definite establishment

[1] Duro's very confused chapter 'Skimmers of the Sea' 1572–85, ii. 333–52, contains no specific mention of Algiers ships except regular fleet which captured Cervantes's squadron.

[2] Duro, ii. 399; V.S.P. 1581–91, pp. 273, 277, and 450–1, mainly Morat's exploits; Morgan, pp. 596–7.

[3] Lane-Poole, p. 222, Morgan's translation of Haedo, i. 84; Duro, iii. 434. Probably Haedo confused Algiers galleys with Christian corsairs and Turkish Levants, which wintered elsewhere.

of Turkish dominion along the North African coast, from Oran eastwards, though it is apt to be ignored or dismissed as 'obscure' by modern historians, is of particular interest, because it coincides with the rise of English influence, at the expense of the French, alike in Barbary and Turkey, and with Haedo's extremely informative and, in the light of other evidence, generally reliable historical and economic presentation of the Algerine state.

Apart from criticism of one ruler, Hassan Veneziano, for avarice and over-indulgence in privateering at the one time that we claimed to have ground for complaint, Haedo's opinion of the bashaws is almost extravagantly flattering. Kheir-ed-din's son Hassan, who held that office three times, was 'eminent for many singular virtues' and was the equal of his father in 'fine qualities and Princely Qualification', but without his vices, which appear to have consisted mainly of alleged cruelty to Christians. He was evidently an intrepid soldier and a liberal—perhaps too liberal—ruler.

Sala Reis was not only an able general, admiral, and administrator but a man of 'noble courtesy', whom the French would have liked to see succeed Kheir-ed-din as Capudan pasha. He is described by a hostile witness as sending away defeated inhabitants of Tlemcen laden with presents.[1] Ochiali, whom it is the fashion to regard as the outstanding ruler of Algiers, was apparently one of the least successful. He was exceptional in that he was a genuine renegade, who is said to have changed his religion merely to gratify a grudge, continued to visit his relatives in Calabria, and, in spite of his naval exploits, apparently never enjoyed the confidence of the Algerine Turks.[2] Brantôme thought him a less estimable character than Kheir-ed-din or Dragut. Hassan Barbarossa, though he appears to have had no record as a seaman, and Hassan Veneziano, described as a 'restless and ambitious spirit', each became Capudan pasha in his turn. Sala died on campaign in western Algeria.

Of Djafer Aga Haedo speaks with the authority of an eyewitness. 'Never did anyone make the least complaint of his administration. Nor has anyone yet remarked him to be addicted to any vice whatever.' A later report from Constantinople

[1] Weir, p. 52.   [2] App. F.

describes him as Jafer Bassa, a eunuch of Hungary, who in his government of Tauris 'showed Valour, Prudence, and Liberality'. Heinrich mentions him as assuring merchants of all nations of a welcome at Algiers and even as issuing an invitation to Spain through the director of the Spanish hospital, which was already a feature of Algiers.[1]

A special tribute is paid to 'their beloved Ramadan Sardo', popular alike with Turks and Moors, under whom the state enjoyed 'such Justice and Equity' and 'more Peace and Tranquillity' than ever before, so that the people were not unnaturally distressed when he was transferred to Tunis. De Grammont gives him a poor character, but a report in Spanish from Valencia described him as a man of much justice and very fair dealing, worried, however, by the fear that he might be suspected of unduly favouring the Christians. As he spent a period of retirement in one of the finest houses of Algiers, we are able to have some unusually personal details of him. A native of Sardinia, aged fifty-five when he left Algiers in 1577, he was evidently a man of culture, since he was said to be keenly interested in Turkish and Arabic literature. He had only one wife, a Corsican, and three children. Both his daughters married renegades, from Spain and Naples respectively. As Bashaw of Tunis he addressed an extremely sensible letter to Henri III in June 1579 about the capture of French cargo, and as Bashaw of Tripoli he was involved in the affair of the *Jesus* in 1584. The victim, perhaps, of his virtues, he was murdered the same year by his soldiers. The massacre of his widow and her household by nominally friendly Venetian ships was a sensational scandal, for which that republic had to make humble amends to the Porte.[2]

It is not unlikely that the vices and deficiencies of the so-called 'Triennial Bashaws', who administered the country after the death of Ochiali in 1587, have been considerably exaggerated, partly in support of a highly questionable theory.[3] According to Haedo, Shaaban was one of the best viceroys, and

[1] Cotton MS. Nero B. xi, f. 4b; Charrière, iv. 320, &c.; Heinrich, pp. 139–40.

[2] Finlay, v. 93 n.; Charrière, iv. 314 n., &c. Admiral Emo was executed at Venice. Aguilar calls Ramadan 'hombre de buena experiencia y discreción'. For letter to Henri, see Grandchamp, *La France en Tunisie, 1582–1620*, i, pp. xi–xii, and for Valencia, p. 108 n. 2.

[3] App. F.

governed Algiers from about 1592 to 1595 'with general Applause and Satisfaction'. The further description of him as 'very gay and jovial . . . he was to all mankind exceedingly affable and well-behaved' indicates that the office was not of an arbitrary or despotic character. Laurence Aldersey had earlier reported that 'the greatest government is in the hands of the soldiers',[1] a condition which may have dated back to the governorship of Ochiali himself.

The problem of placating the janissaries, who really represented the Turkish interest, and keeping them in order was already a difficult one, although many of them were married and engaged in trades, when not employed in the field. It was perhaps as essential then as nearly two centuries later for the apparently absolute ruler of Algiers to be 'mild and his measures well concerted', since an unruly militia could only be governed by a 'prudent Mixture of Severity and Clemency'.[2] A bashaw's diplomatic abilities were further tried by the necessity for composing the quarrels or rival claims of the representatives of England and France or for giving effect to the capricious, and sometimes contradictory, commands which foreign ambassadors contrived to procure at Constantinople.

Shaaban's successor, Mustafa, was 'good-natured and upright' and his 'satisfactory administration' ended the sixteenth century. Although these viceroys are contrasted by de Grammont and Lane-Poole with the so-called 'Great Corsairs' of the earlier dispensation or the 'wise, just and clement rulers' of Moorish days, they administered a state which was steadily increasing in power and prosperity. It is interesting to note that Mustafa's administration was notable not only for the execution of much needed 'repairs and other useful works for the public good', but for the interest he took in the navy, laying the foundations of a fleet of stout sailing-ships for reprisal against Spain.

For a variety of reasons, not the least of which was the progressive decay of the Ottoman administration after Suleiman's death, the powers of the beglerbey—a title that never actually ceased throughout the history of the regency[3]—had been undergoing modification. His authority as the unquestioned

[1] Hakluyt, vi. 45. [2] *Piratical States*, p. 172.
[3] App. F.

representative of the sultan and Turkish interests may have been undermined by doubts as to the wisdom of Hassan's liberal policy in native affairs and by suspicions as to the loyalty of Ochiali. A new era was perhaps inaugurated on the departure of the latter, together with the main Algerine fleet, to Constantinople after the battle of Lepanto. From that time, at any rate, the administration of the regency appears to have been divided between three officers, whose interrelation is often very confusing.

The beglerbey, or bashaw, continued to represent the sultan, by whom he was appointed, but his term of office was short, at times not more than a year, and the physical connexion with Constantinople was slight, actually diminishing as the sailing-ship replaced the galley. Such authority as he exercised was derived from the prestige attaching to the office and from his personal qualities. He was always the nominal head of the regency, but after Lepanto his marine functions, including coastal defence and relations with Christian powers, became vested in the Captain of the Sea or, as we called him by a somewhat false analogy, General of the Galleys, who was appointed directly by the sultan and probably came at first under the superintendence of the Capudan pasha at Constantinople. Already, by the time that England had established relations with Turkey, there are references to the 'Barbary squadron', principally the ships of Algiers, which might be joined in the Mediterranean by a Turkish fleet.

The sultan issued separate directives, sometimes on the same subject, to the bashaw, for communication to the divan or soldiers' council, and to the Captain of the Sea, for transmission to the various sea-captains. Even late in the seventeenth century Mezzomorto, who had been successively Captain of the Sea, Dey, and bashaw, asked the French government to correspond separately with the last two officials on the subjects appropriate to their respective departments.[1] It was to simplify administrative procedure that from 1710 onwards the entire administration was concentrated once more in a single executive officer who, though usually known abroad by his lesser title of Dey, was in reality also the sultan's beglerbey or governor-general.

---

[1] Plantet, i. 136 n.

Haedo describes the unsuccessful attempt of the bashaw in 1574 to substitute for the recently appointed Captain of the Sea the popular and enterprising Morat Reis. The career of this remarkable man, who soon helped to restore Turkish naval supremacy in the Mediterranean at the expense of Spain, and appears to have been a good friend of England, has been strangely neglected by historians. If it is correct to regard Algiers as primarily a maritime state, our slender knowledge of a naval record which begins at least with the siege of Malta in 1565 and ends with the great disaster at Valona in 1638, is certainly surprising. In 1582, *fifty-six years* before his death on active service, de Grammont styles him 'ce vieux patriarche de la piraterie'[1] and the object of almost superstitious veneration. Haedo and Lane-Poole regard him as disappearing from view about 1595, the actual year of his definite appointment as Captain of the Sea. More recent French and Spanish writers make incidental references to him at later dates as an outlaw, pirate, or celebrated corsair.

His official career was, however, an honourable and eventful one, which brought him into contact with French ambassadors, eminent London merchants, the governors of Marseilles, and even James I and his successor. In 1603 he is described as the sultan's admiral in the Mediterranean, and in 1616 he appears to have commanded Turkish forces in the Levant as well.[2] In the interval, when his prestige both in Barbary and at Constantinople was very great, one French ambassador accepted him as arbiter in a dispute with Tunis, and another suggested his promotion to the post of bashaw at Algiers. He did, in fact, serve for some years as viceroy of the Morea. His naval reputation about 1608 was such that the French ambassador reported that he was regarded in Turkey as a 'miracle' and a 'saint', without whom nothing at sea could be accomplished.[3] Staper described him as 'Morat Bey, Admiral of Algier, being now a man of 70 yeares old who heretofore was as much renowned for

---

[1] De Grammont, p. 121. Dispute concerned confiscation of 24 silk bales claimed by *Lyons* merchants and detention of 2 *Breton* ships by Morat, 'chef et capitaine général des forces de mer dudit Alger', Charrière, iv, esp. 123 n. and 459 n.
[2] Knolles, pp. 825 and 939; App. E. Wrote officially to Florence in 1596, Braudel, p. 706 n., and Marseilles, Plantet, i. 2–4. Three mentions in V. von Klarwill, *The Fugger Letters* (Second Series), tr. L. S. R. Byrne, London, 1926.
[3] De Brèves, *Voyages*, p. 323; Heinrich, pp. 196, 198, and 209–11.

his exploite in the Levant seas as ever Drake was for his attempte upon ye Ocean'.[1] Knight witnessed the end at Valona in 1638 of 'Murate a renegade of the Corsica nation, a person of great honour in Algiers, lieutenant general of the armada, father-in-law of Ally the general, a man of 104 years of age, whose desire was to die in the face of the Christians fighting the battle of Mahomet'.[2]

It was apparently at the beginning of the century that the Captains of the Sea at Tripoli, Tunis, and Algiers were removed from the superintendence of the Capudan pasha, whose area of official jurisdiction then ended at Alexandria, Lepanto, and Santa Maura.[3] After the constitutional changes of 1626 the Captain of the Sea at Algiers became the 'greatest personage in the city', with the unusual attributes of a life-appointment and a fixed salary. He had, however, no voice in the all-powerful divan, which controlled the 'preferments, honours, estates and lives' of all officials, 'they of the council being so absolute in themselves that they have infallibility and inde-fectibility, power to make laws and obtrude them, whereby all those aforementioned officers are but as cyphers, serving only as interpreters to them, whose will is their reason'.[4]

The Captain of the Sea at that time, Morat's son-in-law the celebrated Ali Pitchnin, was easily the richest man in the country, but, being the native-born son of a Turkish soldier, he could not be an active member of the army. It was his ambition to be made bashaw, as at least one of his predecessors and successors was during the century.[5]

After the developments of 1626, when they are said to have 'created a commonwealth and chosen officers', the janissaries, or regular soldiers, became unquestionably the most powerful factor in the administration of the regency. The change took place with the formal approval of the Porte,[6] and soon after-wards the new mode of government is said to have given the sultan great satisfaction.[7] These soldiers formed one of the four great corporations or guilds of Algiers, but were obviously

[1] Cotton MS. Nero B. xi, ff. 280 sqq., Aug. 1607. See App. E, and for Morat and Drake, V.S.P. 1581–91, p. 277.

[2] Osborne, A Collection of Voyages and Travels, ii. 477.

[3] Knolles, pp. 960 and 988–9.

[4] Osborne, ii. 480.   [5] De Grammont, pp. 178–9.

[6] Roe, Negotiations with the Grand Signior 1621–1628, pp. 548 and 574.

[7] Osborne, ii. 483–4.

greatly superior in authority and privilege to the other three—the marine, the ecclesiastics and jurists, and the civil service. They actually controlled operations in the arsenal, in the port, and even, in course of time, on all ships at sea.

The regular army was composed mainly of Turks, who continued to regard themselves as subjects of the sultan, and were entitled to take leave in Turkey on full pay or retire on those pensions which enabled them to live with their families 'void of care' or 'gave releef assured whereupon they need not go begging like our soldiers, robbing those they meete and in fine trouble the hangman'.[1] They represented, in fact, a national military organization, which was regarded, even in the early nineteenth century, as remarkable for discipline, solidarity, and self-respect, and also for the care which the government took for the welfare of all, from the time of enlistment up to their deaths. No soldier was ever punished in public or even forcibly arrested. Relations between the various ranks were friendly, but breaches of discipline, especially against 'divan men', were severely punished—only, however, at the aga's official residence, the 'House of Bitterness'.

Discussions or dissensions were settled inside the barracks, 'pieces of excellent workmanship and commodity', which even in Elizabethan times were notable for their size and amenities, and later were recognized by treaty as affording sanctuary for our naval deserters. In public affairs the army appeared to speak with one voice, and remarkable testimony is paid to the harmony existing in its ranks, even when, in the middle of the seventeenth century, they still contained a wide variety of Christian elements.

The peculiar character of this highly privileged organization must have puzzled contemporaries, as it has done many modern critics. Gardiner, for instance, describes Tunis and Algiers as 'seats of independent communities' where the 'turbulent soldiery' and 'uncontrollable hordes, who had long bidden defiance to the Sultan', held the wretched population 'in subjection with all the crushing weight of a military despotism'[2]—a purely theoretical inference drawn from false analogies and

---

[1] Ibid.; Cotton MS. Nero B. xi, ff. 8–12b.
[2] S. R. Gardiner, *History of England, 1603–1642*, 10 vols., 1883–4, iii. 64. See App. L.

the slenderest of data, which is quite irreconcilable with reliable contemporary evidence or the history of those regencies over the next two centuries.

The army was not exclusively military in character, since its members could, and frequently did, follow a trade, a circumstance criticized by Haedo as derogatory to the 'nobility' of the profession, often demonstrated elsewhere by resort to plunder, extortion, and begging. Nor was it too rigidly Turkish in its outlook, since through trade and marriage sympathetic relations could be formed with the local population. Married soldiers are described as living in blocks of flats alongside wealthy merchants, and their children, after the Colougli riot of about 1636, seem to have melted into the native population to a far greater extent than the Eurasian in British India or the mulatto in the old French colonies.

The privilege of active membership of the regular army was successively withdrawn from the native inhabitants, converted Jews, soldiers' sons, and renegade Christians. From about the end of the seventeenth century it and the civil service, which was recruited from the better-educated soldiers, were composed solely of native-born Turks, engaged in Turkey. Many of the more lucrative offices, such as provincial governorships, however, became open to Moors and some of a technical nature, connected with the marine, to Christians or Christian renegades. The chief of police in Algiers was always a Moor and the chief executioner, like many of the principal officers of the bashaw's and Dey's households, was a Christian slave. In the time of the Deys the grand admiral could not also hold the post of minister of marine in their cabinets, unless he was a Turk by birth.

A very different policy was followed in Tunis and Tripoli, where the highest offices became available to Christian renegades and other non-Turks, with the result that the responsibility for ensuring Turkish dominion in North Africa came to rest almost entirely with Algiers, whose administrative system collapsed completely with the repatriation of the Turk soldiers in 1830. During the early history of the regency, however, the great majority of the ruling caste were necessarily, owing to social conditions in Turkey itself, 'Turks by profession', i.e. Christians who, whether born in the empire or not, were from early years trained as Mohammedans and loyal subjects of the sultan. They are frequently, but erroneously, confused with voluntary, i.e. adult, renegades, who in fact seem to have played a small part in Algerine history and practically disappeared during the seventeenth century.[1]

Promotion in the army was automatic and its aga, or official head, had necessarily served in every grade, including the period of very rigorous training as a raw recruit. His term of office lasted only two months, after which he retired from active service. That some discrimination was shown in the selection of so responsible an official is clear from Haedo's statement that three or four senior officers were excluded owing to the morals of their wives, while Dapper says that only a limited number of those qualified by seniority were actually chosen. The aga, who was represented in the field by a lieutenant, was not only the head of the army but military governor of the city of Algiers and its vicinity, and above all president of the divan.

That body rapidly took charge of the administration of the country and, in its peculiar way, appears to have performed its duties with a sense of responsibility, to which Francis Knight soon afterwards bore witness, and a degree of expedition and efficiency unusual in those days. There was no debate at its sessions, and its decisions were made unanimously. It met in private or public session every day of the week, except Friday, the day of prayer, and in course of time only one of the two public meetings, that specially devoted to external affairs, was held at the official residence of the bashaw, when he might communicate to the divan the sultan's commands. These appear to have been treated with greater respect and more careful study than is generally supposed.

The council is said to have had, from very early times, power to decide questions of peace and war, a responsibility which was unavoidable when contact with Moslem neighbours or Christian shores was only a matter of days, in contrast to almost as many months with Constantinople. Indeed, when the sailing-ship came to replace the swifter and more dependable galley, a bashaw might be delayed as much as two years awaiting the arrival of his successor. It is consequently very difficult to know to what extent the Porte intended the 'commands', which appear in many cases to have been dictated by Christian

[1] Osborne, ii. 466. Shaw says about 1730 there were only 30.

ambassadors, to be mandatory or merely subjects for consideration. They were often unreasonable or even contradictory—
the product of ignorance, importunity, threats, bribery, and
even, it was frequently claimed, of forgery.[1] There seems to be
little room for doubt that the regencies were intended to settle
their affairs as best they could, in the interests alike of themselves and the Ottoman empire.

The civil servants were concerned mainly with questions of
supply and accountancy, not only on land but on board warships and privateers. They are said to have been very accurate
and good 'arithmeticians'. Among the state records that they
kept were registers containing the sultan's commands, the texts
of treaties, and detailed particulars of prizes, of the sale of slaves,
and of the collection of taxes. The very informative lists of
men-of-war supplied by Haedo[2] or consuls of Charles II were
presumably copied from official records. Gramaye[3] claims to
have established by reference to the 'rate-books' prior to 1619
that the number of suburban properties at Algiers was precisely
14,698. If our estimates of prizes and Christian slaves are even
approximately correct the volume of book-keeping must have
been very great.

The service was headed by the four secretaries of state, who
were originally attached to the bashaw and later sat on the
aga's right at the divans. Knight describes the first secretary as
'the greatest person in council, or otherwise their sole director
in matters of state'.[4] Not less important to our consuls was the
fourth secretary, whose province was 'Christian affairs'. He was
responsible for the preparation and custody of foreign treaties,
which he is said to have interpreted with meticulous accuracy.[5]

The judicial officers—the muftis and cadis—played no part
in Christian relations, except when they were consulted upon
some religious or constitutional point, such as the abolition of
slavery, or asked to sit in some special tribunal in connexion
with the condemnation of a ship or cargo, when some unusually

[1] Lucas, *La Grèce*, ii. 237; Rousseau, *Annales tunisiennes*, p. 39.
[2] *Topographia*, ch. xxii.
[3] Purchas, *Hakluytus Posthumus*, ix. 270.
[4] Osborne, ii. 480.
[5] *Piratical States*, pp. 189–90. For accurate division of booty, see Morgan, p. 616, and Lewes Roberts, *The Merchantes Mappe of Commerce*, 1638, 3rd ed., London, 1677, ch. xix.

knotty or delicate consideration was involved. The Turkish muftis and cadis continued to be sent out from Constantinople on the recommendation of the chief mufti there.

The unsupported assertions of writers like de Grammont that the countryside of Algiers and Tunis was the scene of frightful and perpetual anarchy are quite irreconcilable with the testimony of Lithgow, Mainwaring, or Gramaye in the reign of James I or, at subsequent stages, of Dapper,[1] Shaw, Bruce, and Venture. Special note is made of occasional strife between tribes on the border of Tunisia and Algeria in the early part of the century[2] and of the civil war in Tunis towards its end. On the whole it would seem that, in spite of external intrigue and violence, law and order were better preserved, travel was safer, and the people more prosperous throughout a large part of the area than in at least the greater portion of Christendom. It is also interesting to observe how Algiers succeeded in avoiding the pitfalls that were to prove so disastrous to the governments of Morocco, Egypt, and Turkey itself.

[1] Absence of 'brawling' and 'cabals' was often noted. Soldiers were 'so well governed and live in such unanimity' that quarrels were rare, Dapper, *Africa*, p. 239, and p. 228 'they live in great concord'.

[2] Osborne, ii. 486–8.

V

THE CITY OF ALGIERS IN THE TIME OF ELIZABETH I

THE city, which our Levant merchants selected for their headquarters on the Barbary coast, was clearly not the bloodstained anarchical centre, maintained solely by the fruit of sea-robberies, which is described by some imaginative writers. The graphic picture painted for us by Haedo[1] is convincing from its wealth of detail, which is largely confirmed, during the following century, by narratives or illuminating sidelights from a series of eye-witnesses of different nations and varied walks of life—travellers, captives, sea-captains, naval officers, consuls, and, not least, a French academician. Corroborative evidence is available from other areas—Turkey, Tunis, and Morocco—and from accounts of Algiers at much later times, even by Scottish and Tuscan poets in the nineteenth century.[2] Its simple narrative, reinforced in this manner, helps to dispel the unfavourable impression created by the bigoted and usually ill-informed Father Dan and de Grammont's imaginary enigma of people living 'rich and happy' in a welter of riot, bloodshed, famine, and disease.

Haedo's account of the city is confirmed moreover by a map made in 1579 and by the detailed legend affixed to an engraving of it dated Naples 1601, both of which are reproduced by Playfair. It describes a prosperous and well-ordered town in an interesting stage of its development from the days of Gomara and Nicholay to the luxurious city, with modern amenities, of which Knight and d'Aranda left us pictures in the reign of Charles I.

---

[1] The *Topography* and *History* were probably written by the Archbishop of Palermo and Captain General of Sicily up to 1581, with a superficial continuation of the *History* by his nephew when settled in Spain. Internal evidence suggests the latter added to the *Topography* ch. xxii and xxiii about corsairs and part of xxxvi about local vices, which is inconsistent with general context. Influx of hostile French and English ships doubtless embittered later portions.

[2] Campbell and Pananti; H. D. de Grammont, *Un Académicien (J. Roy Vaillant) captif à Alger, 1674–1675*, Paris, 1883.

Even in Haedo's time it contained such distinctive features as a mint, a theological school, public baths—two of them particularly handsome—with hot and cold water and various other conveniences, and a hospital for the sick, the gift of Hassan Barbarossa.

The prominent part played by the army was demonstrated by the arsenal, which it controlled, and the five barracks, which housed 2,000 regulars and offered many amenities, including small rooms for separate messes and fountains in the quadrangles. Though already an object of Christian admiration and described by the French mission of 1605, two centuries before we had any at all, as resembling 'great hotels', they were steadily improved until the completion in 1650 of four still handsomer ones by the best architects procurable. They played a very important part in the economy of Algiers, since they provided the more truculent members of the ruling caste not only with lodgings but with parade grounds, recreation centres, and places for political debate. They were kept immaculately clean by Christian slaves, who are even said to have paid for the privilege of working there. D'Aranda tells us of the kindness he received in one, eating from the same dish as a friendly soldier. In Haedo's time 1,600 janissaries lived in their own homes.

The two 'bagnios', or state prisons for captives, closely resembled the barracks in their structural arrangements. The original one, which held about 2,000, could only be left by permission and was guarded night and day. The smaller, built by Hassan Barbarossa to accommodate some of the Spanish soldiers captured in his great victory near Oran, was afterwards used for skilled slaves, employed at the neighbouring arsenal and shipyards, who were apparently free to come and go at will. The only instance of favouritism cited by Haedo was the ability of janissaries or other influential Turks to transfer from the public prison to the greater comfort of the larger bagnio.

In addition to the attractive but not very imposing viceregal palace and the *Casbah* or citadel, where state prisoners were confined, the national treasure kept, and public divans held, there were a number of fine dwellings, 'stupendious and sumptuous edifices' according to Knight, inhabited by Turks, Moors, and renegade Christians, and even by a Jew. The contrast between their forbiddingly plain exteriors, which misled some visitors into believing them the strongholds of robber barons or tyrannical husbands, and the clean, bright elegance within illustrated the frugal and unostentatious character of the Algerine Turks. This, combined with the austerity of their habits and the simplicity of their tables, betrayed Haedo, who really knew better, into saying that no cobbler or artisan in Europe lived so poorly. These interiors surprised and pleased English visitors, even in Victorian times,[1] and their amenities were greatly increased, early in the seventeenth century, by the introduction of running water.

Special features of the houses were the galleried courtyards and, even more, the flat roofs on which the ladies, in particular, might take their ease and receive visits. They also offered the opportunity of fairly long promenades of a pleasanter and more private nature than could be afforded by the streets, which, with the exception of the Sook, a kind of market-place traversing the city, were exceptionally narrow, even for those days, and at first very dirty for want of drainage to the sea. This latter defect was, however, remedied when, early in the seventeenth century, the Moriscos introduced various improvements, including a good water supply, so that the city became 'commodious for her abundance of fountains in all parts of her and concavity for the passage of ordure and excrement from all houses and corners'.[2] In this respect Algiers must have compared extremely favourably with many of our largest cities, including the 'vile haunts' of Portsmouth and Plymouth, even two centuries later,[3] and we can understand why its inhabitants are described as healthier and longer-lived than Europeans.

Their cleanliness in regard to their persons, clothing, houses, weapons, and eating was a frequent subject of remark and even of ridicule or censure. Gramaye lists among their 'foolish conceits' the fact that they 'wash before work, prayer and meals', and we are told that nothing 'disobliged' them so much as to have their clothes touched by the hand of a Christian. Even a drop of blood was looked on as defiling and the removal of shoes on entering a house as 'a great point of civility'.[4] The public

[1] H. E. Pope, *Corsair and his Conqueror*, London, 1860; J. W. Blakesley, *Four months in Algiers*, Cambridge, 1859.

[2] Osborne, ii. 480.

[3] Biographies of St. Vincent; Oppenheim, *History of the Administration of the Navy*, pp. 321 and 323 n. [4] i.e. of civilized manners.

baths at Algiers were made available to persons of all races and creeds, including slaves.

Like many subsequent writers Haedo draws an attractive picture of well-watered gardens and vineyards outside the city, luxuriant with fruits, flowers, trees, and vegetables, each with at least a little white house. These were much used for recreation, especially by the ladies, who picnicked there and entertained their less fortunate friends, and they made a pleasant residence during the summer heat. Haedo puts their number at 12,000, a figure which would seem quite incredible, though it increased steadily up to 18,000 in descriptions over the next two centuries. They were largely responsible for the city's abundant supply of food and for the demand for Christian slaves. Knight estimated that not less than 60,000 were employed on them. However doubtful we may feel about the accuracy of such figures, the very existence and regular use of such amenities indicate a pleasant, peaceful, and orderly way of life.[1]

Seven large mosques, one of them constructed in 1579 by a wealthy Moor, and more than fifty chapels or shrines provided for the religious needs of the Mussulmans at that time. In addition, there were elementary schools—Gramaye gives the questionable number of eighty-six—in which children learned to read and write from the Koran. Women, who for sexual reasons were excluded from the mosques, spent much of their time visiting shrines or taking care of tombs. Haedo mentions two Jewish synagogues, one in each half of the city, but in Gramaye's time there were six. Besides oratories in the bagnios and the French consul's house, a Spanish hospital, established in 1551 and reconstituted in 1612, ministered to the physical and religious needs of Christian slaves. The Algerines, who had a great respect for religion in any monotheistic form, believed that the best slaves were the most devout, and it was partly on this account that Spaniards are said to have been valued at three times the price of Englishmen.[2]

The population of the city, which by 1650 numbered about

---

[1] They were still admired, though damaged during the occupation, Campbell, ii. 94; Blakesley, p. 21.

[2] Partly because Englishmen could be exchanged, or redeemed on conclusion of peace.

100,000, was extremely cosmopolitan. In addition to 'natural Turks', including merchants,[1] from Anatolia and Romania, various native races and three distinct categories of Jews, there were different kinds of renegades or 'Turks by profession', the offspring of Christian parents, who had been converted and are said to have numbered more than all the other free classes put together. According to Haedo there was no country from Muscovy to the Spanish and Portuguese colonies in the East and West Indies that did not have representatives among them, desiring in this way either to escape from slavery or to enjoy a life of greater freedom than in their homeland. Dapper, some fifty years later, describes the amazing harmony in which this strange miscellany of foreign nations lived together, as a result of the military 'policy' of Algiers.[2] Haedo, unfortunately, gives no figures for either janissaries or Christian slaves, but they may in his time have represented half the population of the city.

It is a pity, too, that he makes no mention of the corporations or trade-guilds, as they would have helped to illustrate the parts played by the different races in the city's complex economy. We know, for instance, from later sources, that one tribe from near Djidjelli furnished the bakers; that 'salvage Moors' from the Sahara—probably the negroes to whom Haedo refers—had a monopoly of the trade in ostrich-feathers, and also formed the corporation of watchmen or porters; that the Baldis, or original inhabitants, who by ancient privilege came under the exclusive jurisdiction of the bashaw, were employed in menial occupations, such as carrying the soldiers' arms on campaigns; and that the ever-increasing community of Jews— native, Aragonese, and Italian or 'Christian'—monopolized a number of special trades as goldsmiths, jewellers, exchange-brokers, and money-lenders. The retail sale of contraband goods—wines, spirits, tobacco, shot, &c.—seems to have been reserved for Christian slaves, who thereby acquired a profitable and privileged position and were enabled, *if they wished*, to purchase their freedom.[3] The integration of these corporations with the government through emins, or official representatives,

---

[1] Perhaps 'trading janissaries', Pinkerton, *General Collection of Voyages and Travels*, x. 25 and 619.

[2] Dapper, p. 228. Gramaye attributed the agas' increased power to prolonged peace, p. 14, surely confusing cause and effect, Peysonnel, p. 408.

[3] D'Aranda, Appendix, 'L'Esclavitude Imaginaire'.

ensured the members a fair measure of protection and regulation and the administration a considerable source of revenue.[1]

Haedo was struck by the democratic spirit or absence of social strata. Lineage counted for nothing and family connexions, apart from the very closest, for very little. Turks, Moors, and renegades married indifferently Turkish women from Constantinople, who were very few, native Moors, renegade Christians, and the converted daughters of Jews. Almost simultaneously, in the late seventeenth century, the wives of both the Dey of Algiers and the Emperor of Morocco were Englishwomen, but such cases were probably exceptional.

Various Christians, including the Sieur de Roqueville,[2] who, as water-carrier to one of the baths, claimed to have special opportunities for judging, spoke of the remarkable beauty of the native women, their dazzling white skins and flashing eyes and, perhaps most of all, of their clean and healthy appearance. Female slaves, according to Haedo, were mainly prized for their domestic accomplishments, then rarely possessed by Moorish women, and were often employed in workshops on fine sewing, weaving, spinning, and embroidery. I have seen no reference to their indecent exposure or public sale. On the contrary it seems to have been the rule to treat all women respectfully, and even the very hostile Pananti, in his advice to captives, recommends men on the seizure of their vessel to hand their money and valuables to female passengers, because of the well-known respect always shown by the Algerines towards women.[3] A Christian woman, returning home after, perhaps, years of slavery, might still be regarded as a highly eligible bride.[4]

Haedo's criticisms of Algerine wives and of their relations with their husbands sound strangely modern. They dyed their hair with henna and reddened their nails. Apart from bringing up their children, washing clothes, getting meals, and kneading bread, if they had no slaves, they did nothing but loaf or spend their evenings in dancing and feasts, while their husbands waited patiently for their return. They might also, especially if they came of Christian stock, pass some of the time spinning

---

[1] Pellissier, i. 76–79.

[2] *Relation du royaume et du gouvernement d'Alger*, Paris, 1686.

[3] p. 355, 'The Turks hold their persons sacred'. For land wars, see Pellissier, iii. 435.

[4] Hubac, p. 201, cites Molière, *L'Avare*, Act v, Sc. 5.

or sewing. but a good deal more was devoted to religious duties.[1] There were schools where women could learn trades and a corporation or college for those skilled in prophecy and similar mysteries.

We hear little about polygamy, though Haedo expressed guarded approval of its effect on men's morals, and it seems to have soon died out—at least among the Turkish inhabitants. Wives had their property rights and might even be richer than their husbands. While they could only be divorced for clearly proved adultery, they could obtain their freedom on several grounds, including insufficient maintenance and the drinking of wine. A wife and her women-folk had their private apartments in houses, which were partly planned for their convenience, and the lavish expenditure on her adornment was in striking contrast to the unostentatious austerity of the home. In this connexion Knight quotes a local proverb of the Turks that 'there are three things that destroy the world: the Christians in law, the Jews in feasts, and they upon their wives'.[2]

Although the question as to who should rule the home was said to be decided by a quaint physical contest at the wedding, the husband seems to have been no match, in either the sixteenth or nineteenth century, for the habitual combination against him of 'all that was feminine' in the household. After retailing some scandalous gossip the Tuscan Pananti, like Dean Addison earlier in Morocco, came to the conclusion that Moorish women made good wives and mothers, and various indications confirm Haedo's suggestion that morals were on the whole better than in Christendom.[3] Steps appear to have been taken to safeguard them in the case of female and boy slaves, and the regulation of prostitutes, of whom we hear surprisingly little, provided much trouble for the night police and may in later times have contributed to the mysterious assassination of a particularly severe Dey. They were never punished in public.[4]

The difference between the Moslem and Christian conceptions of slavery was fundamental. In the case of Algiers and Tunis the application of such epithets as 'hopeless' and 'de-

[1] A. Roberts, *The Adventures of Mr. T— S—*, pp. 41 and 55.

[2] Osborne, ii. 479.

[3] Experienced writers, like d'Arvieux, admitted ignorance of domestic and sexual affairs; Leo, p. xlviii. For Addison see Pinkerton, xv.

[4] Haedo said women could be for notorious adultery.

grading' is singularly inappropriate. A Christian slave was, in fact, a prisoner of war and regarded as a victim of temporary misfortune. His servile condition involved no 'contempt of human dignity'. He had his recognized rights and privileges, partly founded on precepts of the Old Testament. In Haedo's time the theory still existed that slavery should be restricted to a period of seven years bondage, and more than two centuries later this was the recognized practice among desert tribes of Morocco. Whether Christians were actually better off as slaves than as free men in their own land naturally depended on circumstances. They were certainly more favourably treated on the whole in the regencies than slaves in Turkey or in Christian galleys and plantations or the generality of prisoners of war. There were various ways of obtaining freedom—by voluntary emancipation, by purchase, by charity, by individual exchange, or by treaty at the end of hostilities. It was a rule throughout the Ottoman empire that, whenever an opportunity offered, any Turkish soldier must be redeemed by the exchange of a Christian slave.[1] Captain Richard Hunt, while in the service of Spain, was three times ransomed from captivity at Algiers.[2] Escape was by no means difficult, the chief deterrent being fear of treachery by fellow slaves.

In Algiers and Tunis domestic slaves were often treated as members of the family and, in accordance with old religious teaching, could alone share with them in the Passover.[3] The beylic, or government, slaves, generally regarded as the least fortunate, did not work on Fridays and had three hours free on other days, in which they might earn money for extra food or for recreation by working, begging, or more usually, according to good authority, by stealing.[4] Contrary to Christian practice a man was normally a galley-slave for only about a quarter of the year, and the total number at Algiers fell from about 4,000 in Haedo's time to 900 soon after the Restoration.[5] The galley had become practically obsolete there, when its use was so intensified by Colbert and his successors.

---

[1] D'Aranda, *Relation de la captivité et liberté du Sieur d'Aranda*, p. 43. (? Found 'mighty pretty reading' by Pepys.)   [2] Cal. S.P.D. 1634–5, p. 223.

[3] Haedo uses Lent and Easter for Moslem fasts and feasts. For Morocco, see Cal. S.P.F. 1575–7, p. 598; for Turkey, Conyers Read, iii. 229.

[4] On Friday they found their own food.

[5] Consul Martin's report S.P. 71. 2, ff. 329–51, 10 June 1675.

The bagnios, which actually had no dungeons,[1] were certainly as good as our best gaols, and served as prisons only at night. Part of the accommodation was appropriated to taverns, where such normally prohibited attractions as drinking and gambling could be indulged in by unmarried soldiers, renegades, foreign seamen, and slaves, and to quarters for officials and a resident chaplain. D'Aranda describes dropping in to these places to listen to the slaves spinning yarns or join them in a game of cards, and the American Foss long afterwards spoke appreciatively of the pork sausages which he purchased there. The priest not only said mass every morning at the altar in the main dormitory but helped to keep order in emergencies, as, for example, when one intervened 'with his wax candle' to quell a riot of the Russians against the Spaniards and Italians. These priests are said to have made many converts among the other Christians.

The bagnio, in which he heard twenty-two languages spoken, was, in d'Aranda's not very elevated opinion, the best school in the world for practical experience. Knight, whose captivity of seven years varied from a life of indulgence to campaigns in the galleys, comments on the quality of the seamen produced in this manner at Algiers, of whom a thousand were better than three thousand of our own. At its worst it might have been preferable to rotting in a Leghorn gaol[2] or dying of 'starvation, cold and stench' in an English one.[3]

Chains were only used in special circumstances to prevent escape, and conversion only conferred emancipation if the master were willing. Bread, clothing, and bedding for slaves in the bagnios were drawn from the army stores.

If male slaves were often as flagrantly dishonest, and many of the females as shameless, as some writers suggest, it is hardly surprising that slavery as an institution lost its attraction for Algiers in proportion as its economic value diminished in what had ceased to be a pioneer state. The number of Christian slaves in the regency fell rapidly during the second half of the

[1] The only dungeons were old grain-pits, e.g. at Ceuta and Oran, called by d'Aranda a 'Spanish custom'.
[2] D'Aranda refused detention at Leghorn, a 'second slavery' according to later Dutch captives, 'principal comptoir de ce trafic infâme', Sue, *Correspondance de H. Esconbleau de Sourdis*, i, p. xxxix.
[3] See biographies of de Ruyter.

seventeenth century. There were in 1700 about 2,000, mainly Spanish, and after peace was made with Spain in 1785, there remained only 500, practically all 'voluntaries', i.e. deserters from the Spanish garrison at Oran. Even in that century Algiers was by treaty not only permitted, but even at times compelled, to condemn nationals of the other party to slavery. Even so, there were probably far more Barbaresques held captive in its later stages in Christendom than Christians in Barbary.[1]

In the neighbouring countries of Tunis and Morocco Christian slaves were to some extent replaced by negroes, but in Algeria free labour came to be used perhaps as generally as in any other part of the world, though slavery there was not officially abolished until the Second Republic.[2] Christian reports of the seventeenth and eighteenth centuries suggest that the problem of manpower was being reasonably well solved.

The generally humane and rational attitude of the Algerines, by contemporary standards, is an interesting revelation of the practical good sense and moral responsibility which were fundamental aspects of their rule. They are to a large extent corroborated in Haedo's generally favourable appreciation of the character of the ruling class, in which it is noticeable that the items of commendation are more numerous and convincing than the criticisms.

He seems genuinely impressed by the careful observance of religious duties and the strict decorum at worship, and cites among the excellences worthy of imitation the good lives led by the old men, adding 'would to God that the Christians were more like them, in reverence to God and his holy commandments'. Included in these exemplary traits were the absence of blasphemy, gambling, quarrels, and duelling; their comradeship and co-operation in camp and field; their obedience to authority; their refusal to tolerate abuse or criticism of either the sultan or their priests; their cleanly habits, abstention from plunder, and readiness to endure privation in war-time—all of which are confirmed elsewhere.

His criticism of soldiers resorting to trade or handicrafts in their spare time has already been mentioned. He illustrates the

[1] Venture, pp. 50–56; Campbell, i. 82–84; Plantet, ii. 486–8.
[2] Pellissier, iii. 355–6.

sin of pride by their contempt for the Christians, which, however, he admits was not entirely unjustified, and of sloth by
their lack of virtuous recreation, which apparently included
military exercises and blood sports, but not craftsmanship of
any kind. According to some observers the dearth of amuse-
ments in Algiers furnished the principal grievance for many
English slaves.

In charging the inhabitants with inhumanity to the poor
and sick he was influenced primarily by accounts of distressing
scenes during the great famine of 1579–80, and contrasted the
callous rapacity of Hassan Veneziano with the careful provision made for a previous emergency.[1] There was good reason
for complaint about lack of hospital facilities, if the celebrated
foundation of Hassan Barbarossa was mainly devoted to the
care of old soldiers. He makes no allusion to various institutions
and funds, including one for the welfare of Christian slaves,
which later attracted attention.[2] His description of exhibitions
of drunkenness as exceeding anything seen in Germany presumably referred to the revelries of renegades or foreign adventurers returning from triumphs at sea, since elsewhere he
commends Turkish abstinence, noting that to have touched
wine once was justification for divorcing a husband or dis-
qualifying a witness. Such orgies may have been a new phenomenon.[3]

Perhaps the most interesting and unexpected characteristic
of Algiers which he records is the spirit of democratic comradeship at the great religious feasts, when members of all the varied
races and creeds rejoiced together. Even the staid and dignified
Turks unbent to join in the dancing and to take part in those
very pastimes which characterized our village fairs some three
centuries later—wrestling, swinging, and walking on stilts. The
Christian slaves not only joined in, but reaped a small harvest
by exhibitions of skill at acrobatics, conjuring, and marksman-
ship. It was even said that the *usanza* or practice of giving
presents to officials or servants on these occasions, which was

[1] Starving soldiers plundered private stocks. Hassan was promptly recalled at
instance of *Moors* sent to the Porte, Haedo, i. 385.

[2] See Campbell, ii. 96–100.

[3] Apparently an unfamiliar problem. Ch. xxiii deals solely with Morisco raids
from Cherchell. Haedo possibly referred to English and French activities at
Algiers from 1581 or the welcome given English ships in 1586, Hakluyt, vi. 56.

later the subject of so much complaint by foreign consuls,[1] was actually introduced by Christian slaves under the guise of Christmas and Easter perquisites. Rather unexpectedly, the 'affability' of Turks and Moors at Algiers is more than once mentioned by both captives and visitors.

Playfair, Plantet, de Grammont, and others insist that Algiers had no trade or industry, and Duro cites Haedo as evidence of its dependence on booty for its prosperity or even its existence. It is true that Haedo does refer bitterly to the corsairs and their sea-robberies, though not necessarily with any suggestion of illegality, but against this must be set his long list of items which went to make up the official revenue of Algiers, and the two remarkable chapters[2] dealing with its merchants and their trade and with its workshops and crafts. His picture of Algiers as a busy port and trading centre is specifically confirmed by Thomas Dallam, who in 1599 found it 'a great place of trade and merchandise';[3] by Gramaye, who twenty years later gives very extravagant statistics of its merchants, shops, and craftsmen; and by Knolles's *History*, which mentions Alexandria and Algiers about 1625 as the commercial centres of Turkish North Africa.[4] In 1597 Davies spoke of its 'great store of gold and rich merchants'.[5] While Lithgow describes it as a 'divelish town grown wonderful rich' by robberies, the London merchants were 'importunate' soon afterwards to resume trade there, and Roe, Knight, and Huett Leate regarded it as a good potential market for English goods.

Another chapter by Haedo, relative to the flourishing Jewish community, is at least suggestive of attractions for international commerce. Such a phenomenon, not unnaturally, evoked comment from nearly all Christian visitors. Some expressed pity for the Jews, others loathed them. Haedo showed unusual intolerance in the remark that, however clean, they and their houses stank like he-goats.

The merchants of Algiers, by which term Haedo clearly meant those engaged in foreign trade, are described as very numerous and consisting mainly of natural Turks and renegades,

[1] S.P. 71. 3, f. 452; Charrière, iv. 75 n.
[2] *Topographia*, chs. xxiv and xxv.
[3] *Early Voyages and Travels in the Levant*, ed. J. T. Bent (Hakluyt Society), London, 1893, pp. 17–18.   [4] Purchas, ix. 272–3; Knolles, p. 983.
[5] *The Travels and Miserable Captivity of William Davies*, Osborne, i. 476–88.

their children and converted Jews. Though most had begun as young apprentices, some were janissaries and Levants, i.e. maritime adventurers from Turkey, who desired a quiet life. We know from other sources that Turkish merchants at this time traded on a considerable scale, not only with North Africa but with Venice, Ragusa, and other ports in the Adriatic. At Algiers there is mention also of Christian merchants receiving royal licences to export goods which were subject to strict regulation. The demand for a French consulate as early as 1564 indicates that trade relations with Provence were active and that some French merchants were resident in Algiers.[1]

Haedo describes how the port, from the time that Kheir-ed-din had welcomed to it traders and ships of all nations, had rapidly developed into a great entrepôt, through which Christian trade was carried on throughout North Africa and even with Turkey itself. He mentions among other things the maintenance of a regular service of galleys between Algiers and Tetuan, and its strategic connexion with the great caravan routes. However exaggerated some of his statements may be, and he was hardly in a position to obtain accurate statistics, the general reliability of the picture he presents is substantiated in various ways. For instance, one of his less probable statements, that Algiers carried on a considerable trade direct with Valencia and Catalonia, while it received contraband goods from Spain by way of Marseilles, finds considerable support in the fact that there was a Corsican merchant residing in Algiers, who had brothers in business at Valencia and Marseilles and, incidentally, supplied the Governor of Valencia with intelligence.[2]

We know, too, from official French correspondence that goods and passengers from Marseilles were at times transhipped at Algiers for Constantinople and that, presumably as conditions in Provence continued to deteriorate, ships from Dieppe began to take part in the trade. We also know that the goods which Haedo mentions as coming to Algiers from England were

[1] Heinrich, p. 140, after famine of 1580, mentions 'la vive impulsion aux affaires' of French merchants with Algiers and Tunis, adding 'la meilleure preuve de la prospérité c'est que plusieurs Compagnies en disputaient les monopoles'. Charrière, iv, and Grandchamp, i, pp. xv–xxi. Saint Tropez and La Ciotat, &c., were busy ports.

[2] Braudel, p. 127. *News from Valencia*, Add. MS. 28359, f. 133, reported on Ramadan, 13 Mar. 1575, the year Cervantes was captured.

almost identical with those sent at first by the Levant Company to Constantinople. Unfortunately, he gives no date or indication as to what proportion of those goods came in our own ships.

What he does tell us is that England furnished much iron, lead, tin, copper, pewter, gunpowder, and cloths of every kind, and that a very wide range of goods, many of them articles of luxury, were imported from Marseilles (especially), Genoa, Venice, Naples, Sicily, and Eastern Spain. The omission of Flanders and the Hanseatic States suggests that the report does not cover the last decade of the century. In exchange for these goods a great variety of agricultural produce was exported, especially grain, animals, wool, and hides. The mention of camels and silk is an indication of the extensive area served by the port. Special reference is made to its pre-eminent position, 'since so many Christian trading vessels do not come to any port of Barbary as to Algiers'.

Normal trade was enhanced by traffic in prize goods—a privilege officially claimed by British, French, and Americans as late as the nineteenth century. Many merchants dealt in the varied wares which the corsairs—presumably of various nations —brought for sale to Algiers, as well as in the profitable traffic in Christian captives. The value of the trade in prize goods has probably been greatly exaggerated, and it is noteworthy that the gold, of which we hear so much, reached Algiers from legitimate sources—the 'Barbary gold' of the interior and the gold crowns with which Spain purchased Algerine produce.

Local manufactures were the products of a wide range of craftsmen—workers in coral and gold, tanners and saddlers, smiths and armourers, masons, stone-cutters, and ship-builders. Elsewhere we hear of the jewellery, embroidery, carpets, fine shawls, dyeing, &c. Even before the Levant Company had established itself at Algiers, hopes had been entertained of mitigating our unemployment problem by taking over part of the manufacture of Tunis caps, for which Algiers was already famous.[1] In its early days, too, the East India Company was investing considerable sums in the purchase of Algiers and Tunis coral through Leghorn and Marseilles.[2]

---

[1] Hakluyt, v. 230. So did the French later.

[2] Cal. S.P. Col. 1617–21, p. 256, regarding purchase up to £30,000. Later the Company appointed purchasing agents there.

When we read these and other particulars, corroborated and even embellished by the later accounts of Gramaye, who speaks of its 3,000 merchant families of different nations and 2,000 shops, or of Knight, who was an intelligent English merchant, or the tributes paid by a number of Christian visitors to the abundance, variety, and cheapness of food supplies, or the competition of Christian merchants and corporations for trading privileges and concessions, or the anxiety of the dukes of Tuscany and Savoy and even the pope to establish similar free ports, we begin to understand why Haedo came to regard Algiers as 'the most opulent place' in the sultan's empire, his 'Indies, Mexico and Peru', and that Knight describes the city as flourishing 'to the admiration of the Turk'.[1]

[1] Osborne, ii. 479–80. See also Gramaye, ch. x, 'Hinc per orbem totum Argela velut nova aliqua India reputetur et imo nominetur a Turcis'. He was a merchant of Antwerp. Soon after Knight described Algiers and 'its original manner of government, increase, and present flourishing state'.

VI

THE LEVANT COMPANY AND THE REGENCIES

THE institution of direct commercial relations between England and Turkey was facilitated by a combination of economic, political, and religious developments. Most important among these were the marked decline of French credit at Constantinople and the imperative necessity for our merchants in the Spanish trade to transfer their operations to a more congenial sphere. Both were, though in different ways, largely the product of religious dissensions. The economic situation had been affected to the extent that England was urgently seeking new markets for its wares in North Africa and the Levant—'more woorth than all the golde of Peru and of all the West Indies'—and that Turkey was in desperate need of those commodities.[1] Politically, the English and Turks had little in common, until both were faced with the threat of a united front from Spain, Portugal, and France, after which anxiety about the fate of Morocco[2] provided a rather vague common interest.

Already by 1570 our trade with Spain had come to a virtual standstill and was being partially transferred to Saffi and Fez. In the same year Jasper Campion wrote from Chios, then occupied by the Turks, recommending the reopening of commerce there and warning against the danger of calling at ports in Spain. Possibly English trade with Constantinople, Egypt, and Syria had already been renewed,[3] either by overland routes or in those ships of Ragusa which added the word

[1] French and Venetian envoys believed metal supplies, broken images of saints, procured our capitulations, Charrière, iii. 907 n. Sherley, p. 9, mentions 'powder and other munition for warre broughte by the Englishe in greate abundans thither, and by noe nation els'.

[2] English, Spanish, Turks, Tuscans, and Dutch tried to occupy El Arisch. Spain secured Portuguese ports.

[3] Beazley, i. 132–8. Hostilities near Malta 1551–65 interrupted trade. English goods reached Constantinople in foreign ships before 1583, when 'great trade' was assured through direct traffic, T. Birch, *Memoirs of the Reign of Queen Elizabeth from 1581*, London, 1754, i. 36.

'argosy' to our language.[1] As regards North Africa, the Dutch rebels are said to have been doing a 'lucrative trade in oars, spars and cordage with the piratical powers' in 1572,[2] perhaps with English assistance. Haedo's account suggests that Algiers was already a market for English goods.

It is, consequently, by no means unlikely that Englishmen were already familiar with trade in various parts of the Ottoman empire before two of our Spanish merchants, the celebrated Sir Edward Osborne and the less known Richard Staper, who is, however, perhaps justly, commemorated as 'the greatest merchant in his time, the chiefest actor in the discoverie of the trade of Turkey and East India',[3] sent Joseph Clements in 1575 and William Harborne in 1578 to negotiate for commercial privileges at Constantinople, and so laid the foundations of the famous Levant Company.

It is typical of the lack of interest in this area that as late as 1910 a leading work of reference could state that in Turkey 'traders of all nations were put under the French flag. It was not until 1675 that, under the first capitulations signed with Turkey, English consuls were established in the Ottoman Empire',[4] while another, which practically ignores the existence of the Levant Company, gives the very distinct impression that consuls were first established in the Levant and Barbary by Henri IV.[5]

It is, in fact, not clear to what extent English vessels did trade under the French flag, either with Turkey or with Syria and Egypt, which were apparently regarded as a separate area.[6] There is, however, no question but that under the capitulations, granted in 1580 and ratified in 1583, William Harborne, in accordance with his authority as the queen's ambassador, appointed consuls at certain places from the latter date onwards.

[1] *Memorial of the Levant Merchants*, Cal. S.P.D. 1650, pp. 106–7. Ragusa monopolized trade after 1565, Charrière, iii. 695 n. and 791 n.; L. Villari, pp. 303–16.
[2] Maxwell, ii. 91. In 1572 Algiers offered to supply Marseilles, Charrière, iii. 287.
[3] Wood, *The History of the Levant Company*, p. 7 n.; J. Stow, *Survey of London*, 1633, p. 135. Closely connected with Spain, Morocco, Turkey, Patras, and Algiers. Co-operated with Harborne 1579, Creasey, p. 227.
[4] *E.B.* vii. 20, but see v. 283–4 and xxvii. 450.
[5] *C.M.H.* iii. 694 and 883.
[6] App. G.

The capitulations,[1] it should be made clear, did not take the form of a treaty, but were a unilateral grant of trading privileges from the sultan to the queen, for the benefit of her subjects, contingent always upon her remaining with him 'in peace, friendship and league, firm constant and sincere'.[2] They contained no political implication, did not specifically recognize the Company, and, except in regard to disputes among the English merchants themselves, did not confer any exemption from Turkish jurisdiction. Infringements of the peace by any of Her Majesty's subjects were punished by an *avania* or collective penalty on the resident merchants.[3] The law of reprisal was still recognized in practice in Christian countries, and the sultan, in particular, had no other means of exercising pressure on a distant government. We know from such experienced persons as d'Arvieux, Chardin, and Dudley North that these penalties might be fully warranted and that the system might have a salutary effect. The glaring case of Kenelm Digby's deliberate violation of Turkish waters and its consequences are strangely ignored by historians.[4]

Unfortunately, the capitulations were in some respects so vague or ill-expressed as to call periodically, though on the whole ineffectually, for further explication. It is probable that none of the envoys of the maritime powers were regarded as ambassadors in the fullest sense of the word. Our own, for instance, were literally the custodians of the English privileges and, at the same time, like the other resident merchants, security for the good behaviour of their sovereign and fellow countrymen.

When the question of the incorporation of the Levant Company was under examination, Walsingham, who had been ambassador in France, foresaw difficulties in the Mediterranean. He pointed out, very justly, that the King of Spain and other—

---

[1] Chalmers, ii. 431–62, begins with clauses of 1593 which differ materially from Latin and English texts in Hakluyt, v. 178–9, and V.S.P. 1581–91, pp. 50–52. Note the phrase 'I grant the request'

[2] The Sultan, acknowledging the Queen's ratification, reminded her that capitulations depended on good behaviour, V.S.P. 1581–91, p. 57.

[3] Chardin derived it from Persian for court sentence, *Journal du Voyage en Perse*, &c., 10 vols., Paris. 1811, i. 18 n.; Masson, pp. 13–14. Birch quotes three instances by France at Rouen, Bordeaux, and Calais almost simultaneous with the Algiers case of 1626.

[4] Roe, *Negotiations with the Grand Signior, 1621–28*, pp. 821–2 and 826–7. Ninety-nine Venetians and French were killed.

officially friendly—Christian princes would employ all means, open and underhand, to obstruct our trade. Our ships should take care not to pass the Straits of Gibraltar, which Philip then commanded from both sides, or the coasts of France, Spain, or Italy 'in time of calm', but rather only in winter. He recommended that an 'apt man' should be sent to Constantinople to obtain an 'ample safe-conduct and impeach the indirect practices of other ambassadors'.[1] He should also 'procure the Turk's letters to the King of Barbary and the rest of the princes of Africa, that the ports there may be free for our merchants, as also in case of necessity to have a safe-conduct of the galleys from Algiers to pass the Straits withal'.[2] The added complication of English depredations in Mediterranean or Levant waters does not seem to have presented itself to him.

His wise advice was evidently ignored or forgotten. English ships may have made their own arrangements with Algiers, where in 1581 we find Edward Cotton selling the crew of a Genoese ship, and, like Edmund Auncell soon afterwards, redeeming English captives,[3] while in 1583 Thomas Shingleton obtained from the Bashaw of Algiers a passport to protect his vessel, when trading in French and Italian waters. There is no evidence as to when, or under what arrangement, John Tipton was first established there as commissary, or factor, of the Levant Company, except that it was before the bashaw had been informed of the capitulations. It may well be that he was the person who left England about the end of 1582 with a letter from the queen to the 'King of Algiers', asking him to assist the Emperor of Morocco in preventing the occupation of El Arisch by the Spaniards.[4]

It seems incredible that Harborne, who left England on 14 January 1583, carrying to the sultan the queen's ratification of the capitulations and his credentials as her ambassador, should have elected to call at an unfriendly Spanish port, where he

---

[1] Harborne was 'agent for the English merchants trading into the Levant' sent 'about merchants' causes', Cal. S.P.F. May–Dec. 1582, p. 365. Elizabeth avoided open political relations with Turkey and Morocco. See Conyers Read, *Mr. Secretary Walsingham and the Policy of Elizabeth*, 3 vols., Oxford, 1925, especially iii. 332; App. G.

[2] Epstein, *Early History of the Levant Company*, p. 245; Read, iii. 229.

[3] For piracies of Cotton and the Burds, see Cal. S.P.F. 1581–2, pp. 423, 433, &c., and A.P.C. 1581–2, pp. 265–6; for Auncell, S.P.D. 1581–90, p. 124.

[4] Cal. S.P. Spanish 1580–6, p. 422.

narrowly escaped capture, instead of taking the opportunity to cultivate cordial relations at Algiers and settle the Company's affairs there. He does not seem to have been well equipped for a very difficult position, in which he encountered the violent opposition of the French and Venetian ambassadors, as well as some of the Turkish ministers, notably the Capudan pasha, with whom he had previously quarrelled.[1] He was very ill advised or unfortunate in his choice of local assistants, and his correspondence indicates unfamiliarity with diplomatic procedure and international practice, as well as, perhaps, inaccuracy of fact. He may have owed his success to his courage, bluster, and tenacity, though perhaps still more to the political and economic difficulties of the sultan and the rivalries of his ministers.

On 5 November 1583 he addressed a letter through a correspondent at Algiers, presumably Tipton, to the bashaw, requiring him to forbid his sea-captains to meddle with English ships, which had been instructed to pass through Barbary (and not Christian) waters on their way to and from the Levant, and to issue five or six passports for their better protection. His correspondent explained in reply that our ships were so apprehensive of the 'gallies of Cartagena, Florence, Sicilia and Malta', which had combined to prevent their traffic with Turkey, that they were wont' to open fire on the galleys of Algiers and Tripoli, when these tried to verify their nationality. His statement that 'all the world doth know that Marchants ships laden with marchandises do not seeke to fight with men of warre' is hardly borne out by our own records or foreign complaints that the Company's ships were indistinguishable from pirates, but there may well have been misunderstandings and over-hastiness on both sides. Harborne, indeed, had recently had experience of difficulties arising in Turkey itself, partly from the violence of our merchant ships. Twenty years later we expressly granted the Venetians the right of search in the Adriatic, and Queen Anne was later advised that any English ships which did not stop to show their passes would be brought into Constantinople 'as good Prize, as some French vessels had been'.[2]

---

[1] Over Foster's misconduct, Charrière, iii. 884, and iv. 55 n.; App. G.
[2] Akdes Nimet Kurat, *Despatches of Sir Robert Sutton, Ambassador in Constantinople, 1710–14*, R. Hist. Soc., Camden Series, London, 1953, p. 197.

After discussion with the bashaw, Hassan Veneziano, and the aga, it was recommended that the sultan should be asked to send commands on the subject—presumably the text of the capitulations, which took the form of instructions to all officers of the Ottoman empire, together with 'favourable letters' addressed to Ramadan, Bashaw of Tripoli, and Hassan, the cadi, captains, janissaries, and Levants at Algiers.

Commands from the sultan to the viceroys of Algiers, Tunis, and Tripoli, together with authenticated copies of the capitulations, were dispatched in June 1584 to Edward Barton, Harborne's secretary, who was apparently inquiring into the case of the *Jesus* at Tripoli. Although Osborne, then Lord Mayor of London, sent the Bashaw of Algiers a copy of the capitulations in a letter of 20 July 1584, which complained of the sinking of a ship, evidently the *Mary Martin*, they do not appear to have been officially registered there until Barton's arrival, some time in the summer of 1585. In the meantime five ships had been taken or sunk by the galleys of Hassan from Algiers and two by those of Ramadan at Tripoli.[1]

Since, from this date, Tripoli disappears from our contemporary records until the Commonwealth, it may be convenient to discuss here the case of the *Jesus*,[2] which contains several points of interest. The vessel was chartered in 1583 by Osborne and Staper, presumably on behalf of the Company, for the voyage from London to Tripoli and back. After a series of misadventures it left Falmouth on 1 January 1584 and, after staying at San Lucar for a month, arrived on 18 March at Tripoli, where the crew were 'well entertained by the King of that country and also of the Commons'.

It, unfortunately, carried a substitute captain and two supercargoes, one of whom was a Frenchman named Sonnings, engaged, apparently, to assist Staper's factor on account of his previous experience of the trade. A ship from Bristol arriving at the same time, its supercargo, Miles Dickenson, and the two of the *Jesus* set up house together. Sonnings swindled Dickenson and perhaps attempted to do the same with the bashaw over the export duties on a cargo of sweet oils. Finally, the ship tried to carry off a hostage, an old friend of Sonnings, and was

---

[1] Hakluyt, v. 280–2.
[2] *Thomas Sanders' Narrative*, ibid., pp. 292–311.

only stopped by gun-fire. Judging by the somewhat confused account of one of the seamen, evidently an intelligent and well-educated man, the bashaw, Ramadan the former Viceroy of Algiers and Tunis, wished to set the seamen free, but the janissaries insisted on the full rigour of the law, with the result that Sonnings and the captain were executed, and the rest of the crew enslaved. The Bristol ship and the *Green Dragon*, at the neighbouring port of Jerba, do not appear to have had any trouble, but the cabin-boy on the latter, who was very unhappy on board, deserted and turned Turk.

A modern description of the occurrence as the brutal seizure of the Company's vessel in defiance of the treaty hardly seems more justified in the circumstances than the accompanying statement that the fate of the vessel was 'long wrapped in mystery', until a letter was smuggled out.[1] The mystery is highly improbable in view of the proximity of two other English vessels, and it does not seem to have been customary to restrict the correspondence of captives with their families. At all events, Thomas Sanders wrote to the ambassador and also to his father in Devonshire, who got into touch with the Earl of Bedford. As a result the queen addressed a letter to the sultan about this and other matters on 5 September 1584, almost precisely four months after the seizure—a remarkably rapid procedure for those days. When the other letter reached Constantinople is not clear, but Barton had left for some 'proceedings in Tripolis with Romadan' prior to 24 June 1584. If it was in connexion with the *Jesus*,[2] he was evidently ill prepared, since he and the Turkish cadi received their instructions from the sultan only at the end of October, and on their arrival at Tripoli on 27 April 1585 immediately obtained the enlargement of the seamen and the payment of some compensation.

In so far as treaty rights were concerned, none could entitle a foreign ship or person to break the law of the land, and it was not contested that such an offence had been committed. Even Harborne approved 'the death of the said Frenchman as a thing well done',[3] but no court would have upheld his contention that the master of the ship, who 'did not returne when he was

---

[1] H. G. Rawlinson, *Embassy of William Harborne to Constantinople* (R. Hist. Soc. Trans., vol. v, Fourth Series), p. 10.

[2] Probably the *Judith*.   [3] Hakluyt, v. 318.

commanded by your honourable Lordship', was innocent of blame, though he might have been only foolish. Whether the punishment of the crew was illegal or unduly harsh is a matter for conjecture or comparison with the penalties which would have been inflicted in Spain or Venice or England itself. The assertion that the oil was intended for the queen's court was, even if true, irrelevant, and looks like an attempt to bolster up a dubious case.

Four things seem clear. The measures taken were not condemned in advance by the sultan, who ordered an inquiry to be made by the new bashaw as to whether or not the English had been guilty of a breach of the league. The crew were *pardoned* for their offence.[1] Restitution was made only of such property as fell to the lot of the sultan's representative. Staper, whose factor's 'lewd behaviour' or 'unjust practices' had admittedly caused all the trouble, was unwilling to reimburse the ship's owners out of the compensation received.[2] Whether English ships had any particular legal status at Tripoli, or whether we had been remiss in not ensuring that they had, can now only be regarded as questions of academic interest.

Barton reached Algiers in the summer of 1585 in order to register the capitulations, but apparently the liberation of captives was not effected until a year later owing to the opposition of Ochiali, who threw all the blame on the English ships for treating the Turks as pirates.[3] He also brought a commission from Harborne, appointing John Tipton 'consul of the English nation in Algiers, Tunis and Tripoly in Barbary'.

In his letter of instructions Harborne informed Tipton that he was enclosing 'the Grand Signior's and our patents for exercising the office of consul there, by virtue of which authority you may without fear proceed as the office doth challenge in defence of our privilege, to redress all injuries offered to our nation'.[4] In spite of some special pleading and strange claim of ignorance about Algiers regulations, he evidently acquiesced in the views already urged by Tipton, as he continues, 'and hereafter *according to your advice* I wil and do give our ships order not to fight with any gallies of Alger but to hoise out their skiffe

[1] Hakluyt, v. 307.   [2] A.P.C. 1586–7, p. 33.
[3] Hakluyt, v. 282–3; Charrière, iv. 527.
[4] Hakluyt, v. 276–80, 30 Mar. 1585.

and go aboord to show them their safe-conduct'—an arrangement which evidently proved very satisfactory. Harborne, however, unlike Barton, persisted in his grudge against Hassan, even when, as Capudan pasha, his goodwill was of the greatest importance.

Playfair makes the unwarranted statement that 'the first English consuls at Algiers were representatives of important commercial corporations or elected by the merchants themselves from their own number rather than nominated directly by the State. Master John Tipton was acting in this capacity on account of the Turkey Company at least as early as 1580'. The Company, however, did not exist in 1580, and a consul, whose *public character* was an essential feature of his office, could only be appointed by, or under express authority from, his sovereign or, in emergency, by the sanction of the local ruler. It was precisely because there was no recognized representative at Algiers, to whom captives could be delivered, that it was necessary for Barton to go there and for Tipton to be appointed, about two years after consuls had been established in Syria and Egypt. A document of 1584 shows that consulage of $1\frac{1}{2}$ per cent. on English goods landed was then payable to a local official, who was 'Justice of the Christians' at Algiers.[1]

Tipton was clearly at the time acting simply as factor for the Company, and there is no reason to suppose that, apart from his assistant, Thomas Williams, there was any other English resident at Algiers. There was evidently no English communal house, as at Tripoli in Syria and Alexandria—perhaps owing to the greater freedom enjoyed by Christians in Barbary—and Laurence Aldersey, who passed through in 1586, would almost certainly have mentioned the presence of any other English merchants. His remarks are, however, of interest as he records: 'I lay with Master Typton, consull of the English nation who used me most kindly and at his own charge; he brought me to the King's Court and into the presence of the King, to see him and the manners of the Court.' The obligations of consuls as official hosts and the courtesy visit with newly-arrived nationals to the chief ruler were regular features of life there for another two centuries. A very informative little memorandum on the trade of Algiers dated 1584, a sort of

[1] Ibid., p. 271.

guide for merchants and commercial travellers, shows that Williams lived separately in a Jewish street, where he apparently provided lodgings for English visitors.[1]

Playfair's statement that 'there is every reason to believe that he is the oldest known consul of English birth' is not even approximately correct. Indeed, it is not unlikely that he was related to Hugh Tipton, whose consulship in Andalusia, duly confirmed by Queen Elizabeth, Philip II, and the Spanish courts, had terminated some fifteen years before. Few of our consulates, however, can compete with Algiers in continuity or historic importance.

It is unfortunate that the recklessness of Playfair's claims should have led de Grammont into the erroneous belief that only France had the right to have a consul there at that time. The passage which he quotes from Gramaye of about 1619, to the effect that the English were only represented by a merchant, is based on a misunderstanding to which de Grammont's remarkable indifference to English sources of information greatly contributed. Quite apart from the manner of his appointment, Tipton's public character is attested by the fact that instructions for the extradition of two defaulting factors from Genoa, who actually seem to have taken refuge in Leghorn, were sent to him in October 1589 and June 1590, not by the Levant Company but by the privy council, whose concluding admonition: 'Hereof faile you not as you will aunswer for your slacknes or defalt to the contrary at your uttermost perills' might seem almost painfully familiar to his modern successors.[2]

Similarly, Playfair's contention that our consulate was actually older than the French, which certainly existed in 1577, is also quite unfounded. The bashaw's refusal to recognize a substitute for the French consul in 1579, as an innovation of great prejudice to the merchants, seems entitled to more discriminating appraisal than it has received.[3]

From the little that is known of him Tipton appears to have been a satisfactory representative, whose successful promotion

[1] Hakluyt, v. 272.

[2] A.P.C. 1589–90, pp. 201–2 and 1590, p. 246; compare Hubac, pp. 186–7.

[3] Plantet, i. 1–2, misinterpreted Charrière, ii. 800 and iii. 930 n. Hassan's action accorded with long recognized principle, Capmany, ii. 274 and 250. Algiers protected foreign interests, see Gramaye, ch. x, and Tanner MS. 78, f. 46, regarding English and French consuls in 1585.

of our commercial interests, especially at neighbouring ports, evidently worried the French. The ungrateful John Sanderson's description of him as a 'wicked atheisticall knave' may be safely disregarded in view of divergent statements by that writer, as well as his incurably malicious disposition.[1] Hasleton's criticism that the consul gave him only 'faire words', instead of practical assistance, carries little more weight. It is, on the other hand, by no means improbable that the cordial reception and whole-hearted assistance given in 1586 to the five English ships, which put into Algiers after a hard-fought victory over a Spanish fleet,[2] were in some measure due to his good offices, as was also the fact that in 1587 out of the great number of Christian captives only fifteen, presumably captured on enemy ships, were Englishmen, who appear to have been cleared soon afterwards.

We know that at some date, after a visit to Constantinople, he was murdered in the Gulf of Venice by the Greek crew of his bark *Diana*. It is probable that the post was vacant when in 1595 the bashaw addressed a letter to Queen Elizabeth about some unfortunate seamen left there as security for the debts of their disreputable captain, Edward Glenham.[3] As this question occupied the attention of the privy council for some years without any reference being made to a consul, we can hardly doubt that none existed.

It is also significant that the visitors to Algiers during the years immediately following—William Biddulph, chaplain at Aleppo, William Davies, barber-surgeon of London, and Thomas Dallam, organ-builder of that city, who had as a fellow passenger John Sanderson, treasurer at Constantinople—make no mention of a consul, as they frequently did at various other places. They, or the ships they travelled in, evidently had no occasion for official assistance, and there can be no doubt that the English during this period, especially as active allies against Spain, enjoyed most favoured treatment there after the queen

[1] *Travels of John Sanderson in the Levant, 1584–1602* (Hakluyt Society), ed. Sir W. Foster, London, 1931, pp. 10 and 12.
[2] Hakluyt, vi. 46–57.
[3] S.P. 71, f. 1; A.P.C. 1595–6, p. 348, to 1599–1600, p. 422. During voyages of 1591–2 and 1593–4 he made Algiers his base, calling Morat 'the admiral'. For second voyage, see J. P. Collier's *Reprints*, i, *News from the Levant Seas etc by R. H.* and G. B. Harrison, *Elizabethan Journal, 1591–4*, London, 1928.

had in 1586 formally secured for English ships free access to the ports of Barbary for shelter and refreshment.[1] This valuable privilege was to prove a source of embarrassment to the Turkish authorities, but hardly seems to have been adequately appreciated by our rulers. Harborne, however, came to realize its value, as did also various adventurers—Glenham, Giffard, and, later, the Fleming Danser—who did not scruple to abuse these facilities.

There is no record of the actual appointment of John Audellay, or Audeley, who, according to a letter from the bashaw to the queen in 1600, 'says he is your Majesty's consul here',[2] and who in subsequent official dispatches is described as the 'Queen's consul' and a 'publique minister for our nation'. The correspondence arose out of the misconduct of his countrymen, and his own behaviour was the subject of criticism, though it probably compared very favourably with that of his successor or of his contemporary colleagues at Patras, one of whom Dallam found absent from his post, because he had gone forty miles away 'to hang a Jew'.[3] The standard of conduct in our Levant communities at the time clearly left much to be desired. Whatever we may think of Sanderson's scurrilous remarks about ambassadors, we cannot ignore the Company's suspicion that some of its factors and officials indulged in 'horedom, incontinency, discourtesies and idellness'.[4]

Audeley, perhaps a relative of William Audeley, one of the absconding factors from Genoa, later found trading from Leghorn to Tunis, was probably a fair specimen of the time and a reasonably good consul. His appointment may not have been strictly regular, as he was quietly superseded by the reconstituted Company in 1606, though he was still in Algiers some years later.

Apart from illegal acts of violence by our own nationals and the fact that the country was continuously involved in war, not only with its inveterate foes of Spain and Malta but also less formally with the ports of Provence, Algiers must have been by

[1] V.S.P. 1581–91, p. 161.

[2] S.P. 71. 1, f. 2; Playfair, pp. 30–32.

[3] Bent, p. 86, Jonas Aldrich, later accused of aiding pirates; imprisoned by our ambassador; agent at Florence; and recommended for consulate at Aleppo.

[4] Cotton MS. Nero B. xi, f. 321; S. G. Chew, *The Crescent and the Rose*, New York, 1937, pp. 159–60.

no means an unpleasant place of residence. The period of wise
rule and strict regard for the laws of war did not, as so often
asserted, come to an end abruptly with the death of Ochiali in
1587.[1] On the contrary, the period which we considered most
unsatisfactory occurred during his lifetime, in the years immediately preceding the definite inclusion of Algiers in our capitulations and the appointment of Tipton as consul.

So far from becoming a den of pirates Algiers was a recognized port of call for English shipping. There is evidence that
a clear-cut distinction was made between the vessels and other
property of friendly and enemy nations, and that the bashaw,
or the divan, endeavoured to adjudicate fairly on conflicting
claims in regard to prizes brought in there. The treatment of
Captain Glenham in 1593 on his arrival with his ships at
Algiers, where 'the King entertained them in the best manner'
and showed 'extraordinary favour' by attending a banquet on
board, may be contrasted with the subsequent imprisonment
of one crew for piracy and of Glenham himself for assaulting
the French consul.[2]

In two cases,[3] of which we happen to have records, because
they were decided against the English, there is no apparent
reason to criticize the award. In one it was substantially upheld
by our own High Court of Admiralty. The queen referred to her
previous experience of the bashaw's 'princely justice', and the
practice regarding the condemnation of cargo, &c. on neutral
ships was very similar to our own today. In some respects it
was more liberal.

In spite of the uncertainty regarding relations with the ports
of Provence, some of which, like Marseilles, might be hostile,
and others, such as Toulon, friendly, the French consul evidently enjoyed considerable prestige.[4] While Morat, the most
powerful and permanent influence in foreign policy, appears
to have been anxious to maintain friendship with both countries,
French reports refer to the loss of some of their commercial
privileges to the English. The absence of complaint from the
Levant Company, in which the queen herself had a large and

[1] App. F.
[2] *Elizabethan Journal, 1591–4*, pp. 311–14.
[3] The Venetian prize which caused criticism of Audeley and the *Marigold*, see
ch. vii.
[4] For intrigue at Paris, see Cal. S.P.F. Jan.–June 1583, p. 186, and App. G.

highly profitable interest, or from other parties, as revealed by the records of the privy council, is very significant. In fact, a very striking feature of the internationally disastrous years which ended the reign of Elizabeth was the amazingly rapid development of our trade with the Levant and the increasing attractions of Algiers and Tunis as ports of call for Christian shipping. Not less remarkable was the competition for permanent commercial concessions in those areas.[1]

[1] Apparently Tipton, Audeley, and Allen 'usurped' French privileges.

VII

ENGLISH SHIPS IN THE MEDITERRANEAN AND THE LEVANT

AN unquestionable feature of the last years of the queen's reign, which may have been obscured by greater events elsewhere, was the emergence of a formidable power in the Mediterranean and Levant seas. Walsingham had formulated as the primary advantage of organizing a Levant Company the ability to 'set a great number of your greatest ships in work whereby your navy shall be maintained',[1] and the 'London ships' employed by the Company did indeed soon prove themselves to be powerful fighting units, which successfully defied Spanish efforts to intercept their traffic in the Straits of Sicily and Gibraltar.

The *Centurion*, for instance, emerged triumphantly from combat with 5 Spanish galleys, and the *Hector* is said to have cowed 7 Dunkirk privateers.[2] When possible, however, the ships sailed together for their better protection, and we hear of the equivalent of naval battles in those narrow waters. In 1586, as already mentioned, 5 ships triumphed over 11 galleys and 2 frigates of Spain off Pantellaria, and in 1590 10 English ships claimed to have beaten a force of 12 powerful galleys under Admiral Doria.[3] Although foreign versions are only partially confirmatory, the fact remains that in each case the enemy failed to achieve its object, while the advantage of being able to refit in Barbary ports before resuming the voyages was clearly demonstrated. The London ships had shown themselves at times capable of taking offensive action and, like our East Indiamen soon afterwards, of combining the attractions of privateering with those of commerce.

The facilities of Barbary ports were not the only advantages derived from Turkish goodwill and co-operation. It has been asserted that the arguments in favour of Turkey sending a large

---

[1] Epstein, p. 245.   [2] Hakluyt, vii. 31–38; Bent, p. 12.
[3] Lediard, i. 277.

fleet to aid us in the war with Spain were 'unanswerable';[1] that it made great promises, but did precisely nothing. Such views appear ill-considered, as they ignore vital geographical considerations and the experience of the past. They are, moreover, inconsistent with definite facts.

The suggestion that Turkey, whose principal interests and dangers were oriental, should send its fleet for nearly two years at a time into the distant Mediterranean, leaving dangerous foes in its rear, had previously been declared impracticable in more favourable circumstances, and Toulon, which *we* offered as a winter base, had been considered quite unsuitable, even when Provence was under effective allied control. The true interest of Turkey may have lain less in a precarious alliance with a distant power than in a satisfactory peace which would deter Spain from stirring up Persia and harassing Turkish trade in the Red Sea and Indian Ocean. Had not Spain been kept in a state of constant anxiety, 100 ships with 30,000 men might have been released for service elsewhere, and also, if we can accept Roe's estimate some forty years later, not less than 20,000 soldiers from garrison duty in Italy alone.[2]

Turkish co-operation was not assisted by the attitude of Harborne, who disliked and thwarted Ochiali and Hassan, though both were anti-Spanish and the principal advocates of action west of Malta. The former had plans for a joint attack on Spain and Italy by Turkish and Barbary forces based on the regencies, but he was overruled, though supported by the agents of Venice and Savoy.[3] The only practicable proposals that we seem to have made were for action on the Atlantic coast of Morocco and constant attack on Spanish territory and shipping. When, however, Hassan attempted the former, apparently at the queen's behest, Harborne broke into a violent

[1] Sir E. Pears, 'The Spanish Armada and the Ottoman Porte' (*English Historical Review*, viii. 439–66), p. 439. Creasey seems equally unreasonable. See, however, V.S.P. 1581–1603; Charrière, iv; Klarwill, *The Fugger Letters*; Braudel, pp. 710–11; Duro, iii. 92 and 237–9; Corbett, i. 7, &c. Charles V would not, for the same reason, send his fleet into Turkish waters, Armstrong, ii. 3.

[2] Duro, iii. 174; *Negotiations*, pp. 197–8, 29 Nov. 1623. In 1587 Spain could only act against England, if Turkey inactive, and the Lisbon armada might be required against Algiers, Charrière, iv. 573–98. See Conyers Read, especially, iii. 328, and V.S.P. 1581–91.

[3] V.S.P. 1581–91 and 1592–1603. Catholic envoys condemned Anglo-Turk alliance, Charrière, iv. 623–6 and 194 n.

tirade against him, and, when the latter was carried out very effectively and in much the same manner as by our own seamen, English and French historians condemn the Barbaresques for their piracies and sympathize with the Spaniards in their sufferings.[1]

In spite of the accession of Portugal, Spain is said to have been internally exhausted, and was evidently as anxious as ever to maintain a truce with the sultan. In 1585 Algiers was at war with Philip's Provençal allies,[2] and in 1586 Turkish galleys are reported to have sacked all the ships at Barcelona. In the same year Morat, whose arrest Harborne had recently demanded, harried the coast of Alicante with ten galleys and also entered the Atlantic to raid Lanzarote in the Canaries.[3] In 1587 he was reported to be making another voyage to the Canaries with eighteen galleys to annoy Spain in concert with Queen Elizabeth.[4] In 1589 he gained a signal victory over the galleys of Malta and Majorca, and is also mentioned in a Venetian report from Barcelona as commanding one of two Algerine fleets, which were blockading the coasts of Spain and inflicting no less damage in the east than the English ships in the west.[5]

Two years later the queen through her ambassador was urging the sultan to attack South Italy, citing the precedent of Barbarossa and suggesting the 'greatest riches', 'infinite glory', and 'vast benefits to the Empire' to be extracted from doing so. He added persuasively, 'this is a question which concerns the faith, for, acting as requested, all idolaters will be undone'.[6] Rather awkwardly, one of the idolaters, the Duc de Mayenne, was simultaneously pressing for the dispatch of instructions to the governors of Algiers and other ports to allow the French to traffic freely. A consular commission was actually issued in the name of Charles X to enable a Catholic to supersede the Huguenot at Tunis, one of whose predecessors was

[1] Cal. S.P.F. 1583–4, p. 40. Ottoman fleets attacked Spanish territory in 1589 and 1591 aided by Barbary squadrons, ? under Morat, Morgan, p. 598. Cal. S.P.F. 1588, pp. 101 and 165.

[2] On sultan's orders, Charrière, iv. 520 n. Huguenots of Aigues-Mortes welcomed Algiers ships.

[3] Duro, ii. 399.

[4] V.S.P. 1581–91, pp. 273 and 277.

[5] Morgan, pp. 596–7; V.S.P. 1581–91, pp. 450–1.

[6] Ibid., pp. 514–15.

executed for treason at Marseilles before he could take up his new post at Algiers.[1]

An invitation for a Turkish fleet of some 600 vessels to use Toulon as a base was consequently less tempting than ever. Some assistance was sent, however, as we hear soon afterwards of a fleet of a hundred pirates (!!) 'under one Cicola' striking a blow at the Spaniards in the Straits of Messina.[2] That an Italian historian should be unaware that he was describing a celebrated Capudan pasha and son of a well-known Italian nobleman is surely significant.

Among the services rendered to the allied cause by the Algerines under Morat must be included his actions during the last decade of the century, on instruction from the sultan and urgent request from Henri IV, in protecting the French coast from the ships of Tuscany,[3] aided no doubt by English and French outlaws, and subsequently helping to save Marseilles from Spanish occupation. Henri, whose oriental policy was as capricious as that of Francis I, gratefully acknowledged these services,[4] and then, after effecting an alliance with the Grand Duke, began to complain bitterly of the piracies of the English and Barbaresques, regardless of the fact that Tuscany was virtually at war with both.[5]

Duro leaves us in no doubt about the extent and result of Barbaresque activities, which he did not regard as illegal, like those of the English in the earlier stages or of the French and Dutch later. There is a remarkable difference, too, between his descriptions, at the end of the queen's reign, of English ships not daring to leave their ports and of the constant ravages inflicted on the Italian coasts by the Barbaresques, which continued even after Spain in 1601 had sent a large composite force against Algiers under the auspices of the pope and in

---

[1] Grandchamp, i, p. xi.

[2] L. Villari, p. 310; Klarwill, p. 230 n., but see Italian encyclopaedias.

[3] 'Avec toutes les forces et galères d'Alger', de Brèves to Henri, Heinrich, p. 164.

[4] Henri regarded relief of Marseilles as an inexplicable miracle, Birch, *Memoirs of Elizabeth*, i. 438. Heinrich, pp. 162–7, records Henri's joy at help of Algiers and p. 168 calls Morat 'vieux pirate' for sheltering at Marseilles from Tuscan galleys. 4 Algiers galleys entered Marseilles under sultan's orders and 'sous la conduite du fameux corsaire Mourad raïs', de la Roncière, iv. 247 and 729.

[5] His hostility, Heinrich, pp. 169–81, and Masson, p. xix, arose partly from our Mediterranean privateers, G. B. Harrison, *A Last Elizabethan Journal, 1599–1603*, London, 1933, pp. 4 and 11.

alliance with a Berber king. Duro relates that, although the Spanish admiral preferred not to attack the port, which is said to have been practically defenceless, or to take any action against the fleet operating under Morat on the Atlantic coast off St. Vincent, a gold medal was struck to celebrate his achievement.[1] In expressing the view that the Barbary corsairs had no leaders of the quality of the Barbarossas, though Morat excelled them all, Duro apparently overlooked the lack of contemporary evidence that any of the Barbarossas ever entered the Atlantic[2] or inflicted any great damage on the coasts of Spain.

Our own attitude to our Turkish allies was not unlike that of Francis I and Henri IV. Cecil, referring to the preparation of a second expedition against Algiers in 1602, felt that as a Christian he might not 'wish a heathen prosperity' but as a Protestant he could hardly wish Philip 'other fortune than the same which his grandfather had at Algier'.[3] Oppenheim even states that Queen Elizabeth never had an alliance with the Turk and would not have been permitted by her subjects to have one, had she wished.

Actually, religious cleavage in both France and England followed conflicting lines, and Englishmen fought on either side in the great Mediterranean struggle. The temptation to prey on the adherents of both sides was often irresistible, especially as the attitude of our seamen towards national or religious allegiance was, throughout the seventeenth century, embarrassingly elastic. Early in the reign of Charles I Roe complained that 'they fly at all without difference' and 'the great licence given or taken by our ships will leave us no friend nor place to relieve with a drop of water'. The contrast drawn soon afterwards by Sir Henry Blount between the 'barbarism' of our seamen and the 'extraordinary civility' of the Turks appears to be endorsed by Admiral Badiley, who had had long experience of the Levant trade, and at a critical juncture warned a colleague of the case of a converted Turk who reverted to his old religion after witnessing the excesses on shore of some English sailors.[4]

[1] Duro, iii. 237–40; see Corbett, i. 7.
[2] Duro, iii. 237.
[3] Cal. Carew Papers 1601–3, p. 319.
[4] *Negotiations*, pp. 825–7; Osborne, i. 536; T. A. Spalding, *Life of Admiral Badiley*, Westminster, 1899, p. 135.

Corbett's statement that 'during the later years of the Elizabethan war the Mediterranean from the Archipelago to the Straits had rung with the piracies of English merchant men' finds corroboration in the well-known dictum of Scaliger[1] and in our own official archives, which, however, appear to discriminate carefully between 'Turkes galleys', as lawful belligerents, and 'pirates of the sea'. His implication that these illegalities were mainly due to the 'way roving privateers pressed their rights over Spanish goods in neutral ships' is somewhat misleading. Similar complaints of the 'licentiousness', 'piracy', or 'sanctioned robbery' by our privateers continued in that area up to 1814. Complaints of illegal attacks on Turkish ships and property date from 1580 and were the alleged ground of Ochiali's hostility to England. A Constantinople report of January 1587 refers to the damage done at Algiers by an English ship which 'looted a lot and kidnapped many Turks and Christians'.[2] A somewhat similar occurrence towards the end of the reign appears to have led to the closing of Algiers to English traffic.[3]

Complaints came from the Adriatic, the 'Sea of Provence', and Sicilian waters,[4] together with a news item from Portugal referring to 'the infinity of goods, merchandise jewels and treasure taken by our English pirates daily from Christians and carried to Allarach, Algire and Tunis to the great enriching of Mores and Turks and impoverishing of Christians'.[5] In the same year, 1602, Henri's ambassador was instructed to present to the queen on behalf of the Marseilles merchants 'un gran mémoire des grandes volleries desdits Anglais'.[6]

Our own merchants were seriously alarmed at the danger of reprisals or the closing of markets by Turks and Venetians. Perhaps as a result of the increasing volume of remonstrance, the queen issued a proclamation on 3 March 1602, forbidding any ship or vessel furnished in warlike manner to pass into the

---

[1] 'Nulli melius artem piraticam exercent quam Angli' surely refers to privateering. In Sec. 18 of our first capitulations 'piratae aut alii liberi gubernatores navium' are clearly privateers who should make restitution if *shown to have done wrong at sea.* Sec. 21 deals with 'latrones et fures', who must be *searched out and punished* severely. For 'pirate' with commission and flag of King of Poland, 1686, see Mifsud, *Knights Hospitallers of the Venerable Tongue of England in Malta*, p. 257 n. For uncertainty of public law after 1581, see Charrière, iv, Tanner MS. 74, f. 46, &c.

[2] Klarwill, p. 125.   [3] App. F.   [4] Klarwill, pp. 255–6.

[5] Salisbury MSS. xiv. 246.   [6] Masson, p. xxvi n.

straits or Mediterranean Sea or any English men-of-war to dispose of goods taken at sea 'either in Argier, Tunis, Zant, Patrasse or any other place in Barbary, Greece, Italy or else-where'.[1] This was an amplification of instructions previously sent by the queen to her consuls in Ottoman territory.[2] The new method of entrusting merchant ships with the duty and means of suppressing piracy in the Mediterranean was a desperate remedy, as the cases of the *Marigold* and *Merchant Royal*[3] soon showed. The proclamation was evidently ignored by the ships which operated from Leghorn, probably under the hostile flag of Tuscany, and by those based on Tunis, where a year later one of our captains is alleged to have found twelve English privateers defying Her Majesty and leading a life of licence.[4] It may have diverted some adventurers to home waters or the Atlantic coast of Morocco, but can have done little to regulate the powerful, and apparently aggressive, ships of the Levant Company. Before the queen's death English maritime power had clearly become recognized in the Mediterranean. Unwel-come evidence of the fact was soon forthcoming in the increasing use of the Cross of St. George by foreign vessels to cover illicit trading or treacherous attacks on friendly nations.

Some details of the experiences of English ships, which called at Algiers and Tunis, may help to illustrate conditions in those waters. It would be tempting, if space permitted, to try to trace the career of Shakespeare's *Tiger* from its first recorded voyage to Tripoli (Syria) in 1583 to the final journey, which ended thirty-one years later in its capture in Tunis harbour by French ships, variously described as men-of-war, Marseilles pirates, or an official peace mission. In 1587, in the course of an apparently satisfactory voyage to the Levant, it made Algiers its first and last port of call in the Mediterranean and stayed nearly a month at Tunis.[5] Like the *Mayflower*, it had trading connexions with both the latter port and the new world.[6]

Playfair mentions the case of a ship putting into Algiers with

[1] *Last Elizabethan Journal*, p. 270.   [2] A.P.C. 1599–1600, p. 744.
[3] 'A very brave and good shippe and of great report', in 1586, Hakluyt, vi. 47. Under Tuscan flag took a Turkish galleon 'of infinite price', bringing tribute from Egypt, 1605. Its owner was imprisoned, T. Birch, *Court and Times of James I*, 2 vols., London, 1848, i. 45 and 59.
[4] V.S.P. 1592–1603, pp. 550–1; de Brèves, p. 308.
[5] Hakluyt, vi. 35–38.   [6] Rowse, p. 230; Grandchamp, iii. 234.

a Spanish prize and receiving favourable treatment, but gives no details, except that the captain's name was Griffon (? Giffard). Hakluyt also relates that the *Moonshine* sold a Spanish prize with its cargo at Algiers in December 1586.

In 1600 the bashaw complained to the queen of the action of her subjects in bringing in a prize of great value, which proved to be an illegally captured Venetian vessel. A Turkish guard was placed on board pending delivery to the rightful owners, but the Englishmen, taking advantage of a Friday when the Turks were absent at worship, set fire to the vessel and came near burning all the shipping in the harbour. The bashaw had great difficulty in protecting the English from the fury of the soldiers, and wrote to the queen asking her to punish them suitably and 'to advise the consul here to take care not to help or allow your subjects to treat in this fashion your Majesty's friends and allies'.[1]

On 29 September 1602 a letter was addressed to the 'Consul of Argier' by the lord high admiral and 'my master', presumably Sir Robert Cecil, drawing his attention to the numerous cases of hard usage of our ships calling at Algiers, either for relief or trade, and to his duty 'being a publique minister there for our nation' to protect them or obtain redress.[2] This letter Playfair characteristically claims to be 'the first communication addressed by the British government to a consul', though Henry VIII had written to his consul at Chios nearly a century before, and there are various indications of early correspondence with consuls in Spain. The immediate object of this letter was the detention of the ship *Marigold* and the removal from it of forty (? fourteen) chests of indigo 'without', in Playfair's words, 'any form of justice, on the mere suggestion that some of his master's subjects were interested therein'. The letter ended with instructions to inform the King of Algiers of the queen's 'princely resolution to protect all her oppressed subjects' and, if necessary, to complain to the sultan, pointing out at the same time the advisability of assessing damages in the early stages as high as possible.

While Playfair gives the substance of this letter, other sources

---

[1] S.P. 71. 1, f. 2: Two English captains were imprisoned at Constantinople, V.S.P. 1592–1603, pp. 455 and 459.

[2] S.P. 71. 1, f. 9; Salisbury MSS. xii. 351.

of information—all English—place the affair of the *Marigold* in a very different light. From the outset there had been a conflict of interests and objectives between the captain, who claimed authority under a letter of marque to prey on traffic between the Netherlands and Spain, and the merchants' representative, who was anxious that nothing should interfere with a trading voyage to the Mediterranean. In that sea the *Marigold* boarded a Hamburg ship and took out some chests of indigo and other property belonging to Dutch shippers. On its arrival in Algiers from Zante the French consul, presumably as representative of all Christians with no consuls of their own, insisted on the delivery of this property to him. It is hardly likely that the Algerines would show undue favour to the French at such a time, and the decision was substantially supported by a subsequent award of Dr. Julius Caesar in our High Court of Admiralty, while Staper had already complained of the captain's proceedings and the danger in which they placed his factor and the consul.[1]

There seems to have been a curious elasticity about the ship's commission, which is in any case hard to reconcile with the recent proclamation. Its official instructions actually read 'for the apprehending of such English pirates as do impeach the quiet trade of her Majesty's friends in the Levant Seas', but, according to Cecil's endorsement, it 'goeth for reprisal of pirates and Spaniards',[2] and not even the still wider scope claimed by the captain could possibly justify his proceedings in this case.

Such considerations did not, however, prevent the queen two months later sending the consul instructions to complain to the viceroy of his unkindness to our privateers in respect of Spanish goods captured in French ships, pointing out the favour that he showed to their common enemy, the Spaniards, and adding the futile threat to forbid her subjects to have any further intercourse with Algiers.[3] As it was presumably in the local interest to stimulate the sale of prize goods, and the viceroy was being simultaneously reprimanded by the sultan for helping English ships to prey on the French, he must have been somewhat bewildered, and apparently thought it advisable to send

[1] Cal. S.P.D. 1601–3, pp. 118–19, 247, and 253.
[2] Salisbury MSS. xii. 551; also pp. 68 and 75 and xi. 377-8.
[3] S.P. 71. 1, f. 10; Cal. S.P.D. 1601–3, p. 247.

an ambassador to London 'in token of good will and friendship' to explain the true situation.[1]

Where more legitimate trading ventures were concerned the queen had apparently no cause for complaint in respect of the conduct of the regencies. Of the seven ships listed as sunk or captured prior to 1585 specific complaint was only made in two cases, and in both we happen to have narratives of members of the crew. The *Jesus*, as we have seen, was 'confiscate by the lewd behaviour' of its supercargo at Tripoli, and the *Mary Martin* was sunk in 1582 on its return from Patras, because the master maintained a steady fire upon the galleys of Algiers in spite of the protests of his crew and the possession of the sultan's safe-conduct. The resolute determination of Richard Hasleton, one of the survivors, to return to slavery in Algiers after his treatment by the Spaniards is worthy of comment, and his repatriation in December 1592 on the *Cherubim*, in company with other English ships, provides interesting evidence of the volume of our traffic with that port.[2]

Laurence Aldersey evidently had a pleasant visit to Algiers in 1586, as John Evesham also had the following year. In the winter of 1598 William Biddulph, on the way to his chaplaincy at Aleppo, recorded a friendly reception from the bashaw and Captain Morat,[3] and Thomas Dallam, escorting the great organ presented by the queen to the sultan, appears to have had no trouble, either going or returning. On the outward journey in 1599 it is noteworthy that the latter took only fourteen days from Plymouth to Algiers, where his ship called for fresh meat and water, and about *four months* from that port to Constantinople.[4] For purposes of sea-travel Plymouth was about equidistant from London and Algiers, which was actually much nearer to the capital of England than to that of its own empire. In accordance with custom Dallam's ship took on Turkish passengers at Algiers.

Two other vessels were less fortunate. The *Francis* of Saltash left England in January 1597 for Civita Vecchia with a cargo of fish. It then proceeded to Algiers and Tunis,[5] and at one or

[1] S.P. 71. 1, f. 11, sealed by Bashaw, Captain of Sea, Aga, Consul, &c.
[2] *The Miserable Captivity of Richard Hasleton*, Beazley, ii. 151–80.
[3] Osborne, i. 768.   [4] Bent, pp. 13 and 14.
[5] Osborne, i. 478.

both of those places also embarked Turkish passengers and goods for Chios, 'for we traded as well with the Turk as with the Christian'. That, however, proved its undoing, as it was captured by some Tuscan galleys on that score, and the crew condemned to the oar at Leghorn, where their lot was a hard one. Even innocent Christians looked in vain for justice or mercy at the hands of those champions of the Faith, who for years to come were to be a special thorn in our side. It seems somewhat hard that Davies should now be described as enslaved at Tunis, where he was in fact much better treated than at Leghorn or Naples.

The voyage of the *Angel* was somewhat longer, more instructive, and almost as disastrous. It was chartered in September 1602 by five London merchants for £130 a month and carried a cargo of broadcloth, kerseys, tin, lead, and other goods valued at £6,480 and consigned to Walter Glover & Co. who travelled on the ship. The orders were to sell the goods in Algiers, Tunis, and Alexandria, with liberty to carry to the last port any passengers they could pick up at Algiers and Tunis. It was also to touch at Zante to deposit with an English merchant 4,000 pieces-of-eight, the standard currency of the Levant, which were to be forwarded to Aleppo by the first English ship. On arrival at Alexandria the agents were instructed to try to secure a cargo for Leghorn and in August or September to load the vessel for home, by means of the money earned in Algiers and Tunis, with currants from Zante or cotton and gall-nuts from Syria.

At first all went reasonably well. Glover & Co. wrote from Algiers in November, December, and January to the effect that they had sold some goods but had been underbid by a Flemish ship for the hoped-for passengers to Alexandria. The bashaw had earnestly requested them to take on board a Turkish ambassador, who was returning to Constantinople, and promised, in return for the courtesy, the unusual privilege of loading corn on their return voyage. At Tunis passengers were embarked for Alexandria at an aggregate fare of £300, and a call was made at Zante to land the ambassador, but it was thought wiser to retain the pieces-of-eight, since a great uproar had been created by the depredations of an English pirate, and the governor threatened to arrest the ship and seize its cargo in reprisal. The last recorded report received by the owners was in May 1603 from Alexandria, where most of the goods had been disposed of and arrangements had been made to sail for Tunis and Algiers fully laden with Turkish merchandise, as soon as the passengers were on board.[1]

It would appear that the *Angel* was seized off Strivali on 2 July 1603 by Venetian galleys for alleged failure to salute, and that its cargo from Alexandria belonging to Turks, Moors, Jews, Greeks, and English was unloaded into the Lazaretto at Zante. Much trouble had apparently arisen about this time from the failure of English vessels to salute, i.e. submit to a visit from Venetian ships in Venetian waters, where pirates were said to be doing great damage.[2] What precisely happened to the cargo or the Turkish passengers is not clear. Discussions about the former were still proceeding in April 1605. The *Angel* itself returned home safely.

It is interesting that, while our Levant traffic suffered during the last years of the Elizabethan era from the piratical or high-handed actions of Christian ships, not least of them our own, and English privateers were alleged to 'robbe, spoil and kill Mussulmen',[3] even in Turkish waters or on Turkish soil, no evidence has been brought forward of illegal acts of violence against English lives or property by the ships or rulers of Tunis and Algiers. Moreover their judicial methods apparently offered a remarkably favourable contrast to the procrastination, corruption, and expense so notoriously characteristic of English and most other Christian courts of Admiralty. While we seldom have the advantage of being able to examine the Turkish point of view the mutual recriminations or glaring discrepancies in English, French, and Venetian reports and histories afford a student much food for thought and often considerable enlightenment.

[1] V.S.P. 1603–7, pp. 92–93.
[2] Ibid., p. 60.
[3] Wood, p. 25; V.S.P. 1603–7, p. 206; Sherley, pp. 9–11.

VIII

THE MEDITERRANEAN IN THE
EARLY SEVENTEENTH CENTURY

THE conventional representations of the Mediterranean as a peculiar hotbed of piracy during the first half of the seventeenth century and of Barbaresque illegalities as a constant problem for the government and merchants of Britain find little support in records of the period, contained in our State Papers (Foreign, Domestic, Colonial, Scottish, and Irish), the Calendars of Venetian State Papers, two very illuminating chapters by Spanish and French naval historians, particulars of French and English negotiations for treaties of peace and commerce with Algiers and Tunis, and a number of contemporary narratives.[1]

In particular, the course of trade—English, Dutch, and French—during that period seems entirely inconsistent with the picture painted by Masson of waters infested not only by Barbaresques but by Christians, most of whom are in turn described as even more treacherous and cruel—English, French, Dutch, Majorcans, Tuscans, Savoyards, Uscoques, Mainotes, and Maltese.

The introductory chapters of Masson's illuminating work indicate how many other adverse factors, besides insecurity at sea, French traders had to contend with. The records of the Levant and other English companies trading southwards or of the very vulnerable Newfoundland fisheries[2] or of the privy council indicate even more clearly how little the Barbaresques contributed to our trading difficulties. So far as concrete evidence goes, the losses inflicted on English commerce by Barbaresque operations, legitimate or otherwise, alike in the

---

[1] Duro, iii. 353–68; de la Roncière, iv. 425–8; Masson, pp. 13–47; Finlay, v; Napier, v, &c. deal mainly with Levant. For Mediterranean see Grandchamp, Salisbury MSS. ix–xviii, and *Discourse of Pirates* ? 1616 in G. E. Manwaring, *Life and Works of Sir Henry Mainwaring* (N.R.S.), 2 vols., London, 1920–1.

[2] Cal. S.P.D. 1650, pp. 71–72; D. W. Prowse, *History of Newfoundland*, 2nd ed., London, 1897, and report for 1574–1718, A.P.C. (Col) vi. 109–19, showing 50 English ships in 1578, 250 in 1615.

Mediterranean, Atlantic, and our own waters, were by the standard of the times surprisingly small and are often characterized, not unreasonably, as reprisals. The first incursions by the Salletines in 1624–5 and Algerines in 1631 caused alarm, not on account of their destructiveness or illegality, but of their *novelty*. Both were recognized about that time as entitled to the use of English ports.

De la Roncière describes the oceans of the world as so infested, in the early years of the century, by the pirates of England, Holland, and other Christian countries that French adventurers had no other field for their operations than the Aegean, where they were soon terrifying and demoralizing the Greek islanders and preying on their Turkish 'allies'—usually under cover of the Maltese or Tuscan flag. Very tardily Henri IV forbade the fitting out of private men-of-war in his ports, and the one thing that seems definite about the alleged exploits of the Sieur de Beaulieu-Persac in 1609–10 was that he had no other status than that of a pirate, naked and unashamed.[1]

Duro shows that Algiers only began to be regarded by Spain as a piratical port when, after the capture of Mamora in 1614, Christian adventurers, formerly based on that port, transferred their activities from the Atlantic to the Mediterranean. It was almost immediately afterwards that Spain tried to replace by a regular navy those locally recruited privateers, whose use had originally been forbidden in the fifteenth century, and that, under Spanish influence, England first—and very briefly—applied the term 'pirate' officially to the Algerines.

To the ordinary Briton, Barbary meant simply Morocco, and the Barbary pirates were those adventurers, mainly English, who during the war had established a base at El Arisch, from which to attack Spanish shipping. Soon after the conclusion of peace, which coincided with civil war in Morocco, they were joined by other ships from the Mediterranean and our own waters, and formed a considerable organization operating from Irish and Moroccan harbours. Periodical raids on the Newfoundland fisheries furnished supplies of food, naval stores, and seamen, volunteer and impressed.[2] Among the more celebrated leaders were Peter Easton, who settled down as a wealthy

---

[1] De la Roncière, iv. 371–87.
[2] Prowse, pp. 100 n.–136, but no Turk violence, pp. 145–6.

Catholic and marquis in Savoy, Sir John Fearne,[1] and Sir Henry Mainwaring. None of these had any connexion with the regencies, apart from the fruitless tour of northern Africa and southern Europe which terminated Mainwaring's piratical career.

These piracies had greatly troubled Morocco, the Dutch who traded there, and the Spaniards. The emperor arranged with the Netherlands government for their expulsion from El Arisch and Mamora, but its accomplishment was forestalled by the Spanish occupation of those ports, which seems to have presented little difficulty. The physical characteristics of the coast, which are described as so especially facilitating piratical operations—the sand-banks, creeks, and shallow lagoons—are a feature of the Atlantic coast of Morocco, and it is noticeable that Monson, who often speaks of Morocco as the 'Kingdom of Barbary', tells us that the Barbary coast was faced by the Atlantic ports of Cadiz and Seville.[2] The rugged shore-line of Algeria bore no resemblance to such descriptions, and it is surprising how little Algiers, in whose harbour its marine was concentrated, figures, at least as an aggressor, in our annals of the early part of the century. English merchants were resident and our ships trading there in 1620, the year of Mansel's attack.[3]

Our privateers had little encouragement to return home on the death of Elizabeth, since they laid themselves open to reprisals by the Venetian secretary or other foreign officials. While Cecil maintained that these were matters for the lord admiral, as the offences, if any, had been committed in war-time, presumably under authority of letters of marque, the secretary described that officer as merely an accomplice and insisted on dealing direct with the king, who declared our laws barbarous and unworthy of a civilized nation. It is quite likely that James's actions at first, however well meant, were illegal, and there is little room for doubt that Venetian officials in the Adriatic failed to distinguish between lawful trade and piracy, taking care to extract good profit in the process and further

[1] Oppenheim (? wrongly) calls Fearne 'Algerian pirate'.
[2] K. Heeringa, 'Een bondgenootschap tusschen Nederland en Marokko', in *Onze Eeuw*, Amsterdam, 3 July 1907, pp. 81–119; de Castries (Pays-Bas), i and ii.
[3] Grandchamp, iii. 362. Bashaw reported death of English merchant, IND. 13395, 1620.

their policy of diverting to Venice our direct trade with the Levant. James seems to have been very susceptible to the blandishments of Venetian and Spanish diplomacy.

While in the Adriatic we were prepared to grant Venice maritime rights quite incompatible with our national tradition,[1] in London its secretary seems to have taken matters largely into his own hands. One captain, reputed to be not a bad fellow, was arrested and 'brought to my house like a murderer with a mob at his heels', and, after examination there, 'I have had him put in prison that he merits, loaded with all the irons and chains that he can carry, for so runs the warrant that was granted to me. *Time and torture will make him speak and declare something that will allow the interested parties to recover some damages for loss which must here be clearly established.*'[2]

Actually, in spite of indignant protestations and asserted 'detestation' of piracy, little regard was paid to the ethics of the question. Piracy had long been endemic in England, though it is said to have only taken on its savage character as a result of the Reformation. Religious strife reinforced normal covetousness with fanaticism or hypocrisy. When the Bishop of Salisbury assured Queen Elizabeth that it pleased God that she should spoil the Spaniard, he probably did little more than enunciate a national sentiment, of which not only men of the type of Drake and Grenville but the queen herself took advantage.

Drake, who seems in some respects to have been unusually humane and politic,[3] frankly admitted that he set out on one of his famous voyages to the new world in his 'good ship well equipped for war' without a commission of any kind, since, 'as England and Spain were not then in the best terms of friendship, he thought the general Licence of the Times would be his justification'.[4] Even so, it is said that some of his fellow countrymen, unlike the queen, regarded his voyage round the world as illegal from its inception and refused to accept any share in the fruits of piracy. It was precisely because they carried

[1] V.S.P. 1607–10, p. 4; Osborne, i. 486.

[2] V.S.P. 1603–7, p. 66. For other cases, see V.S.P. 1607–10, p. 474; Salisbury MSS. xvii. 472, and, for pressing to death, ibid., p. 296.

[3] He repatriated 100 Turks and Moors liberated from Spanish ships, and sent Ochiali a present, V.S.P. 1581–91, p. 149.

[4] Burchett, *A Complete History of the Most Remarkable Transactions at Sea*, p. 344.

no papers that the Spaniards treated French and English adventurers as pirates.[1]

Warfare of the most illegal kind appears to have been carried on openly in the channel itself—and even apparently in the Thames. Among the more notorious places had been Dover, the most important of the Cinque Ports, and Plymouth, the headquarters of the Vice-Admiral of Devon. The former witnessed in 1570 the sale of friendly French and Spanish ships and their cargoes and even the auction in the market-place of Spanish seamen.[2] At the latter the queen impounded the bullion carried by Spanish ships, which had taken shelter there from the hostile operations, it is said, of ships belonging to its own mayor. Close by, Torbay appears to have been a pirate stronghold, where in the next two reigns the notorious John Nutt[3] flourished in defiance of the government, until he was hanged by the Spaniards or, according to other authority, by the French in 1632.

Privateering, which so easily degenerated into piracy, became an important industry during the war with Spain, to the great detriment apparently of our marine, our economic position, and our foreign relations. Before the death of Elizabeth Scaliger cited the English as the arch-pirates, our waters were infested by the privateers of neutral nations seeking reprisal, the country began once more to lie under the shadow of Spanish invasion,[4] and even Venice and Turkey sent missions to complain of English pirates as 'the disturbers of the world'. The vent of English produce, especially cloth, had become a pressing problem, and Turkey and Barbary were looked to hopefully as promising outlets. The sale of fish—cod, herrings, and pilchards—to Mediterranean ports may have been no less important.

Neither law nor ethics, but success or profit to the crown, appears to have been the prevailing criterion. 'No man', said Raleigh, 'is a pirate for millions', and Sir Henry Morgan

---

[1] Duro, ii. 209–30, 'Piraterías' in Atlantic by English, French, and Dutch. For Oxenham, see ibid., p. 343 and Burchett, p. 345.

[2] J. Bavington Jones, *Annals of Dover*, Dover, 1916, p. 299.

[3] J. Forster, *Sir John Eliot, 1590–1632*, 2 vols., London, 1865, i. 44–86. Nutt was 'old friend and patron' of Secretary Calvert. Cals. S.P.D. from 1623 to 1631, and T. Birch, *Court and Times of Charles I*, 2 vols., London, 1848, ii. 186 and 197.

[4] Duro, iii. 217.

realized the truth of this saying more than fifty years later. The ships of the East India Company were declared to be pirates by James I, if they did not pay him his share.[1] So far from any leading pirate being severely punished, apart from the exemplary execution of the notorious Danser by the Dey of Tunis,[2] such offences could easily be compounded, if not actually rewarded, so that 'the trade' became a recognized field for naval training and official advancement. The simultaneous membership of the admiralty board by Richard Giffard,[3] Sir Henry Mainwaring, and Sir John Pennington[4] speaks for itself.

The results of such a system are exemplified by the fact that in October 1603 the Venetian ambassador was robbed by English pirates on his journey to London and only with difficulty extracted some of the plunder from the lord admiral, and that in 1614 James's own brother-in-law, the King of Denmark, was attacked by pirates on a voyage to Yarmouth. The Dutch in the pursuit of pirates did not hesitate to land on English or Irish soil. In the west piracy flourished almost unchecked—in Devon and Cornwall, in the Severn estuary, Milford Haven, and above all, in Ireland, that 'Nursery and Storehouse of Pirates', which provided among its other facilities 'good store of wenches'. If Wentworth or Cromwell did in fact suppress piracy the effect was very transient. Indeed, when Blake made his famous voyage of 1654–5 he passed by the 'pirate' stronghold of Brest, French pirates created alarm in the channel, and English privateers in the Mediterranean were described by a French historian as more barbarous and sanguinary than the Barbaresques.[5]

That English adventurers played an important part of very varying legality or loyalty in the Mediterranean between 1580 and 1620 is generally admitted, but, whereas one modern historian represents their 'outrages, rapines and roberries' as ending with the Anglo-Spanish peace of 1604, contemporary writers such as Mainwaring, John Smith, and Venetian officials describe their numbers and activities as greatly intensified by that event. The Venetian State Papers and our own records suggest that their operations were continuous throughout the

---

[1] Cal. S.P. Col. 1622–4, pp. 125 and 294.

[2] In 1611. Previously blackmailing French in Tunis, Grandchamp, iii. 1 and 5.

[3] Called in 1627 our best seaman; earlier proclaimed 'rebel and pirate'.

[4] Lithgow mentions French seizure of a Captain Pennington's ship for piracy off 'coast of lower Barbary'.   [5] De Grammont, p. 197.

period, though there was an increasing tendency to throw the responsibility for them upon the rulers of the ports from which they operated.

Algiers seems to have exercised a surprisingly effective control over the operations of foreign vessels, a practice for which its old viceroy and admiral Ochiali became noted at Constantinople,[1] and its example was imitated in this, as in other ways, at the neighbouring ports of Tunis and Leghorn. Watson speaks of Naples under Osuna as a centre of piracy, and it is possible that no large city in the Mediterranean surpassed Marseilles for lawlessness.[2] Christian piracy moved from the Mediterranean to the Archipelago and the 'Bottom of the Streights', where the rich traffic between Egypt and Turkey afforded an easy prey.

Evidence of the extent to which it had been developed during the second half of the century can be found in the writings of d'Arvieux, Spon, Chardin, Vandal, and Paul Lucas.[3] Eventually the sultan had to create a special fleet to protect his coasts from 'the corsairs',[4] whose operations had undoubtedly contributed to the previous general discredit of Christians at Constantinople. In addition to the English and French, the ships of the 'Religion' from Malta and Tuscany, as well as Majorca and Villefranche, were operated by a desperate class of seamen and consequently greatly feared by the Christians as well as the Turks.[5] According to d'Arvieux the most dreaded were the Mainotes of ancient Sparta, whom about that time it was proposed to ship in large numbers to our colonies in North America.[6]

It was largely on account of the depredations of these various enemies that the Turks, whose navy was increasingly involved in the Black and Red Seas, periodically entrusted the 'auxiliary' fleets of Algiers and Tunis with responsibility for patrolling the

---

[1] V.S.P. 1607–10, p. 490. For Algiers, &c., see Manwaring, ii. 25–29.

[2] The normal obstacle to French commerce was not insecurity at sea but local lawlessness and maladministration, see works of Sue, and Masson; *H.H.W.* xi. 537.

[3] Masson, pp. 45 and 47; Finlay, v. 57 and 90, &c.

[4] Lucas, *La Turquie*, i. 19.

[5] Finlay, v. 95 and 106 n.; *C.M.H.* iii. 398–9; Napier, *Florentine History*, v. 387, 396–7, &c. For 1683 see A. Vandal, *L'Odyssée d'un ambassadeur. Les voyages du Marquis de Nointel*, Paris, 1900, p. 324.

[6] 'Peuple méchant, cruel, sans foi, sans humanité, en un mot Grec', d'Arvieux, *Mémoires*, i. 33; Finlay, v. 162 n.; Cal. S.P. Col. 1675–6, pp. 235–6.

waters of the Levant.[1] It was, by a curious irony, precisely from
this circumstance that historians have drawn their conclusions
that in 1624 'the pirates of Algiers and Tunis had cast off all
obedience to the Sultan and even attacked his territory and
best ports'.[2] The grand vizier, however, made it quite clear at
the time that the ships of Tunis, which alone were involved,
were acting with his authority and approval, adding, in the
words of Roe, that 'those of Algiers and Tunis were raysed by
their prophett in the later tymes, to protect the Ottoman State;
that they were the only true Mussulmen' but for whom '*in
these tymes of their distraction*'—described by our chaplain at
Aleppo as 'civil broyles', evidently due to a rising of the Druses
and not unconnected with Christian intrigue—Turkey and
even its capital would have lain open to Christian attack. Roe's
account is corroborated by the reports of the French consul at
Aleppo, perhaps a partisan of the Druses, and of his ambassador,
who said that the Barbaresques were regarded by the Turks as
their right arm and main strength at sea.[3] A hundred and
fifty years later Algerine ships and soldiers were employed in
suppressing revolts in Syria and Egypt.

When cases are cited of Barbaresque piracies in the Levant
Sea it would be well to ascertain whether these were not in fact
legal repressions of illicit activities. For instance, when we hear
of a Dutch ship being captured by an 'Algerine pirate', while
bringing grain from the Archipelago to Leghorn, it would be a
fair assumption that it was in fact arrested for a serious breach
of Turkish law,[4] just as in 1633 the Capudan pasha himself was
killed trying to seize the *Hector* and the *William and Ralph*,
ships described as engaged in the Levant trade and furnished
with letters of marque, which were loading corn in those
islands.[5]

[1] (Sir) Henry Blount, *A Voyage into the Levant*, ?1638, Osborne, i. 535: the 'Barbary fleet' was 'the more warlike' part of the Sultan's navy who 'keeps him an
exercised fleet for war'; Knolles pp. 960 and 988. 'The auxiliaries of the Turks
Forces by Sea are the Pyrates of Barbary from those three towns of Tripoli, Tunis,
and Algier', ibid., iii. 102.

[2] *Advices from Constantinople*, enclosed in Roe's letters, *Negotiations*, pp. 243-55.

[3] Ibid., p. 227; Masson, pp. 29 n. and 44; Rev. Charles Robson, *Newes from
Aleppo*, 1628, p. 17 (B.M. 1425 g. 5).

[4] H. J. Bloom, *The Economic Activities of the Jews of Amsterdam in the 17th and 18th
centuries*, Williamsport, 1937, p. 98.

[5] V.S.P. 1632-36, p. 121 n.; Rycaut, *The Turkish History*, p. 22.

The difficulty in dealing with charges of piracy by the ships of Algiers and Tunis arises from lack of substantiation by specific detail and reliance on sweeping denunciations of the character of their people, which are almost entirely inconsistent with contemporary evidence and are indeed remarkably similar to descriptions of Christian ports or of our own ships. Theirs were regarded as 'piratical towns' because they were for a time the ports most favoured by Christian adventurers for refitting and the disposal of prizes and captives. This practice was in principle recognized by the maritime powers,[1] authorized by the sultan,[2] and imitated by other ports, especially Leghorn and Villefranche. If the activities of a ship were illegal, it was the duty of the consul to make representations to the local authority or otherwise prevent them. It would seem that early condemnations at Algiers and Tunis were recognized in France.[3] Indeed, Christian treaties usually provided for reciprocity in such matters.

The value of having a consular representative at Barbary ports is shown by the testimony of many contemporaries, including St. Vincent de Paul (about 1605),[4] James Frizell (1624–9), John Comberfort (1628), and Francis Knight (1631–8), the petitions of London merchants, especially one (? 1622) setting forth seven 'reasons for keepinge constantlie an Agent or Consull at Argier',[5] and the opposition of rival powers to such appointments. It was the duty of consuls to maintain good relations, for on their ingenuity and integrity might depend peace and war; to see that treaty provisions were observed,

---

[1] By Britain, France, and, later, the United States.

[2] 'Ministers of Porte have introduced custom of affording refuge in different parts of the Empire to English vessels and bertons which go about spoiling ships, property and merchandise of our subjects and others and take them to ports of his Majesty to sell to our great prejudice', V.S.P. 1613–15, p. 206. Lewes Roberts said Algiers had to admit privateers of friendly nations, as well as 'Levents whom we call Pirates and they call natural Turks', ch. xvi. Algiers was a 'port of refuge', Julien, *Histoire de l'Afrique du Nord, Tunisie–Algerie–Maroc*, p. 525.

[3] French practice varied, de Grammont, p. 198; Hanotaux, p. 306.

[4] St. Vincent de Paul was legally captured on a Spanish ship, 'otherwise we should have been freed by the Consul who is kept there by the King to safeguard French trading', P. Gosse, *The History of Piracy*, London, 1932, p. 83.

[5] S.P. 71. 1, f. 116. Most important were: 'to keepe a Corispondence with them as other Nations do that are in League with them', and 'to have a free porte for any of our ships to retire to in the Streights, where they may be secure, furnisht and refresht with what they need, beinge almost debard of all others'.

especially to safeguard the ships, goods, and persons of their nationals, and to compel or persuade these last to act in conformity with the law of nations and the interests of their country. Such functions are also clearly enunciated in Elizabethan records. French treaties contained a reciprocal clause for the appointment of agents of Tunis and Algiers at Marseilles, and Knight recommended the establishment of a senior Algiers army officer as consul in England.[1]

Law and order seem to have been exceptionally well maintained in the regencies for that age. The strict discipline of the ruling class and the absence of brawling, blasphemy, gambling, and drunkenness were noted by visitors. Travel was safer on the whole than in Europe or other parts of the empire. Lithgow's account of his journey from Tunis to Algiers in 1615, passing apparently through a region which Playfair was deterred from entering more than 250 years later, 'in all this way of twelve score miles, I payed no Tribute, neyther had I any eminent perrill, the country being peaceable though the people uncivill', i.e. uncivilized, evidently held good for the rest of his journey to Fez, and was in striking contrast to his experiences in lawless and poverty-stricken regions of Europe and Ireland.[2] So far as Tunisia was concerned his reaction is confirmed by Mainwaring at the same time, while Gramaye appears to have wandered about Barbary without difficulty a few years later. The former tells us that the people at the outlying ports of Algiers and Tunis were 'very just' and obedient to the central authority. Dapper was able, about 1670, to give a detailed and by no means unfavourable account of administrative and economic conditions in the regencies.

The practice at Algiers in connexion with neutral shipping and the condemnation of enemy property was in principle not unlike the system which we recognize today, and was so far ahead of the time that Mainwaring thought it must conceal some subtle snare. In case of suspicion ships were taken into Algiers for examination, and the consul was invited to take part in the proceedings. If enemy-owned cargo was found on a neutral vessel, which had not violently resisted search, it was

[1] Osborne, ii. 488.
[2] Lithgow, pp. 316–17. Compare N. Taubman, *Memoirs of the British Fleets . . . in the Mediterranean*, London, 1710, p. 98.

confiscated, the ship and crew being allowed to proceed un-molested and the master receiving compensation for loss of freight.[1]

Justice at Algiers and Tunis, as in other countries where Mohammedan law was practised, for example in Turkey and Crim-Tartary, was 'prompt and without cost', chicanery, or 'multiplicity of lawyers', and found to be no less equitable than in the best Christian courts.[2] Evidence that ships were not seized or men enslaved arbitrarily or 'without any form of justice' is furnished involuntarily by the vehement denunciations of Paul Rycaut in 1663 or Pananti 150 years later. In spite of the former's declaration, in connexion with admitted illegalities on our part, that 'these Pyrates and ungracious Villains would find a knot in a Bull-rush and a scruple where none was', and the latter's description of the admiral delivering to the court, specially summoned on the day of the ship's arrival, though the day of prayer, a long harangue replete with the artifices and chicanery of 'pirate law', it is noteworthy that the represen-tations of our consul prevailed in both cases.[3] Collingwood, who was well aware of our constant abuses of neutrality and the treaty rights and legal practice of the Algerines, wrote Castle-reagh his belief that 'it would be advantageous to the general interests, if the same disposition were more manifest in the Admiralty Court of Malta'.[4] A French consul said he never approached the divan without a copy of the treaty in his hand.

In Christian countries it was not merely a question of pro-crastination or corruption in the courts but of extra-legal religious considerations. Tuscany's attempt openly to observe incompatible religious and municipal codes had entailed a stinging rebuke from the great Suleiman, and proved an effec-tive bar to the participation of its ships in the Levant trade. In the later seventeenth century the Grand Duke could only show his disapproval of the seizure of Tunisian property on an English ship by refusing to accept his official share. In 1622 the cargo of a friendly French vessel carried into Rye was

[1] Manwaring, ii. 42; Grandchamp, iii. 406. Neither realized that only *enemy-owned* cargo was taken.

[2] Osborne, i. 541–2; Smith, *True Travels*, ch. xv.

[3] Rycaut, p. 258; Pananti, p. 67.

[4] G. L. Newnham Collingwood, *Correspondence and Memoir of Lord Collingwood*, London, 1828, p. 384.

unceremoniously disposed of as 'being Papist goods', and in 1626 England welcomed the arrival of 'a rich prize of Jew goods, valued at £100,000'. As late as 1665 our merchants complained of the difficulty in getting any information about ships taken into Toulon and Marseilles.[1] In Spain the Inquisition, which was superior to law or royal authority, seized English vessels, cargoes, and crews on the flimsiest pretexts. Little protection was forthcoming from our consuls, who were expected to be good Catholics and Spaniards, and were even at times officials of the Inquisition or a 'mass priest'. The French complained that they suffered no less in peace than in war time from English and Majorcan privateers.[2]

That the Barbaresques kept their treaties, which as late as 1662 were concluded with the official approval of the sultan, better than France or England is incontestable. In 1609 we find an intolerant and fire-eating ambassador of Henri IV expressing surprise at the failure of France to implement the recently concluded treaties with Algiers and Tunis by the return of captives, mainly galley-slaves, and complaining of Morat's ability to proclaim the better faith of his countrymen. Very illuminating was his advice to invade those regencies, regarding whose strength he was woefully ignorant, or, failing that, to comply with the terms of the treaties.[3] How well, in comparison with ourselves, the Algerines kept treaties made by Roe in 1623 or Cason in 1646 is shown by our own records. The reactions of merchants or casual references in the journals of such seamen as Coxere and Barlow indicate that Algerine observance of a peace was relied on as a matter of course in the reign of Charles II.[4]

Sir Henry Blount's striking contrast between his experience of the 'incredible civility' of Turkish mariners, the best of whom according to Knolles's *History* were trained in Barbary, and 'the barbarism of other nations at sea, and above all others our own',[5] finds support from other contemporaries. John Smith, Wotton, Roe, and Badiley express strong views about the

---

[1] Cal. S.P.D. 1619–23, pp. 380 and 383; Birch, *Charles I*, i. 164; Cal. S.P.D. 1665–6, p. 58.

[2] Masson, pp. 13–17 and 45.   [3] Heinrich, pp. 212–15.

[4] *Adventures by Sea of Edward Coxere*, E. H. W. Meyerstein, Oxford, 1945, pp. 54 and 85; *Edward Barlow, Journal of his Life at Sea from 1659 to 1708*, ed. B. Lubbock, 2 vols., London, 1934.   [5] Osborne, i. 536.

conduct of English seamen and ships, which appear to be corroborated by official documents. We complained bitterly of the barbarous behaviour of Dutch seamen, and de Ruyter's chaplain at Algiers described his ship's company as *ecclesia porcorum* or congregation of swine.[1] Some of the methods employed by the principal organizers of the French navy, Richelieu and Colbert, reflect little credit on their good faith or humanity.[2]

In spite of the withering denunciations, so commonly repeated today, of the Barbaresques as barbarous renegades and outlaws, 'gens sans loi et sans foi', a remarkably flattering distinction is made between the strangers, Christians or Moriscos, who operated from ports in Barbary, and the Turks and Moors resident there. John Smith calls the former 'the most cruell villains in Turkie and Barbarie, whose natives are very noble, and of good nature, in comparison to them'.[3] In the same way French treaty negotiations of the period differentiated very clearly in favour of the Turk and Moor residents of Algiers and Tunis as men who could be relied on to keep their treaties and obey their rulers.[4] Spain adopted much the same attitude by giving no quarter to Christians or Moriscos commanding Barbary ships. In the royal letter carried by Mansel to Algiers specific mention is made, not of our losses, but of the commanders of ships with their countries of origin.

There is ample testimony to the fact that renegades or 'Turks of profession' could be very estimable characters who were quickly moulded into harmonious units of the Turkish military and administrative organization, of which Dapper draws a surprising but not uncorroborated picture. There is also good evidence of the strict control exercised by the rulers of Algiers and Tunis over Christian adventurers. Those who sought refuge there, as also at Amsterdam or Leghorn, in search of greater freedom or opportunity, quickly went elsewhere if they found

---

[1] Blok, *Life of Admiral (Michiel) de Ruyter*, p. 152.
[2] e.g. Sue, *de Sourdis*, i. 77 and 90.
[3] *True Travels*, ch. xxviii. 'Pirates in true sense of word who disgusted Venetians, English, and even Dutch', Duro, iii. 330. For pirates at Mamora, see Cal. S.P.D. 1611–18, p. 55, and H.M.C. Downshire MSS. iv. 302, and for complaints by Sallee de Castries (England), iii, p. 111.
[4] Rouard de Card, *Traités de la France avec les pays de l'Afrique du Nord: Algérie, Tunisie, Tripolitaine, Maroc*, p. 18. De Brèves, p. 325.

such conditions unpalatable. We find various references in the years following Roe's treaty to the patience and forbearance of the Algerines in spite of 'just provocation' to a rupture and the 'civility' of their ships at sea. It is ironical that Pepys's impetuous and singularly ill-advised outburst against 'that heady and faithless people' should still be quoted, while his more sober judgements on other occasions are forgotten.

There is apparently little reason to doubt that the army and marine of Algiers continued to be, as in the previous century, better organized and disciplined than those of Christian countries, and that conditions throughout the regency, in spite of Christian intrigue, were on the whole more peaceful. Of its Christian opponents Spain seems to have shown the greatest sense of responsibility and regard for the law of nations, but there is at least some ground for a more comprehensive application of Prescott's dictum that the Mussulmans appeared to be 'the better Christians of the two'. Some such sentiment was expressed at times during the century even by ecclesiastics. During the régime of Madame de Maintenon a chaplain on the French galleys had the temerity to end a eulogy of the Turks and Moors on board with the words 'You would say that the Turks are Turks in name only but Christians in fact and that the Christians are the real infidels. So that when the Turks are spoken to regarding Christianity they reply "We would rather be transformed into dogs than embrace a religion which practises so many abominations" '.[1]

Such sentiments seem to find confirmation in our own estimates of Christian 'corsairs'. We find something romantic in Sir Francis Verney, a singularly despicable character, and Mainwaring, a not very successful pirate, subsequently described as dishonest, untruthful, and quarrelsome, is transformed into 'no unworthy successor' to Drake himself or his 'very incarnation'. We are even told that a Spanish adventurer, whose Confession[2] shows that his daily pursuits in the Maltese galleys were, according to a conservative appraisal, 'robbery, abduction and piracy' and his life 'one continuous succession

[1] C. Taylor, *The Camisards*, London, 1893, p. 10.
[2] *Confession of Alonso Contreras*, D. Ogg, *Europe in the Seventeenth Century*, 5th ed., London, 1949, pp. 15–18; Hubac, pp. 158–80; J. B. Trend, *Spain from the South*, London, 1928, pp. 210 and 214.

of quarrels, fights, escapes, intrigues and murders', must be regarded 'by the standard of the time 300 years ago and the standard of the state of war' as 'an epitome of the Castilian spirit'. Though specially commended by the pope and the Knights of St. John, he was outlawed by Spain and Sicily. I know of no reason to believe that such a character would have been tolerated at Algiers. He does not seem to have cut a good figure beside Morat.[1]

No account of the Mediterranean or reference to corsairs would be fully intelligible which did not differentiate carefully between the Mediterranean and Levant Seas as distinct spheres. Between 1574 and 1732 at least the knights took no official part in the war between Algiers and Spain, but operated east of Sicily in Levantine waters, where they were apparently less antagonistic to Tripoli and Tunis than to the Greeks or, perhaps, English traders. During Contreras's career the Aegean, like the Caribbean, became the great field of maritime adventure—to the ultimate advantage of France, which at first showed less concern for 'political morality' than Venice or Spain. Finlay clearly overestimated the damage done to Greek commerce by the 'indefatigable corsairs' of Malta or the Christian pirates who, unlike the ships of the regencies in the Mediterranean, 'acknowledged no allegiance to any government'.[2]

The knights and their associates are represented in Charrière's correspondence and travellers' narratives up to 1732 as minor irritants—'little barking dogs', according to Blount—who might sting Turkey to reprisals.[3] Their illegalities in Cretan waters caused Venice constant anxiety. Extravagant claims by French naval historians about unauthorized adventurers, who defeated fleets single-handed and became the 'terror of the Turks', contrast strangely with the futility of operations against Barbary and the low level of French prestige at Constantinople. Paul's chief recorded success consisted of sinking an English vessel with French cargo. The 'aventuriers de Provence qu'on appelle Levanti, gens accoutumés d'aller à la mer avec des corsaires de Malte . . . ces vagabonds de la gloire n'étant avoués de

---

[1] Hubac, p. 165.

[2] Finlay, v. 90–94; de la Roncière, v. 174.

[3] Charrière, iv. 425 n., 431 n., &c.; Osborne, i. 536, compare Cal. S.P.F. 1560–1, p. 433, C.M.H. iii. 124.

personne, usant comme subterfuge de tous les pavillons' did little to assist the Venetian cause or raise the credit of Louis, either as 'Grand Turc' or 'eldest son of the Church'.[1] The humiliating result of Duquesne's illegalities at Chios in 1681 served as a warning in 1729.[2] In 1718 an *Ordonnance du Roy* forbade persons trading in Turkey under French protection to receive anything taken from Turks by Maltese corsairs or others.[3]

The religious obligations of a knight commander in the later seventeenth century are indicated by his admission that he was, in fact, a Dutchman and Lutheran.[4] From about 1731 the knights appear to have been more friendly to the Turks than to the English, until in 1795 they renewed their depredations along the Turkish coast.[5] In 1798 Bonaparte divided the Ottoman world by his invasion of Egypt and termination of Maltese slavery.[6] In the interval activities of corsairs had been restricted to championship of the Greek cause in the Adriatic. In Britain the title became familiar largely through Scott's interest in William Davidson's *Bloody Journal* (1788–9) and Byron's poem (1814).[7]

[1] Lacour-Gayet, *La Marine militaire de la France, 1624–61*, pp. 168–85; de la Roncière, iv. 266–80.

[2] H.M.C. MSS. of Lady Du Cane, p. 244. Louis paid compensation. See Vandal, Sue, d'Arvieux, &c. Tripoli's special responsibility for combating Venice and Levantine piracy requires study. Downshire MSS. i. 348, &c.

[3] A. Devoulx, *Les Archives du Consulat Général de France à Alger*, 1865, p. 29. See also F. Charles-Roux, *Les Échelles de Syrie et de Palestine au dix-huitième siècle*, Paris, 1928, pp. 54–56, and Pinkerton, x. 578, 581–2, 596, &c.

[4] Chardin, i. 4.

[5] Mifsud, *Knights Hospitallers of the Venerable Tongue of England in Malta*, pp. 257 sqq.; *G.M.* 1795, p. 607, and 1802, p. 263.

[6] Plantet, ii. 486–8.

[7] Finlay, v. 269–76; *D.N.B.* xiv. 130; *G.M.* 1797, p. 701; Masson, *18ᵉ siècle*, p. 609 n.

IX

THE MEDITERRANEAN IN THE
EARLY SEVENTEENTH CENTURY
(continued)

TWO outstanding features of the Mediterranean in the early seventeenth century are found in the constant Christian aggression, open or disguised, against the Turks and the development of international trade, in spite of very unpropitious conditions. From 1601 to 1621, prior to any hostile action in our waters, the African coast from Algiers to Hammamet in Tunis was under almost continuous assault,[1] often of the most barbarous and treacherous character, in disregard perhaps of treaty or the laws of war, by men or ships of Spain, Sicily, Malta, Tuscany, France, Holland, and England.

In 1607 the Tuscan Knights of St. Stephen, whose forces usually included a number of English ships, burned Bona, the principal commercial port of Eastern Algeria, killed 470 Turks and carried off enormous booty and 1,500 captives. In 1610, in addition to other depredations, they burned the town of Bresk, which remained a ruin, massacred the garrison, and kidnapped 2,000 men, women, and children.[2] Slave-raiding appears to have been frequent, and at times was officially encouraged,[3] but such hostilities were by no means approved by the mercantile interest. The London merchants persuaded James to protest to the Grand Duke, and those of Leghorn and Marseilles often sent advance warnings to their correspondents in North Africa.[4]

The relations of these two ports with the regencies were very close and played a very considerable part in the development

---

[1] By 1621 the shattered Turks had deserted Italian waters, Duro, iii. 366–7. The French entered enemy ports at will to 'prendre, brûler, ravager et piller', de Sourdis, i. 25.

[2] Bresk (Biskra) was 'filled with fire and blood', Knolles (Nabbes), p. 1299; de Grammont, pp. 48 and 150.

[3] By navies, Duro, iii. 342; Calmon-Maison, Le Maréchal de Château-Renault (1637–1716), Paris, 1903, p. 11.

[4] De Grammont, p. 145; Masson, p. 47; Gramaye, ch. x; Calmon-Maison, p. 12 n.

of English and Spanish trade with Turkish Barbary. The East India Company had its own agents at both for that very purpose. Free ports were established in competition at Villefranche and Civita Vecchia. Venice, by its equivocal attitude in Turkish affairs, was reduced from its old commercial preeminence to carrying on much of its business through Leghorn and Ragusa. While its own island possessions were remarkable, even in those days, for lawlessness,[1] it lost no opportunity of denouncing the ports of Barbary and the Morea as 'piratical' or their Christian rivals as traders in 'pirate goods'.

Such insinuations have involved in much unjustified criticism those enlightened popes who tried to provide their subjects with facilities for traffic in the produce of Barbary, as also with the ships and goods of English Protestants.[2] It was a similar, and still more liberal, commercial policy that developed the surprising prosperity of Leghorn as a centre of international trade, to the admiration of, among others, the great economist Thomas Mun, who as consul or merchant had watched, and taken part in, its expansion from the previous century, and Colbert, who planned to establish a free port at Marseilles on similar lines. Such developments were largely dependent on the very liberal practices in the regencies, of which we have special evidence at Tunis.

Even more remarkable is the friendly relationship between Barbary and Sicily, whose inhabitants expressed their desire about 1640, and again some forty years later, to be placed under Turkish rule.[3] Such a possibility had been a source of anxiety to Spain from the time of Charles V. In the early years of the seventeenth century there was a Tunisian merchant established at Palermo, and the Bashaw of Tripoli also had a sister living there.[4] The Genoese maintained relations with Barbary ports through their much-envied concession at Tabarca, for which the Lomellini family paid tribute to the rulers of Algiers and Tunis. Even Naples and Malta maintained some direct rela-

---

[1] For Crete, see V.S.P. 1636–9, p. 344; for Zante, &c., Coxere, p. 53, Finlay, v. 94.

[2] At Civita Vecchia. Compare Ranke, *History of the Popes during the Sixteenth and Seventeenth Centuries*, ii. 260, and Masson, p. 29, with L. Roberts, ch. clxix.

[3] Osborne i. 532; H.M.C. App. Sixth Report, p. 286; Reinach, *Recueil des Instructions données aux Ambassadeurs de France*, vol. x, pp. lxxvi and 5.

[4] Grandchamp, iii. 11 and 47–48.

tions. The establishment of the coral-fishery in the waters between Sardinia and North Africa, which brought Torre del Greco such great prosperity and renown, dated from about 1580 and could hardly have survived, much less flourished, in the face of continuous Moslem hostility.[1] Communication with Malta was carried on not only in neutral ships but, according to Sandys (1610) and d'Arvieux (1655), in Barbaresque and Maltese vessels.

Prize goods were of relatively little value, as can be ascertained from the French consular records at Tunis. They usually consisted of fish or grain, which were in little demand and often had badly deteriorated before they could be disposed of. The only valuable commodity was silk, which was shipped in Syria and apparently consigned to Spain. The great bulk of the trade between Mediterranean ports or from them to the Levant was carried under the French flag, and the criterion for the condemnation of cargo, or part of it, was not its nature, origin, or destination, but enemy ownership, a fact not easy to determine. There could, however, be no room for doubt with regard to such cargoes as ammunition shipped from Malta to Sardinia, then a Spanish possession. Evidence, of perhaps doubtful authenticity, was normally obtained from the crew either voluntarily or by the bastinado. Nationality, as French treaties with the regencies show, was determined solely by domicile, the proof of which was residence and marriage. Ships described as 'taken' by the Barbaresques were in fact brought into port for examination.[2]

About 1605, when Henri was fulminating about piracies on French shipping, his ambassador at Constantinople reckoned that 1,000 ships were trading to the Levant under the French flag and earned over 500,000 crowns annually by the carriage of enemy goods.[3] For various reasons, including the depredations of French adventurers under the Tuscan and Maltese flags on Turkish goods, ships, and territory, as well as, perhaps, the difference in treatment of Morisco refugees to Barbary by French and English ships, the French marine decreased rapidly

---

[1] P. Colletta, *Storia del Reame di Napoli 1734–1825*, Paris, 1837, pp. 102–3; Charrière, iv. 459 n.

[2] Confirmed by Grandchamp, iii. 406.

[3] De Brèves, pp. 29–30.

and preference was given to English and Dutch vessels, even for passengers and goods from Marseilles. It is significant that, while French writers are apt to attribute this to the fact that their ships were small and weakly defended, both the Levant Company and the Ragusans complained at different times of unfair competition by the Dutch who dispensed with strong hulls or armament.[1] The very dubious use of the English flag, which brought considerable profit to the Rycauts and other Genoese in London and also to the Levant Company and its ambassadors, was so beneficial to the owners as to secure a reduction of 80 per cent. in insurance premiums.[2]

About the same time, however, the Venetian charterers of English ships were accused of flying the Cross of St. George, when attacking Turkish territory, and their own flag in Levant ports to avoid paying consulage, to the collection of which the English and French appear at times to have attached more importance than to the development of national commerce. The abuse of the English flag was so great, sometimes for the express purpose of damaging our relations with the Turks, that the extent of English piracy may have been less than supposed.[3] Wotton describes the crew of an allegedly English ship as a 'ramass of rogues of every nation', which tallies closely with Collingwood's description of our Mediterranean privateers two centuries later. We ourselves maintained that the nationality of the majority of the crew was sufficient evidence of the nationality of our ships, though we also complained of the readiness of English seamen to marry and settle down in foreign countries—as, indeed, men like Ward did in Tunis. The age which was ushered in by Henri, as Catholic King of France, or James, as head of the Anglican Church, was not remarkable for loyalty to country or religion—as witness the remarkable case of Robert Sherley.[4] Seamen,[5] whose condition was little better than slavery, sought redress from numerous injustices in changing their allegiance or their religion, sometimes whole crews at

---

[1] Cal. S.P.D. 1580–1625, p. 548; L. Villari, p. 314.

[2] Roe, p. 450.

[3] Ibid., pp. 278, 451, &c.

[4] Cal. S.P. Col. 1617–21, pp. 13–14.

[5] S.P. 98. 18, 11 Apr. 1695. Jal, i. 522–3, calls English seamen 'race fort nomade et qui, sans patrie, pour ainsi dire, allaient où les marchands ou les souverains payaient mieux'.

a time, in which respect Innocent XII sympathized with our consul at Leghorn, or in the 'running away' with their ships.

Gardiner's account of the regencies, drawn not from our records but from a German history of Turkey, depicts 'the uncontrollable hordes, who had long bidden defiance to the Sultan', falling, in obedience to the 'duty of making war upon the infidel', with their powerful fleets upon the 'full stream of European commerce, passing before their eyes'. Why 'swarms of foreigners', usually described as impious outlaws, should be guided by any such religious obligation is obscure. Even more so is the statement that this part of the Turkish empire 'called imperatively for the interference of the maritime powers'.[1]

Actually, the Mediterranean appears to have been at this time a highway of commerce, which compared extremely favourably with the lamentable conditions prevailing throughout Christian Europe, the scene during the first half of the century of the longest and most barbarous war in modern history and of ruinous internal dissensions, amounting often to anarchy. Traders from the North Sea may well have felt relieved when they safely passed Finisterre and still more when they entered the Straits of Gibraltar. The development of prosperity by western ports, such as Bristol, was remarkable, and so was the expansion of English commerce in the Mediterranean, as shown by the establishment of, or demand for, English consulates at Malaga, Alicante, Marseilles, Genoa, Leghorn, Pisa, Naples, Civita Vecchia, Palermo, Messina, Trapani, Gallipoli, Zante, Venice, Tunis, and, perhaps, Malta. As regards the Atlantic, which is often pictured as infested by the rovers of Algiers and Sallee, both the seat of English consulates, our countrymen enjoyed a degree of prosperity and prestige in the Canaries which they never recovered after Cromwell's war with Spain, and developed with surprising speed a valuable trade in cod and pilchards, which were normally carried in very small craft.

The Levant trade, which Harborne, Roe, and others stated to be dependent on the goodwill of Algiers and Tunis, especially during strained relations with Spain, is described at different times—sometimes simultaneously—as the principal foreign commerce of England, France, and Holland. During the very

---

[1] S. R. Gardiner, *History of England, 1603–42*, 10 vols., London, 1883–4, iii. 64.

eventful decade ending 1620 the trade of Provence with the
Levant averaged 30,000,000 livres a year, the highest figure—
the decreasing value of money notwithstanding—for more than
a century to come. In 1614 exports from Marseilles alone to
Turkey, which probably included the regencies, amounted to
7,000,000 crowns.[1] There are amazing descriptions about this
time of Aleppo as a prosperous centre of foreign commerce,
and long before *Macbeth* was published it was 'as well known to
England (or at least to our English merchants) as Kingston
upon Thames'.[2] By 1614 the *Tiger* may have been as familiar
to Barbary ports as to Shakespeare's public. Levant merchants
made large fortunes and the French consul in Egypt collected
200,000 livres in consulage in 1638. Ten years earlier Wyche
had been greatly impressed with Leghorn as a port for our
Levant trade,[3] and Kenelm Digby was dispatched with a
naval squadron to deal a destructive blow at French shipping
in the outport of Aleppo. He made use of the facilities of Algiers
on his way out, but did not risk doing so on his return. The
prosperity of Aleppo was gradually rivalled at other ports,
especially Smyrna, which became a great centre of Christian
trade, and Sidon, which was much favoured by the French.

In spite of many adverse factors, prosperity in the Mediterranean and Levant Seas continued to develop, until after 1648
the maritime powers began to transfer their *naval* rivalries to
that area, as may be seen by a study of, among other things,
the Levant Company's memorials of 1649, 1650, and 1657.[4]
The maintenance of Commonwealth warships in the Mediterranean was only made possible by the co-operation of our consuls and factories on its shores, particularly at Leghorn, the
great 'Magazine of the Streights', and at Tunis, 'the only safe
refuge for all the Levant Navigation', a 'plentiful' source of
supply for our warships and the inhabitants of Provence.[5]

A few words about Tunis may be appropriate, since it is
usually represented as playing a negligible part in our foreign

[1] Masson, p. 133; V.S.P. 1610–13, p. 180; de la Roncière, iv. 396–7.
[2] *Voyage and Travels of Captain Robert Coverte*, ? 1612, Osborne, ii. 241–66;
'wonderful, great trading', ibid., p. 263. Confirmed by Lithgow, L. Roberts, Pietro
della Valle, Fermanel, &c.
[3] S.P. 98. 3, f. 79, 27 Feb. 1628; Masson, pp. 124–5; Napier, v.
[4] Cals. S.P.D. 1649–50, pp. 11–12, 1650, pp. 71–72, 1657–8, pp. 95–96.
[5] Boothouse Report S.P. 71. 25, ff. 1 sqq.

relations, apart from events connected with John Ward and Admiral Blake, and because we have so much contemporary information about it which illustrates conditions in the regencies.

Mainwaring creates surprise by holding it up to King James in 1616 as a model of administration, just as one of our consuls did nearly two centuries later.

In the little observation I could make in my small travels I have noted those Countries best governed where the laws are most severely executed; as for instance in Tunis, where no offence is ever remitted but strictly punished according to their customs and laws. In five months together, when I was coming and going, I never heard of Murder, Robbery or private Quarrel. Nay a Christian, which is more than he can warrant himself in any part of Christendom, may on my knowledge travel 150 miles into the country, though he carry good store of money, and himself alone, and none will molest him.

This striking contrast to the environs of London at that time, as described by Roe and James himself, is amply confirmed by Consul Boothouse some forty years later and, in a practical form, by Lithgow, who returned to Tunis after his tour of Barbary and made it his residence for some weeks.[1] Even Dan speaks relatively well of the regency.

While Mainwaring attributes such conditions to the rule of the Dey Yussuf (1610–37), 'a sterne man' and 'very just of his word', of whom French writers usually speak highly, the social and administrative fabric of the regency, which is described as having quickly developed from 'un vulgaire repaire de brigands' into 'une sorte de confrérie de trafiquants, présidée par le Dey', appears to have largely been created by his predecessor and collaborator Cara Osman (1593–1610), who, in common with John Ward (? to 1622), has been the subject of so much ill-informed criticism and even abuse. A French history of 1689, quoted by Lucas, tells us that Osman's rule, which was all too short, was characterized by 'douceur et justice' and 'une tranquillité profonde'.[2] He made an exceptionally enlightened treaty with the French, including reciprocal renunciation of the right of search and the expulsion of English adventurers, and on his

---

[1] Manwaring, ii. 42; Roe, p. 574.
[2] *Histoire des dernières révolutions*, pp. 29–30.

death he was lamented by his people. In 1609 a very hostile French captive spoke highly of his personality, his popularity with the janissaries, and his domination of subversive elements. Alphonse Rousseau also commends the intelligent interest which he displayed in the minutest details of administration.[1] The conventional sneers at his origin are ill-founded. He was a Turkish janissary who, like the greatest officials of the Ottoman empire, had passed through the various army grades and, in accordance with common practice, followed a trade in his spare time. The rule of the Deys for a period of some seventy-five years, i.e. until the beginning of the active contest between Ottoman and Moorish conceptions of administration, appears to have been effective, popular, and peaceable.

The conventional view of John Ward, who is generally regarded as the leader and personification of Tunisian 'piracy', also rests on very slender foundations—indeed on no reliable first-hand evidence at all. If he is the person described by Andrew Barker,[2] who, however sincere, is mainly a retailer of gossip, he obviously could not have been the first to teach Tunis the use of the round ship. So much of the information about him is contradictory or demonstrably untrue that he has probably been confused with other adventurers of the same and similar names. Corbett's singular theory that Ward's arrival in the Mediterranean in about 1604 paved the way for the permanent establishment of our naval power there in the next century is based on dubious assumptions that by the beginning of 1609 this new-comer was admiral of the Tunis fleet, which was not the case; that his presence there was 'an out-rage not to be endured' by Spain, which was at war with Tunis, on the brink of war with England, and only too ready to enlist into its service maritime adventurers from England or elsewhere; that Tunis constituted a formidable naval power; that it was preparing a cruise against the American treasure fleet; and that Fajardo's attack in June 1609 was 'the heaviest blow that the pirates had received since Lepanto'.

This action, for which not only the Spanish admiral but the French corsair Beaulieu-Persac and the English Captain

---

[1] Grandchamp, iii. 389–96; *Annales tunisiennes*, p. 35.
[2] *A True and Certaine Report of the Beginning, Proceedings etc. of Captaine Ward and Danseker, the late famous pirates*, London, 1609 (B.M. C. 27 c. 6).

Hunt[1] claimed the credit, was one of those unheralded and indiscriminate raids to which ships anchored in the defenceless roads of Goletta were so constantly exposed. There appears little ground for believing that 'all Christendom rang' with the exploit or that it had any marked effect on the naval activities of Tunis. The report of the Venetian ambassador at Madrid that Fajardo had burned all the ships at La Goletta under cover of darkness and that unpleasant consequences were feared from the fact that these included some French merchant vessels is unexpectedly confirmed by the complaint of a French captain, recorded in the consular register at Tunis, that fifteen Spanish warships had burned all the ships in the roadstead, 'tant corsaires que marchands'.[2]

It was not until some months after this action that Ward turned Turk, i.e. became a naturalized Tunisian, and received a commission from the sultan. From that time he seems to have been mainly, if not entirely, occupied on shore in training gunners and casting cannon until his death in the great plague of 1622–3. Lithgow evidently liked him and appreciated his kindness. He appears, after his conversion, to have been well and not unfavourably known at the French consulate. He cuts a much better figure than Giffard, Elliott, Verney, or at least two of the Sherleys. But for the accident that some Venetian goods captured by him were brought to England he might never have achieved any notoriety there, and his name would not have figured so inappropriately in the royal proclamation of 1609 about English piracy in general.[3]

The registers of notarial acts at the French consulate at Tunis for the period 1582 to 1620 throw an exceptionally interesting and valuable light, because entirely factual, on the foreign relations of Tunis, and offer a striking contrast to the paucity of official records regarding the regencies preserved in France and England. Their editor, who unfortunately does not seem to have had access to the best of outside authorities, admits that the French merchants lived there *assez tranquilles* up to the beginning of the century, when references to English corsairs become frequent, as also to Christian aggression. While Ward is only

[1] Cal. S.P.D. 1634–5, p. 223.
[2] V.S.P. 1607–10, p. 41; Grandchamp, ii. 152, and iii. 45–46.
[3] He did not capture them, V.S.P. 1607–10, pp. 17 and 23.

mentioned once prior to December 1610, there are, between 1605 and 1616, records of ten attacks on the regency or its galleys, in which France appears to have had some share.

One of these de la Roncière describes as a well-merited reprisal for the action of a Tunis corsair, which lay in wait off Marseilles for an enemy ship sheltering there, in much the same way as our cruisers did off New York in 1914. The same writer, faithfully followed by Charles-Roux, describes Tunis replying in 1614 to a message of peace, brought by Vice-Admiral Théodore de Mantin ('pirate of Marseilles', according to a Venetian envoy), by seizing twenty-two Provençal vessels and imprisoning all the French residents. The consular records, however, mention two visits that year. In February he came with two ships and committed 'plusieurs ravages contre le Sr. Issouf Dey et autres commandans en ce pays', which led to reprisals. During the night of 29–30 May he attacked ships anchored in the Goletta road and carried off one English vessel (the *Tiger* with its valuable cargo) and one or two French.[1] So far from any indication of the imprisonment of the consul and his flock the register contains, in its published form, no less than 65 pages of acts between 4 April 1614 and December 1615, and Tunis was visited during that period by English ships and merchants, including Mainwaring and Lithgow. The *Tiger* was apparently never restored nor any compensation paid to its owners. Its consort had already been attacked in Gibraltar by French ships, which Lediard about this time describes as 'men of war (or pirates or at best privateers)'. De Mantin's peace negotiations later at Algiers, like those of Narborough and others, seem to have been based on aggressive violence. He cut a very dubious figure subsequently in our own waters.

These registers which, according to their editor, contain entries regarding redemption of captives, freighting of ships, partnerships or companies, receipts, powers of attorney, loans, minutes of meetings of the French community, copies of notarial acts drawn up in France, &c., throw much light also on Christian trade, marine insurance, the behaviour of consuls, and relations with neighbouring countries. There are frequent references to English and Dutch merchants and ships, though in

[1] Grandchamp, iii. 103–4; A.P.C. 1613–14, pp. 618–19; V.S.P. 1613–15, p. 155; Roe, pp. 821–2.

1618 the Dey relieved those nations of French jurisdiction. It is interesting to find the *Mayflower* trading there under the well-known Captain John Goodlade.[1]

A close relationship existed between the European and African shores of the Mediterranean, not only on account of their historic economic interdependence but because of the existence in both areas of a large number of captives. The demands for the service of the galleys, which were many times more numerous at Christian than Barbaresque ports, and the increasing number of raids to meet their requirements or to provide material for exchanges and profitable ransom evidently gave rise to a serious problem at this time. Though it is usually represented as a unilateral one, arising out of Moslem religious exigences or cupidity, it is quite possible that the number of Moslem slaves was the greater, and there can be no doubt that the position was aggravated by dubious Christian practices. The system of ransoming prisoners of war was still recognized between Christian countries. We had an agent, a Scotsman, at Dunkirk in 1627 for the redemption of prisoners,[2] and the practice of kidnapping or deporting men, women, and children for sale in our plantations was just beginning.[3]

The description, used frequently by writers so authoritative as Gardiner and Oppenheim, of captivity in Barbary as one of 'hopeless' slavery is clearly contrary to fact.[4] Captives, whether enslaved or not—apart, perhaps, from young boys, who, as brands to be plucked from the burning and potential champions of Islam, received special treatment—were under Mohammedan law prisoners of war, who should be surrendered at the conclusion of hostilities. This the Turks were prepared to do, and actually did to a large extent, regardless of any discrepancy in numbers, following de Brèves' treaties with Tunis and Algiers of 1606 or Roe's treaty with Algiers of 1623. The unwillingness, however, of French galley commanders to release Turks and Moors, who were specially prized for physical and other qualities, and the heartless cupidity of English captains in selling their captives into Spain, where owing to religious

---

[1] Grandchamp, iii. 234; Roe, p. 448.
[2] A Scott named Ross, Birch, *Charles I*, i. 197.
[3] *Prowse*, p. 147; Fitzmaurice, p. 32.
[4] There was always hope, Pananti, p. 355.

scruple they became irredeemable,[1] necessarily involved an alteration in the practice of the Barbaresques, though the principle was never abandoned.

The result was a complex system of traffic, partly through individual exchanges, partly by redemptions, of captives, who in this manner had acquired a permanent value. It was carried out by brokers, usually Italian Jews, and Catholic organizations, which had their own representatives in Algiers and Tunis, including ecclesiastics or even sometimes renegade Christians.[2] Naples and Sicily did not share the scruples of their Spanish masters about the redemption of Moslem prisoners, and the natives probably keenly regretted the reciprocal practice of slave-raiding. On the Christian side this appears to have been officially conducted for the purpose of replenishing the galleys, while from the African shore it was normally carried on for speculative or retaliatory purposes in small native craft unconnected with the Turkish marine. At Leghorn and Valetta, the ports serving the galleys of St. Stephen and St. John, international slave markets were developed, which facilitated exchange or supplied the galleys of other countries, including France and, for a short time, England.[3]

Apart from the governments, which received head-tax or percentages, and the brokers, the return to the captors was probably, as in the case of prize goods, only small. But for the efforts of Colbert and others to recreate a powerful force out of the galley, then regarded in Algiers as obsolete, the traffic would for all practical purposes have died out during the century.[4]

Except perhaps in Spain, where captivity was regarded by the Algerines as the legal equivalent of decease, and Malta, where the treatment of galley-slaves was peculiarly inhuman, the system may have created a relationship no less close, and in many ways more personal, than the more normal forms of commerce. Slaves communicated with their families and made provision for their welfare through powers of attorney, transfers of property, and even cash remittances, while their relatives in turn might work in various ways for their redemption. Redeemed slaves often corresponded with their old masters in Barbary and sent them presents. A Bashaw of Tunis, according

---

[1] Duro, ii. 53–54.
[2] See Grandchamp and Riggio.
[3] Mifsud, pp. 251–2.
[4] D'Arvieux, v. 263; Morgan, p. 517.

to d'Arvieux, never forgot the kindness of a Frenchwoman when he was a galley-slave at Marseilles, where Barbaresque captives appear to have got on well with the inhabitants. In Morocco, cases are recorded of Englishmen after liberation continuing to reside there for business purposes, but in Algiers and Tunis they generally found it more advantageous to remain in nominal slavery. Captives often complained that they suffered most from fellow Christians, including their own countrymen. The Algerines were frequently struck by the callousness of the English towards the plight of their nationals, which contrasted with the devoted efforts of the Catholic missions.

In considering the extent of the so-called 'depredations' of the Barbaresques, regard must be had to the small size of their marines and the fact that the cruising period usually lasted less than three months in the year, and was often unsuccessful. Their real naval strength consisted in their galleys—normally eight of Algiers and six of Bizerta. These operated as a rule in squadrons, sometimes jointly. Their high degree of discipline and training compensated to some extent for their relatively small size and armament. When their triumphant campaigns of 1637 and 1638 along the coasts of southern Spain and Calabria went to their heads, the entire joint fleet was annihilated by the Venetians, and the naval power, which had so long given the Turks of Barbary periodical supremacy in the Mediterranean, passed away. By the time that Colbert went to such lengths to revive the use of the galley the Barbaresque navies consisted almost entirely of light sailing vessels.[1]

It was very soon after the Anglo-Spanish peace of 1604 that the foreign ships operating from Algiers and Tunis were brought under effective government control. At Tunis they may have operated for the account of an official syndicate. At Algiers, where, partly for protection and partly for regulation by the divan, all the sea-going marine made its headquarters, the government was the chief participant in the spoils, gave permission for departures, furnished the ammunition and armament, appointed the commander of the fighting men and the purser, who were required to furnish reports on each voyage, and in course of time selected the captain as well. I can find no mention in English or the more reliable French contemporary

[1] D'Arvieux, v. 263; Morgan, p. 517.

records of the *Taiffe*, which is so often today represented as an all-powerful association of ship's-captains, forming a 'state within a state'.[1]

In contradistinction to other countries neither Spain nor the Barbaresques approved of the privateering system of those and later days, whereby ships, particularly in the Mediterranean, were commissioned in the most haphazard manner and could pursue their calling with almost complete 'licence' and irresponsibility. It was a question not only of principle but of practical utility. One of the arguments adduced in Spain against the use of privateers was that they made captive only men, women, and children who, unlike the prisoners of royal ships, were useless for service at the oar.[2] Slave-raiding in North Africa seems to have been at this time a function of Spanish men-of-war, as also of the government of Oran. Privateering was forbidden by the Anglo-Spanish treaty of 1604, but this was of little avail if ships could obtain commissions from other countries. It was, moreover, impossible to keep the terms of a treaty if ships could sail with 'double commissions', i.e. under the authority of two different governments. One Spanish privateer is actually mentioned as the possessor of three separate commissions. The international status at sea of the great Duque de Osuna was at one time distinctly dubious.[3]

The number and power of Barbaresque ships were obviously greatly exaggerated from various motives in Christian reports. Osuna's description of the meteoric increase in a few years of the sailing ships at Tunis from none to 'eight and forty great ships' was probably an invention designed to deceive his king. In 1609, before Fajardo is stated to have destroyed between 22 and 33 ships, Captain Foucques in somewhat inflammatory reports put the total number at 12 large ships. Tunis had in fact no harbour for sailing ships, which had to lie in the unprotected road before La Goletta and Porto Farina. The strength of these great ships may be judged from 'a typical episode in the constant struggle of Mediterranean trade against Moslem piracy' when, it is alleged, the *Dolphin* of London in 1617 with a crew of 38 and 28 guns defeated 5 Turk (apparently

---

[1] *Taiffe* at Tunis meant corporation of regular soldiers, Lucas, *La Grèce*, ii. 161 n. Haedo called individual ships republics of co-partners.

[2] Duro, iii. 342.   [3] Cal. S.P.D. 1666-7, p. 60; Duro, iii. 335-50.

Tunis) men-of-war and a *sattee*, 'all vessels of great burden and strongly manned', and commanded by Walsingham, together with the celebrated Samson and another English captain. It is noticeable that, though we were then at peace with all Ottoman countries, the *Dolphin* opened hostilities.[1] It is even more remarkable that the Levant Company, for which the vessel was operated, was at this very time complaining of unfair competition by unarmed Dutch ships, and official circles in London were telling the merchants of the ruin of their trade by pirates of Algiers and Tunis, who are even represented as spreading terror in English waters.

There is a singular dearth of reliable figures for Algerine ships between Haedo's detailed list of 36 galleys, mostly very small, in 1581 and the numerous lists after the Restoration. In 1634, however, Dan saw 28 ships in, or leaving, the roadstead, and in the same year Knight says the number had temporarily fallen below 30. The very restricted harbour of Algiers could accommodate at that time, according to a French historian, 30 vessels or, according to Monson, only 20.[2] During the latter part of the century the Algerine fleet usually approximated the lesser number.

Like their light galleys of the previous century their ships were designed entirely for speed, with a view to overtaking and boarding their adversaries. Their armaments appear, even very much later, to have been of little value; the powder was often scarce and of poor quality; the gunners were either renegades or inexperienced slaves. The Algerians had no use for our merchantmen, which were too slow and clumsy for their purpose. Their ships were no match for ours individually. Knight describes their surprise at the surrender of an English vessel at the beginning of the war of 1630.[3] The three Algiers cruisers, which caused so much consternation in Cornwall in 1640, showed no superiority collectively over a Virginia trader.[4] In the reign of James I the French, Dutch, English, and Spaniards are credited with destroying their fleets in almost monotonous fashion.

[1] Beazley, ii, p. xiv.

[2] *Tracts*, iii. 91. He thought it unsuited to privateering. See plans in Dapper, Plantet, Lane-Poole, *Piratical States*, &c.

[3] Osborne, i. 536, and ii. 488.

[4] Cal. S.P.D. 1640, p. 321; Chew, p. 362.

It may be that the chief insecurity at sea was derived, not from piracy in its normal sense, but from revolutionary forces and their abettors, from the civil wars and rebellions in Morocco, Spain (the Moriscos and Catalans), France (de Soubise and the Rochelois), Naples, England, Greece, and Syria. Special reference is often made to the serious damage inflicted on trade by the privateers, or pirate ships, of Prince Rupert.[1]

[1] Cal. S.P.D. 1649–50, pp. 11–12; Lacour-Gayet, p. 172.

X

OUR RELATIONS WITH THE REGENCIES
1603 TO 1620

THE London negotiations for the Anglo-Spanish peace of
1604 showed little concern for our Turkish allies. They
began with a characteristic invitation from a Spanish
delegate to 'all European princes to peace among themselves
and . . . to a common resistance of the Turk, the common
enemy of Christendom'. Salisbury, however, was opposed to
commitments or reciprocal guarantees which might be incompatible with other treaty obligations. While he pointed out the
danger of including generalities in a treaty, Northampton
contended that anything should be regarded as permitted that
was not expressly prohibited.[1]

Whether specifically mentioned in the final text or not, the
cardinal principles enunciated at the prolonged discussions—
the abolition of privateering, the position of consuls, the non-
molestation of merchants, 'either by sea or land for matters
of conscience'—were in practice disregarded. While James
exercised little or no control over his sea-going subjects, the
privateers of Dunkirk, Biscay, and Majorca contrived for many
years to come to inflict great damage on our ships or coasts.
The situation with regard to the appointment of consuls in
Spain, the interference of the Inquisition, and the requisitioning
of English ships continued to be most unsatisfactory.

A union of Christian princes against Turkish aggression or
for the division of Turkish territory was still regarded as a
panacea for a distracted Europe, in spite of past experience
and obvious detriment to the trade of England, France, Holland, and Venice. Unanimity between Christian princes, however, seldom went further than the consistent prevention of any
permanent understanding between Turkey and Spain.

James's own son-in-law later spoke bitterly of the advantages

[1] R. Watson and W. Thompson, *History of Philip III*, 2 vols., London, 1786, ii,
Appendix; *Pol. Hist.* vii. 21–22.

that might have accrued to him if English money and influence had been used in helping him, instead of antagonizing the Turks in the interests of Spain. The attitude of our merchants was very similar. James considered relations with Turkey as coming purely within their province, and paid little heed to remonstrances about piracy in our own waters. He, however, soon won over the London merchants, especially those trading to the Levant, by an extension of their privileges, but it was not until some of the great figures of the Elizabethan era, notably Salisbury and Staper, had passed away that he was able to give effect to his new policy.

His attitude is the more surprising in view of the apparent absence of specific grievances against the Barbary States at the time and the stream of complaints issuing from our merchants and representatives in Spain against the proceedings of the Inquisition, the machinations there of the English Jesuits and the Irish refugees, who were 'murderers in the guise of Catholics', and the general miscarriage of justice, of which our ambassador's dispatches are full. Applications from the merchants for assistance and redress have, according to Cornwallis, 'almost worn out the mind of myself and the leggs of poor Cottington my secretary', while the unfortunate applicants pine away in 'Fears, Irons, Diseases and Misery'. According to the Inquisitor himself, in spite of solemn treaties, 'for such as fall into that Gulfe there is no labour to be made nor better Meanes to be used than Sylence and recommending them to God'. Staper about this time told Salisbury how much better Englishmen fared trading among the Turks than among the Spaniards, and the experiences during the reign of Charles I of Giles Penn in Morocco were in striking contrast to the sufferings of his son George in Andalusia. While in the early years of King James the Spaniards complained bitterly of the activities of English pirates on their coasts, we were almost equally apprehensive of a surprise attack from the Spanish fleet.[1] At least three times during his reign there was danger of war between the two nations.

The indifference alike of the Levant Company and of our government to the affairs of Turkish Barbary is indicated by

[1] E. Sawyer, *Memorials of Sir Ralph Winwood*, 3 vols., London, 1725, ii and iii; H.M.C. Downshire MSS. iii and iv.

the almost complete absence of records. Except for three or four letters in 1607 and 1608 to Richard Allen, whom it had appointed consul at Algiers in 1606, there is no sign of correspondence by the Company with the regencies until after Mansel's expedition of 1620 nor of any by our government after 1608. Apart from certain troubles, which are not altogether easy to elucidate, the interesting points in the letters to Allen are a reference to the suppression of 'interlopers', which suggests that the trade had some attractions, some unfavourable comment on his manners, and the determination not to appoint a consul at Tunis. Foreign commerce at that place, though perhaps still smaller than at Algiers, was evidently very considerable, and English interests were protected about this time by the French consul, Hugues Changet, 'there residente both for the French and English nation'.[1]

Whether the Company had any more interest in promoting normal trade relations with Algiers and Tunis than with Egypt is extremely doubtful. Its policy appears to have been conservative and timid, and its trading operations were soon practically confined to its factories at Aleppo, Smyrna, and Constantinople.[2] While the French sneered at its intrigues and trade in contraband, it would appear that the strategically important position of English merchants at Tunis, Algiers, and Tetuan was achieved in course of time in spite of it rather than with its assistance.

It must have been late in 1608 that Allen made his surreptitious departure from Algiers—possibly on account of failure to maintain certain English commercial concessions in the face of French pressure. It is interesting that our records and histories contain no allusion to them, although this form of preference had proved so embarrassing to the Algerines, and the conditions under which they were enjoyed were cited later as a precedent in a treaty with France.[3] They hardly suggest an atmosphere of ill will towards the English.

It can only be assumed that James Frizell, who later claimed to have carried on the consulate for seven years, apparently up

---

[1] C. H. L'E. Ewen, *Captain John Ward 'Archpirate'*, Paignton, 1939, p. 4; Grandchamp, ii and iii.

[2] 'Our unintelligibly prudent Company', Downshire MSS. i. 431 and 303.

[3] Coquiel Treaty, 1640, permitted exports 'du temps que les Anglais avaient les échelles', Masson, *Établissements*, p. 107.

to the beginning of 1618, acted in a somewhat informal manner and conducted his correspondence directly with Nicholas Leate, the deputy governor of the Company, whose factor he was. There is little doubt that there were then other English merchants settled in Algiers—the death of one there is recorded in 1620—and probably also in Tunis, or that our ships and travellers were welcome at both ports.[1]

Apart from Morat's letters of October 1603 to 'Sir Horatio', and of November 1607 to Richard Staper, the patriarch of the Levant Company, which are indicative both of friendship and a desire for peaceful commercial relations, official correspondence at this time relates almost entirely to complaints arising out of violent and illegal proceedings by the king's subjects. A joint letter from the Bashaw of Algiers and Morat,[2] described as 'General at Sea', received by King James on 2 February 1607, requests his assistance in effecting the release of some 'poor soldiers', passengers on an English vessel who had been 'betrayed under your Majesty's colours' and sold into slavery at Leghorn. Such glaring bad faith was evidently all too frequent, as the Maltese agent at Naples boasted of secret arrangements with English captains to deliver up their passengers to his country, and Venetian reports frequently rejoice at any opportunities for breeding suspicion or dissension between the English and Turks.

Further evidence of hostile English operations under the protection of Tuscany is afforded by a letter of June 1606 from the Turkey merchants,[3] i.e. the Levant Company, expressing gratitude for Lord Salisbury's intervention with the agent of the Duke of Florence 'about these hard courses which his master takes in setting out our ships and merchants against the Turks', and which were very prejudicial to our merchants in that trade. Indeed, it would seem that for a short time the port of Algiers was actually closed to them. In this letter, as in one from two merchants to the privy council in 1608,[4] specific complaint was made about Captain Richard Giffard, who, though his operations from Leghorn were more than questionable and decidedly

---

[1] A.P.C. 1621–3, p. 345; Grandchamp, iii. 163 and 362.
[2] S.P. 71. 1, f. 12.
[3] Salisbury MSS. xviii. 187.
[4] S.P. 71. 1, f. 13. Proclaimed a pirate 1605 and 1606, Salisbury MSS xvii. 465 and 472 and xviii. 164.

harmful to us both materially and morally, was eventually recommended for a baronetcy and given a seat on the Commission of Admiralty.

This ruffian—for it is hard to give any other name to him and some of his associates at that time—was stated in the former letter to have enticed 20 Turks on board his ship at Bougie, under a flag of peace and pretence of trade as English merchants, and then tried to burn some galleys in front of Algiers, where 20 Englishmen were held in prison as hostages, until the Turks taken to Leghorn were restored. After mentioning that 9 Englishmen had been executed and much money seized on that account, the Company requested that the 20 Turks might be delivered to Edward Turner, an English merchant at Leghorn or Pisa, to send to Algiers. It subsequently informed the consul that the Duke of Florence had undertaken to restore the Turks as soon as the galleys, in which they were serving, returned from sea, but it is at least doubtful if the promise was kept.

The second letter referred to the unfriendly fly-boat belonging to Giffard which was loading at Algiers and was reported to have done damage to both English and Turk under the alleged authority of a letter of marque against Spain.

Again in 1609 Captain Henry Pepwell[1] reported the ill treatment of his ship by the Tuscans with the result that on arrival at Algiers his crew joined the 'pirates'. About the same time even our consul took part in a gross act of treachery, which Playfair relates as follows:

Another ship came to Algiers and according to custom the Consul Richard Alline and Mr. William Garrat went on board with an Algerine officer to search it; they drowned the officer and the consul escaped in the vessel to Bougia, another port on the Algerine coast where the captain of the castle, two of his sons and sundry other Mohammedans were enticed on board, carried off and sold as slaves at Leghorn. Another ship carrying Turks and Moors to Tetuan had changed its course for Alicante and had there sold them as slaves.[2]

It is significant that Allen and Garrett were in due course appointed consuls at precisely those ports of Leghorn and Alicante. Such charges would seem to have been recognized as substantially true, but no help was forthcoming from the

---

[1] Cal. S.P. Ireland 1608–10, pp. 278–9.   [2] p. 42; S.P. 71. 1, f. 24.

Grand Duke of Tuscany, who ceased even to reply to King James's remonstrances.[1]

Christian adventurers using the facilities of Algiers, as indeed they were legally entitled to do, if not hostile, were also a source of trouble to English traders. In November 1608 the Company wrote to Allen to complain of Ward taking a trumpeter by force out of the *Darling* at Algiers,[2] and at about the same time, apparently, supported the Venetian denunciation of him, though perhaps on very slender grounds.[3] In January 1609 a letter from John Audeley, 'sometymes Consull in Argier', reported the arrival of Simon Danser in a ship built at Lübeck 'of great force' and manned by Turks and about twenty Dutch and English seamen, which, together with some English ships, had captured about thirty vessels, some of them our own. He was forcing Englishmen to serve with him and importing Dutch seamen from the Netherlands, and Audeley feared that he was 'like to overthrow all the merchants here' and 'bring the name of Englishman into great disrepute'.[4] Such adventurers were probably as embarrassing to the Barbaresques as to ourselves, and it is a curious fact that, about the very time that what the sultan called this 'fresh leaven'[5] had been either eliminated or brought under control, English denunciations of the 'pirates' of Algiers and Tunis really began.

Indeed, while our records indicate that we had merchants and consuls established at Algiers, as well as a community at Tunis, and that such complaints as were made were directed by the Algerines or our merchants against the irregular prac-tices of Christians, usually of our own nation, a concerted attack seems to have begun late in 1616 against Algiers as the 'common enemy', who must be suppressed by 'an unanyme consent' of

[1] The Venetian ambassador, reporting a conversation with the queen about 'the wealth of the Turkish prizes captured by ships of the Grand Duke', enclosed the proclamation against English pirates, V.S.P. 1607–10, pp. 224–5, and p. 4.

[2] Ewen, p. 9 n.

[3] Cal. S.P.D. 1603–10, p. 469.

[4] S.P. 71. 1, f. 17; V.S.P. 1607–10, p. 182.

[5] To Louis XIII, 23 July 1618, 'In the past our subjects have been most obedient, but now through the relations with your nation, England and Flanders a fresh leaven has been introduced which renders them less obedient than before', V.S.P. 1616–18, p. 274; and to Henri IV, Aug. 1603, Salisbury MSS. xv. 225–6. Pro-vençals complained 'les pirates et les Turcs et autres déguisés en Turcs' carried their people into Barbary, 2 Dec. 1626, Lacour-Gayet, p. 23. Algiers was officially at war with France.

Christian princes. This development evidently had its origin in the increased pressure applied in the summer of that year by the Dutch ambassador, Noel Caron, for the suppression of piracy in British waters. James assured him that a committee of London merchants had just been appointed to study that problem.[1] At almost the same moment Raleigh's projects and Southampton's restless ambition were giving great concern to Don Diego Sarmiento de Acuña, who had been sent by Spain as ambassador in 1613 for the purpose of diverting England from aiding the Protestant states in Europe or attacking the Spanish possessions in America. His success was apparently recognized in 1617 when he was created Count of Gondomar. His efforts may well have been supported by some of those adventurers who had about this time returned to England, after having outstayed their welcome on the Barbary coast.

The hand of Spain was also discernible in other ways. In 1616 Sir Francis Cottington, our newly appointed ambassador at Madrid, who, oblivious of previous experiences there, had become an enthusiastic member of the Spanish party, wrote the dispatch to which so much prominence has been given by Playfair, Lane-Poole, and Pepys.[2] His new bias, as well as his ignorance, is illustrated by the sensational statement that 'the strength and boldness of the Barbary pirates is now grown to that height, both in the ocean and the Mediterranean sea, as I have never known anything to have wrought a greater sadness and distraction in this Court than the daily advice thereof. Their fleet is divided into two squadrons; one of 18 sail remaining before Malaga in sight of the city; the other before the Cape of Santa Maria, which is between Lisbon and Seville.' This sensational account not only reveals a change of attitude on the part of the writer but is very hard to reconcile with Spanish accounts. At this very time they criticize the depredations of their privateers on Christian vessels in the Levant trade and

---

[1] J. L. Motley, *Life and Death of John Barneveld*, 2 vols., London, 1874, ii. 58. A proclamation against piracy, issued 16 July 1616, A.P.C. 1615–16, p. 682, followed one by Holland against English pirates in the Channel in 1611, E. de Meteren, *Histoire des Pays-Bas*, The Hague, 1618, p. 719; *Tracts*, iii. 376–9; Downshire MSS iii. 108–47.

[2] Morgan, pp. 629–31. Spain argued the Barbaresques would prove more harmful to England than to Spain, since they had few Christians on board and 'do *now* profess themselves the common enemies of Christendom'.

extol the amazing successes of their navy, which, after a triumphant raid on Tunis, gained a series of victories in Greek waters, in sight of Constantinople, and, most especially, one off Cyprus which was regarded as a landmark in naval history.[1]

It is noticeable that, while Duro dates 'piracy in the Mediterranean' from the expulsion of the Christian adventurers from their Morocco bases in 1614, Spain was able to denude its defences in the very next years for Osuna's schemes in the Adriatic and this campaign in the Levant. By 1619 not only had the navies of France, Holland, and Spain been credited with inflicting heavy losses on the Barbaresques, but the privateers of Biscay alone are said to have taken 1,600 prizes in the Mediterranean and Atlantic. Accounts of this period are, indeed, very conflicting and obviously unreliable. They are particularly hard to reconcile with the remarkable prosperity of Christian trade at Aleppo, the growth of Dutch competition, and the interest shown by the East India Company in that area, both for the purchase of Algiers and Tunis coral and the dispatch of correspondence to Persia and the East Indies.[2]

Both Cottington and his government might well have known that no such organization as the 'Barbary pirates' still existed, if indeed it ever had, and that the two squadrons clearly represented distinct navies engaged in a normal activity, which we had long recognized and often encouraged and with which Spain had long been familiar. The operations off Malaga were presumably conducted by the ships of Algiers and those on the Atlantic coast by the Emperor of Morocco's fleet, recently commanded by Joseph Pallache, whose activities were well known in England.[3] Both countries were at war with Spain, and the only irregularity could have been in any participation by Dutch or English vessels. Mainwaring, who received his pardon that year, had, as 'no unworthy successor' of Drake,

---

[1] Duro, iii. 342–6; Cal. S.P.D. 1611–18, p. 432.

[2] Playfair's 'complaint' that in 1609–16 Algiers took 466 British ships and enslaved their crews is based on a memorandum of 1628, S.P. 71. 1, f. 91, designed to show by contrast how well it was keeping Roe's treaty. Precisely in that period Corbett describes its sea-power as 'broken', and there is no official record of English losses or complaints. A dubious Constantinople report of November 1616 mentions 5 ships lost in recent years, V.S.P. 1615–17, p. 352. The 936 ships captured by Algiers in 1613–21 included 60 English, Garrot, p. 454.

[3] Three of his prizes reached Plymouth in 1614, Birch, *James I*, i. 352, and received Admiralty sanction, de Castries (Pays-Bas), ii. 425–30, 433, and 519.

been attacking the Spaniards from Morocco, as Walsingham may still have been doing from the North African coast.

Madrid was, however, singularly ill adapted to serve as a centre for marine intelligence. In Cottington's earlier days our embassy admittedly had little or no information regarding events at seaports, or even in the English communities of Seville and Lisbon. In their dispatches of 1608 and 1609 Cornwallis and Cottington attributed the attacks on Spain to Christians, and tried, rather irresponsibly, to identify the principal assailants by name—Ward, Danser, Fearne, and Verney —perhaps in the hope of convincing Salisbury that their intelligence system had improved. Circumstances, however, had changed and on this occasion accuracy of detail was hardly a consideration. The account of the damage to English ships by the Malaga squadron is remarkably vague: 'three or four from the West of England' taken and two 'big English ships' driven ashore and burned. The lack of essential details— the names of the vessels, the fate of their crews, the unexplained inability to put up the usual effective resistance—these omissions, combined with the absence of any corresponding complaint from owners or relatives at home, arouse grave suspicion as to the authenticity of the information, which was probably supplied by the Spanish authorities as obligingly to Cottington as five years later to Sir Thomas Roe. The account from the Atlantic coast, which is more convincing and partially confirmed by other evidence, may well have been furnished by our consul at Lisbon, the embassy's only reliable source of information at Spanish ports. In this case the blockading squadron 'met with seven sail of English ships but laden only with pipe-staves. Five of these they took and the others escaped; they robbed them only of their victuals, their ordnance and of some sails and so let them go.' In the absence of complaint, it is not unlikely that the Moors took from the ships such supplies as they badly needed—food, powder, and canvas—and may possibly have done so, as on some other occasions, civilly and with adequate payment. It is by no means improbable that the three or four also described as 'taken' off Malaga met with somewhat similar treatment, especially as the bashaw told Mansel four years later that his people had only taken some fish from English vessels.

The currency given to dubious and alarmist reports in court and official circles may be gathered from the correspondence of so experienced a man as Lord Carew[1] with his friend Sir Thomas Roe at the court of the Great Mogul, where the latter was himself greatly embarrassed by complaints from the Turks of English piracies. It was not until October 1616 that Carew makes his first reference to Turkish pirates and Algiers, when he also tells of 7 ships bound from Newfoundland with fish for Italy and attacked in the straits by 30 Turkish men-of-war, which sank 2 and pillaged the cargo of the other 5 and enslaved their crews. This might well be a gross distortion of the incident reported by Cottington, and it is significant that, according to the records of Newfoundland, its traffic during that reign suffered only from Christian, mainly English, pirates, including Mainwaring and his associates.[2]

The most interesting feature of the letter, however, is the evidence of growing alarm as to the security of our shores. Carew cites Mainwaring's claim to have captured a Turkish pirate, who had been in the Thames as high as Leigh, and freed its captives, 'but', he adds with unusual caution, 'of any hurt he did uppon the coast of England I have not heard'. Nor, apparently, had anyone else, and this, like so many claims of that plausible but, I fear, unreliable adventurer, seems to rest solely on his own very dubious assertions. The evidence of Sir William Monson, then commanding in the channel, and the records of the privy council definitely rule out such a possibility.[3]

The theme is further developed by Carew the following month, after the receipt of 'letters out of Spain' and, apparently, further disclosures from Mainwaring. He describes the recent development of sailing ships by the Turks 'who in former time knew not any other than the Mediterranean Sea', but now 'not onlye take and spoyle all Christians that trade to the Levant (which our English marchantes to their great loss have felt) but the coasts of Spain and Barbary (without the Straits) receives incredible damage by them'. After a pathetic

---

[1] *Letters of George Lord Carew to Sir Thomas Roe, Ambassador to the Court of the Great Mogul*, Camden Society, London, 1860, pp. 51–130; *Letters written by John Chamberlain*, ed. N. E. McClure, 2 vols., Philadelphia, 1939.

[2] Prowse, pp. 101–8 n.

[3] App. H.

account of the recent desolation of the island of St. Mary in the Azores by eighteen Turkish ships he expresses the fear that 'this next sommer they will seek purchase uppon the coastes of England and Ireland'. He adds that 'in the towne of Angire (as heretofore) the English are well enough intreated but if they be taken at sea either outward or homeward bound they are esteemed good prize without redemption', which we know to be untrue.

The hand of Spain, which always assumed that Christian and Spaniard were synonymous terms, is seen in the conclusion that 'if the Christian princes do not by an unanyme consent endeavour there suppression there coastes will be daylye infested and trade in to the Levant [at that time, apparently, the subject of keen competition] will be utterly destroyed for the numbers of pirates increase like Hidraes'. About the same time the 'Commissioners for the Spanish business' were also urging joint action by the Christian princes.

A few days later Carew reports the sacking of villages near Malaga and the 'supineness' of the Spaniards, and on 16 December 'every day we hear of our shipps taken in the Levant by the Turkish pirates and very lately they have taken two merchant ships of London'. Perhaps one of these was Captain Pennington's, captured that year by the French, who, according to Duro, were inflicting heavy losses on the Turks.

Then we begin to see another side of the picture. First the penalties imposed on the Company by the sultan for certain offences are cited: 'in briefe the Turks begin to breake all the conditions of the contract between us and them'. Then we hear of anxiety about 'certayne piracies' committed on the Turks in the 'bottom of the Levant' by two Englishmen in the service of the Duke of Florence. News also reaches him that the pirates are flocking to Tuscany, and, indeed, about that time there is a record of one of Raleigh's captains selling in Leghorn the cargoes of seven vessels of the Newfoundland fleet.[1] Carew's account of the 'spoyles and robberies committed (as the Turks alledge) upon the Grand Signor's subjects in East Indies, whereof daylie complaints and infractions come to Constantinople' could hardly have been news to Roe, who was 'told to his face by the enemies of England that they were all thieves'.

[1] Prowse, p. 103.

Then come further complaints of high-handed requisitions by Spain of English ships for a secret expedition and signs of nervousness as to where this 'blow will fall'. As the French had for some time been plundering English ships in the Mediterranean and Spanish ones in the Atlantic, and the Dutch were 'publicly robbing all nations', Christian solidarity in the cause of law and order was evidently little more than a mirage. The rival countries were clearly more interested in the profit to be extracted from embroiling each other with the 'pirate states' than in uniting for their extirpation, and even within some of those countries themselves there was sharp division between commercial and political interests.

How ignorant of the area itself and how out of touch with our merchants and their views were Carew and other members of the government can be judged from the next two letters. In the summer he writes of Turkish pirates on the coasts of England and Ireland—presumably an exaggeration, as he only mentions their having met with our fishermen between Ushant and Scilly. He expressly says that they did no hurt, that they only captured some vessels off the coasts of Spain, and that they treated our ships civilly, paying generously for anything they received. This in itself he considers suspicious; he can only conceive that they came to discover our coasts and that 'hereafter . . . we shall have to (*sic*) much of there custome and less civiltie'. His knowledge of Morocco was clearly very imperfect, since we had received an embassy from it not long before, and the Barbary Company, one of the joint signatories of the petition for the suppression of piracy, renewed its charter the following year. Otherwise, he would have realized that they were not Algerines at all but Sallee Rovers. Of their existence he appears to have been entirely unaware until at the end of August he learns by reports from The Hague that the Moriscos, refugees from Spain, who had recently established what Roe later called the 'new plantation' at Sallee, were doing great damage in the Atlantic. The estimate of the rovers' strength at sixty ships is obviously a gross exaggeration, as is probably the account of the 'havoke' they had wrought and the number of prisoners they had taken in the Canaries and Madeira, as well as in the 'weak maritime towns' of Spain.

It is indeed clear from Carleton's correspondence that about this time the governments of England and the Netherlands, which had just failed in its ambitious scheme to obtain a fortified base in Morocco and was now trying to strengthen its position in the Ottoman dominions, were engaged in egging each other on to a complete breach with Algiers. On 31 March 1617 Carleton, whose extensive instruction of a year earlier had contained no reference to Barbary, reported about Dutch negotiations through their admiral and consul for a peace with Algiers and Tunis based on the right of search and confiscation of Spanish goods. Both our secretaries of state already showed signs of alarm at such an event, expressing particular concern at reports that the Dutch were to furnish those 'pirates' with gunpowder, 'an offence so notorious that all Christendom speaks shame of it'.[1]

Winwood[2] begins with the extremely disingenuous statement that the Levant merchants had presented to His Majesty 'a humble petition complaining of their irreparable losses and craved aid and assistance from him to protect them against the violence of these miscreants'. Both he and Lake[3] stress the need for a 'concurrency between all princes' for their suppression, since otherwise not only 'our trade must cease in the Mediterranean sea', but they 'will adventure to possess our seas and assail us in our forts'. A large sum was alleged to have been collected for a powerful armada; an expedition had been decided upon; and it was hoped to obtain active assistance or financial contributions from such discordant nations as Spain, Venice, Savoy, France, and the Netherlands.

Carleton had the temporary satisfaction of reporting[4] that treaty negotiations were suspended because of the 'disgrace and difficulty' of the right of search, which was, however, permitted under our capitulations, and of a newly developed fear of Spain. It seemed to the Dutch preferable to join with us 'as against a common enemy,' and the idea of selling powder was repudiated with horror. Carleton, while saying that this was a common practice of the Dutch, who 'if money be stirring in hell will not fear to fetch it', did his best to make the breach

[1] *Correspondence of Sir Dudley Carleton at the Hague (1627)*, ed. Earl of Hardwicke, London, 1757, pp. 115 and 135.
[2] Ibid., p. 125, 1 Apr. 1617.
[3] Ibid., p. 116, 17 Apr. 1617.
[4] Ibid., pp. 138 and 143, 13 June and 7 July 1617.

irreparable. When he saw that they were once more ready to come to terms with Algiers, he advised them rather to rely on old friends, adding a warning that the Algerines would abuse the right of search to quarrel with their seamen and take their ships. By 1619 both France and Holland were making treaties with Algiers while Spain and Venice were at daggers drawn. Under cover of hostilities against Algiers Spain was preparing to attack Venice, and England to assist the republic.[1]

The conclusion seems inescapable that English policy at that time was to stir up animosity against Algiers, with which we were still ostensibly on good terms, not only among other nations but in England itself. The 'irreparable losses' of the Levant Company were evidently figments of Winwood's imagination, and his description of its petition was, to say the least, decidedly misleading. It was in fact not aimed solely or specifically at Algiers or Tunis but at the suppression of piracy in general, which was probably most serious in our own waters, and was signed jointly with a number of other trading organizations, including the Muscovy, Eastland, and Flanders companies. These had no connexion with the Barbary States at all and tried to back out as soon as 'Turkish pirates' were mentioned as the specific objective. Trinity House attempted to collect its quota from ships 'trading to all seas'.

This document is the only one which could be construed as an application on the subject from the Levant Company to the council in the period following 1613, when the latter's records again become available, although it made petitions about the alleged decay of its trade through different forms of *competition* and against the 'barbarous usage by the Turks', i.e. an *avania* or fine by the Sultan of Turkey.[2] That the initiative did not come from the Company is evident from a letter written by it to its governor in, apparently, August 1618. It begins 'Upon receipt of the Council's letter to you *desiring our resolution* that their Lordships might proceed to suppress *pirates and robbers at sea* we assembled and considered the project which two years since was petitioned by us and the merchants of this city.' It goes on to say how much its trade (which three years before it alleged to be decaying from Dutch competition) was being reduced, first by competition of the East India Company and then by the prospective loss of the silk trade, to about a third of its normal volume. Then, after a pathetic reference to 'that little remainder of trade left us', which rival petitions suggest was still extremely valuable, it points out that, as a result of its policy of using none but 'extraordinary good ships' going in convoys, 'we stand in little fear of pirates; neither have had any great losses that way'.[1] Actually, its ships had long been so strongly armed as to be regarded with considerable distrust at Constantinople, and were more than a match for the light-built Turks, even under English captains. Its chief recorded loss up to that time was occasioned by the capture of the *Tiger* in Tunis harbour in 1614 and of the *Salamander* at Milo about 1606, both by French ships.[2]

The East India Company[3] adopted a similar attitude. On learning that the objective was the Turkish pirates, it first wanted a *quid pro quo* in return for a contribution, and later expressed the opinion that it was very well able to protect its own trade. The Bristol merchants tried to excuse themselves from contributing on the score of their 'great loss of late, one ship taken by [unspecified] pirates and one casually burned'.[4] Judging by their conflict with the Levant Company at this time, they would appear to have shared the opinion of the Plymouth merchants that their trade was injured 'still more by the encroachments of the Londoners . . . who engross the commerce of the world'.[5] The Yarmouth merchants eventually refused to pay their quota[6] on the very valid ground that their real enemies were the pirates of Dunkirk.

Up to January 1618 when they come to an end the Carew letters, in common with contemporary records, contain surprisingly little evidence, and that usually of a somewhat vague nature, of any losses inflicted on English ships in the Mediterranean. The writer continues to dilate on 'Turkish' ravages of the Spanish coasts and Canaries, and, owing probably to the lukewarm attitude of the trading companies and complications in the East Indies and the Adriatic, the projected expedition

---

[1] Ibid., p. 599.   [2] Roe, pp. 821–2.
[3] Cal. S.P. Col. 1617–21, p. 255, and p. 47.
[4] A.P.C. 1617–19, p. 63.   [5] Cal. S.P.D. 1611–18, p. 476.
[6] H.M.C. App. Ninth Report, pp. 306, 309, and 319, for 'utter overthrow and extirpacion of the Pirates at Algiers and Tunys'.

may have been abandoned. Whereas we had been brushing aside complaints of Dutch cruelties against our ships and apparently regarded with satisfaction accounts of their hanging prisoners from the yard-arm in sight of Algiers or throwing overboard from one prize seventy or eighty Turks,[1] the protest from the East India Company that 'the Dutch know better how to tyrannise over us than the Moors, which already our experience findeth' could hardly be ignored. Soon afterwards Carleton had his hands full with the controversy over 'the inhuman massacre at Amboyna . . . that shocking scene of barbarity', which nearly resulted in a complete rupture between the two countries.[2] A change of policy seems clearly indicated by the issue in July 1619 of a commission to Buckingham as lord high admiral 'to repress the pirates and sea-rovers', apparently in home waters, as he was to 'attack and bring the pirates into port and to commit the men to prison'.[3]

In the meantime such a provocative attitude can hardly have failed to have had its effect upon our relations with Algiers. The Venetian correspondence, which is hardly likely to be partial to the Barbaresques, suggests that it was the openly hostile preparations against them by France on the one hand, and England, Spain, and Holland on the other, that provoked them to action. The ambassador in London, whose colleague at Constantinople was, we may be sure, making the most of the situation, reported in June 1616 that the people of Barbary, having heard that the Christians were preparing a great fleet, had mustered their forces, about 30,000 soldiers and 80 large ships, at Algiers for its defence. They had expelled the consuls of France, England, and Holland, because through collusion with the bashaw they were taking slaves away from their owners on various pretexts.[4] In July 1618 the sultan wrote to the King of France protesting about the preparations he was making against Barbary, 'a Mussulman country in our dominions'.[5]

Our consul, presumably James Frizell, who claimed to have filled the post for seven years, evidently returned to England,

---

[1] Carleton, p. 423, 23 Nov. 1619, and earlier Carew, p. 62. For 'very courteous letter' from Algiers and treaty, early 1619, see Carleton, pp. 336 and 381. *Life of Cornelius van Tromp*, p. 157.

[2] Cal. S.P. Col. 1617–21 is full of Dutch outrages.

[3] Cal. S.P.D. 1580–1625, p. 615. See p. 187, n. 4, and Gardiner, iii. 286.

[4] V.S.P. 1617–19, p. 230.   [5] Ibid., p. 274.

but his French colleague was soon back in anticipation of the successful conclusion of a new peace. Shortly afterwards the Dutch, who alone of the Christian powers appear to have taken the practical step of sending a considerable naval force to the Mediterranean, came to the conclusion that it was better to make terms with Algiers than to take part in joint operations 'to extirpate that wicked generation and secure the common trade', which might involve the risk not only of sacrificing their property in Turkey, but of putting the Spaniard in possession of Algiers and so making him 'too absolute a master in the Mediterranean'.[1]

Whether the final decision to dispatch a fleet under Sir Robert Mansel towards the end of 1620 was in any way influenced by events in France is a matter for speculation. Scanty French records merely indicate that, in spite of the massacre of an Algerine mission by the Marseilles mob in March of that year, negotiations continued until attacks by the royal galleys in July precipitated a war which was clearly not desired by the officials of either Algiers or Marseilles.[2] There is no suggestion that it produced any improvement of Anglo-French relations, or that either government took any real interest in the regencies.

At all events, the fact is recorded on 11 June 1620 that a satisfactory agreement had been made with the Spaniards, the use of whose ports was essential to us, 'and the plan is the old one against Algiers'. Spain, whose 'abiding dread' is said to have been the possibility that one of the Protestant powers might discover the secret of naval predominance in the Mediterranean, had finally put an end to its tergiversations and decided that an English expedition against its enemies there was the better risk of the two, especially as our naval prestige was no longer high. Perhaps, too, more or less satisfactory assurances were obtained from King James as to the scope of our operations there.

The object of the expedition was stated to be the suppression of piracy and 'as Algiers is known to be the nest and receptacle of the pirates every step is to be taken to destroy that nest', but the admiral's instructions prohibited an 'open assault' on account of the known strength of the place and the fear of

[1] Carleton, pp. 341 and 491–2.
[2] Plantet, i. 5–12; Masson, p. 31. Forty-five were killed.

offending Turkey.[1] There was also the realization that any action which permanently deprived us of the facilities of the Barbary ports in future emergencies, especially a war with Spain, could only be regarded as the height of folly. Lediard in his *Naval History* expresses the prevalent view of the origin of the expedition. 'Count Gondomar, the King of Spain's Ambassador in England, had now gained so great an Ascendant at Court that he governed the King at his pleasure; And at his sollicitations there was fitted out a Fleet for the Mediterranean . . . to humble the Algerines *who much infested the Spanish Coasts.*' We were evidently not inclined to attempt any more ambitious or drastic measure.[2]

How little general enthusiasm there was in England for the project may be inferred from the lukewarm responses received from official bodies and commercial associations to attempts to stimulate interest or collect the stipulated contributions and from the issue of a warrant calling on justices of the peace to help in impressing pipers and drummers for service in the merchant auxiliaries. Money was very scarce and might have been more logically and beneficially employed for similar purposes nearer home. The precise usefulness of such an expedition was never made clear, but it must have been obvious in well-informed circles that, however complete and gratifying to national pride its outcome might be, it would be attended by consequences of a very embarrassing nature, despite the fact that in his letter to the bashaw King James more than once stressed the approval which he professed to have received from the sultan.[3]

It evidently was not justified by commercial considerations, judging by the attitude of the East India and Barbary Companies, and still less by the 'Discourse' published in 1621[4] by Thomas Mun, the celebrated economist and former consul of the Levant Company at Pisa, which describes the very flourishing condition of our trade with Turkey at that time. The historian of Cornwall, allegedly the area most affected, is probably correct in stating that the expedition was 'more immediately occasioned by European politics than by the

[1] Monson, *Tracts*, iii. 107.   [2] Lediard, ii. 459.
[3] p. 189, n. 1.
[4] Macpherson, *Annals of Commerce*, ii. 306.

sufferings of King James's subjects'.[1] Playfair's statement that it originated from 'the urgent petition of the Turkey Company' seems no better founded than his other assertions that the Company contributed £20,000 to the cost and that Gondomar employed his whole influence to induce England to take possession of Algiers.[2]

It is significant that, while James had tried to persuade the merchants at other ports that he was acting under pressure from the Londoners owing to their heavy losses, he actually thanked the latter for their 'submissive carriage' in the matter.[3] If further evidence of the hollowness of his claims were required, it would be found in the contents of Digby's letter to Buckingham of 5 April 1619, which stated plainly that any grievances which the merchants might have had against Barbary no longer, on their own admission, existed, and that it would be unwise for us at the moment to 'pick that thorn' out of the King of Spain's foot.[4] A similar conclusion might be drawn from acts in the French archives at Tunis, which showed that English vessels were still trading freely to Algiers and English merchants residing there, and also from the absence of specific charges in the letter brought by Mansel from the king to the bashaw, who evidently had written a friendly message in that year.

[1] *Victoria County History, Cornwall*, i. 496–7.
[2] Playfair, p. 38 n. Actually £8,000, hoping to recover half from Spanish merchants.
[3] Cal. S.P.D. 1611–18, p. 464.
[4] De Castries (England), ii. 511–12.

XI

OUR RELATIONS WITH THE REGENCIES
1620 TO 1645

FEW commanders can have been better equipped with technical advisers in olden days than Sir Robert Mansel when he set out on his mission to suppress piracy at Algiers, and demand exemplary punishment of its principal perpetrators. His assistant admirals, Hawkins and Button, had had considerable experience of oversea marauding and also, like Mansel himself, of trying to control our own pirates in the channel. Several of his captains had been engaged in piracy on the Barbary coast, and another had been a captive in Algiers. He had, moreover, the expert advice of James Frizell, who had for many years been employed there as merchant and consul, and, apparently, expelled for fraudulent practices.

Some similarity is noticeable between Mansel's instructions and those of Blake and, perhaps, subsequent commanders in that area. There was no question of negotiations or other action than presenting the bashaw with a very abrupt letter from King James. In the event of non-compliance he was at liberty to do little more than destroy any Algiers ships that he might happen to meet. His orders were, indeed, so conflicting that, while they read that 'as Algiers is known to be the nest and receptacle of the pirates every means should be taken to destroy that nest', he might not make an 'open assault' on it because of its known strength and the fear of offending Turkey and involving our merchants there in reprisals.[1] There was also great anxiety to avoid a definite breach with Algiers itself or other Barbary States, whose ports would be of vital importance to England in the event of a war with Spain. As Mansel had no authority to negotiate a satisfactory settlement, even apparently by renewing the old capitulations, there can have been little prospect of his mission proving more than what one of his officers called a 'fruitless errand'.[2]

[1] Monson, *Tracts*, iii. 107.
[2] *Algiers Voyage*, by J. B., 1621 (B.M. 1093 b. 82).

Though James was at great pains in his letter[1] to insist that he was acting with the sultan's approval in presenting his demands for the restitution of English property and the punishment of the principal offenders, the bashaw not unnaturally refused to recognize the validity of any instructions not addressed by the sultan to himself, or to lay them before the divan. The claim was probably disingenuous, as the Turkish attitude had been that the troubles in Barbary were largely due to the failure of King James and other Christian rulers to control their subjects, and we were also at this very time complaining of English treatment at Constantinople. It would seem from Mansel's own report that the king's letter was finally sent ashore just before he sailed away.

The fleet arrived at Algiers only on 27 November 1620 after calls at three Spanish ports, where it failed to allay entirely local suspicions about its real objective, and caused panic among the citizens of Malaga, who mistook it at first for a Turkish invasion.[2] Its stay lasted about two weeks, of which only three or four days appear to have been taken up by actual negotiations.[3]

Mansel's demands, presented by Captain Roper, Captain Squibb, the ex-slave, and Frizell, for whose safe return hostages were sent on board, required that compensation be paid for 150 ships alleged to have been taken by the Algerines during the previous six years; that the 'pyratts and their armadores who ar the harborers might be by them cutt of by the swoarde of justice, or handed over to the Admiral to receave condigne punishment'; that all English vessels then in harbour with their cargoes should be delivered up; and, lastly, that all His Majesty's subjects whether slaves, renegades, boys, or freemen should be sent on board the flagship.

The Algerines on their side pressed a number of somewhat more specific claims, mainly referring to the treacherous kidnapping and sale of their countrymen by the king's subjects.

---

[1] Latin draft to Mustaph(a) Bassa, 16 Aug. 1620 (Letter Book of Thomas Read, 1619–23), Add. MS. 38597, f. 23. Roe was later instructed to desire the sultan 'to take some order with the Pyrates of Tunis and Algiers who shelter themselves under your Royal protection', Knolles, p. 967.

[2] Lithgow, p. 393.

[3] S.P. 71. 1 contain a *Journal of Proceedings at Algiers* of 8 Dec. 1620, and Mansel's dispatches of the 16th and 17th.

Though these had been the subject of official correspondence and were subsequently admitted by Roe to be substantially valid, they were airily dismissed by Roper on the ground that they had not previously been mentioned, and that 'the authors of the deeds were persons beyond the King's jurisdiction'. The latter excuse, which incidentally was frequently proffered at much later dates, was in strange contrast to the 'long arm' of royal authority of which the Stuart kings were apt to boast and to the attempts to extradite and punish defaulting merchants, as far afield as Algiers and Morocco. It should not have proved as difficult to punish the captains of English vessels who had enslaved Moorish and Turkish pilgrims entrusted to their charge or left them to perish of cold and hunger on a desert island. Of the offenders Giffard was the recipient of honours and high office in England, while Garrett and Allen were made consuls at Alicante and Leghorn where their victims had been sold into slavery.

The Algerines only admitted having spoiled some of our pilchard vessels of their cargoes, which may have been substantially true, as the main grievance soon afterwards was the not very serious damage done to 'our western fishermen', and legitimate, if they were consigned to enemy countries. They suggested that such ships and goods as were still in the place should be given up; that a proclamation should be made to all who possessed English slaves or boys; and that the *captives* should be delivered up at once. Here, I think, a misunderstanding arose, as it frequently did on subsequent occasions.[1] Neither the bashaw nor the divan had power to dispose of slaves or other prize goods once they had passed into the possession of private individuals. The 'captives' were probably men who had not been enslaved, including the crews of two ships which had just been brought in, and the same consideration may have applied to the goods which were available for delivery. Frizell would have understood the position, but perhaps his advice was ignored. The demand for the surrender of renegades, who had presumably become Ottoman subjects, would appear to be quite inadmissible. The fact that there was still in the city a number of English 'freemen', mainly, it is to be presumed, captives on parole, is at least interesting, as is also the absence

[1] See in 1634, Osborne, ii. 471; 1637, *de Sourdis*, ii. 381–94.

of any further reference to them, unless they are the Englishmen whose clearance is reported a year later by the consul.[1] Playfair's mention of 'the many hundred English captives known to be in the place' seems to be supported by no evidence, even if it includes slaves, and is at variance with subsequent reports.

The bashaw and divan were most anxious for the appointment of a consul, which was indeed the outward symbol and guarantee of peace, and was in accordance with the capitulations, but Mansel objected that he had no authority. Finally in response to a request 'to send a Person of Figure and Distinction in Quality of Consul with his Majesty's letter' he landed 'one Foard, an ordinarie saylor', 'a common man', 'a Person of meane Condition handsomely dressed with the Title of Consul whom they received respectfully'. The unfortunate man's unenviable position was not made any easier by the fact that before sailing 'the Admiral sent a Letter on Shoar with Instructions to the pretended Consul and another to the Bashaw to let him know how ill he took his perfidious dealing', or by his attempt some five months later to fire the shipping in Algiers harbour.

The news of the first operations was not received in London with much satisfaction, and, according to the Venetian ambassador, the merchants anticipated little advantage from so great expense. Peace had not been established, as Mansel still threatened to seize Algiers cruisers, and 'the appointment of this consul also causes dissatisfaction here as it seems by no means honourable to this nation owing to the character of the nominee', previously described as 'a person of the lowest condition who had been condemned to death by the commander for his misdeeds'.[2] Although Richard Forde, as he signed his name, remained in office for at least a year and wrote two official dispatches,[3] which do not indicate that he was an uneducated man, his appointment appears to have been ignored alike by the government, Company, and ambassador at Constantinople, who all left him without instructions or funds. The £200 which Mansel had given him had, it is hardly

---

[1] 50 in 3 Nov. 1621, S.P. 7. 1, f. 33.

[2] V.S.P. 1619–21, p. 618.

[3] S.P. 71. 1, f. 33, 'To Glorious Sovereign', reports he has 'suffered imprisonment and many other abuses'. The second, 24 Feb. 1622, recounts his financial distress 'and many other extremities', besides Algiers successes in the war.

necessary to say, proved insufficient for even the early calls upon him.

The result of the expedition was the very reverse of that intended, as it amounted to an open declaration of war which legitimized and intensified the operations of Algiers cruisers. In December 1621 Roe reported from Messina[1] that the Algerine pirates, if not checked, 'will brave the armies of kings at sea and *in a few years* attempt even the coasts and shores with peril', and Forde wrote about the same time in a similar strain from Algiers.

Attempts have been made to attribute the ill success of the expedition to pure bad luck, and stress has been laid on the crash of timbers and groans of the wounded on mysterious cruisers encountered in the dark. The reader of a journal of the voyage is asked to imagine that he hears 'the Cannon playing and Turkes by hundreds tumbling into the Seas, our owne stretching out hands to save a miserable number of poore Christians made slaves to the barbarous Turk and crafty Moore but delivered from that servitude by us, God assisting our labours'.[2] There seems, however, no question but that the result was a miserable fiasco, the expense and loss of life being offset by a few prizes, including a French bark captured on the coast of Morocco and a ship—nationality unspecified and perhaps immaterial—carrying a Dutch envoy and very innocent cargo from Leghorn to Algiers.[3] A small number of Algerine captives were also delivered to the consul at Alicante to be sold as slaves, an incident which was to cause complications in the future.[4]

The severe indictment of Sir William Monson can hardly be considered unjustified: 'Though the Design of it was to find out and destroy the Pirats of Algiers, yet, the fleet sent out for that Purpose, beside their going and coming, did not spend twenty days at Sea whilst they continued in the Streights but retired into Harbour where the Pirats might find them but not they the Pirats: A Practice not forgot in later times.'[5] The pity was, indeed, that useful lessons were not drawn from this experience

[1] Roe, p. 7; Playfair, p. 45. See, however, Duro, iii. 366–7.
[2] *Algiers Voyage*, introduction.
[3] Some money, Venetian cloth, and Leghorn dishes, Lediard, ii. 462.
[4] *Algiers Voyage*, 13 June 1621.
[5] *Tracts*, iii. 94–98.

for the better conduct of our future relations with that area. It is lamentable to find our ambassador at Constantinople only a few years later citing as a precedent the fact that Mansel was able to destroy the shipping in Algiers harbour without any resentment being shown by the sultan![1]

The curious variance between the attitudes of the government and the Company is strikingly illustrated at this time. The latter was 'importunate' to make a peace with Algiers as its Dutch rivals had done, but the king thought it dishonourable to have dealings with 'pirates'.[2] Less than five years later the position was reversed, the Company washing its hands of Algiers and Tunis, and King Charles actively soliciting their goodwill and co-operation. It might be added that, while King James showed no disposition to punish any of the leading English pirates, some of his officers, including Calvert, one of his secretaries of state, were openly accused of protecting and aiding them.[3]

Playfair tells us that Roe, who had been appointed ambassador to the Porte, 'was instructed to call at Algiers on his way to Constantinople in March 1622. He then concluded a treaty.' In fact, he never set foot in Algiers at all, and had reached Sicily before the end of 1621. His instructions referred only to 'the suppression of those insolencies', and 'that wicked crew' of Algiers and Tunis. His credential letter reminded the sultan of 'those common rovers of the seas, who are enemies to the lawes of nations and spoilers of the quiett and peaceable merchant' and 'traitors to your honor'.[4]

He himself had no desire to have any dealings with the Barbaresques, about whom he seems to have known nothing. He was, however, in correspondence with Gondomar, whose credit in London was greater than ever, and, as he had not yet begun to have his suspicions of *fides Hispanica*, he seized the opportunity of a call at Malaga to collect information, which the Spaniards there, as later at Messina, were delighted to give him.[5]

He learned that the pirates had taken 'near forty' English

[1] V.S.P. 1636–9, pp. 445 and 514.
[2] Cal. S.P.D. 1637–8, p. 255; Roe, p. 29.
[3] Forster, ii. 28–29.
[4] Playfair, p. 46; Roe, pp. 2 and 4.
[5] Roe, p. 4.

ships since Mansel had left. Of these 'about fourteen' were in the roadstead since, having made no resistance, they had been released after being rifled.[1] Those that resisted, he reported, were 'burned men and all, taking none to mercy', though, curiously enough, the Spaniards had recaptured 'four or five', which they were holding there as prizes, and we also know that others were retaken by their own crews. He dilates on the 'disgraceful barbarous usage such as I am loath and ashamed to mention', 'much the worse since our late unhappy and unperfect attempt', 'now enraged doggs'. He was in fact easily influenced by Spanish propaganda at the moment, and, though he was never really in touch with Barbary, where he does not seem to have been aware of Forde's existence, and was much more interested in European affairs and the fortunes of the Queen of Bohemia, the gradual change in his point of view, as revealed in his letters from Constantinople, is very instructive. His revised estimate of the damage to our ships by the Barbaresques in 1620 and 1621 at about £1,000, or perhaps £15 per ship, is particularly revealing.

He soon found that the Company, so far from sympathizing with his 'fire and sword' policy or sharing his pessimism about the future of the Levant trade, had actually been trying to induce such men as Nicholas Leate, its deputy governor, or Sir Thomas Glover, its ex-ambassador, to go as consul to Algiers.[2] As, moreover, England was admitted to be 'too weak to do any exploit at sea', the privy council could make no better suggestion than a threat to recall Roe and other subjects from the sultan's dominions unless 'speciall and speedy order taken'. Confronted with this dilemma Roe, having 'chosen rather to make some tryall than to leave it at the worst . . . procured capitulations and commands', which were sent with a Turkish official and a member of his own staff to Algiers and Tunis—'though I had rather seene them buried in their owne ashes'—to arrange conditions of peace and restitution with them.[3] He had already begun to suspect that he had been the dupe of Spanish guile.

Tunis, with which we do not seem to have had any real quarrel, agreed to renew the peace on condition that no English

[1] Roe, p. 574.
[2] S.P. 105. 148, f. 65.
[3] Roe, pp. 29–38.

ship began to fight with its people or transported their enemies' goods, and actually restored some slaves and a quantity of merchandise.[1] There may already have been an English merchant there acting unofficially as consul. At all events Roe appointed one provisionally in 1622.[2]

Algiers, which was doubtless well aware that the sultan was not likely to be acquainted with the facts or mindful of its true interests, since there seems to have been another of his messengers working on behalf of France, rather than of Turkey, and against England, refused to accept the message, whose authenticity might well be doubtful. It was, however, willing to send a deputation.[3] At this Roe expressed satisfaction, since being 'a kind of dependinge skirt of empire and not in absolute obedience', he could there bind them 'in faster chaines than on their own dunghill', an expression of somewhat unjustified self-confidence and hardly compatible with his previous 'promise that we will trade and resort to those parts in *friendship as in tymes past*'.

His principal problem proved to be not so much the conclusion of treaties with the aid of twelve commissioners of Algiers—though apparently of only two assistants from Tunis—as in overcoming the king's reluctance to make peace with pirates, pleading 'the common ease of your merchants and fishermen' and the consequent 'great advancement of traffique'. The composition of the commission is instructive, as its members were not solely Turks, and represented interests and activities which were not at all naval nor exclusively military. Those who signed or approved the treaty on behalf of Algiers[4] were: the 'Provincial Mufti and Mufti of the City, 2 Caddees Judges of Provinces, 2 that have been Governors, 2 Colonels of the Army, 2 Captains of Foot and other Antients both Burgesses and Souldiers'. The army officers were of course members of the

---

[1] Fourteen government slaves, Roe, p. 118. About 20 remained, the Company having no redemption fund. Secretary Conway to 'Magnificent, famous, Honoured and esteemed' Dey of Tunis mentions only 6 captives, S.P. 71. 26, ff. 1–2.

[2] Roe, p. 118, ? William Cooke.

[3] Plantet, i. 16 and 18 n.; Masson, pp. 31–33. The Dutch consul, 'a knowne knave', was recalled in 1625, Roe, pp. 381–2.

[4] Ibid., pp. 24–25. Originally to be signed as 'obligation' to the sultan by 'beglerbeys, beys and officers of both towns', a copy going from Algiers to London as 'quicker, cheaper and more honourable than any treaty from England with people of so base a condition'—? subjects.

divan, or executive council, and the burgesses were presumably Moors, of whom Roe says there were two.[1]

It is particularly interesting that, though he had yielded the points for which Algiers had contended, Roe was at pains to explain to the privy council how much we were gaining for nothing that was not contained in the existing capitulations. Eight hundred slaves were to be restored against forty Turks on the arrival of a consul, while we promised not to protect their enemies or carry arms or goods for them.

If any do transporte such goods it shall be at their own perill, without prohibition absolute or breach of peace, and this is incident and agreed in all treaties *That enemyes goods are lawfull prize.* Neither could I refuse to agree to *what is right in itself neither attempt to bridle them.* . . . I avoided an absolute contract and left it to the adventure of those who for their own gayne would hazard it.

In other words, instead of binding them 'in fast chaines', he resorted to quibbles and obscurity to save the king's honour, setting a precedent in treaty-making which resulted in serious and sometimes very costly difficulties in the future.

Of the various obstacles to be surmounted, which almost certainly included the bitter hostility of other foreign representatives at Constantinople, not the least was the task of obtaining the co-operation of the Company in providing any funds that might be required. Roe, whose previous experience had left him few illusions on that score, wrote without delay to Calvert, beseeching him 'that so good a work, now allmost perfect, may not perish for want on our parts who complayne and yet do nothing; least I say to the merchants (whose slowness I know) "I have piped but ye danced not"'. His apprehensions were only too well founded.[2]

It is remarkable that so important a treaty—a landmark in our relations with Algiers—should have been the subject of so much misinformation. Playfair says that this 'Utopian Treaty', which the Algerines never attempted to keep, was concluded

---

[1] Roe, pp. 118 and 177; S.P. 103. 1, ff. 67 to 71. The preamble read: 'Notwithstanding the privilege of free trade there have happened some discontents and quarrels between the said English nation and the souldiery of Tunis and Algiers', ibid., f. 67. The articles were confirmed at Algiers by the bashaw, divan, mufti, cadis, and captains of foot, who sent a messenger to the king 'with their letters and instruments sealed', Roe, pp. 336–7.

[2] Ibid., pp. 139–40, 143, and 177.

at Algiers in March 1622; according to the *Dictionary of National Biography* it was 'patched up' in 1624; Lane-Poole simply records that 'Sir Thomas Roe made a Treaty which turned out to be waste paper'. The State Papers at the Public Record Office, from which Playfair appears to quote, show, however, that it was ratified and signed by the Grand Signior Mustapha at Constantinople in March 1623 and was reconfirmed by Sultan Morat, who succeeded in August 1623, and by King Charles on his accession in 1625. The minutes of the privy council record its ratification by us in July 1623. An endorsement on our copy of the treaty reads: 'This peace thus concluded was *well and exactly observed* for five years and not one English ship assayled or taken and at least 600 mariners released from a miserable captivity.'[1]

There is, indeed, abundant evidence in the form of letters from Frizell and Leate or complaints from Morat and other officials of Algiers or correspondence of the secretary of state with the council or a royal proclamation of Charles I that the treaty was well kept by the Algerines and constantly broken by us. Even Roe, who has been quoted to the contrary and was gradually profiting by experience, reports late in 1626 'in generall the peace hath been kept' by Algiers and 'I do believe it will be dayly better observed', and he is increasingly conscious of the shortcomings on our part. Nothing could, however, be more explicit than the statement of Francis Knight: '*I am certain that the last peace was broken by the English, by whom those of Algiers received many injuries and long suffered them before they sought the least revenge.*'[2]

Indeed these states seem to have been only too anxious to make peace, for as early as November 1622 Calvert wrote to Roe: 'I cannot but beleeve you have settled all things well at Algiers and Tunis, for the safety of the Levant merchants from pyratts, for I have no complaints from them at the boorde now a dayes.'[3] Experience taught Roe that they might be well-intentioned and even profitable allies, and that our interests might be prejudiced by the aggressive acts of Christian ships, including our own, of which he writes 'if these courses be

---

[1] S.P. 103. 1, f. 71; Knolles (Nabbes), p. 1444.
[2] S.P. 71. 1, ff. 91 and 99 b; Roe, p. 574; Osborne, ii. 488.
[3] Roe, p. 107.

continued we shall shortlie have no port nor trade in the Levant'. His experiences on his return journey from Constantinople to Venice may have taught him as much on that subject as his seven years residence in Turkey.[1]

The provision in the treaty for the appointment of a consul, which Roe left as vague as possible, was intended as a concession, not to ourselves who already enjoyed that privilege under the capitulations, but to the Algerines who insisted, as a condition precedent, on the dispatch of a suitable person, 'discreet, wise and of good quality', to watch over the fulfilment of the treaty or, as the Dey of Tunis later expressed it to Charles II, to 'do justice' between the two countries.[2]

Roe's action in appointing a provisional consul at Tunis was apparently ratified by the Company, when on 21 August 1623 it issued a commission to William Cooke as consul there with a small salary, consulage on ships, and permission to trade, but not in 'pirate goods', presumably because it had twice been in trouble—in England and Turkey—on that very account.[3] The appointment may never have become effective in its eyes. It was soon cancelled owing to Cooke's failure to furnish the required security for his 'good carriage', but he probably continued to act, as there was an English consul there in 1626, through whose efforts the captain of one of our ships was released.[4] It is not unlikely that it was to fill a vacancy caused by his death or departure that King Charles appointed William Woodhouse in 1638.[5] Though the Company refused to have anything to do with that affair, it did not scruple later to complicate matters by interference, and even came to claim the appointment as a part of its prerogative.

The appointment on 24 July 1623 to Algiers of James Frizell on the same terms but at a somewhat higher salary[6] caused considerable stir. The Venetian representative in London reported on 18 August that 'the English merchants have made a compact with the ever formidable pirates of Algiers and for the greater security they have chosen a consul to reside in

[1] Roe, pp. 825–7. Travelling in Rainsborough's ship he and his wife suffered slightly from a Maltese corsair, Knolles (Nabbes), p. 1498.
[2] Roe, p. 140; S.P. 102. 1, f. 67.
[3] S.P. 105. 148, f. 96; in 1607 and 1617.
[4] V.S.P. 1626–8, pp. 117–18.   [5] Thurloe, *State Papers*, i. 2.
[6] S.P. 105. 148, f. 93.

Algiers', adding, however, that his departure had been deferred on account of Spanish objections. A further report of 9 September, which is remarkably consistent with Roe's correspondence, states that the consul has left, that the peace will be arranged, that the ambassador began the negotiations, that the king disliked the proceeding but yielded out of compassion for the slaves, and that 800 English were to be surrendered against 40 Turks sold, by Mansel and others, into Sicily and Spain, ending with an echo of Roe's rather incongruous argument 'they say the pirates will gain more from trade than piracy'.[1]

Whether the Company ever made any real attempt to open up trade with Algiers or whether its interest was confined to the prospect of regaining those commercial privileges, which the English enjoyed at the expense of the French for some years prior to 1608, is not clear.[2] It certainly had no intention of assuming any public obligations, if that could be avoided. It soon lost interest in a post which showed no promise of immediate profit, and might entail some responsibility for the clearance or redemption of slaves with which Frizell's letters were mainly concerned. It is significant that, unlike most other countries, England had no fund at Constantinople for the redemption of captives, and that King James, whose conscience was so tender about dealing with pirates, could do no better, when importuned by the wives and kindred of those who should have been delivered under the treaty, than treat them to 'hard usage both in words or worse'. Frizell complained bitterly of the Company's 'neglect of so naughty a business', and Roe spoke of Leate, to whom it tried to transfer its responsibilities, as 'a sad example to warne others not to serve the publique at their owne hazard and ruyne'.[3]

In April 1626 the Company wrote to Frizell, whose transactions may have become somewhat confused, 'we know not what to make of your letters', which do not seem to have been even acknowledged, and that 'we did suppose that your presence there would have wrought better effect but we see that you

---

[1] V.S.P. 1623–5, pp. 95 and 107.

[2] 'Les Agents de la Compagnie de vingt bateaux qui trafiquaient dans les pays barbaresques' endeavoured by lavish gifts to recover their concessions at Bona and Collo, Plantet, i. 14 n.; de Grammont, pp. 136–7; Masson, *Établissements,* pp. 107–8 n.

[3] Cal. S.P.D. 1623–5, p. 13; S.P. 71. 1, f. 154; Roe, p. 574.

prevail little'.[1] This vague criticism is the more unexpected in view of the fact that we had made little attempt to keep the terms of the treaty, in contrast, as the records of the privy council show, with the conduct of the Algerines; that the secretary of state could not 'charge his mind' with ever having had a copy of the treaty; and that King Charles had behaved so discourteously to the Algiers ambassador that there was fear of his leaving in a rage after receiving, in the words of the Duke of Buckingham, 'injury upon injury'.[2]

The Company lost no further time in deciding to sever all connexion, consular or commercial, with 'those barbarous places', and to notify the privy council of the closing of the consulates or, more strictly, of the cessation of its responsibility for them. While its action was approved, it was apparently ordered to indemnify Leate for part of his expenditure.[3]

From this time the connexion of the Company with Barbary may be said to have ceased. As in the case of Egypt some time before, it was not interested in maintaining trade relations 'even if it rayned gold', and the French, who were in some respects less well equipped for the purpose, reaped the benefit.[4]

It may be that it realized its inadequacy to deal with such problems and had already begun its policy of restricting activities to Turkey proper, since at about the same time it ended its consular responsibilities in Italy. It would otherwise seem inexplicable that it did not consult its own ambassador, who was taking a rosier view of the situation in Barbary and of the abilities of Frizell,[5] or fall in line with the policy of the government, which was extremely anxious to secure the good-will of the peoples of the Barbary coast since the outbreak of the war with Spain. Perhaps it was deterred by the possible risks and additional expenditure entailed by this new complication, as it must have been clear that the political orientation of Barbary had become quite different from that of the Ottoman state. The conduct of relations with Tunis and Algiers

---

[1] S.P. 105. 148, f. 142.

[2] Cals. S.P.D. 1628-9, p. 322, and 1625-6, p. 113. Sent to inquire why the Turks in England had not been restored, he brought presents and over 100 freed captives, Birch, *Charles I*, i. 11 and 15.

[3] S.P. 105. 148, f. 143; Cal. S.P.D. Add. 1625-49, p. 7; A.P.C. 1623 to 1626. Fees due to the Porte had to be paid.

[4] De Grammont, pp. 165-75.   [5] Roe, pp. 517, 548, and 574.

through far-distant Constantinople, where they had no form of representation, had become an obvious anomaly, if not absurdity, and the abolition of the Company's monopoly removed restrictions on more enterprising merchants.

The relief felt by the Company must have been immediate, as two questions arose at once in which it had no desire to be involved. Roe had apparently decided that an annual allowance should be made to the bashaw at Algiers for the maintenance of the peace, and the privy council was investigating the question of the source from which this payment should be made, though the money might have been better employed in arranging for the clearance of the unfortunate captives and the fulfilment of other provisions of Roe's treaty.[1]

An even more serious and ominous development, following on our hostilities with Spain, was the plundering of an Algiers cruiser by one of our ships engaged in the attack on Cadiz. Such an unfortunate incident, coming on top of a series of infractions of the treaty and the 'ancient Capitulations', previously excused as the work of 'private men', may well have seemed the last straw. An *avania* or fine of about £6,000 was imposed in retaliation, and the consul and merchants temporarily imprisoned.[2] Shortly afterwards the bashaw, in whom Roe had placed so much reliance, was deposed for his misconduct by the soldiers, whom Roe reported to 'have erected a commonwealth and chosen officers'.[3]

He indeed, rather surprisingly, tended to condone the occurrence, which he attributed in the first place to 'some occasion' for resentment given by our fleet, on the grounds that 'the injurye was done by the violence and necessitye of one man against the will of the councell of that towne'; that the deed had been disavowed and reparation offered to Frizell; and that 'in generall the peace hath been kept'. As to the question of *avanias*, which according to such authorities as North and Masson were not necessarily unwarranted, he points out that 'such like and greater extortions have bene here against Constantinople and Aleppo where they yet continew'.[4] He was soon to see our Aleppo merchants pay a very much larger one

[1] A.P.C. 1626, pp. 123 and 354.
[2] Cals. S.P.D. 1625–49, p. 478, and 1628–9, p. 425.
[3] Roe, p. 574.   [4] Ibid., pp. 820–1.

on account of the illegal acts of Digby's squadron. The sultan informed King Charles in reply to his letter of complaint that he had ordered that the goods impounded should be released, and that 'your consull sent into those ports according to ancient custome, shalbe enterteyned and honored'.[1] Such commands were, indeed, little more than ratifications of accomplished facts, and the authority of the sultan in Algiers from this time, except in matters affecting the empire as a whole, may have become negligible. He was in fact unable to keep order in his own country.

The two persons principally affected, Frizell and Leate, do not appear to have held the Algerines but their own country-men, including the Company, responsible for their ensuing difficulties, and our government evidently did not regard the affair as a breach of treaty or at least as entirely unjustified.

At all events the importance of securing the goodwill of the Barbary States, which was already recognized in Roe's dis-patches, was officially emphasized by the issue on 22 October 1628 of a royal proclamation, calling on His Majesty's subjects to refrain from acts of violence against the people or ships of Algiers, Tunis, Tetuan, and Sallee,[2] and by a remarkable letter from the secretary of state to the privy council, recom-mending not only the appointment of consuls at those places, but that no letters of marque should be issued without a clause *specifically prohibiting* any action against those peoples.[3] A pretext had been found for inducing King Charles to give a gracious farewell audience to the Algiers ambassador,[4] who, contrary to Playfair's statement, made a very favourable report on his reception in England. The bashaw soon afterwards thanked His Majesty for sending him some guns, but intimated the acceptability of a gift of ammunition as well.[5]

More substantial and consistent measures were, however, essential if the peace was to be secured. It is clear that no

---

[1] Roe, p. 604. The 'free pratique and commerce in those ports' were 'very profitable and commodious to both our kyngdomes'.

[2] Cal. S̆.P.D. 1628–9, p. 356.

[3] S.P. 71. 1, f. 87.

[4] Treatment of Governor Wyatt with 'so much equity and humanity', Cal. S.P.D. 1625–49, pp. 47–48.

[5] S.P. 102. 1, f. 18. Charles had earlier requested 'subsistence and assistance to Buckingham's fleet', ibid., f. 10.

effective control was exercised over our shipping in those waters, and no attempt seems to have been made to return the captured Turks in spite of frequent pressure and the actual presence of some of them in England.[1] The maintenance of a suitable consul was the corner-stone of the treaty, but Frizell's urgent requests for official recognition and financial assistance were ignored, although Leate and Roe were agreed that he should be given every encouragement to remain, since they knew of no other 'instrument so fitt', because of his industry, his patience, his popularity, and his influence.[2] He had indeed rendered great assistance in arranging the return of six hundred captives and redeeming a Spanish friar, who was exchanged for forty English seamen in prison at Dunkirk.[3]

As he had foretold, however, his usefulness was rapidly coming to an end, partly through lack of funds and partly through our illegalities. In a letter of 20 May 1629 he complains to the ambassador at Constantinople of the violent acts of English ships, particularly the *Adventure* trading to Tetuan and Sallee, in seizing the prizes and Christian slaves of the Algerines, who have now given *twelve months notice of a rupture*. A letter of 8 December to the secretary of state indicates that the peace has been broken, and the following year it is recorded that 'those of Algiers were so incensed' by direct violations of the treaty 'that they seized upon Mr. Frizell the Consull and the rest of the English and their goods with intent to spare neither lyves nor goods', in spite of the consul's plea that 'these acts were done by private men without the knowledge of his Majesty'.[4]

Such action was not regarded as entirely abnormal in those days or as constituting a definite rupture. It merely impressed on our government the necessity of taking at long last some remedial action. In view of the fact that 'some violences were committed on both sides to the breach of the peace and it cannot be denied but the English have in some things directly violated the Conditions', it was proposed to rectify the situation by punishing the guilty, sending an agent to Algiers 'to doe the

[1] List of Turks and Moors 'wandering and begging about the City of London', S.P. 71. 1, f. 74. Some returned in 1628, S.P. 98, Bu. 3, f. 79.
[2] Roe, p. 574.
[3] Cal. S.P.D. 1627–8, p. 101. Part of compensation by bashaw?
[4] S.P. 71. 1, ff. 93 and 95.

offices required', appointing a consul 'to reside there', and sending royal letters in reply to those of the bashaw.[1]

The views of Francis Knight, who was captured and enslaved in 1631 and had an exceptional insight into conditions at Algiers, are always illuminating. It was his belief that the Algerines had 'a just propension to a good firm and constant peace', which would best be preserved by the appointment of a suitable person as consul there and of an Algiers army officer as agent in England.[2]

To his contention that a peaceful accommodation was impeded or frustrated by vested interests in England might have been added the obstinacy and inconsistency of King Charles, at that time on friendly terms with the rulers of Tetuan and Sallee and supplying powder to our most dangerous enemies at Dunkirk.[3]

The people at Algiers do not seem to have been particularly hostile or vindictive. Frizell and the merchants were evidently soon at liberty, and in 1632 two traders of Yarmouth refer casually to their factor in Algiers.[4] Knight's statement that 'England is admired by all Turks' is generally supported by our own records or experiences of Barbary over two centuries. His belief that there were good opportunities for English trade with Algiers at that time is confirmed by events at other ports of Barbary and also by a petition of Huett Leate in the year 1638 requesting that, to offset his father's losses, he might be granted the monopoly for some years of trade to Tunis and Algiers, 'places that will vent good store of cloth'.[5] Leate seems to have been even then agent for the redemption of slaves there, probably in conjunction with Frizell who continued to function up to that year, though presumably in a very restricted manner, as Knight makes no mention of him.

Apart from the fact that conclusion of peace with Spain had lessened the importance of close relations with Algiers, English initiative may well have been temporarily paralysed by the desperate and humiliating plight to which the country was reduced when, after the failure of the Rochelle expedition, the

[1] *Memorial of the Business of Algiers*, 1630, S.P. 71. 1, f. 137.
[2] Osborne, ii. 488.   [3] Fulton, p. 327.
[4] Cal. S.P.D. 1631-3, pp. 478-9.
[5] Cal. S.P.D. 1637-8, p. 255; S.P. 71. 1, f. 159.

channel and adjacent seas were, according to Burchett, infested with the privateers of neighbouring countries, as well as, it may be added, our own pirates. Money, too, was described as a 'great consideration', and neither the Company nor any other body was prepared to provide for the maintenance of consulates in Barbary, the redemption of captives, or the settlement of claims. Frizell's plea for the dispatch of money to release him 'out of thraldom and gett home and discharge his duties to his Majesty' fell on deaf ears, now that the number of captives had increased to 340, including 20 men and 89 women and children from the recent raid on Baltimore.[1]

A surprising amount of publicity has been given to this raid and also to the smaller one in 1640 on the Cornish coast, which seem to have been regarded as quite new developments. They were, however, in accordance with the spirit of the times, and could not be compared with earlier ones—in which English ships probably played a leading part—on the Algiers towns of Bona and Bresk or some which the Algerines had made on the Canaries and Gibraltar—the latter nearly a century before. The occurrence of such a raid, in time of open war, had long been predicted; the chief concern seems to have been its exposure of our naval weakness; and it did not reach the king's ears until some months later. Quite apart from a considerable variety of marauders from Christian countries, there were at the time flourishing establishments of pirates at Torbay and Milford Haven, as well as in Ireland. Indeed, Baltimore, which Playfair represents as a peaceful village, had had the reputation of being one of the principal pirate bases, and the expedition was, in Knight's appropriate phrase, 'pilated' by a native son. Father Dan's pathetic picture of the arrival of the helpless captives is at best drawn at second hand, as his short acquaintance with Algiers only began three years later. Knight, who arrived in January 1631, makes no allusion to it at all.

It may, however, have helped to make the breach more definite and also, perhaps, have suggested a facile solution of the problem. In 1632 proposals were made by Roe, Pindar, and Wolstenholme, who might be regarded as leading representatives of vested interests, and by Captain Rainsborough, who supplied the naval knowledge—though there is no evidence

[1] Ibid., f. 99 b, 10 Aug. 1631. App. H.

as to what personal experience, if any, they had of the area in question. They recommended, as the best way of reducing Algiers, Tunis, and Sallee to reason or of suppressing the pirates of Algiers, that 'the King grant Commission to make full prize of all the shipps and subjects of Algiers, Tunis and Sallee without any duty to the Admiralty and to sell them as slaves; to land in any part of their dominions to waste burne and spoyle; to take women and children and doe to them as they have done unto us'. The grounds for the inclusion of Tunis and Sallee in this recommendation are not given. The privy council approved of the general idea of sending a 'fleet to take enough prisoners to redeem the slaves', since 'it was both impossible and inconvenient to think of redeeming captives by collection, contribution or at all by ransom' and 'bodies should not be gainful merchandize', especially as 'at Frizell's price', £50,000 would not suffice.[1]

Though the Levant Company was alarmed at the risk of molestation of trade and the Chief Justices of Ireland hoped that the English consul now 'lieger' at Algiers might do something for the captives,[2] and a suggestion was made two years later, in 1634, that ship-money might appropriately be used for the purpose,[3] this optimistic proposal continued to hold the field. By 1636 it had progressed to a decision that 'Algiers must certainly be taken by a compounded force of Christians', despite reports that 'Turkish' cruisers were enjoying the facilities of Breton ports. In 1638 the original plan was revived, with, however, the benefit of some maturer reflections. Rainsborough, for instance, recommended a blockade of Algiers which he estimated would be a matter of three or four years, while Roe and his colleagues made the even more unpractical suggestion of sending a 'strong fleet' as far east as Alexandria in order to paralyse the trade of Algiers, though we were unable to check piracy in our home waters and had no dependable ports of supply in the Mediterranean.[4]

---

[1] S.P. 71. 1, ff. 111 and 152.   [2] Cal. S.P. Ireland 1625–32, p. 646.

[3] Cal. S.P.D. 1634–5, pp. 401 and 610. Allegedly for protection from pirates and others, 'Turks enemies of the Christian name', Gardiner, vii. 369; Fulton, p. 253, though actually friendly to Turkey, Tunis, and Sallee. For official ignorance, see Cal. S.P.D. 1635, pp. 68–69.

[4] Cal. S.P.D. 1637–8, pp. 187 and 192; Fulton, pp. 327–8. Mention of Alexandria suggests deliberate piracy.

Meanwhile the war with Algiers was causing considerable damage to our trade and giving rise to constant complaint, especially from our western ports. The actual harm done seems, however, to have been considerably overestimated.[1] It was certainly caused in part by the ships of Sallee, now evidently a greater thorn in our side, or by those of France, Biscay, and Dunkirk, and in part by the panic or at least timidity prevailing in our ports, where people at times lay quaking in their beds and fishermen dare not put out to sea.

A historian of Cornwall suggests that, at a time when it was officially reported that 'Egypt was never more infested with caterpillars than the Land's End with Biscayners', the imagination was more impressed by Mohammedan pirates 'as messengers of life-long slavery and torture'.[2] Some years later, when very alarmist rumours of Turkish activities in western waters were current, our admirals regarded them as existing only in the minds of the inhabitants who 'fancy the crescent in all colours', even in the ensigns of His Majesty's ships sent for their protection.[3] The relatively little damage that appears to have been done at the time, mainly to very small fishing boats, evidently arose from the *combined* efforts of France and Sallee. The number of English ships taken into Algiers, mostly small, during some twelve years of warfare was, according to English reports, surprisingly small.

The number of captives taken was evidently also considerably exaggerated. The 3,000 petitioners mentioned in 1640, a number curiously identical with that very erroneously alleged to be there in 1626, represented about four times the number actually found by Cason in 1646.[4] The distress was probably aggravated by the periodical sermons and collections for captives on 'Brief Sundays' at the parish churches.

It was not until parliament got the upper hand that really effective steps were taken. In 1641 Charles was induced to

[1] In 1629–36 53 English ships were taken, S.P. 71. 1, f. 157—the exact number taken by France in peace 1674–6, p. 263 n. 5. In ?1640–5 five English ships were brought in, a fact disregarded by Oppenheim, p. 277, *Autobiography of the Rev. Devereux Spratt*, London, 1886.

[2] App. I. *Victoria County History, Cornwall*, i. 495. Compare reports of English 'cruel piracy' in the Red Sea and 'torturing the poor Mahometans', Birch, *Charles I*, ii. 265.

[3] Cal. S.P.D. 1636–7, pp. 151, 407, and 434.

[4] Cal. S.P.D. 1640–1, p. 134.

give his reluctant consent to an Act which earmarked a per-
centage of the customs receipts—henceforward frequently
known as the 'Algiers duty'—for defraying the cost of naval
expeditions to Barbary and the Levant or redeeming captives
there.[1]

Whether the former alternative was ever seriously considered is far from clear. It would rather seem that warships
were required at home for protection against possible Algerine
attacks, and that Barbary ventures would be left to private
ships, since in May 1641 the Venetian ambassador reported
that permission had been given to English ships to blockade
the Barbary coasts and plunder all vessels going there. He
added that twenty well-armed ships expected to extract great
profit from it, and that *those with most experience* fear they will
attack ships of friendly powers on the plea that they are going
to Barbary and carrying spoil to pirates'. The next year he
reported that ship-money was being levied on the pretext of
suppressing the pirates of Algiers and the rebellion in Ireland.[2]

In 1643 the Houses of Parliament dispatched an agent to
Algiers with a letter to the bashaw and instructions for 'Mr.
James Frizell, residing as consul at Argeir', regarding the
redemption of thousands of poor English captives remaining
there 'in cruel slavery'. Whether Frizell was still there is extremely doubtful, as he had apparently not been heard from
for about five years, when he had lamented: 'I doe verily
believe that never any of his Majesty's Ministers hath been so
neglected as I am.'[3] Official ignorance regarding Tunis seems
to have been still greater, since, though it was consistently
coupled with Algiers as one of those dens of pirates against
which drastic, and if possible lucrative, action must be taken,
our relations with it were, apparently, friendly and not un-
profitable. It was a port of call where we had a considerable
trading community, and Woodhouse continued to perform his
consular duties, until in 1650 he was replaced by a parliamentary nominee.

The mission to Algiers was completely successful. An account
of 25 August 1643 shows that 112 Englishmen and 22 strangers,

[1] Cals. S.P.D. 1640–1, p. 443, and 1641–3, p. 159.
[2] V.S.P. 1640–2, pp. 172 and 289.
[3] Playfair, pp. 50–51.

apparently taken on English ships, were actually redeemed. Arrangements were made for the redemption of others as soon as the money was forthcoming.[1] It was evident that nothing else need stand in the way of a resumption of amicable relations with Algiers or, indeed, with the rest of Barbary.

[1] Add. MS. 5849, f. 85 b. Spratt's much quoted denunciation was written 40 years later. He was better treated than previously in Ireland, see also W. Okeley's account in Harris, *Navigantium atque Itinerantium Bibliotheca, or a Compleat Collection of Voyages and Travels*, ii, Appendix.

XII

OUR RELATIONS WITH THE REGENCIES
1645 TO 1660

CONDITIONS in the Mediterranean can hardly have been as bad during the fifth decade of the century as might have been expected from some of the sensational reports in our archives or the constant references to piracy by Christian writers of various nations. Until Blake's appearance in 1655 the waters along the Barbary coast may well have been more peaceful than the English Channel, where French 'pirates' continued to be active.[1]

In 1641 de Ruyter began a series of voyages to the Barbary coast, principally to Sallee, and in 1651 'by trade and successful privateering' was able to retire in comfort. In 1641 the English were said to have monopolized the trade of Spain, and in 1645 they acquired their extraordinary privileges in Andalusia and the Canaries. In Italy, especially Tuscany and the Venetian Republic, we had developed important interests. In Turkey, notwithstanding the civil war at home, the Company was able to spend enormous sums to settle its internal differences. It required the new ambassador at Constantinople to give security in the sum of £10,000 and the consul at Patras of £3,000. Of special interest is the fact that Huett Leate appears to have been trading, or controlling our trade, with Algiers and Tunis from 1636 to 1645, in spite of a state of war with the former. Even as late as 1646 there was keen competition for our trading rights with Morocco.

It was consequently in a spirit of reasonable optimism that the Houses of Parliament in August 1645 dispatched Edmund Cason, one of the charter members of the Barbary Company, as their accredited agent to treat with the rulers of Algiers and Tunis for the release of English captives and the settling of a

---

[1] B. Whitelock, *Memorials of the English Affairs, 1625–60*, London, 1682, pp. 607 and 621. H.M.C. App. Sixth Report, pp. 436–43; Cal. S.P.D. 1655, p. 567; 'Pirateries réciproques' ended Nov. 1655, Lacour-Gayet, p. 198.

future peace 'for the security of the Merchants and the Mariners' Voyage'. He was provided with a 'ship of strength', the *Honour*, carrying a cargo of money and goods, but unfortunately it got no farther than Spain, where it was looted and accidentally set on fire.[1]

The following year the two houses sent him out again with the *Charles*, and on 1 September 1646 he reached Algiers, where he was welcomed by the bashaw and divan. A 'long and difficult treaty' was negotiated, after a detailed examination of the register of captives, and prices were agreed on. There were about 650 captives in the city and 100 more absent on service in Cretan waters. Difficulty arose because the owners did not wish to part with the captives at the 'first cost' or officially recorded purchase price; some of the English youths had turned Turk 'through beating and hard usage'; and some of the children, 'which they keep very galant', may not have wished to return. However, after the bashaw had 'entertained me with all courtesie, feasted me at his house and afterwards in his fields', everything was satisfactorily settled; 244 men, women, and children were redeemed and sent home in the *Charles* before the end of October. Ten thousand dollars were paid on account, and concessions were granted regarding rates of interest and export taxes.

Arrangements were then made for the dispatch of two ships with a greater cargo. Cason urged speed, as he was most anxious to complete the transaction before a change of bashaws took place, in view of the natural reluctance of the owners to part with their property, especially the women, who were usually worth double the original price, and the skilled craftsmen, including surgeons, who were greatly esteemed. Of those redeemed the highest price was paid for a woman.

The treaty, which was signed and sealed by the bashaw, divan, mufti, cadi, and 'Shoudes which be principall Justices of the peace', contained little that was new. Any ships might come to Algiers, 'as in former times, to buy and sell and no man to give Englishmen bad word or deed'. English ships were not to be harmed on the high seas, and no Englishman was to be bought or sold as a slave, though this was, as usual, qualified by the implications of another clause that 'no English subject,

[1] *Relation of Edmund Cason* (B.M. 1434. i. 4).

passenger on board any prize, was to be enslaved'. No corsairs of Tunis, Tripoli, or Sallee were to sell English prizes there, an important safeguard against possible double-dealing, and the usual privileges were assured for the personal and religious freedom of the consul and the guardianship of estates of deceased merchants.

It will be seen that no specific provision was made for maintaining the right of search or for punishing the English who engaged in contraband trade, points which Roe had admitted in principle. The bashaw did, however, make the not unreasonable stipulation that he 'expected our ships not to defend any other Nation who shall be in our Company from ships of the place'. He also insisted that, as Cason had secured a definite list of slaves with their agreed prices, he should remain until he had cleared them all.

Unfortunately, although parliament approved Cason's actions, the work of redemption proceeded slowly, either because money was scarce or, more probably, because the allotted funds were used for other purposes. Such procedure was of course by no means satisfactory to the slave-owners nor presumably to Cason, who died at his post some eight years later, and least of all to the hapless slaves. The work involved was probably considerable. Humphrey Oneby, who was also a Barbary merchant and perhaps a business associate of Cason, arrived as agent for the redemption. In 1649 he was appointed consul at the instance of the navy commissioners who were charged with that business, which had been repudiated by the Levant Company as a matter of purely 'publique concernement', and paid him a small salary. He and Cason seem to have lived together in a large house, apparently rented to them by the Algiers government, and presumably maintained a fairly large establishment by means of their business transactions and consular fees.

Playfair makes the customary accusations that 'it was hardly to be expected that this state of things would be of long continuance; however fair the promises of the Algerines might be they were made with the firm intention of breaking them on the first opportunity'. He goes on to say that Blake was sent out with very precise instructions to require instant restitution of English captives and ships. He has been faithfully followed by more authoritative historians in defiance of recorded facts and even of dates.[1]

Our own records, though disappointingly meagre, provide indubitable evidence that such difficulties as arose were not due to the ill will or misconduct of the Algerines or indeed of the Tunisians. That might be inferred from the letters of the committee of the navy relative to the appointments of the agents, Humphrey Oneby and Thomas Browne, as consuls at Algiers and Tunis, to facilitate the redemption of captives and 'promoting that good work' and a 'work of great charity', but such letters as we have from Cason and Oneby[2]—as also from Boothouse of Tunis[3]—leave no doubt on the subject.

In December 1652 Oneby writes to thank the committee for some of his arrears of salary and reports 'at present we have good quarter with these people which it is hoped may continue'. On the same date Cason presses for a remittance 'as I know not where to provide any money', except from some trade transaction, and gives particulars of the delivery of Englishmen taken on foreign ships. Cason's letters of April and May 1653, the latter of which reports the death of Oneby on the 16th, probably from the plague epidemic, show that the principal trouble was the failure to send ships for the transportation of captives, some of whom he had been holding for *four years*.

Oneby's letter of 4 April—his last—is very explicit.

We have fair usage from the Bashaw and Duana who promise that all things shall be performed by them according to the peace whereof we have no cause of complaint, for in the last six months they have given us eight of our men taken in their enemies ships and their ships being abroad they met with several English ships and commanded some but used them in a very friendly way and did them no harm so that we hope the peace will be maintained. I hope that you will give order to the commanders of your ships not to abuse any of the ships belonging to this port as Captains Wadsworth and Badiley formerly did which brought trouble and charge on us.

Badiley had himself reported taking English slaves out of Algerine ships, a high-handed proceeding which was contrary to our treaty, as they were presumably among those listed for redemption.

[1] July 1656, S.P.D. 1656–7, p. 49.
[2] S.P. 105. 150 and 151; Cals. S.P.D. 1649 to 1654.
[3] S.P. 71. 25, ff. 1 sqq., report of Sam Boothouse ?1656.

In August Cason reports that freed captives have been embarked on a ship for England, and that he does not intend to lodge any more in his house, as some of them have been troublesome. Since there are said to have been sixty English captives, 'earnestly waiting for liberty', in addition to ten others taken from Dutch ships and detained for 'port' charges,[1] it can hardly have been a very happy household. The long and virulent plague epidemic of those years cannot have added to its amenities.

Cason's death on 5 December 1654 was reported by Abraham Smedmore, his 'servant', to whom the bashaw had entrusted his property after an inventory had been taken. A letter was also transmitted from the divan expressing their desire to have another consul sent and confirm the peace with England. Cromwell replied, stating what arrangements had been made for the administration of the estate, expressing 'our resentment of their great care and endeavour', asking their further assistance in the settlement of Cason's affairs, and adding 'so shall the Divan perfect their good intentions and do a respect which will be acceptable unto us who shall be ready to return the like upon all occasions'.[2] It is probable that all the *English* captives had then been cleared. The final settlement of Cason's account in 1657 for the redemption of captives at Algiers showed a total payment out of Algiers duties of nearly £40,000, including a sum of £400 to Richard Cason who had assisted in the work.[3]

Cason never went to Tunis, where a new peace was probably not required, but merely passed on the necessary instruction to the merchants. We already had a consul and a considerable trading community there. An official report informs us that its government was 'civil and quiet', and that, 'though the people are rude to excess yet their Natural Fierceness and Barbarity is [so] subdued and moderated by the Magistrates' Rigour and Severity that the people may walk the citty and stray the country as quietly as in and about London'.

Unfortunately the same writer, the ex-consul Boothouse, when he first arrived at Tunis in 1650, 'found such unnatural discords or rather deadly feudes' between 'ye Consul Woodhouse, Mr. Brown and the rest [of the English merchants] as

---

[1] Cals. S.P.D. 1652-3, pp. 62 and 255, and 1653-4, pp. 52, 476, and 130.
[2] Thurloe, iii. 157 and 500-1.   [3] Cal. S.P.D. 1656-7, p. 282.

were indeed scandalous to the Christian profession' and rendered his countrymen 'contemptible to Turk, Jew and Gentile'. This was the more regrettable as the city of Tunis and the environs provided a good market for foreign goods and it was the only safe refuge 'for all the Levant Navigation'.

That was a difficult time in all English communities, but at Tunis conditions had probably been aggravated by ill-advised intervention from without. At all events a local merchant, Thomas Browne, had been selected as agent for the redemption of captives, perhaps because Woodhouse had received his commission from the king. Since, however, it was found that even the status of a navy agent was inadequate for the purpose, the Levant Company was instructed in November 1648 to arrange for the consular recognition of Browne at Tunis and of Oneby at Algiers. The company was, however, reluctant to be involved in the Barbary States, and the ambassador seems to have been so definitely obstructive as to confirm Woodhouse instead, an action which evidently placed the Dey in a quandary, and may have checked the delivery of captives.

It can only have been late in 1650 that Browne received the appointment. Almost immediately the Company began criticizing him and evidently superseded him by Boothouse, who, after temporarily acting as consul at Smyrna, had been sent to Tunis to protect a valuable estate belonging to the Bowyer family from Browne's alleged maladministration. There is nothing to show that the Company's action was sanctioned either by the Porte or by the council of state, which had been entrusted by parliament with all such matters. Apparently Boothouse, unfortunately for himself, assumed control, while Browne, who had previously committed the cardinal sin of inviting the Dey's intervention in the affairs of the English community, sent his brother to England to protest.

Some time in 1651 Stephen Mitchell, master of a ship most inappropriately named the *Goodwill* and engaged in the Levant trade, contracted for the conveyance of thirty-two Turks from Tunis to Smyrna. His intentions may have been dubious from the outset, as he would not wait for an armed escort as far as Crete. At all events, soon after leaving he met some Maltese galleys, and though, according to Boothouse, these had neither the legal right nor the physical power to enforce a search, he voluntarily delivered up the Turks for a large sum of money after his crew had plundered their persons and belongings. When news reached Tunis of this occurrence and the enslavement of the passengers in the galleys there was not unnaturally an outburst of indignation. Boothouse was thrown into gaol as security for their redemption and perhaps also for his own protection, for in those days even ambassadors in Christian countries, including our own, enjoyed little security.

As it chanced, Admiral Penn's squadron arrived five days later and was not ill received. He evidently found the merchants at liberty, as they supplied him with some provisions—at least he thought they did—and he tried to arrange through Browne for other supplies, which were not then available. Browne, however, warned him soon afterwards that the Dey would not be willing to let him have provisions on his return, unless he sold his prizes there, that being in fact the only practical method of paying for supplies, except at those very few ports where the Admiralty could arrange a credit.[1]

Boothouse was allowed to proceed with Penn to Sicily, so as to negotiate for the release of the captives, and, according to his account, was nearly murdered by Browne in the street. He found the ransom demanded by the Maltese to be exorbitant and was only able to obtain some relief for the unfortunate men, before proceeding to London to take up the case there. In this he was unsuccessful and, though Mitchell was arrested, he was soon released, presumably because he had committed no offence under English law. The Dey, seeing no prospect of compensation, evidently adopted, after considerable delay, the course which had long been sanctioned in such cases, especially by our own practice, authorizing the capture of an English ship in reprisal. I have found no evidence for statements that more than one was seized or that the Dey issued instructions for their indiscriminate capture—which was obviously not the case—or even that this ship was actually taken on the high seas.

The ship was the *Princess* (or *Principesa* recently taken from Spain, presumably also in reprisal). It was returning from

---

[1] *Memorials of Sir William Penn*, ed. Granville Penn, 2 vols., London, 1833, i. 345–6 and 350. Penn wrote the Grand Master, 29 June 1651, requesting the Turks' return, Mifsud, pp. 247–8 n.

Zante with a cargo of currants and represented a venture by Admiral Badiley and some of his associates into that privileged market. The Venetian agent in London jumped joyfully at the conclusion that Badiley would gladly take command of the expedition, which was, however, eventually entrusted to Blake, 'not only from a detestation of piracy but in the hope of recouping his own loss'.[1] It may, indeed, be that trouble first arose from uncertainty as to the true status of the vessel, since the only official record is of the capture of a 'Dunkirk frigate' with a cargo of currants for London.[2] Probably the crew were not enslaved but held as hostages.

Whether any negotiations took place to adjust the matter is not clear, but very little time for them can have elapsed before Cromwell instructed Blake to present a demand for the restitution of the ship, cargo, and crew, though not apparently of any other English property. The instructions seem to have been based on the same strange conception of negotiation as contained in Mansel's orders or practised by French and Dutch commanders. An ultimatum was to be delivered—in this case in the form of a letter from Cromwell—without any provision for negotiation or the consideration of counter-claims, and in the event of non-compliance pressure was to be applied by capturing the country's ships, thenceforward designated as 'pirates', special care being taken not to infringe Turkish sovereignty on shore. This practice proved on the whole costly and usually unsuccessful.[3]

Blake evidently did not arrive at Tunis, February 1655, in a conciliatory mood, as he immediately blockaded the nine ships, possibly a Barbary contingent bound for Turkish operations in Crete,[4] which he found anchored off Porto Farina. He was probably in a hurry to proceed with more important business, and the refusal of the Dey to comply with his demands or facilitate his stay by furnishing him with water and provisions placed him in an awkward position. He hoped to solve it by destroying the ships which, unmanned and dismantled, were anchored as close as possible to the protecting fort, justifying

---

[1] V.S.P. 1653–4, p. 231.   [2] Cal. S.P.D. 1653–4, p. 313.
[3] Corbett, i. 271 and 275–6.
[4] *Blake's Letters* (N.R.S.), ed. J. R. Powell, London, 1937. A composite Barbary squadron operated there from 1645.

this extension of his official instructions (with Cromwell's eventual approval) by the insolence and intractability of the Tunisians 'denying us all commerce of civility and hindering all others as much as they could from the same' and by the plea that 'these barbarous provocations did so work upon our spirits that we judged it necessary for the honour of our fleet, our nation and religion, seeing they would not deal with us as friends to make them feel as enemies'. The Dey's reported protest 'trouble me with no more papers' suggests that he was steadily served with an inflexible ultimatum in the shape of Cromwell's letter.[1]

How far Blake was justified in claiming that 'the barbarous carriage of these pirates did turn the scale' may be judged from the fact that Browne continued to act as consul, that English merchants were trading ashore, and two English merchant ships visited the port during Blake's visit. It is also worth recording that, though Browne left with the fleet, there is evidence that trading and consular activities alike were carried on during the ensuing years of hostilities, and that both Boothouse and Browne were anxious to return to the consulate. There seems no reason to assume that the attitude of the Dey was either unreasonable or undignified, and it surely compared more than favourably with the 'shameless craft' of the policy towards Spain, which Blake was about to put into execution. D'Arvieux later reports having heard good accounts of him. He showed himself very friendly to the French vicar general who actually at this time was administering sixteen Catholic places of worship in Tunis in addition to five at Bizerta. A year later Boothouse went on record that we had not suffered 'any private or publique detriment which hath not partly or totally derived' from our own actions there, and one of his successors paid a tribute to the friendly attitude of Tunis, referring to the French and Dutch as the pirates and to this particular Dey as 'the good old King'.[2]

Both the scope and ultimate success of Blake's brilliantly executed operation seem to have been greatly exaggerated. Weale's enthusiastic description of it as 'a peece of service that

---

[1] *Journal of John Weale* (N.R.S.), ed. J. R. Powell, London, 1952, p. 109.

[2] S.P. 71. 26, f. 147; Rycaut, p. 138. Once a galley-slave in Malta, he was as Dey (1653–65) commended for his 'bonne conduite et belles actions', *Histoire des dernières révolutions*, p. 32. See L. Misermont, *Études sur Jean le Vacher*, 1917, p. 32, and the Company's grateful letter of 25 Sept. 1654, Cal. S.P.D. 1654, p. 371.

has not been paralleled in this part of the world', which he was then visiting for the first time, would have amazed the Algerines and Tunisians, who had suffered much worse blows during the century, sometimes at that notoriously vulnerable spot and sometimes apparently by English ships. Even the exaggerated reports which reached London seem to have made no permanent impression. Ten years later a French admiral, after a similar but smaller action at the very same place, remarked complacently that the English had never done anything like it.[1]

The immediate and subsequent result of the action has been consistently claimed by modern writers as a signal triumph for our naval power and the foundation of our national prestige in the Mediterranean. A typical description shows Blake making the round of the Mediterranean with an irresistible fleet, showing the flag, insisting on the settlement of old accounts, and letting princes and pirates see the force which could and would come to the help of every aggrieved subject of the rulers of Great Britain and Ireland. At the time of his death, however, our position in Barbary was very critical and our stock very low. An appreciation of 1816 seems to be approximately correct: 'The success of Blake (who never failed) in burning the Tunisian fleet at the Goleta was as detrimental to our Mediterranean commerce as the failure of Mansel.'[2]

So far from being able to dictate terms to Tunis Blake was reduced to approaching the Dey again through Consul Browne, only to be informed that he must settle with the sultan for the damage done to the ships and fort and that 'we have our subsistence from the land without needing aught from the sea, neither do we expect anything from sea and therefore he that will negotiate with us let him come ashore and he that will not let him chose (*sic*)'—a position that seems to have been strictly correct.[3]

Blake, who was in desperate need of provisions, 'now drawing very near to expiration', decided to leave at once for Algiers, the only place where he could expect to obtain any, 'if they will', and left Tunis without securing 'the least compensation'.

---

[1] Jal, *Abraham du Quesne et la marine de son temps*, i. 344.

[2] *A.R.* 1816, p. 325. Compare Madrid report, 24 May 1656: 'The Barbary pirates puffed up by their late victory are cruising about those waters with audacious licence', V.S.P. 1655–6, p. 221, with Carlyle, iv. 231; see p. 11, n. 2.

[3] *Blake's Letters*, p. 319.

A common variant of the story relates that 'the Dey of Tunis was thoroughly cowed and, when Blake returned from Tripoli where he had obtained satisfaction, he received the complete submission of the Dey'. In fact, however, he did not ever go to Tripoli, though that had been his original intention, or see Tunis again. From that time we were at war with both. He lost no time, however, in sending an explanation of his proceedings through our ambassador to the sultan, who was probably already fully occupied with his own troubles. It was doubtless with considerable relief that the London merchants learned that the earlier reports of the execution of their factors and confiscation of their property in Turkey were without foundation.[1]

The following year a petition from Richard Badiley and his associates referred to a plan to send a merchant vessel to Tunis to redeem the cargo of the *Princess*, which suggests that as far as they knew, it had not actually been condemned.[2] It is quite possible that the proposal was carried out, since the total number of captives finally redeemed by Admiral Stokes after three years of hostilities was only seventy-two, of whom three were women. Under Stokes's treaty, which was enthusiastically welcomed by the Admiralty, there was no question of the restoration of ships or cargoes or even of that valuable property which had been entrusted to Boothouse and subsequently sequestrated by the Dey. In 1661 the ambassador at Constantinople, who seems to have placed all the blame on the captain of the *Goodwill*, desired that a warrant should be granted to the English consul at Tunis—once more Browne—to make a moderate levy on English goods there and so compensate the London owners.[3]

Among other provisions of that treaty, which could hardly have been palatable to our self-esteem, was the express stipulation that 'if any English ships receive on board any goods or passengers belonging to the kingdom of Tunis they must defend both them and their goods as far as in their power and not deliver them to the enemy'. A similar clause was subsequently inserted in our other treaties with Barbary, thereby entailing new duties and responsibilities for our consuls and recurrent embarrassment for our government. Another infraction at

---

[1] App. Sixth Report, p. 439.   [2] Cal. S.P.D. 1656–7, p. 502.
[3] H.M.C. Finch Papers, i. 100.

Tunis some forty years later may have necessitated an innovation in the procedure of the High Court of Admiralty.[1]

The conventional pictures of Blake's triumphant proceedings at Algiers are equally erroneous. He did not find the city 'in such consternation that he liberated the whole body of British slaves for a trifling sum', nor is there any foundation for the claim that

his exploit had already told. Within a week of it, while still before Tunis, he had received a deferential invitation from the Dey of Algiers to negotiate. . . . His stay lasted barely a fortnight, but so great was the effect of his lesson to Tunis that it was enough to do his work and do it well. So far from finding any resistance he was received with marked respect. Victuals, water, everything he asked for was readily furnished.[2]

The receipt of the invitation in time was a physical impossibility—it is even possible that the news of the action had not reached Algiers before the arrival of Blake, who was clearly uncertain as to the nature of his reception there—and there was no question of negotiations. In fact the real purpose of Blake's visit to the coast seems to have been the confirmation of treaties or the renewal of peace after Cromwell's elevation to the rank of Protector. We were on very good terms with Algiers, as is evident not only from Cromwell's letter of about this date, but from the courtesies which Blake's fleet had received from Algerine cruisers on entering the Mediterranean, including the delivery of Englishmen rescued out of Sallee vessels.[3] The unwarranted assumption that the Algerines, whose ships are said to have been granted by the Commonwealth government facilities at two English ports,[4] were pirates and necessarily at war with us has induced such eminent historians as Gardiner and Corbett to try to alter as 'impossible' the very natural date —July 1656—of Cromwell's instructions to Blake to take strong measures against Algiers—instructions which Blake and his successors were in no position to implement.[5]

[1] F.O. 335. 1, Bu. 11, Dec. 1689.
[2] Corbett, i. 311–12, but *Merchant's Delight* arrived before the action.
[3] *Weale, Journal*, pp. 93–94; Whitelocke, p. 609.
[4] V.S.P. 1647–52, p. 42. Stokes's treaty provided for reciprocal treatment at English and Tunis ports.
[5] Gardiner suggested 1654, *History of the Commonwealth and Protectorate, 1649–*

He arrived at Algiers, apparently for the only time, on 28 April 1655, more than three weeks after his action at Porto Farina, with the evident intention of being conciliatory. His report of the visit could hardly have been briefer. After stating that he had left Tunis for Algiers to supply himself with victuals —for it seems clear that he did not succeed in getting anything but water at Cagliari on the way—he continues, 'the tenth May (having well refreshed our men, taken aboard a considerable store of bread and as much beef as we could spend while it was good, placed an Agent (the former being dead) and renewed the capitulations with those of the place) we put to sea'. Even this very inadequate report was not written—at sea off Cape Mary—until 12 June, probably because his mind was occupied with new and more important developments, and he had obtained what he wanted at Algiers.

Unfortunately he did not realize the consequences of this negligence until more than a year later, when he found it necessary to trouble Cromwell 'with an old business', and to relate in rather more detail those proceedings at Algiers which urgently required official confirmation. He recalls that

having been at Algiers *for the relief of the fleet* I was necessitated to send one Mr. Browne ashore for the speedier procurement thereof; and also for a *further confirmation of the peace between us and them*, to appoint him in the quality of an agent to reside in that place, until the approbation of your Highness could be obtained. We had a good effect of our desires there, having received a seasonable and competent supply of victuals. And to the terms of the former peace there was added an article in favour of the Scots and Irish likewise, as your Highness may be informed by a paper which at that time was sent from the King and Divan of that place unto your Highness upon their importunity.

This second and slightly more informative letter was written as the result of a report from Browne—who, we learn elsewhere, was Robert Browne, a brother of the late consul at Tunis— 'complaining that for want of an answer from your Highness to that paper and confirmation of that warrant, which Mr. Browne had from me, they began very much to slight him,

1660, 3 vols., London, 1894–1903, iii. 373 n.; and Corbett, 1655, i. 276 n., regardless of relations with Algiers.

were in great aptness to break the peace'. Blake humbly
suggested that a letter should be promptly written, and that
money due to the Algerines—perhaps both for the captives and
for the supplies—should be duly paid, drawing attention at the
same time to the increasing size of the Algiers navy which, if
Venetian reports can be trusted, had in the meantime been
helping us against Spain. Instead of complying with this
advice or the sentiments of gratitude he had so recently
expressed, Cromwell appears to have sent, or at least drafted,
the very intemperate instructions of July 1656 already mentioned.[1]

How little importance Blake attached to his proceedings at
Algiers, apart from obtaining supplies, may be judged from the
fact that even in his second letter he gives no information about
Browne or his qualifications, though he does go to the length
of supplying his surname. While he refers to the extension of
Cason's treaty to the Irish and Scots—a relatively unimportant
matter—he makes no mention at all of the two articles which he
specifically added to it and which read as follows:

(1) That all Englishmen, Scotch, and Irish serving for wages
in any strangers ships *were to be slaves*; and
(2) that ships arriving from Leghorn and *Marseilles*, &c. with
passes of the bashaw and Duana were not to be molested.[2]

This peace appears to have been duly ratified. In December
Browne was oppointed 'His Highness' Consul' at Algiers with
a salary of £400 a year out of the captives' redemption fund.[3]
The first article must certainly have met with approval, as it
was inserted in Stokes's treaty with Tunis three years later and
also specifically or by implication in all subsequent treaties with
the Barbary States up to the reign of George III. It had been
recognized in substance by Roe, though he carefully avoided
express mention of it in his treaties, as also did Cason. The
French long tried to avoid the adoption of a similar clause, and
our acquiescence was probably not unconnected with the
Navigation Acts or the spirit that prompted them.

The number of captives actually redeemed at Algiers was
twenty-seven, at a cost of £1,435. 15*s*. 10*d*.[4] Since, in an

---

[1] *Blake's Letters*, pp. 297 and 362. [2] S.P. 103. 1, ff. 249 and 253.
[3] Cal. S.P.D. 1656–7, p. 194. [4] Cal. S.P.D. 1655–6, p. 129.

attempt to magnify Blake's achievements there, this sum has been described as 'trifling' or 'moderate', it should be pointed out that, not only was the price several times as much as Cromwell demanded for his Irish slaves, but that Stokes considered the rate to be embarrassingly extravagant and succeeded with some difficulty in obtaining better terms from Tunis.[1] Mountagu the next year refused to consider any payment for captives at Sallee, 'as dishonourable for us that appear before their port with the English standard'.[2]

Even that small amount seems to have been paid only after considerable delay, though the Commonwealth government did show itself more punctilious in this respect than the Stuart kings who preceded or followed it. In view of the grossly exaggerated estimates of British captives (who were not necessarily slaves) it may be added that the number whom Stokes redeemed at Tripoli, after three years of hostilities, appears to have been roughly the same as at Tunis or about 150 at the two places.

If the issue of Blake's activities and Cromwell's policy in this area proved a triumphant success, neither of them lived to see it. On the contrary they witnessed confirmation of Roe's warning: 'If these courses be continued we shall shortly have no port nor trade in the Levant' or 'no friend nor place to relieve with a drop of water'. The old maxim that the goodwill and facilities of the Barbary ports were essential to our ships in the Mediterranean, 'Spain being enemy', seems to have gone unheeded.

The first sign was the change in attitude towards Sallee, even when its ships were causing annoyance. 'A good composition' or 'an accommodation' or 'bringing them to amity' or 'to terms of compliance' or to 'terms of amity and agreement' are phrases which hardly suggest a dictatorial spirit. One of Blake's last recorded actions was the conclusion of a peace at Sallee, of which no particulars seem to be available beyond the fact that he redeemed all the English captives.[3]

Some months earlier a consulate and naval supply base had been established at Tetuan, which enabled Stokes and others to keep their station in the Straits of Gibraltar. Within the Mediterranean, however, the situation had become so unsatis-

---

[1] Cal. S.P.D. 1657–8, p. 307.   [2] *Blake's Letters*, p. 418.
[3] Thurloe, vi. 368; Cal. Clarendon, iii. 310.

factory that, when Stokes was at Tunis, he found his ships too foul to do good service and his men 'daily falling down for want of refreshments'. He was even less well situated than Blake at Algiers, and felt that the 'accommodation and benefit' of the place fully compensated for the ransom money paid out and also, presumably, for the important concessions he had to make.[1]

In the last years of Blake's life the Levant Company was petitioning the Admiralty about the interruption of its trade in the Mediterranean by the piratical fleets of Tripoli and Tunis and informing the ambassador at Constantinople that 'our trade was never in so languishing a condition as it is now by reason of the swarms of Turkish and Spanish pirates (!) pestering those seas'.[2] At the same time Browne at Algiers was reporting that Cromwell could only hope to obtain compliance with his curious conception of international law by the use of force.[3] In the year that Cromwell died the secretary of the navy warmly congratulated Stokes on the peace treaties which he had been able to make with Tunis and Tripoli, however unsatisfactory they might be to national pride, since they now opened up some prospect of our being able to deal with the dreaded privateers of Majorca.[4]

Meanwhile the position at Algiers reflected anything but awe of English sea-power or respect for our national integrity. The 'colouring' of foreign ships adopted by Cromwell, in defiance of international usage, delighted our new French allies, who were amazed at their commerce receiving any help from England.[5] This not unnaturally infuriated the Algerines. Browne complains of their reprisals for injuries done them and of the change of attitude towards the English 'since my confinement'. The people affront them on the street 'and they stick not to tell us to our faces that Englishmen are not as they were'.[6]

[1] Cals. S.P.D. 1656–7, p. 302, and 1657–8, pp. 307–8.

[2] Cals. S.P.D. 1657–8, p. 95, and 1656–7, p. 272.

[3] Thurloe, vi. 543, 1 Oct. 1657. Algiers would not return ships taken under 'forran collers', but would continue to take them. It had peace with England, but not with France and Holland.

[4] Cal. S.P.D. 1658–9, p. 141. For treaties, see ibid., 1657–8, pp. 307–10, and Sloane MS. 2755.

[5] Masson, pp. 46–47.

[6] Thurloe, vii. 566–7, 16 Dec. 1658, due to misconduct of *Angel*: Playfair, pp. 75–77; V.S.P. 1657–9, p. 289.

A letter from the divan to Cromwell foreshadows those ultimatums addressed later by the same state to Charles II and even to Louis XIV at the height of his power. After recalling their loyal and friendly treatment of the English and its requital by bad faith and violence the divan announce their intention henceforward to hold the consul personally responsible and, in default of satisfaction, to search all English ships at sea and take out enemy persons and goods. 'We cannot believe that our peace should be understood a good peace with so much treachery and falsehood nor can we imagine that you, their great king, should approve it, wherefore be pleased to be speedy in the remedy hereof and God prosper you.'[1]

What lasting impression the violence of Cromwell's policy or the might of his navy may have had on the North African states is conjectural. It is certain that the treaties of both Stokes and Blake were of very brief duration and their actual contents have been ignored by our historians. The terms that Stokes had to concede to Tunis and Tripoli show that the fleet was unable to impose its will on those states. One of his final reports before leaving the Mediterranean suggests, as was indeed the case, that he was in no position to subdue the increasing resentment at Algiers: 'From thence for Algiers to see if I can quieten these people the very noise of their inclination to a breach with us being prejudicial to our commerce'. The measure of his success is indicated by the precautions taken soon afterwards for the protection of our Levant and Mediterranean convoy and by the consul's complaint about the 'insolence and rigour' of the Algerines towards the English and the unfortunate consequences of 'the little regard that our masters at home have for our affairs'.[2] Morocco was not deterred soon afterwards from strenuously opposing our occupation of Tangier.

It would, indeed, appear that a great opportunity had been lost of establishing ourselves advantageously on the North African coast. One of the principal objects of the revolutionary measure at Algiers, which in 1659 replaced the rule of the bashaws by that of the agas, was the improvement of foreign

---

[1] Thurloe, vii. 566–7.
[2] Cals. S.P.D. 1658–9, p. 338, and 1659–60, p. 337.

relations, especially in regard to trade.[1] It was, however, France that ultimately reaped the benefit and succeeded in gaining a firm footing in the ports of Eastern Algeria. Even more regrettable, however, was the failure to take advantage of the opportunity to oust the Spaniards from at least some of their strongholds on the Barbary coast. Had we retained the goodwill of the Algerines, instead of wantonly antagonizing them, it might not have been difficult to follow the advice of the far-sighted Longland at Leghorn and create at Oran a naval base, where our ships could refit and refresh themselves.[2] Such a proceeding would normally have been welcomed alike by Algiers and Morocco, and would have helped to solve one of our principal problems in the Mediterranean.

As it was, our position at Algiers, the political and strategic centre of the coast, was anything but encouraging. The question of the right of search had unnecessarily been resurrected in an acute form, and the work of Oneby and Cason had been undone, since soon after the Restoration there were said to be 1,200 slaves in Algiers awaiting redemption. It was not long before our prestige reached its nadir with the tragic spectacle of our consul and merchants harnessed to carts in the quarries, and for more than twenty-five years after Blake's visit our relations with the Barbary States were to be a source of constant anxiety, expense, and embarrassment.

The long-term consequences of Cromwell's policy were, however, more advantageous. The continued presence of a fleet in the Mediterranean and the periodical visits of warships were to prove in time to come a valuable factor in the maintenance on a permanent basis of good relations between Britain and this remote but strategically important area. The manner in which the royal navy acquired a diplomatic character, as the principal instrument of official communication and negotiation with those states, provided an interesting, if not unique, feature of that long period, during which the destinies of France and Britain were being decided by the struggle for supremacy in the Mediterranean. The foundation for such procedure—and perhaps also for the development of a modern consular service—may be found in the combination at this time

[1] Plantet, i. 56-59.
[2] To Badiley, 4 Oct. 1656, Cal. S.P.D. 1656-7, p. 227.

of the functions in that area of a consul and navy agent, a practical arrangement of which Cromwell's royal successors took full advantage.[1]

[1] At Algiers, Tunis, Tetuan, Marseilles, Lisbon, and Cadiz. At Leghorn Consul Read and Longland co-operated closely. Luke at Tetuan received commissions as consul from the Council and as navy agent from the Admiralty. His naval instructions dealt not merely with furnishing supplies to warships. He was to inform commanders in the Straits of 'anything you shall judge may assist them in their service', and 'to observe any further orders we may issue and render us account of your proceedings', Cal. S.P.D. 1656–7, p. 302.

XIII

OUR RELATIONS WITH THE REGENCIES
1660 TO 1672

THE situation in the Mediterranean inherited by the royal government at the Restoration was neither simple nor happy. It was further complicated by our strained relations with Spain, by the demonstration of imperialistic ambitions of both France and England, and by the outbreak of war with France and the Netherlands. An additional complication had just been introduced into our relations with Algiers by a change in its form of government, which was inaugurated in 1659 and may have been completely misinterpreted by us. Though it placed all the power in the hands of the soldiers, its object is said to have been the improvement of foreign relations, to which the corruption of the bashaws was believed to be the principal obstacle, and more especially the development of overseas trade.[1] It did not, however, involve any change of loyalty to the sultan, whom the Algerines continued to help in his Cretan war.

Our method of dealing with a very unsatisfactory situation on the Barbary Coast left much to be desired. Cromwell's high-handed practices had involved England in open war with Algiers and in settlements with Tunis and Tripoli which, however sound in themselves, could hardly be regarded as gratifying. The first attempt to conclude a peace with Algiers was almost foredoomed to failure, especially as it was considered essential that no better terms should be granted than under the Commonwealth.[2]

It consisted in instructing Lord Winchelsea, the new ambassador to Constantinople, to visit Algiers for the arrangement of a treaty of peace. How hopeful the prospect was may be gauged by his ignorance of the country, his intolerance (especially towards its 'democratike' methods), his refusal to set foot on shore, and his conception of the great condescension

[1] De Grammont, p. 210; Plantet, i. 57 and 58 n.; d'Arvieux, v. 244–5.
[2] Cal. S.P.D. 1660–85, pp. 29–30.

shown in even staying in the roadstead, but perhaps most of all by the express stipulation that he was not to recognize the right of search,[1] though it was conferred by, or inherent in, the Turkish capitulations and was believed to be conceded by Stokes's treaty with Tripoli. What the Algerines clearly were seeking was a definite guarantee of English, Dutch, and French neutrality in their war with Spain. Their objection to one clause in Winchelsea's draft, though it was welcomed in subsequent treaties, was based solely on the fear that it might be regarded as equivalent to giving English ships a monopoly of its foreign trade, and so prove a source of friction with the other maritime powers.[2]

Winchelsea's methods were not likely to inspire confidence. He sanctioned provisional agreement to the right of search simply in order to gain time. He brought Browne, who had been continued in the consulate despite his original appointment as the Lord Protector's consul, instructions from King Charles to confirm the peace and, if necessary, to spend a sum not exceeding £200 on 'such in power there as have best interest'. He then sailed on after advising Browne to fob off the Algerines with 'what faire words and hopes you can of a conclusion', so as, if necessary, to 'secure your own person and estate', even under pretence of carrying a draft treaty to England.[3] He seems in fact to have taken very little interest in the regencies, especially after he had learned that the consulships there were not to be in his gift, as he had been led to believe. Paul Rycaut, who, as his secretary, negotiated on shore in his behalf and three years later brought the ratifications of Lawson's treaty to Algiers, was equally ignorant and intolerant, as his continuation of Knolles's *History of the Turks* shows only too clearly.

Browne, accordingly, in December 1660, concluded a treaty which was rejected in London owing to its recognition of the right of search and confiscation of strangers' goods on payment

---

[1] Nicholas to Browne, S.P. 71. 1, 17 Oct. 1660; Winchelsea to Charles, 13 Dec. 1660, n.s., 'the only difficulty being concerning searching our ships and pillaging of such goods and passengers as should appear to be strangers and not English . . . only that difficulty about searching of English ships'.

[2] Winchelsea to Charles, 26 Jan. 1661, S.P. 103. 1, ff. 264–87. In ff. 268–9 he proposed to allow seizure of foreign goods, paying double freight. Compare Dutch treaty 1662, f. 303.

[3] *H.M.C. Finch Papers*, i. 82 and 87.

of double the freight lost. The following June Winchelsea was advised by the secretary of state that

my Lord of Sandwich is gonne with a fleete of 14 or 15 good ships (and 5 or 6 others) into the Mediterranean to offer peace to those of Algier, Tunis and Tripoli which if they refuse to accept uppon honourable terms (the cheife is that of not searchinge our ships) he hath commission to doe them all the mischiefs of warre and if that happen it may perchance startle you at the Porte but you may assure them that his Majesty intends no breach of allegiance and amity with the Grand Signior nor hath any designe or intent to make any attempt upon any of the cityes under his dominion or protection but only to reduce and chastyse those pyrates.[1]

Sandwich, who had apparently not profited much by his previous experience in the Mediterranean, and was presumably partly responsible for this somewhat distorted account of our relations with Barbary, failed to improve matters by methods which were both provocative and futile, and the results do not appear to have met with the approval of his usually admiring kinsman Pepys or his government. He apparently brought Browne away after holding a 'Full Council of War with Consul at Algiers' in July 1661, and failed to resettle him there the following December.[2]

Admiral Lawson, however, handled matters with greater understanding. In 1662 he brought Browne back and made treaties with Algiers, Tunis, and Tripoli, which would probably have proved satisfactory, if the first could have been assured of our good faith, and if we had been wiser in our treatment of the consuls at the other two places. It was also unfortunate that advantage was not taken of the opportunity to make uniform treaties with all three states, which appear to have kept themselves informed of the various negotiations.

Had the necessary articles been drawn up, as they so easily might have been, in simple straightforward and identical terms, much misunderstanding and mutual recrimination could have

---

[1] Morice to Winchelsea, 16 June 1661, ibid., p. 129. The regencies were observing the treaties. Tunis wished to recover, as Tripoli had, right of search under 'the ancient articles', S.P. 71. 26, f. 12.

[2] *Sandwich Journal* (N.R.S.), ed. R. C. Anderson, London, 1928, pp. 91 and 110. Extraordinary variations are in Cal. S.P.D. 1666–7, p. 77; Jal, i. 237; de Grammont, pp. 212–13; A. Strickland, *Queens of England*, 8 vols., London, 1857–82, v. 497.

been avoided, and the historian's task greatly simplified. As the French consul d'Arvieux remarked soon afterwards, the French, modelling their procedure on Lawson's treaty with Tunis, preferred to include matters which were unpalatable in separate agreements, tending to concentrate on *les formalités* or face-saving, while the Barbaresques were more interested in *le solide* or matters of essential importance to them. Actually the French treaties seem on the whole to have been more explicit and comprehensive, and we find no reference to those subsidiary verbal explanations or qualifications in which we indulged.[1]

In fact, our negotiation of treaties with these states was at times so casual that it is little wonder that our own authorities were often unaware of their contents or correct interpretation. It is quite possible that Lawson's work was actually above the usual standard. Turkish copies of his treaties were brought to London, presumably for ratification at Constantinople, and translations are said to have been made 'word for word out of the Turkish'.[2]

His treaty with Algiers contained two novelties. One was that (like the Duc de Beaufort's treaty with Tunis of 1665) it contained a separate clause regarding the redemption of captives, which was, however, printed with the formally agreed articles and read:

His Majesty, out of his princely and tender care, having since the conclusion of this treaty recommended the redemption of all slaves, his subjects, in Algiers, unto the lords bishops of this kingdom; their lordships have (in this truly Christian and pious design) proceeded with such alacrity and expedition that, for the effecting thereof, £.10,000 are already prepared to be transmitted into those parts for redemption of all captives, according to the tenour of these articles, at the rate they were first sold in the market.[3]

Evidently the bishops intended to ensure that this money should not stray into other channels, as the Algiers duties had done. Two churchmen, Dr. John Bargrave and Archdeacon Sellecke of Bath, were dispatched to superintend its proper expenditure with the assistance, as agent general, of young

---

[1] D'Arvieux, iii. 396; Finch, ii. 170–5.

[2] S.P. 102. 1, f. 24, divan's complaint of 'contention and strife and on your part fighting or war'.

[3] Chalmers, ii. 365.

Francis Baker, who in his old age alleged that there were 1,200 captives awaiting redemption, almost certainly another exaggeration.[1] In 1672 the fund still showed a balance of £4,441.[2]

The other clause provided for the free passage of the ships of both countries—in our case on the production of a pass 'under the hand and seal of the Lord High Admiral of England' or, in default of a pass, of evidence that the major part of the company were subjects of the King of Great Britain. The peculiar feature was the requirement that the pass should be issued only by the lord high admiral or, in other words, should bear the easily recognizable seal of the anchor, regarding which Lawson found the Algerines very 'jealous'—not without reason, as the usual pass, issued by some unknown official such as a mayor or customs officer, would have been of little practical use. As an additional safeguard it was printed on a perforated form, which enabled it to be identified by a detached 'top' or counterpart, hence the designation of 'scolloped passes'.[3]

This provision was reciprocal to the extent that Algerine ships were likewise to proceed unmolested, if they had passes from the chief Governor of Algiers and 'a major part of the ship's company be Turks, Moors or slaves', such passes being in practice authenticated by our consuls. The visit was to be effected through the medium of a rowboat with only two 'sitters' besides the oarsmen, a very wise arrangement which was unfortunately nullified by the alternative regarding the majority of the crew. This must have had its origin in some misunderstanding, though the Algerines attributed it to the trickery of the consul. It was in their case meaningless, and in our own such a fact was not easily capable of proof or, indeed, necessarily in accordance with our navigation laws. By their treaties a few years later with Tunis and Algiers *all French ships*, even naval ones, were specifically required to carry and produce on demand passes from the Admiral of France, a practice designed to leave no room for doubt as to the true nationality of the vessel.

As among the more normal provisions we find agreement that no restitution or compensation for damages previously inflicted should be required from either side, that it should not be 'lawful to break the peace on account of grievances till satisfaction be

---

[1] S.P. 71. 3, f. 699.   [2] S.P. 71. 2, 29 Nov. 1672.
[3] App. J.

denied', and that His Majesty's ships might sell prizes without paying customs-duty and buy victuals freely at the market rate, it might have been expected that matters would proceed smoothly, as they did at Tripoli, apart from the non-payment of the consul's salary, or at Tunis, despite the fact that Thomas Browne, being removed from his consulship very belatedly in 1663 because he 'was for the usurper', had tried to make matters as difficult as possible for his successor.

Robert Browne at Algiers was probably a better representative than his brother at Tunis and more adequately remunerated than the unfortunate Tucker at Tripoli, for, though his salary, which was originally payable out of the 'Algiers duties', seems to have expired with them at the Restoration, the consulage on the redemption of slaves must have supplemented his income from more normal sources. His chief troubles arose from breaches of neutrality and failure to put into practice the system of passes or, perhaps, to arrive at a clear understanding as to what that system was to be.

As early as 15 June 1662 Lawson had reported the desire of Algiers that all ships should carry His Royal Highness's pass, and that each of its cruisers should have a copy with his 'Seale of the Anchor' for purposes of comparison and to avoid counterfeiting by other nations, 'for these are very jealous people'. It was, however, not until 29 September 1663, presumably on the receipt of an indignant letter from the divan brought by Rycaut, that the privy council resolved that the customs should notify all ship-masters and that blank passes should be prepared and sent, not only to all ports in England, Ireland, and the plantations, but 'to such other foreign ports as his Royal Highness thinks fitt for the better conveniency of *all shipps* trading from any of his Majesty's ports to and through the Levant seas to be deposited in safe hands and not to be parted with nore delivered unto any but upon Oath that such *shipps and lading* (for whose safe conduct such Passes shall be given) belong to his Majesty's subjects only'.[1]

An oath, however, as we know from Pepys, was valueless as a guarantee in such matters, and the genuineness of this attempt to conform with treaty requirements receives little confirmation from a letter of instructions which Sir William

[1] P.C. 2/56, f. 631; Rycaut, pp. 139-40.

Coventry at the admiralty sent on 30 November 1663, together with some blank passes, to three leading merchants at Malaga, evidently in substitution for the consul recently deceased.

After pointing out that divers masters of English ships, by neglecting to take passes, 'have not only hazarded their own Safeties but given a Pretence to those of Algiers to infringe the peace lately made with them', he continues that until a fleet could be sent into the Mediterranean 'we must expect that the Perfidiousness of those of Algiers will put a damp upon our Trade; I wish it prove not fatal to some particular Persons who have Stocks abroad, *without knowledge of the Practice of these Pirates*'.[1]

It is also illuminating that one of the earliest passes was apparently issued to a *Genoese* ship, the *Cala di San Paulo*, whose master told Narborough in 1676 that he 'had fourteen years gott free of all Barbary Corsairs with his Royal Highness' pass',[2] a practice that became far too prevalent, even as late as 1815.

The anger of the Algerines on the receipt of the ratifications of the treaty from Constantinople seems to have been not unreasonable, judging by Arlington's attitude, which had been very curious and, in fact, highly suspicious. In sending nine ratifications of Lawson's treaties with the three states, as well as the three signed originals, he wrote Winchelsea that they were considered 'exceedingly beneficial and advantageous to the trade and commerce of his Majesty's Kingdoms', and that, if the Porte refused to ratify them, 'you are to make the least noise possibly you can of it for the ill-fame it will have'—the more secrecy, in fact, the better.[3]

As he told the Levant Company, which was presumed to be the principal beneficiary, that these ratifications involved 'so much secrecy' that they could not be communicated to it, there can be little doubt that they contained something peculiarly offensive, which probably affected the spirit of the treaty. The ratification clause as given by Rycaut, even if it reproduced substantially the Turkish text, really effected no radical alteration in a situation which had existed in practice for a century, and was said to have been recognized in early

---

[1] *Memoirs of the Duke of York, 1660–73*, London, 1729, pp. 41–43.
[2] Sloane MS. 2755, f. 24.
[3] Finch, i. 245–6, 23 March 1663.

French capitulations.[1] The real trouble may have arisen from communication by the sultan of the new article which Winchelsea, following the French technique, had contrived to insert in our capitulations, to prohibit the searching of our ships by the regencies. It was, in fact, quite unrealistic as applied to the Mediterranean, especially at that particular time, and in Queen Anne's reign the Porte itself found it necessary to adopt the Algerine procedure.[2]

As the rulers at both Tripoli and Tunis, including Blake's old adversary, greeted the arrival of the ratifications in a friendly manner, it seems likely that the resentment at Algiers was caused by dissatisfaction at the clause about ship's passes, especially as willingness was expressed to accept the treaty if it was eliminated. It is noteworthy that no such clause appears at all in the treaty with Tunis, while in that with Tripoli it is free from any restriction or qualification.

At all events the Algerines, who were well aware of the manner in which such 'commands' were normally obtained, and only the previous year had had experience of Winchelsea's high-handed methods in the treatment of deputies, sent to complain at the Porte of English violence, refused to accept the treaty as ratified. This marked a new stage in our relations with the regencies, as it was apparently the last time on which we approached Constantinople in connexion with them, until new complications were introduced through Napoleon's invasion of Egypt. No further attempts were made there to influence newly-appointed bashaws, and applications for consular _exequaturs_ ceased. It was also almost precisely at this moment that Christian prestige and credit sank to its lowest level at Constantinople, and that 'the Sultan's government complained, not without reason, that no treaty of peace with a Christian monarch afforded any guarantee for its faithful observance'.[3]

It would appear from Browne's letters that the Algerines, on the other hand, acted fairly and reasonably, according to their conception of the treaty, applying to those ships which were not covered by passes the terms of Winchelsea's provisional treaty, which represented, in fact, their traditional practice. Rycaut, arriving at Algiers early in September 1663 on the same

[1] Rycaut, p. 137, and pp. 115 and 128.
[2] _Despatches of Sir Robert Sutton_, p. 197.   [3] Finlay, v. 165.

ship which brought the ratifications, wrote Winchelsea, who was clearly ignorant of events there, 'it seems that since the peace with Algiers it hath been agreed that all English ships shall carry passports from the Lord High Admirall, and the Algerians having of late met with several of our ships at sea without passports sent them into this place but through the diligence of the consul most of them have been cleared'.[1] On the same day the divan addressed a letter to King Charles notifying him that ships were continuing to be found without passes and that enemy goods or men would in future be taken, compensation being paid for loss of freight, and asking for an immediate reply. The arrival of this letter, which evidently stimulated the privy council to take its hasty, though belated, action, was duly recorded by Pepys.[2]

What precisely followed is not clear. Charles may have been too indolent or too proud to reply to the letter, and Coventry's promised fleet did not materialize—at any rate in sufficient strength to prove more than provocative. The government of Algiers was perhaps at its weakest at this time, and the aga, whom d'Arvieux describes as very old but sensible,[3] may very well have been unable to control an angry mob, which appears to have murdered him. The outbreak of a severe plague epidemic and the French invasion of Djidjelli were hardly calculated to improve matters.

Such information as we have comes from the Dutch, whose admiral, de Ruyter, had followed Lawson's example in trying to conclude treaties with the regencies at about the same time and with very similar results. From Tripoli he succeeded only in getting 'friendly attention', but at Tunis, with the help of Thomas Browne, he concluded a treaty on the basis of 'free ship, free goods, free crews' and mutual facilities for shipping at their respective ports—much the same terms, in fact, as the French had been offered there sixty years before.

With Algiers he made peace in November 1662 on the basis of its right to search Dutch ships, which it undertook to do 'civilly and without threats and violence'. The situation there was said to be very satisfactory, and the Algerines gave 'many proofs of friendly behaviour towards Dutch merchant men'.

---

[1] Finch, i. 276.   [2] *Diary*, 9 Nov. 1663.
[3] v. 245.

The conclusion of peace gave 'great joy'; 130 Dutch captives were redeemed; and de Ruyter, while describing the Algerines as 'rogues and scoundrels', made them a gift of guns and powder. The peace was at first well kept, but, apparently owing to the non-arrival of either ratifications of the treaty or the ransom money and anger at Van Tromp's capture of two of their ships, though the sequence of events is not quite clear, the Algerines broke out into 'piracy' or, as they probably termed it, 'reprisals'.

The Dutch, it should be pointed out, had on their own admission been playing fast and loose with Spain and engaging in a 'mysterious' or dubious form of trade on the Barbary coast; and the practices of their agent for the redemption of captives were very suspect.[1] De Witt's avowed policy was tricky in the extreme,[2] and King Charles accused the Dutch of a direct breach of faith in regard to agreements about Algiers and Guinea. In 1667 our consul at Tunis refers to the ships of both Dutch and French as pirates.[3]

The position of the English and Dutch consuls as security for the observance of their respective treaties was obviously both unpleasant and hazardous. By the end of 1663 the Algerines were reported to 'have an eye' on Browne to ensure that he did not escape on any ship, and by the following June he and his Dutch colleague were confined in the bashaw's palace. Before that he and the English merchants are reported to have been insulted and 'made to draw carts like horses'.[4] Possibly the detention of the consuls in the palace, which has been described, somewhat curiously, as a 'breach of international courtesies', was adopted as the best method of securing and protecting their persons during these admittedly irregular hostilities.

At all events the Dutch consul's release was effected through an exchange, after which he returned temporarily to his post, but Lawson with his twelve ships was unable to secure the liberation of Browne, who, however, was permitted to live under strict supervision in his own house. It is not without interest that the 'very polite' attitude towards the Dutch,

[1] Blok, pp. 157–89.
[2] Macpherson, ii. 472. Louis urged de Witt to attack 'les pirates des Régences barbaresques', while allying himself with them, Jal, i. 459 and 482, 1666–7.
[3] S.P. 71. 26, f. 173, 27 Jan. 1667.
[4] Ibid., f. 61, 10 May 1664. In a long dispatch, Mar. 1664, Browne reported 8 ships taken at Algiers in 1663, S.P. 71. 1, ff. 268–9.

during their not altogether unsatisfactory negotiations, was made the subject of criticism—'it is with such an appearance of saintliness that these barbarians do make shift'.[1] Striking evidence of the conciliatory and reasonable attitude of the Algerines appears in a news item of 22 April 1664, according to which the divan assured the Earl of Teviot, who as Governor of Tangier seems to have won the respect of both Turks and Moors, that the many English ships seized were being kept safely and could be restored together with the men and goods, and compensation paid if anything were missing.[2]

The only solution appeared to the Christian powers to lie in joint action,[3] and a stranger assortment of bed-fellows than the proposed combination of England, Holland, France, and Spain for the suppression of piracy it would be hard to imagine. We were at the time helping the Portuguese army against Spain, which in its turn was aiding the Moors to drive us out of Tangier. Within less than a year the English and Dutch were engaged in hostilities either in the West Indies or off the Guinea Coast, and so were the English and French in the Mediterranean. It is difficult also to see how our haphazard methods of issuing commissions to privateers and condemning prizes can have helped in the diminution of piracy.[4] In Spain our consuls—and on occasion those of Holland—were thrown into gaol, either on account of violations of neutrality by their men-of-war or merely to suit the humour of the local governors.[5] Only a few years before the Dutch had suffered far more at English hands than they probably did in the whole course of their history from the Barbaresques, and we were to have a similar experience from the French privateers of Dunkirk.[6]

The proposed co-operation came to nothing, and in August 1664 the Duke of York issued the customary unrealistic orders to Allin, who was to relieve Lawson:

You shall insist upon punishing . . . the Persons principally guilty of

[1] Blok, pp. 172, 173, and 180.
[2] H.M.C. Heathcote Papers, p. 151.
[3] To attack Algiers jointly 'without having any regard to any former Treaty of Peace or Alliance', *Van Tromp*, p. 230, and 'shuffling conduct' of Charles II, pp. 231–2.
[4] Cal. S.P.D. 1664–5, pp. 62–63 and 202.
[5] Heathcote Papers, V.S.P., &c.
[6] *Van Tromp*, pp. 190–4, 239–40, 445–6; Blok, p. 184.

the Inhumanity lately used towards the Consul: in which if you shall not be able to obtain those Offenders with Death it is left to your Discretion (with the Advice of the Consul) to accept of the Infliction of such other Punishment on them as you shall think sufficient for vindicating his Majesty's honour and securing a better Observation of the Peace for the future. In the meantime if there shall be Opportunity of procuring the release of the Consul you are to endeavour it

—by exchange of prisoners, if necessary.[1]

As there was little hope of Allin being able to accomplish more than Lawson and de Ruyter together with about thirty warships had achieved, it is not surprising that, though Allin found on arrival that Browne was already dead, apparently of either plague or dysentery but perhaps not unfairly described as 'so barbarously used, even to the death', and though his envoys were instructed 'to press for satisfaction for damages, breach of peace and insolences committed upon the Consul', it had already been decided at a council of war 'not to take any notice of the Consul's death'. To all intents and purposes the Algerine contention was accepted that 'the Consul . . . was the main instrument of the first breach and deserved to be hanged'.[2] The outcome was the confirmation of Lawson's treaty in its unsatisfactory form, and, as the Algerines insisted on the appointment of a new consul, Allin left Captain Nicholas Parker of H.M.S. *Nonsuch* behind in that capacity, though only after having 'much adoe' in obtaining his consent.

Parker, who had achieved distinction some years before in the war with Spain, was given a complimentary reception by the divan in the presence of his fellow captains and an abatement of '85 pieces of eight of the rent of the house of what the other Consul paid, being the King's house'. Apart from the fact that he was completely neglected by his own government, who provided him with no funds or instructions, he had little ground for complaint. Later, when trying to claim reimbursement, he not unnaturally stressed the fact that he had 'very expensively and uncomfortably resided' at Algiers, where he had been appointed to 'undertake the Carefull and Chargeable Imploy-

---

[1] *The Journals of Sir Thomas Allin, 1660–78* (N.R.S.), ed. R. C. Anderson, 2 vols., London, 1939–40, ii. 215–18.

[2] Ibid. i. 172; Cal. S.P.D. 1664–5, p. 53, 4 Nov. 1664. He died about 6 Sept. 1664, S.P. 71. 1, f. 270.

ment of Consul in that troublesome station'.[1] Although argument about Algiers prizes at Tangier gave rise to his comments on 'how ticklish these people are' in regard to treaty rights, 'so ignorantly covetous', and their 'frivolous pretences', probably from imperfect information, as we know that the governor was hostile and unjust, the chief local difficulty was reported to be that the Algerines 'seem troubled that since the peace the English have had little or no trade with them'.[2] The aga, according to d'Arvieux, was 'un homme d'esprit et d'un mérite singulier', who made a very advantageous peace with France in 1666 and governed the country for seven years (1664–71) 'avec assez de tranquillité'.[3] He was eventually killed by the militia, because he was more interested in meeting the Moorish menace on land than in maritime activities, and was succeeded by Spragge's late adversary.

Certainly there are some interesting tributes to the goodwill shown by the Algerines at this time from a variety of sources, including news-letters, which contradict in the most categorical manner the assertions in Routh's *Tangier*. We hear, for instance, of a Bideford vessel bound for Portugal being rescued from a French man-of-war by an Algiers cruiser, which refused to accept any reward.[4] Pepys too was evidently impressed by Allin's statement in 1668 that 'he wishes all we are told to be true, *in our defence*; for he finds by all that the Turks have, to this day, been very civil to our merchantmen everywhere and, if they would have broke with us, they never had such an opportunity over our rich merchantmen as lately, coming out of the Streights'.[5] Allin seems to have reciprocated soon after by planning to burn the Algiers fleet treacherously at dead of night.[6]

---

[1] S.P. 71. 1, ff. 271 and 290.

[2] H.M.C. Heathcote MSS., pp. 201–14. Evidently Arlington instructed the governor to make peace, ibid., p. 212. See also Cal. S.P.D. 1660–85, p. 103, and News-letter, 12 Jan. 1666: 'Several Argiers frigates are at Tanger. That Divan has agreed with Lord Belasyse for the cargo of the *Margarita*', Heathcote, p. 232; Routh, *Tangier, England's Last Atlantic Outpost, 1661–84*, pp. 87–88. For abuses by Tangier, see S.P. 71. 1, ff. 286 and 301 b.

[3] v. 246.

[4] Cal. S.P.D. 1666–7, pp. 443 and 472; *London Gazette*, 30 Sept. 1665; News-letter (Muddiman), 21 Feb. 1667; S.P. 71. 1, f. 306; Coxere, pp. 84–85.

[5] *Diary*, 7 Aug. 1668.

[6] Barlow, i. 152; *Journals*, ii. 48–49; S.P. 71. 1, f. 357.

A year later Allin, who says he had full powers to 'conclude Peace and make War' with Barbary, could apparently do no better than adopt the latter alternative with Algiers, which, on his own evidence, does not appear to have been unreasonable or unconciliatory. That the peace had until then been well maintained by it is clear from the steps that Allin took to advise our various consuls of the rupture and from his instructions to offer the bashaw 'a fair compensation of differences'.[1] The ensuing position was an anomalous one, since Allin continued to correspond freely with our consul there as long as he remained on the station.

Quite apart from their own constant intrigues against each other, there were a number of considerations, which might seriously affect the relations of England, France, and Holland with any of the Barbary States. One of the most important was the failure of those governments to make suitable consular arrangements, a vital consideration in the eyes of the Turks in particular. Niggardliness in regard to consular emoluments gave rise to constant trouble. It may suffice to say that apparently the only payment made for our consuls' maintenance during the first ten years of the reign was £100 at Tripoli, and that the total contribution for that purpose at Algiers from 1660 to 1683 was only about £1,000.[2]

No less serious were the dissensions and disloyalty in our community at Algiers. In the time of John Ward, who replaced Parker when he was recalled to command a ship in the Dutch war, both Admiral Allin and the Duke of York were incensed at the hostile conduct of some of our residents. His successor, Samuel Martin, in his last letter from his confinement in Algiers in 1679 seemed mainly concerned with the treatment he had received from his own countrymen.[3]

This was the more unfortunate in that both consuls were capable of rendering valuable service, and Martin appears to have enjoyed the confidence of the Algerines to a remarkable degree. The French were apparently even worse off. D'Arvieux, for example, during his few months at the consulate, managed, on his own showing, to estrange all his colony, and finally

---

[1] *Journals*, ii. 112–16; Cal. S.P.D. 1668–9, p. 357; H.M.C. Wombwell MSS., var. ii, pp. 138, 140, 156–7.   [2] Cal. Treasury Papers, i.
[3] *Martin's Narrative*, S.P. 71. 2, 30 Oct. 1672.

resided with Martin, of whose conduct and abilities he had a high opinion.

Our government was not blind to the important part played by a consul in maintaining good relations with Algiers, and was perhaps unlucky in the course of events. In 1666 William Leavitt, a merchant who had been attached to the fleet as victualler, was appointed to the post but died before he could proceed. Another suitable man selected by the London merchants was not immediately available. A third—perhaps to please the aga, who had set his heart on having for consul another 'officer from the fleet', like Parker—was superseded, after appointment, by Lieutenant (or Captain) Richard Acton (or Aston), who, however, never got any further than drawing the sum allotted to him for his outfit.

John Ward, to whom Parker had entrusted the office in 1666, appears to have received little support from his government. Recommended in 1667,[1] on account of his wide experience and linguistic abilities, by thirty-six London merchants including Sir John Wolstenholme, the chief farmer of the customs, and Captain Robert Starr, who had already been Commonwealth agent in Morocco and later received a royal commission as consul at Algiers, Ward's career proved sufficiently eventful to attract considerable public interest. In July 1668, the same month that his mother petitioned for his retention in the consul-ship, Williamson was informed from a Western port, evidently as an item for his London Gazette, that 'several merchantmen from Cadiz and Lisbon are waiting for a convoy, being afraid to proceed alone because of the Turks on account of what happened to the consul at Algiers'. Ten days later we hear that 'a hot discussion at St. Malo as to whether the consul at Algiers had been killed' had been satisfactorily settled by later advices.[2]

In May 1669 Williamson's faithful correspondent at Leghorn reported 'we have noe Consull in Algier',[3] though Ward had been very active the previous January in pursuing 'the release of ships unlawfully taken'. He was in constant correspondence with Admiral Allin until October, but was apparently placed under protective arrest later, probably after Admiral Spragge's

[1] Cal. S.P.D. 1666–7, p. 443, 8 Jan. 1667.
[2] Cal. S.P.D. 1667–8, pp. 494 and 510.
[3] Thomas Dethick, 20 May 1668, S.P. 98. 9. He was not consul.

burning of the ten ships at Bougie in May 1671. On that occasion, according to de Grammont, whose account of this period is frequently inaccurate, the consul and principal English merchants were thrown into gaol and the consulate looted,[1] but Spragge and others would certainly have dilated upon this, if it had actually occurred.

A news-letter of 26 September 1671 reports: 'We hear from Leghorn of the murder of the Consul at Algiers by the mob. He had long been kept in security by the Divan but was lately set free and sent to his own house. He had hardly entered when the rabble broke in, murdered him and dragged his body through the streets.' Perhaps not for the last time he had been the victim of rumour or journalistic imagination, for on 4 December the Venetian ambassador wrote: 'Good news has arrived from Algiers by letters from Admiral Spragge. . . . He adds that the English consul was at liberty *with all his effects* and he hoped *soon* to report an advantageous peace.'[2] This was more than six months after the action at Bougie, which is usually represented as immediately bringing Algiers to its knees.

Spragge did not in fact make the advantageous treaty that he hoped for—indeed, his first reception at Algiers was by no means conciliatory—and may well have owed the re-establishment of peace on reasonable terms to Ward's diplomacy. De Grammont attributes the aga's murder to the strange policy and violences of the French, and claims that England profited by the resultant ill will towards France to secure a peace, but Algiers, in addition to the threat of invasion from Morocco, certainly required a breathing-space to re-create its navy.[3] This it did with surprising speed, thanks in part to timely aid from the sultan.[4]

Spragge's treaty contained little that was new. He failed to obtain, as he expected, the free liberation of English captives, who were, however, to be redeemed at their original cost—'a very intricate business' according to Ward, but a substantial,

[1] De Grammont, p. 219. Spragge's report is in S.P. 71. 2, 8 May 1671. See also Cal. S.P.D. 1671, pp. 234–5 and 249–51, and d'Arvieux, v. 236–41.

[2] H.M.C. le Fleming Papers, p. 84; V.S.P. 1671–2, p. 127.

[3] De Grammont, p. 220. The revolution occurred 5 months after Spragge's action. The defeated Admiral was elected Dey. Spragge made some unpalatable concessions, S.P. 71. 26, f. 333.

[4] S.P. 71. 1, ff. 329–51; Sloane MS. 2755, ff. 53 sqq.

though not uncommon, concession, when a mutual exchange was impracticable. He unfortunately renewed, in a still more categorical manner, the provision that an English ship which had no pass should be allowed to proceed freely, if 'the major part of the seamen' were subjects of the King of Great Britain. It can only be assumed that this was insisted upon—actually for the last time—out of regard for 'the King's honour', just as the article providing that 'all subjects of Great Britain in Algiers shall be set at liberty and delivered up on paying the original price and no more made slaves' was qualified by a verbal 'explanation' that Englishmen serving on board foreign vessels were to be sold as slaves. There seems to have been no question of restitution of property, and exchange of prisoners was out of the question, as the Algerines taken by us had been sold to Spain and other countries.[1]

It might have been expected that Ward would have received some encouragement from the king or his ministers. They did on 29 April 1671 go to the length of granting him a salary of £100 a year with arrears from Christmas 1666, and even supplied him with a warrant for £250 on account on 24 November. Some time, however, in the latter part of 1672 Samuel Martin was appointed consul, and on 15 May 1673 the Treasury issued a warrant for £150 to 'John Ward, late consul at Algiers for 1½ years to Xmas last on his allowance'. Presumably Ward, whose last known dispatch from Algiers is dated 18 April 1673, had then returned to England. At all events there is no further record of him.

There is apparently no foundation for the belief that he was cut in pieces by the mob before the Dey's palace—presumably a repetition of the rumour of 1671—except a grimly jocular remark in a letter from Martin to Williamson in August 1675 that 'unless his Majesty will be pleased to support my staggering condition I can expect no better fare than befell my predecessor, only he had the good fortune to be cut in pieces and I may chance to escape with burning, a death that lately befell a brave Genoese merchant. I fancy I am too lean to be roasted.'[2] How

---

[1] The treaty is in Sloane MS. 2755. Williamson later mentions the verbal 'explanation' of Article xii, S.P. 29. 366, f. 77. It was cancelled in 1765.

[2] Playfair, p. 120. In his *Handbook for Travellers in Algeria and Tunis* (London, 1891), p. 334, he dates his second version 20 July 1674.

far his dispatches can be taken literally is very doubtful. It is significant that d'Arvieux, who arrived in Algiers the following month and was very envious of Martin's financial position, makes no reference to either of these deaths, on which he would almost certainly have enlarged.

It seems incredible that the murder of one of our consuls, the only one in the history of Barbary, could, if it had occurred, have passed unnoticed, more especially in the case of a man so well known as Ward, or that our relations with Algiers could have been as friendly as they appear to have been in 1674. There is a curious gap in the Algiers dispatches between April 1673 and July 1674, but it is evident from Pepys's letter to Martin of 28 September 1674 that the latter had been there for some time and that the existing relations were those of peace and amity.[1]

It is not the only time that the death of a consul at Algiers—even by roasting or boiling alive—has been recorded by persons who were surely in a position to know better. In a later work Playfair, who is so largely responsible for the propagation of this rumour, which, perhaps, really referred to the last of the agas, tells us that Ward, after he had ceased to be consul, shot a Jew in the presence of the Dey and was promptly cut down by the guards. That version, however, seems to be open to the same objections. As far as I can learn, only one Englishman was killed in peace-time in the regencies during at least two centuries, the worthless victim of a drunken brawl,[2] and burning alive may have been a threat rather than a reality.[3]

Relations with Tripoli and Tunis during this period seem to have been singularly uneventful, and Lawson had little difficulty in confirming the peace there. While our interest in the former was purely negative, the latter was an important port of call and supply, not only for merchant vessels in the Levant trade but also for our warships during hostilities with Algiers, France, and Holland and strained relations with Spain. Rycaut, who met with a friendly welcome from Blake's old antagonist when he visited it in 1663, commented on its economic value to Italy.[4] D'Arvieux soon afterwards describes the value of its products

[1] Tanner, *Descriptive Catalogue of the Naval MSS. in the Pepysian Library*, ii. 362–3.
[2] S.P. 71. 3, f. 227.
[3] Morgan, *Several Voyages to Barbary*, pp. 50–51; Hubac, p. 188.
[4] Rycaut, p. 251.

to Provence. The principal occupation of the English community was the sale of wheat and other produce through associates in Marseilles, Leghorn, and other Italian ports.

Although he feared that Browne might have been working against him, John Erlisman, reporting his first audience in May 1663, found 'these People in general very willing and desirous to keep the peace with his Majesty and enjoy the benefit of trade'.[1] Neither he nor his assistant Francis Baker, who succeeded him in January 1673, had any reason to alter their opinion. Indeed, the latter, owing to his experience and knowledge of the language, received special marks of the rulers' friendship.[2]

Local goodwill took a practical form that must have been vexatious to the French. In March 1666 the consul reports that 'our frigates will be heartily welcomed for we have a good old king who often tells me that what the country affords is ours and provision of all sorts is cheape'. The death of this Dey and election of a new one evidently made little difference, since a report a few months later expressed the opinion that in spite of differences Tunis would maintain its friendship. The Dey was beginning to allow the export of corn—on recovery from a scarcity which had seriously affected Italy—'the country abounding through most seasonable rains'. Allin reaped the benefit on his visits in 1668 and 1670. A year later Spragge was 'very plentifully regaled with all sorts of refreshments'.[3] The chief problem for the future was our ability to prevent the French enjoying similar advantages.

Reports at this time throw a little light on much that is puzzling. Tunis, for instance, could give friendly assistance to ships engaged in fighting Algiers and be itself at war with France, which was in league with Turkey, while both Algiers and Tunis were actively assisting the sultan in Cretan waters. Both d'Arvieux and one of the Deys pointed out that Tunis was always open to trading ships of all nations, even enemies of the Porte. As soon, however, as French ships actually took part in the Cretan war under a thin disguise, the Barbaresques had no

[1] S.P. 71. 26, ff. 59 and 61.
[2] Ibid., f. 390. After his appointment 'the King and principal men' came to visit him and were 'very pleased and friendly'.
[3] Ibid., ff. 147, 173, 249, and 333.

option but to attack them.[1] This by some curious process of reasoning has often been cited as a breach of the recently concluded treaties with France.

Although the confirmation of Erlisman's consulship and the ratification of Lawson's treaties, both in 1663, were the last occasions on which we approached the sultan in connexion with Barbary affairs, prior to Bonaparte's invasion of Egypt, this did not indicate any radical change in the relationship between the regencies and the Porte. Baker, reporting in 1675 the death of the Dey, adds that the election of his successor has been confirmed by the sultan, and that he hopes soon to send details of the 'Ingredients to make up the Composition of the Government'.[2] This was almost precisely the form of government that was being developed in Algiers and which the Algerines tried to preserve in Tunis during the coming civil wars.

[1] On 10 Feb. 1669, ibid., f. 251, Erlisman reports Dey's friendly attitude, adding 'these people take all the French they can meete and the King hath told the French Consull that he should acquaint his master soe much and bids them do the worst they can'. The sultan called the French 'plus ennemis que nos ennemis mêmes', de la Roncière, v. 282; de Grammont, p. 220.

[2] S.P. 71. 26, f. 317, the people were 'strict and observing the peace'.

XIV

OUR RELATIONS WITH THE REGENCIES
1673 TO 1682

THE appointment of Samuel Pepys in 1673 as 'secretary for naval affairs' was an important and opportune event, since he was among the first English officials to show an intelligent and sympathetic interest in Barbary. It only preceded by a year the transfer of control of the southern department from Arlington and Williamson, the real founders of our modern consular service, to the gouty and choleric Sir Henry Coventry, commonly known as 'Hector Harry', who apparently knew nothing of either consular or African problems.

Pepys evidently liked Martin, who was clearly an able and active consul, with a considerable capacity for ingratiating himself with both English officials and the Algerines. They probably knew each other previously in London. In his first extant letter to Martin Pepys writes that he 'has from all hands (the King himself as well as Lord Arlington and others) met with a general good liking of his behaviour and discretion in his present difficult employment with regard both to the honour of the service and the content of the merchants'. He had a constant reminder of him in a lion which lived in his house and was 'as tame as you sent him and as good company'.[1]

Martin, however, made some bitter enemies among the London merchants, especially William Bowtell,[2] who held the profitable agency for the redemption of slaves, which Martin had tried to annex, and who, together with his agents in Algiers, constantly and bitterly attacked him. Whether there was any substance in their charges is not at all clear, but they certainly added to his difficulties and in course of time weakened his influence with his own government. At the end of 1674, however, both Pepys and the king were pleased with his conduct,

---

[1] Tanner, ii. 362–3, 28 Sept. 1674.
[2] 'A notorious villain'. Bowtell's charges against Martin are in S.P. 103. 1, f. 672 b. Later Rycaut applied for the agency.

and Sir John Narborough also seems to have approved of him. In a narrative of that admiral's visit to Algiers at the time a naval officer made special mention of the 'good services rendered by the consul who was not only prudent but greatly beloved by the people',[1] whereas one at least of Bowtell's agents did little to develop goodwill for the English or their prestige.[2]

That Martin's personal relations with the government of Algiers were extremely good is beyond doubt. Bowtell in a lengthy indictment specifically cites this fact among his queer assortment of charges, adding that Martin boasted that he was practically a member of the council.[3] D'Arvieux, despite his arrogant and critical nature, pays several tributes to Martin's ability and diplomacy, and evidently endorsed the testimonial which the Dey in a letter to King Charles made to his 'zeal and prudence'.[4]

Playfair says of Martin 'unfortunately he was permitted to trade', regardless of the fact that too many of his own Victorian colleagues were little more than sinecurists or 'amateur consuls', holding 'ministerial jobs' and often doing more harm than good in return for their consular salaries. There is no reason to think that Martin's conception of consular duties and behaviour was in any way inferior to the standard of that rather lamentable period. It was, in fact, because he was in business, disposing of funds of his own and conversant with the ways of the people, that he was able to smooth over difficulties caused either by mutual misunderstanding or by our violations of the treaty and failure to make good our financial obligations.

It is interesting to note that the consulship of the non-trading d'Arvieux, despite his very exceptional qualifications, quickly ended in a complete failure and that he envied Martin his financial resources. Few of our salaried consuls in Algiers in the next century did any better. If Martin was dishonest or had unscrupulous rivals in London, that was another matter, but, so far as our relations with Algiers were concerned, the fact that he was a substantial merchant clearly proved helpful. Evidence of his local standing is furnished by the case of a well-

---

[1] Playfair, p. 117.
[2] James Crofts, killed brawling in 1688, owed £30,000 in Algiers. The Dey said he wanted no more English merchants, S.P. 71. 3, f. 227.
[3] S.P. 103. 1, f. 672 b.
[4] v. 162.

known merchant, whose release at the outbreak of war in 1677 was procured by the consul, described as 'great with the King'.[1]

Pepys was well informed regarding many important aspects of the situation—the indiscipline in the navy, the duties of consuls, the unreasonableness of merchants, and conditions at Tangier. Except for his exaggerated regard for the 'King's honour', and perhaps the influence of Sir James Houblon, who as a leading merchant and ship-owner represented vested interests in the Mediterranean area, he appears clearly as an honest, well-informed, and highly intelligent public servant.

In accordance with tradition, it has been stated that 'in the spring of 1672 it soon became evident that the Algerines had no intention of keeping the treaty, for they recommenced their attacks on English shipping immediately',[2] a statement for which I can find no more justification than for similar ones made in connexion with the treaties concluded by Cason and Roe. It is, in fact, by no means consonant with our contemporary records nor with a private report to Williamson of April 1672, which states that the Algerines in spite of some provocation were well inclined to keep the peace. England's attitude towards treaty obligations at this very time may be judged from Spragge's attack on a rich Dutch convoy from Smyrna in advance of any declaration of war and various other derelictions on our part in connexion with Algiers. In any case Martin's own account of events up to 1677 may be taken as conclusive evidence of the good faith and peaceful attitude of the Algiers government.[3]

A problem peculiar to the English arose out of our occupation of Tangier in pursuit of a policy of imperialistic expansion, which France had abandoned after the disaster at Djidjelli in 1663. It is improbable that the Algerines objected to the action in itself, since our presence there could hardly have been as

---

[1] H.M.C. Tenth Report, App. iv. 412. Martin arranged Thomas Salwey's departure, carrying 'letters from their King to ours', notably the declaration of war.

[2] F. E. Dyer, *Life of Admiral Sir John Narborough*, London, 1931, pp. 140–1. Ward, Bowtell, and Martin warned of danger to peace from non-redemption and abuse of passes.

[3] S.P. 71. 2, 30 Oct. 1677: 'Almost four years I mett with so good success and so well found the temper of these people that I never made any one demand in the King's name without obtaining full satisfaction', giving instances.

unwelcome as that of the Portuguese or Spanish or even the Moors, who were regarded as a very real threat from the West. They did, however, keenly resent the hostile attitude of its governors and inhabitants after the unfortunate death of Lord Teviot in 1664. Its record seems to have been peculiarly bad in both its internal administration and its foreign relations. 'The drunkenest place that ever I came into in my life' is Rycaut's description in 1663, and twenty years later Pepys gives an appalling account of the debauchery and corruption there.[1] Concrete evidence is afforded by the fact that soldiers were often ready to risk slavery in Morocco rather than endure the tyranny of garrison life, and our *consul at Cadiz* was specially commissioned to ensure that supplies were properly applied to the use of the garrison.

After Teviot's death the attitude of Tangier towards Algiers appears to have been definitely provocative. Colonel Norwood, who acted as deputy governor, and wrote of the 'excellent peace with Algiers' in December 1664, actually bragged a few years later of a treacherous attempt to inveigle into port and capture an Algiers cruiser in search of water, and that at a time when its ships were reported to have given so much proof of goodwill towards us.[2] Teviot's successor, Lord Belasyse, when dealing with Algerine prizes, frankly admitted his partiality for the Spanish and French, though they were then recognized as either covert or open enemies, and apparently condoned the lawlessness and rapacity of his own people. Even before the war with France and Holland privateers were equipped so as to 'busy troublesome heads' and to open 'an honest way of livelyhood to those Englishmen whose necessities have debauched them to unable and shifting wayes of living'.[3]

It is small wonder that the Algerines insisted on the removal of Lord Belasyse or complained of the inhabitants, who threw stones at their seamen. The cities of North Africa are said to have 'shuddered at the name' of Admiral Herbert, who, according to Pepys, starved to death 500 Turks, while, he suspected, continuing to charge their subsistence to the government, 'for his cruelty exceeded their own', but Narborough actually was

---

[1] Finch, i. 280; S.P. 104. 188.
[2] To Allin, S.P. 71. 13, f. 643; Routh, pp. 135–6.
[3] Heathcote, pp. 201–24; Routh, pp. 86–87.

regarded at Algiers as the less humane of the two.[1] The trouble was, however, of longer standing, and Pepys proposed to the Admiralty committee on 27 December 1674 that the government of Tangier 'might be directed from time to time to see that all fitting respect and friendship be shown to any ships and vessels of Algiers which shall happen to put into that place . . . the civility of that people everywhere requiring it'.[2]

Charles apparently had been too busy with his cynical war on the Dutch and attempt to destroy their trade to attend to obligations in Barbary. His attitude to Tripoli had been negligent, if not discourteous, and he had not displayed any appreciation of the friendliness of Tunis to both Allin and Spragge. More important for the moment, he had made no attempt to implement Spragge's treaty with Algiers either by securing the neutrality of his subjects or by paying the redemption money for those English slaves whom their owners were bound to deliver up, not at their market value, but at a very considerable sacrifice. They had now for nearly three years been in the nature of frozen assets, and had given rise to 'several mutinies on the part of their present owners, who were prevented from selling them at a profit'. Charles's indifference to the sufferings of his unhappy subjects was quite inexcusable, for there had been for over two years a balance of between £4,000 and £5,000 lying idle in the redemption fund. Bowtell had already expressed the opinion that the delay was very unfair to all parties concerned,[3] and both he and Martin felt that it seriously endangered the peace, a contingency which both the government and merchants regarded with dismay.

The Dey, perhaps at Martin's suggestion, addressed two ultimatums to Charles, insisting that the slaves must be redeemed before the end of November 1674, their prompt redemption having been the 'first and cheef poynt of our Peace', a matter on which Spragge may at the time have given verbal assurances. Charles took the attitude that the treaty did not compel him to pay by any definite date, was very reluctant

---

[1] (Sir) A. Bryant, *Samuel Pepys, Saviour of the Navy*, London, 1938, pp. 77–78; d'Arvieux, v. 161–2. Up to 1680 Moslem prisoners were, by our naval instructions, treated as 'marketable commodities'. For pitiful details see Allin, *Journals*, ii. 116 and 242–3.

[2] Tanner, ii. 419–20 and iv. 120.

[3] S.P. 71. 2, f. 127; Rawlinson MS. A. 185, f. 351.

to pay out the money himself, and could obtain no contribution from the merchants. Yet 'so tender is he of giving any the least occasion of a breach with that government' that he ordered Narborough to sail as quickly as possible, so as to arrive at Algiers with the redemption money before the term fixed. He was then to proceed to Tunis and Tripoli for the overdue renewals of the peace with them. A letter was also hurriedly dispatched to Martin to advise him of this decision, but, owing to the misconduct of the captain of the *Deptford* ketch, it never reached him.[1]

The unusual speed with which Charles proceeded on this occasion to settle a financial obligation was clearly a tribute to the importance and reality of Algerine goodwill, of which the Pepys papers contain much evidence. The Venetian diplomatic reports, which usually reflect accurately feeling in court and commercial circles, related 'the demand does not seem unjust though it is a rude way of protesting to the king of England'. They illustrated the subsequent anxiety of the government to preserve its prestige by issuing information to contradict reports that 'even these corsairs treated the crown of England with disrespect and to maintain the repute of the flag and commercial activity which is of such vital importance to the exchequer'.[2]

A board of commissioners consisting of Narborough, Martin, and John Brisbane, the judge advocate of the fleet, who had had considerable experience of the Barbary coast, had, with the assistance as secretary of Lieutenant Cloudesley Shovell, little difficulty in arranging matters, the 'very intricate' work of listing the slaves with their proper prices having been already done by Ward and Martin with the help of local officials. Some trouble arose at first through an attempt by Brisbane, with an eye, according to d'Arvieux, to his own pecuniary benefit or, according to his own account, to save His Majesty's purse, to substitute some depreciated local currency for the Spanish dollars obtained for the purpose at Cadiz, the recognized medium of exchange on the coast.

---

[1] Pepys to Martin, depending on his 'discretion and good husbandry', 19 Oct. 1674, Tanner, ii. 380. Narborough's instructions were drawn up at a 'special meeting. Sunday morning' of the Admiralty Committee, 18 Oct., ibid., iv. 69.

[2] V.S.P. 1673–5, pp. 304 and 337.

Another unfortunate episode occurred through Narborough sending back seventeen Englishmen, whom Brisbane had arranged to redeem from a Sallee cruiser, which arrived in the port. The Dey was shocked at what he regarded as an act of inhumanity and, in accordance with the treaty, refused to let the captives be sold on shore. His son-in-law, out of pity, is said to have purchased the freedom of a young member of the group, and Herbert and another captain ransomed the rest by means of a collection in the fleet.[1] Altogether about 200 captives were redeemed, and in a letter, which d'Arvieux was asked to translate from the Turkish, the Dey expressed his appreciation of Narborough and Martin, though Martin himself feared that the meanness shown by his two colleagues in small matters might leave a bad impression.[2]

Of all the questions, however, affecting our relations with Algiers the most important and persistent was that of neutrality in general and of the Mediterranean passes in particular. Pepys from the time that he became secretary lost no opportunity of condemning 'the universal loss of discipline among the seamen of England' and the corrupt practices of naval commanders, some of whom he tells us could not even read or write. The consuls were apparently more reliable, as Pepys was constantly finding new duties for them, including the task of controlling the activities of commanders in or near their ports.[3]

Thanks largely to his keen interest in anything even remotely connected with naval affairs and to the reports of his friend Martin, who also, to Coventry's great wrath, kept in close touch with Williamson, he was well acquainted with events and reactions in Algiers, though unfortunately not yet with those of Tripoli. Except in one or two instances he seems to have displayed both moderation and common sense, and shared the

[1] D'Arvieux, v. 161–2; S.P. 71. 2, 12 Dec. 1674.

[2] D'Arvieux, v. 163. 'That tedious and troublesome labour' was completed within two months of date of instructions. It gave general satisfaction, and 'they have been very civil and kind and inclineable to continue the peace in general', Narborough to Pepys, 13 Jan. 1675, S.P. 71. 2.

[3] Consular efficiency resulted from royal interest, departmental ability under Arlington, Williamson, Pepys, Jenkins, and Hedges, and especially co-operation by experienced merchants throughout the Mediterranean area. On 3 June 1664 Read (1630–65) reported from Leghorn about Rome, Alicante, Toulon, Tripoli, Algiers, Malta, Naples, and Milan. In 1664 he also corresponded with Tunis and Lawson and wrote about Dalmatia, Tangier, Spain, and convoys.

king's anxiety to avoid the expense and risk of any entanglements in the Mediterranean or any unnecessary dependence on
the port of Leghorn.

The scandalous laxity in the issue of Mediterranean passes,
which had gradually ceased to conform to the terms of Lawson's
treaty, and the failure to implement the verbal understanding
relative to service on enemy ships had placed both the Algiers
government and our consuls in a very embarrassing position.
The fraudulent 'colouring' of the Venetian ship *Horologio di
Mare* in 1672 was too blatant to be overlooked, and in response
to indignant protests from the Dey and Ward the culprit, John
Dodington, our resident at Venice, was ignominiously recalled,
though it is quite likely that the personal animosity of the Duke
of York contributed to his fate.[1]

The opening sentence of a vitriolic circular addressed on
10 January 1676 by Coventry to our consuls and ministers at
sea-ports in the Mediterranean may perhaps give a highly-
coloured picture of the position: 'Such daily Complaints are
brought his Majesty of Forraine Vessells passing for English by
Passeports or Allowance from his Majesty's Agents or Consuls,
a practice so highly prejudiciall to the honour of his Treatys
and the safety of the Trade and his Subjects', adding that any
of them who connived at such violation of the treaty should
'feele the Uttermost effects of his Majesty's Indignation'.[2]

The Dey seems to have been very patient and our consuls
very persuasive. At one time Martin reported that over fifty
Englishmen serving on enemy ships had been allowed to go
free, on the plea that they only did so because they were in
distress at foreign ports, but this excuse began to wear thin. He
himself expressed the opinion that the prospect of slavery would
be 'no ill thing' in deterring our seamen from deserting or
giving preference to foreign ships.[3] In the same way it was
obviously undesirable that we should facilitate foreign competition by enabling other vessels to use our passes.

The determining factor at Algiers was, as usual, the attitude
of the army, which felt that it—or the nation that it repre-

---

[1] Reports from Algiers by Ward 12 Dec. 1672 and Francis Baker 17 Dec.,
S.P. 71. 2; V.S.P. 1671–2, pp. 220–1.

[2] S.P. 104. 185, f. 28; Add. MS. 25121, f. 32.

[3] 28 Nov. 1674, n.s., S.P. 71. 2.

sented—was being defrauded of its just rights. It is a tribute to the administration that it had for three very difficult years been able to control the indignant slave-owners, soldiers, and shipping interest. The much-quoted control of the government by a 'cunning covetous English woman who would sell her soul for a bribe'[1] was, I fancy, largely the product of Martin's imaginative pen, and used as one of those specious arguments by which consuls sought to obtain increases of their very inadequate allowances, though it did become usual and politic to compliment the wives and daughters of the Deys. 'Woman hath her Empire even among these unpolished nations. . . . She must be nobly Presented for our Purpose', writes a later consul, when a plan for engaging Algiers in an active alliance against France was on the carpet; but actually we only hear of the influence of women on such occasions, and Martin makes no other reference to this one.[2]

D'Arvieux describes her at the time as a young Englishwoman who had recently married the aged Dey and borne him two sons. He adds, with apparent accuracy, that the state was really managed by Baba Hassan, the Dey's son-in-law. Although d'Arvieux had frequent altercations with the latter and always spoke of him as *ce brutal* and of his rough manner, he later summed him up, in spite of his faults, as a man of intelligence, good judgement, and ability in the conduct of state affairs, fairly popular with the army and a *bon ami*.[3] As his father-in-law's assistant and successor he ruled Algiers during more than ten years of critical history, and lost his life eventually owing to his willingness to treat with the French during Duquesne's savage bombardment in 1683. It is possible that the bluntness and directness of his manner was better suited to Martin than to the punctilious French consul, who had very extravagant ideas as to what was due to the King of France and his official representative, and managed to quarrel with everyone in Algiers except his English colleague.

According to Martin 'the last Haricano was a Mutiny of ye Souldiers about the English captives', which compelled the Dey to 'write in a severe strain to his Majesty' early in October

---

[1] Ibid., 6 May 1676.
[2] S.P. 71. 3, f. 496.
[3] v. 248, and elsewhere 'avide d'argent et d'honneur'.

1674.[1] This letter, together with one from Martin, was by command read by Pepys to the Admiralty committee on 27 December. After describing 'the quiet state of affairs between his Majesty and that Government and the likelihood of their continuance', they suggested that the king should forbid his subjects to continue to serve on enemy ships, and that genuine passengers and their goods should be protected by certificates under the hand of any minister or officer of the king known to the consul. This proposal 'appearing very reasonable to his Majesty', Pepys was ordered to prepare a proclamation on the subject.[2] It is interesting to note that while Martin recommended the measure as being in the interest of our shipping, Pepys suggested for the same reason a restriction of the privileges offered to English passengers rather than 'take the benefit of the Argereens' offer to the utmost extent of the words', thus in effect according Algiers a preferential treatment under the treaty, which was to puzzle Collingwood 130 years later.

In spite of the urgency of avoiding ground for 'just complaint', 'just matter of quarrel', 'provocations' to a rupture, and a variety of similar phrases, to the Algerines, the 'Proclamation Relating to Articles of Peace concluded between His Majesty and the Government of Algiers' was not issued until 22 December 1675. It provided that 'if any offenders contrary to this His Royal Proclamation shall be taken His Majesty *will not require any release of their persons or estates* from the said Government of Algiers but that they must expect to be excluded (as they were intended) out of all benefit of the said articles'. It also instructed 'Passengers in foreign ships or vessels to take care that they have passports with them signed by His Majesty's proper Ministers in England or His Ministers or Consulls abroad expressing the names of their persons and the contents and qualities of their Goods at their perils'. This regulation or agreement remained in force until at least 1765, and the only trouble appears to have arisen from negligence in issuing or obtaining passenger certificates.

On the same date appeared another proclamation of even

[1] S.P. 71. 2, 10 Oct. 1674.
[2] Tanner, iv. 189 and ii. 419–20. The Dey's letter greatly pleased Charles, 'putting him in great quiet in reference to the trouble and charge which an untimely breach with that people might have occasioned'.

greater importance, relating to the carriage of Admiralty passes, but unfortunately not so well conceived. Pepys, who had been entrusted with drawing up the necessary rules for their form and method of issue, was well aware of the abuses prevalent at the time and the dangers to which they might give rise—'the great temptation and provocation to the Algerines and the Turks of other places in amity with us to see foreign ships pass by them under English colours . . . the consequences whereof is very much apprehended, it giving the Turks too just an occasion of a rupture with us when it shall seem seasonable on their parts to make it'. It must be remembered that the arrangement represented a great concession by the Algerines, which a later secretary of state frankly described as 'inequitable' to them during their blockade of Oran, since the production of a pass enabled our ships to proceed freely, even though carrying enemy persons and supplies.[1]

Good faith and strict regulation were essential to the system, and it was most unfortunate that Pepys or his committee should have been so influenced by some doctrinaire consideration or regard for the 'King's honour' or perhaps the complaints of leading ship-owners, of which both had had experience, as not to render the new rules really effective. The most obvious—and indeed inexplicable—flaw was rectified shortly after Pepys had been removed from office, but it is significant that even in 1805, in spite of numerous royal proclamations, orders in council, and protests from Deys and consuls, the articles in the treaty of 1682 relating to 'proper passes' are described as 'neither well understood and (*sic*) observed'.[2] This could hardly be said of the French system based on their treaty of 1666, which was drawn up in such explicit language as to leave no room for doubt or special pleading.[3]

The principal regulations for the issue of these passes, which remained substantially in force up to the reign of William IV, were that they could be issued only by the Admiralty and only to 'English-built ships or foreign built ships made free' and to none 'whereof the master is not his Majesty's natural subject

---

[1] Harrington to Waldegrave, 1733, Add. MS. 32779, ff. 358–62.

[2] Bruce, *Travels*, i, p. lx n.

[3] 'Les navires, Galères et autres Bâtiments tant de guerre que de marchandises' must carry the passes of the Admiral of France.

or foreign Protestant made denizen and whereof two-thirds of
the mariners are not his Majesty's subjects'.[1] They were issued
only for a limited period after the master had taken the usual
oaths and given bond for their surrender. They were to be
'printed upon a certain size of parchment . . . that so they may
be distinguished from all other passes', and they were 'in-
dented' or 'scolloped', i.e. perforated, so that the tops or
'counterparts' could be detached and the Algerine commanders
on the high seas or the consul, if necessary, in port might be
enabled to check their authenticity.

They were prepared by Pepys, who kept a special register
for the purpose, and very strict rules were made about their
issue at any ports outside London. The form of the pass was
probably the same as that employed by the Duke of York in
1663, and the Admiralty fee was also the same. The rules for
issue, however, were considerably improved. As, unlike other
ship's passes, they could only be signed by the lord high admiral
himself, they were in the reign of James II issued under the
hand and seal of the sovereign, with the counter-signature of
'S. Pepys'.[2]

The issue of these two proclamations seemed likely to have
the desired effect of allaying 'the apprehensions his Majesty
hath had of the inconvenience which a rupture with Argeir
would be attended with and the consideration of the little
security we can long expect to have with that government *under
the provocations daily given them* by the King's subjects abroad
in sailing and protecting of foreign ships and either counterfeiting or selling of their true passes to ships of foreign property'.[3] Martin expressed his satisfaction, and described how,
after he had displayed the pass at the public divan, Baba
Hassan made an oration, 'telling that now it pleased God to
continue a peace', which had proved so beneficial for four
years, and pointing out that the abuses of the flag, &c., were
really no 'fault of the King of England'. As Martin went along
the street even the children cried out 'English Christians are
good men'.[4]

---

[1] App. J. Shipowners sought its extension to Danish trade, Cal. S.P.D. 1677–8,
p. 33.
[2] Signed by Charles II ?1684–5.   [3] Tanner, iii. 174 and 152.
[4] S.P. 71. 2, 6 May 1676.

Disillusionment quickly followed. The discipline which Charles threatened to impose on his subjects abroad was far from effective. In June the secretary of state was reprimanding our consul at Venice for having 'presumed to give men that you know to be seamen passes as passengers',[1] and Pepys was inquiring of the merchants about 'the practices still on foot of applying passes granted for the benefit only of his Majesty's own subjects to the colouring of foreign ships and goods' and for particulars of a foreign ship at Leghorn and the name of the 'English house by which she is fathered'. Only through prosecution, he pointed out, could these frauds be stopped, but the efficacy of even that procedure was dubious. Only a year before he had stated that the colouring of foreign ships was 'compassed with so much villainy in the false oaths and other indirect ways of procuring denizations that no course can be thought too severe for the suppressing of it'.[2] It continued, however, apparently with impunity into the nineteenth century.

How little attention was paid to denunciations of the colouring and protecting of foreign ships was shown the following summer by His Majesty's own ship the *Quaker* ketch, which escorted a Dutch ship flying English colours through Algerine waters. Both ships were arrested and towed into Algiers, but the ketch was released after examination. It is significant that the commander was not blamed for this flagrant breach of treaty obligations or the king's published orders, but only for 'suffering himself to be carried away and towed into that port'. Pepys even goes so far as to say 'such an affront cannot, I think, be remembered to have been ever offered to, much less borne by, any other', despite the fact that our own ships do not seem to have hesitated to use violence on very slender grounds to the warships of other countries, and the *Quaker* had itself been captured, apparently with less justification, by an Ostender earlier *in that very year*.[3]

It is hardly surprising that when Martin demanded satisfaction for 'this shameful insult', as Playfair calls it, he was answered with 'bad words and violence'. He was in fact told that England might declare war if she liked, but he thought it more prudent to accommodate matters. There is, so far as I am

---

[1] Add. MS. 25121, f. 43.   [2] Tanner, iii. 212 and 54.
[3] Ibid., pp. 287, 290 and xxxviii; Coxere, p. xi.

aware, no foundation whatever for the statement that he was nearly burned alive, or indeed suffered any physical violence, and it is clear from his subsequent statements that he was still influential with the government.[1]

The main trouble, however, arose out of what was obviously a misunderstanding about the Admiralty passes. The Algerines evidently thought, as probably anyone would who read Pepys's rules, that all English ships were required thenceforth to carry them, and consequently those that had none were promptly stopped and brought into Algiers.[2] That did not necessarily involve seizure, and we know that Martin managed to clear them, but the Algerines, who felt that they were being tricked, were no longer in an accommodating mood, though a French observer has commented on their patience at this very time.[3] Pepys was in a rage when a valuable ship belonging to the Houblons, 'English built of English propriety . . . and manned wholly with his Majesty's subjects is carried into Algiers upon no other score than that of her not having a pass to the manifest violation of the treaty of his Majesty and that people by which her being manned with English expressly exempts her from the necessity of having any passes'.[4]

In other words, no genuinely English vessel manned according to the requirements of our Navigation Laws (or even, according to one interpretation of the treaty, some that did not conform) needed passes,[5] but that did not prevent one from being taken into port, since in the absence of a pass only the consul would be in a position to verify its bona fides. The fundamental object of the pass was to enable a ship to proceed freely without any further verification, and it is noticeable that in the next treaty passes were made obligatory.

Anxious as Charles was to avoid entanglements, no alternative seems to have been considered but the immediate use of a show of force, which had seldom proved effective in the past. Instructions were promptly sent to Narborough at Cadiz to proceed to Algiers with his squadron and, if necessary, to

---

[1] Playfair, pp. 122–4; S.P. 71. 2, 17 Aug. 1676, n.s.
[2] They said this was 'His Majesty's wish', S.P. 71. 2, 21 July 1676.
[3] *Un Académicien*, p. 22.
[4] Tanner, iii. 229 and 242.
[5] Interpretations varied between 'all', two-thirds, and 'a majority'. Algiers only claimed right to remove foreign goods.

declare war. The dates are interesting. 'The merchants of good quality' only made their complaint in July 1676, a warning letter was sent to Narborough on 10 July and his definite instructions on the 14th.[1] He could presumably have been at Algiers by the end of the month but he did not actually arrive until 23 November 1677, or about sixteen months later, having spent the previous three months picking up Algiers ships as prizes[2] and perhaps seeing what help he could give the Spaniards at Oran.[3]

According to Martin the heads of the Algiers government were anxious for peace, but the arrival of a badly battered cruiser brought things to a head. A general divan of an exceptional composition was called, and war was declared, contrary to the wishes of the rulers, in October 1677. The vessels whose clearance Martin had obtained were again seized. Charles had presumably received the Dey's notification some days before Narborough arrived at Algiers.[4]

It is hardly surprising that the Algerines were in no mood to treat with him, especially as his force was by no means an imposing one. It is interesting to note that, while we were prepared to go to war with Algiers on what was really an arguable point, Narborough and other officials did not regard his proceedings in capturing prizes or fighting bloody actions as acts of war and make no reference to hostile actions at the time by the French and others.[5] Even when we had forced war upon Algiers the operations of its cruisers, normally referred to by Pepys as 'Turkish privateers', are still designated in modern histories as 'piratical'. It was, however, the Algerines who insisted on the restitution of all Turkish captives as a preliminary to negotiations with Narborough, and it would be hard to find in the official correspondence, Parliamentary speeches, or

---

[1] Tanner, iii. 229–30.
[2] See F. E. Dyer, *Journal of Grenvill Collins* (*Mariner's Mirror*, xiv). Ships not warned received passes in which they 'had full confidence'.
[3] Cal. S.P.D. 1677–8, p. 541.
[4] S.P. 71. 2, 30 Oct. 1677. The Clerk of the Privy Council mentions, 20 Sept. 1677, 'new war declared with Algiers' which, 25 Dec., was 'very galling', H.M.C. Ormonde Papers iv. 17 and 390. Algiers cruisers received munitions, &c., at Brest, Cals. S.P.D. 1678, p. 378, and 1680–1, p. 636.
[5] *A List of Several Ships, belonging to English Merchants taken by French Privateers, since December 1673*, Amsterdam, 1677, containing complaint from Charles to Louis and details of 53.

instructions of King Charles, who described the war as beginning through a 'certain misunderstanding' on both sides and
ending with 'a very honourable peace', any indication that it
differed from the hostilities in which we were apt to engage so
unceremoniously with Christian powers.[1]

The war, which Martin thought quite unnecessary and Pepys
had prayed 'God may avert', proved neither glorious nor
successful; for, though we may at times have administered some
hard knocks, Algiers is said to have thriven on it. Their cruisers
caused considerable consternation in our own waters, apparently with French connivance. Robert Cole, who was later
consul and was evidently at large in Algiers at this time, estimated that they took 157 of our merchant ships and 3,000
seamen and that the war cost us £300,000,[2] while French
writers quote much higher figures. Clearly the situation did
not deter their government from sending an ultimatum to
King Louis, then described as the arbiter of Europe, and
declaring war on him, a circumstance to which one French
historian attributes our ability to buy a peace with them.[3]

Certainly Captain Shovell, acting for Admiral Herbert,
Narborough's successor, found Baba Hassan anything but
anxious for peace at any price. The Dey in laying Shovell's
proposals before the divan maintained that England had broken
the peace by not demanding satisfaction through negotiation,
and told Shovell he would rather be at war with a potent
prince than with his own subjects.[4] Sir James Houblon had
complained not long before to Pepys: 'We are (God help us)
totally without Guard in the Mediterranean . . . not one man
of war there', and Pepys himself speaks of 'the King's incapacity
to maintain the war longer'.[5]

Herbert's treaty of April 1682, however much criticized by
Pepys and also by Finch at the Admiralty, appears to have

---

[1] Credentials of Philip Rycaut, ? April 1683, Rawlinson MS. A. 257, f. 67, refer
to 'ancient friendship established upon just and lasting terms'. For Lord Mayor's
peace proclamation, see Cal. S.P.D. 1682, p. 196. Instructions for letters of marque
against Algiers include 'none to be killed in cold blood or by torture or cruelty or
inhumanly treated contrary to the common usage of war', Cal. S.P.D. 1680–1,
pp. 617–18.   [2] Treasury Papers 1702–7, pp. 250–1.

[3] De Grammont, p. 247; Morgan, p. vi.   [4] Add. MS. 28093, ff. 190–1.

[5] *Letters and Second Diary of Samuel Pepys*, ed. R. G. Howarth, London, 1932,
p. 104; *Tangier Papers of Samuel Pepys*, ed. E. Chappell (N.R.S.), London, 1935,
p. 203.

been ratified by Charles with great satisfaction. Its most important provision was that the rule about a majority of English seamen was abandoned, and that all British merchant ships were required 'not being in any of the seas appertaining to his Majesty's dominions to produce a pass under the hand and seal of the Lord High Admiral of England and Ireland or of Scotland or of commissioners executing those offices'. Except for the addition of the Scottish Admiralty, Pepys's arrangements for passes remained unaltered, though the fee was reduced.

Another article hardly seems very creditable, since it provided that the redemption of slaves need not take place immediately and, instead of at cost price as in Spragge's treaty, 'only at a reasonable price as usually paid for the redemption of slaves of other nations'. It was presumably on account of this clause, and perhaps of a verbal understanding regarding the return of slaves who might take refuge on our ships, that Charles's 'very honourable peace' was stigmatized by the venerable French vicar general as 'the most shameful peace imaginable'.[1]

Certain important points were left deplorably vague—so far at least as the English text of the treaty was concerned. It is, however, clear from subsequent correspondence that vessels without passes might be condemned, together with their cargoes and crews, and that the king's subjects serving for pay on foreign ships could be made slaves, facts which were often unknown to our naval commanders and even secretaries of state.[2] Whatever its defects, the treaty served its purpose, as it endured with some amendments for nearly a hundred and fifty years. From the time of its conclusion until after Waterloo we had no armed conflict, or I think any really serious trouble, with Algiers or either of the other regencies—surely a very satisfactory record for those or any other days.[3]

Our previous relations with the smaller and more distant state of Tripoli, which was then under the joint rule of a Dey

---

[1] De Grammont, p. 247. Playfair, p. 140, says quite incorrectly that 'similar terms were agreed to by every European State at this time'. Pepys expected Charles would object to the clause and criticized the treaty's 'imperfections' and 'extravagancy'. It was examined very carefully at the Admiralty and Council Board, Finch, ii. 170–5.

[2] Amended by treaties of 1700 and 1765.

[3] *A.R.* 1816, p. 335.

and bashaw, call for some mention because it was the one occasion on which one of these states was largely in the wrong, and restitution or compensation was finally exacted. It helps to illustrate defects in our attitude towards these states, until, after the conclusion of Herbert's treaty, a markedly different point of view was adopted.

As frequently pointed out, the basis of peace was the appointment of a consul. Stokes authorized Sam Tucker to act at Tripoli after making his treaty of 1658, and Lawson confirmed him in 1662, apparently promising him an ample allowance. As, however, he actually received nothing, Tucker was given nine months' leave of absence by the bashaw in 1667, in order to obtain in London some amelioration of his situation. Although the Treasury recognized the necessity for making some financial grant, in order to maintain a 'good correspondence' with the country, and the government recognized the seriousness of the position,[1] no satisfactory offer was made to him. It was not till late in 1671, after a warning from Leghorn, that his successor Nathaniel Bradley arrived in Spragge's ship with instructions to apologize for the 'knavvery of Sam Tooker who after shuffling delays was obliged to return and ought to have been there two years since'.[2]

The atmosphere of resulting suspicion and resentment was not improved by Charles's failure to take any notice of the Dey, who was elected soon afterwards on the death of his predecessor, or even to make the customary renewal of the treaty of peace and friendship with him. In consequence, the Dey, after due warning, declared the treaty at an end, and proceeded to bring into port the *Hunter,* carrying goods from Leghorn to Smyrna, and the *Martin,* described as a rich ship bound from Venice to Cadiz. The very considerable enemy-owned portions of the cargoes were then removed, but no other loss was suffered apart from some petty pilfering and the consul's charges.[3]

When, in November 1674, this news reached London, unfortunately in an exaggerated form, Narborough had already left for the Mediterranean with the customary present and in-

---

[1] Treasury Books 1667–8, p. 211. He received only £200 until in 1669 a royal commission was issued, S.P. 104. 174 B, f. 195.

[2] S.P. 71. 22, 31 Mar. 1671. An earlier draft, ?1670, contrasted Tucker's betrayal of trust with Tripoli's 'constant goodwill', ibid., f. 211. Barlow, i. 156.

[3] Rycaut, p. 242, consul at Smyrna.

1673-82 OUR RELATIONS WITH THE REGENCIES 267

structions to renew the peace. Orders were immediately sent overland in triplicate, via Cadiz, Marseilles, and Leghorn, to obtain restitution, but to avoid a rupture, if possible, by first using 'all fair means of satisfying the people of Tripoli'. This instruction the admiral apparently ignored. He refused at first to send anyone ashore to discuss matters, saying that his letter demanding restitution was quite sufficient. Finally, he did send two officers, in whose presence the sea-captains were consulted in turn, but all voted against restitution.[1]

Narborough's force was inadequate to maintain an effective blockade, even with the aid of the neighbouring base at Malta, where at first he was hardly a welcome visitor. The Tripoli cruisers managed to sally forth on occasion and inflict a little damage,[2] but a more serious consideration was the expense of what Narborough called this 'chargeable war'. The government at home was greatly worried, partly because the merchants complained of their losses through unduly precipitate action, and Narborough was authorized to lower his terms, though the principle of substantial compensation was never abandoned. There was, however, no longer any question of 'heads rolling'. We were prepared to offer, if necessary, some of the concessions contained in Spragge's treaty with Algiers, including the verbal understanding regarding the enslavement of Britons serving on enemy ships.[3]

Actual hostilities lasted about a year and included few events of consequence—Lieutenant Shovell's celebrated destruction by fire of four ships in Tripoli harbour, a brush with four more of their ships, the sinking of five vessels laden with corn and, on the Tripolitan side, the capture at sea of the *Bristol Merchant* with its rich cargo. In March 1676 peace was concluded, largely through the good offices of a former Dey of Tunis.[4] Tripoli restored all British captives, except those taken on enemy ships, and also paid compensation equivalent to £18,000, partly in money, partly in goods, and partly in Christian slaves, mainly Maltese, in recognition of our use of Malta as a base. Narborough appears to have used good sense and made no attempt, like Blake at Tunis, to dictate terms from his flagship. The final terms were negotiated and ratified in the

[1] S.P. 71. 22, f. 163. [2] V.S.P. 1673–5, pp. 479–80.
[2] S.P. 29. 366, f. 77. [4] Rycaut, p. 245.

bashaw's palace, in accordance with local ceremonial, including the removal of shoes. The proceedings were only marred, after the conclusion of the treaty, by an undignified wrangle about a present of horses for King Charles, which threatened to lead to another rupture.[1]

Two months later the Dey, who had apparently never been popular, fled from Tripoli, and the opportunity was taken of adding some extra and rather more abject clauses to the treaty, which do not, however, seem to have been recorded in the Turkish register, particularly the one conferring the right to fly the national flag on the consulate.

The conclusion of peace was received with general acclamation. Both Charles and the people of Tripoli were delighted. Pepys described its terms as 'such as had never been granted before to a Christian prince', not unjustly, since they contained an admission of wrong-doing and provided for compensation, however inadequate. The rewards given, especially to Shovell and his flotilla, were generous and to some extent unprecedented. It was, however, regarded as an uncomfortably costly affair, and probably Will Hewer's comment on Herbert's treaty a few years later was equally applicable to this: 'a Peace for saving charges at this time is not, I believe, unpleasing to the Treasury'. Both wars had the disagreeable effect of reminding us that, despite our occupation of Tangier and the, perhaps grudging, permission to make use of forward bases at Malta and Port Mahon, we were still essentially dependent in such crises on supplies from Leghorn and the goodwill of the Grand Duke.

Fortunately, instead of damaging mutual relations, these two wars contributed to better understanding and ushered in a remarkably long period of peace. The treaty with Tripoli evidently achieved Narborough's objective of an 'honourable and last(ing) peace', which was consolidated by the happy appointment of Thomas Baker, with improved emoluments and the rank of agent and consul general.[2] That small state, indeed, was ready soon afterwards to throw in its lot with King William, when his stock in Europe was very low. Its amazing resilience,

---

[1] *Journal of Augustus Holsteyn*, Sloane MS. 2755, ff. 12 sqq. James Houblon wrote of 'an honourable peace', Cal. S.P.D. 1676–7, p. 67.

[2] S.P. 104. 185, ff. 158–9.

or the conventional under-estimation of its strength and resources, is demonstrated by the fact that, within five years of
the conclusion of Narborough's treaty, it had thrown down the
gauntlet to France. Though Masson draws a tragic picture of
its subsequent derelict condition, it was still capable of making
a decided contribution to the new assessment, by England and
France at any rate, of the strategic importance of the Barbary
States in the imminent struggle for supremacy in the Mediterranean.

Our relations with Tunis, though on the eve of its long civil
war between the Deys and the Beys, continued to be of a friendly
nature. Our merchants continued, unaided, to maintain our
commercial pre-eminence, despite the special French interest
in that area, and to conduct at their own expense our consular
affairs in a creditable and satisfactory manner.

XV

OUR RELATIONS WITH THE REGENCIES
1682 TO 1712

ANY ill will that might have been engendered in Algiers by the operations of Narborough and Herbert was quickly effaced by the conclusion of a peace that promised to be satisfactory; by the intelligent and sympathetic attitude of King Charles's government, attributable doubtless in large measure to the influence of Sir Leoline Jenkins,[1] the new secretary of state; and by the rapid deterioration of Algerine relations with France and even with Holland, despite the treaty so recently negotiated.

Martin is last heard of in confinement after the declaration of war, treated, he claimed, like a 'condemned criminal', though he had no difficulty in writing voluminous letters, including a narrative of his consulship addressed to his 'Noble Lord and Patron'—presumably Arlington. In this he lays the blame for the rupture on Narborough's violence—'seizing cruisers and banging others'—so different, apparently, from the reasonable attitude of the Algiers government.[2] He himself said that he had many good friends among the principal Turks. It is clear that the Dey was well disposed towards him, and that he was, as he himself suggests, confined for his own protection during an outburst of public indignation on the arrival of an Algiers cruiser with much damage and many casualties, as a result of which war was declared. He must have died soon afterwards, as his widow was awarded a pension in July 1680.[3]

The post was filled temporarily by Captain (later Admiral) John Nevill until the arrival of Philip Rycaut, who came on a diplomatic footing, with the title of agent and consul. Most unusually, he brought with him a letter of extremely sensible

---

[1] He probably influenced Charles's decision that consulates in Barbary were more valuable than legations in Italy, P.C. 2/69, p. 333, 28 July 1681; S.P. 104. 190, 23 Feb. and 30 Sept. 1683; S.P. 98. 16, 6 Apr. 1683.

[2] S.P. 71. 2, 30 Oct. 1677.

[3] Treasury Books, 1679–80, p. 643.

instructions, telling him, among other things, how he was to behave towards the local authorities and the consuls of friendly countries and how he should be careful to conform to the laws and customs of the land.[1] After a very short stay and for no apparent reason, except perhaps the necessity of finding employment for his successor, he was replaced by John Erlisman, formerly consul at Tunis and controller at Tangier, whose instructions were even more extensive. He had a larger salary than Rycaut and was prohibited from trading.[2]

Rycaut had hardly arrived when trouble arose out of Dartmouth's violation of the treaty and differences of opinion about the status of English slaves purchased from Sallee. It was most unfortunate that advantage was not taken of the presence of two such intelligent and experienced seamen as Nevill, then stationed at Tangier, and the new Dey Mezzomorto,[3] who was soon afterwards commanding a fleet of a hundred ships against Russia, to adjust various clauses of the treaty.

Nevill had formed strong views on many points, including the use of passes by all south-bound ships and the high-handed conduct of our men of war, drawing the conclusion that, if the steps he advocated were not taken, the French would make peace with Algiers and force it to make war on us, which was precisely what France tried to do almost immediately afterwards.[4] Mezzomorto, for his part, was very anxious to have certain clauses amended, since, he said, the treaty had been concluded by Baba Hassan, who had no experience of maritime affairs, and must inevitably give rise to misunderstandings. Nothing, however, was done, and on the accession of James II Herbert's treaty was confirmed without any textual alteration, apart from the elimination of any references to Tangier.[5] Even

---

[1] IND. 13396, 26 April 1683. He was to 'desire an audience of the Divan' and 'deliver them Our Letters Credentiall'.

[2] IND. 13396, June 1684.

[3] Cal. S.P.D. 1690–1, p. 332. Turkish soldier, successively Admiral, Dey, and Bashaw at Algiers and Capudan Pasha. See d'Arvieux, v. 127; Lucas, *La Grèce*, ii. 142–3; *H.H.W.* xxiv. 404. Sir Roger Strickland reported 'peace will be strictly observed while in the same hands', IND. 13396, 1 Nov. 1686.

[4] IND. 13396, 5 Jan. 1684, also discussing better interpreting, Englishmen on French ships, and expulsion of disaffected English.

[5] 'Wrangling', reported by Soames and Grafton, resulted from ignorance of verbal assurances, which included return of fugitive slaves, see Playfair, pp. 149–51, and Downshire MSS. i. 273.

Pepys, who had originally been one of the critics of the treaty, does not seem to have fully understood it or, perhaps, possessed no copy.

Ample warning might have been provided by the war which had broken out between France and Algiers, partly owing to the fact that some of the terms of their treaty of 1666 were not sufficiently explicit or reasonable and partly through the hostile attitude of King Louis's subjects and officials.[1]

While the clause about passes and the conduct of warships at sea was much more ample and specific than in our treaties, the position regarding Frenchmen serving on enemy ships was, from the Algiers point of view, most unsatisfactory. According to Louis's interpretation, all his subjects were to go unmolested, regardless of the flag under which they were taken, while the Algerines maintained that, when captured in the service of the enemy, they had forfeited all claim to French protection.

The marked difference between the attitudes of Charles and Louis on this point, as on others, may have been very confusing to the government of Algiers and was complicated further, perhaps, by verbal assurances and inadequate translation. The question, which was a serious one for Algiers, in view of the nationality of so many of the Knights of Malta, seems to have developed into a point of honour for the French. The utmost concession that they were prepared to make, prior to the renewal of the treaty provisions in 1790, was to allow the capture of those actually taken with arms in their hands—clearly a very unsatisfactory compromise.

This point, however, though hardly indicative of goodwill, was of far less immediate importance than the suspicion of bad faith. A French historian has criticized the unreasonableness of the Algerines in not realizing that Louis, whose omnipotence was in fact loudly proclaimed in and out of season, was unable to control *his own officials in his own ports*, a procedure which was so easy and natural under the highly centralized system of Algiers, elsewhere condemned by the same author as anarchical.[2]

The chief trouble arose from the commanders of galleys, who seem to have actually owned their crews of oarsmen, evading restitution of the promised Turks, or from the illegal issue by

---

[1] de Grammont, p. 248.
[2] Plantet, i. 139 n., 335 n., and 355 n.

consuls and others of French passes to enemy vessels. It must have been exceedingly difficult for a Dey to restrain his soldiers when they found that their comrades continued to remain in slavery, perhaps for years after their return had been promised, or saw vessels, which had been released on the strength of a French consular pass, run up the Spanish flag in derision, as soon as they were in safety, or noted serious discrimination in favour of their Christian enemies in the French definition of territorial waters.[1]

So pressing was the need for galley-slaves that Colbert is actually said to have appointed a consul at Canea on condition that he supplied the galleys with 300 or 400 Turks a year at a fixed price. In defiance of treaties or those capitulations of which they made such convenient use, the French continued to enslave Turks and Moors who had been illegally captured, purchased in Malta or Leghorn, or rescued from captivity in Spain. This procedure, which continued almost up to the Revolution, long after Algiers had rejected the galley as obsolete, on such a scale as to justify a special place for Mohammedan worship and burial in Marseilles, was in striking contrast to our own practice, after Herbert's peace, of restoring all Turks and Moors who fell into our hands and trying to effect the liberation of any taken in our ships. During his war with Morocco King William did his best to persuade our naval commanders to refrain from the old practice of treating their captives as booty and selling them to Spain.

The French, indeed, seem to have played their cards very badly, perhaps out of overweening vanity and over-confidence in their dominant position in Europe, and were provocative rather than conciliatory. It is hardly likely that the Algerines, already engaged in war at sea with Britain and until very recently with Holland, in addition to their traditional enemies, and threatened on land by Tunis and Morocco, would voluntarily seek to add to their troubles. It would appear from various accounts that they had lived up to their treaty obligations reasonably well, and that they actually found themselves, in Masson's words, *poussés au bout* by the *mauvaise foi* of the French government.[2]

---

[1] Ibid., pp. 138-9.
[2] Masson, pp. 227-8; Plantet, i. 79 n. and 81; O. Teissier, *Correspondance du*

Finally, in October 1681, after Louis had ignored an ultimatum regarding the return of some Algerines illegally enslaved in the galleys, the vicar general Père le Vacher, who
had been acting as consul since the departure of d'Arvieux five
years before and was greatly respected in Algiers, was summoned to an extraordinary meeting of the divan, which was
attended not only by its ordinary members but by the ships'
captains and officers of the militia. Fresh complaints having
been heard from Turks and Moors about their unwarranted
detention in the galleys, it was unanimously resolved to end the
peace with France. Both Père le Vacher and the French commercial agent Dusault seem to have sympathized to some
extent with the local feeling and would have wished to prevent
the rupture. The evidence of a French academician, which has
been generally ignored, furnishes some startling information
regarding the forbearance of the Algerines, and the *procédés plus
que douteux* of the French, who treated their shipwrecked vessels
as pirates, looting and burning them, and condemned their
crews and other refugees to the galleys, while the Algerines
respected French ships and returned prisoners.

Louis was, however, already at war with Tripoli; he may not
unnaturally have regarded himself as invincible; and he had
a new weapon in the bomb. Algiers, was, like Guérnica in our
own time, intended to illustrate to the world at large the power
and resources of a superior civilization. It is remarkable how
quickly a 'bombardment' came to be regarded as a panacea
for troubles with those weaker countries which were so unfortunate as to possess a coastline, though it was severely
condemned by the French when inflicted by us on Brest.
Duquesne, who arrived in July 1682 with a fleet of thirty-three
ships and refused even to discuss terms through le Vacher, was
at first doomed to disappointment, since he had to depart
without obtaining any satisfaction, 'notwithstanding the extraordinary din he had made', and Louis had to change the date
of the medals already struck to commemorate the destruction
of Algiers.

P. *Jean le Vacher* (*Mélanges historiques*, iv. 757–84), confuses the issue. Savile reported from Paris: 'the Algerines had declared warr against this King for detaining
their subjects in his galleys; perhaps as Christian a ground for quarrel as *pour
ma gloire*', *Letters*, p. 235.

A second bombardment, opened the following June without any preliminaries, quickly brought the acting Dey Baba Hassan to his knees, and 570 captives were promptly surrendered. Duquesne was, however, too exigent, and what promised to be an abject submission was arrested by Mezzomorto, the Algiers admiral, who had been regarded as a friend of the French. By the exercise of considerable duplicity he managed to rouse the soldiers against any further act of surrender, with the result that Hassan was assassinated, Père le Vacher and twenty other French residents were blown from guns, as a protest against the continued bombardment,[1] and Mezzomorto, as the new Dey, conducted a spirited defence. Once more Duquesne found his efforts fruitless, but the following year Dusault, who seems to have remained peacefully in charge of the French concessions, informed his government that Mezzomorto would be disposed to negotiate a settlement, but not through Duquesne, *homme sans parole*.[2]

A peace, rather optimistically designated 'for a hundred years', was concluded with Admiral de Tourville, but it proved an uneasy and short-lived one. Presents and captives were exchanged ; an ambassador was sent to France, partly to apologize for the action of an excited mob in murdering Père le Vacher and his compatriots and partly to ensure the complete liberation of Algerines from the galleys at Toulon; and Louis wrote to the divan that he had ordered his subjects to treat their people as 'les amis de notre Couronne Impériale', a style which French kings affected when dealing with the Turks.[3]

The old troubles persisted, however, as may be seen in the long letters written by Mezzomorto, first as Dey and then as bashaw, by the divan and by the new Dey, Ibrahim Khoja, to the king, to the secretary of state for the marine, to Admiral Tourville, and to the intendant of marine at Toulon. Further

[1] A historian of India calls a similar punishment in cold blood a 'wholesome lesson'. Englishmen used it to a French prisoner in 1590, de la Roncière, iv. 97. The Algerines were apparently ashamed of the act, first executed by a Dutch renegade, Morgan, p. 511 ; de Grammont, pp. 249-52.

[2] Plantet, i. 85 n.

[3] Rycaut ridiculed it. Louis constantly urged admirals to restore prestige in the Levant by some 'action éclatante', Routh, p. 142 n.; Corbett, ii. 74 and 99; de la Roncière, v. 300.

fuel was added to the flame by the frequent escape of slaves on board French vessels, which insisted on anchoring too near to the shore, a procedure earlier disapproved by Colbert, and by failure to pay the stipulated rent of the concessions. It may well be that the English and Dutch did their best to embitter feeling, but it is noticeable that it was a Frenchman who was accused of helping the English to usurp some of the French privileges.[1] The disorder in the French community, and even in the consulate perhaps, formed the subject of a letter from Louis to the divan, and was corroborated by the dissensions between the privileged companies in Algiers and Tunis.[2] Some light is thrown on the state of feeling by an official complaint that French members of the crew of a captured Dutch vessel were treated worse than their English comrades.

Early in 1687 mutual reprisals on a considerable scale were already taking place, and in July 1688 Marshal d'Estrées with 15 warships, 16 galleys, and 10 bomb vessels inflicted on the town an even more severe bombardment, which, apart from displays of inhumanity on both sides, led to no definite result. For the second time Algiers proved capable of much more effective resistance than the unfortunate port of Genoa had done. While the damage inflicted on civilians in Algiers and on French commerce in general was very great, and the cost of the expeditions very heavy, the military results achieved appear to have been negligible, and the Algiers fleet remained virtually intact. According to French figures seven mosques had been destroyed in the city, and out of 10,000 houses only 800 were left habitable. Among the buildings described, with perhaps some exaggeration, as destroyed were the English and French consulates.[3] This was the last real test of the defences of Algiers until in 1816 they were subjected to the concentrated fire of much heavier artillery, reinforced by the Congreve rocket.

As France was now engaged in a war with both England and Holland, and the situation on the main land frontiers of Algiers was very serious, it was not unnatural that both sides were prepared to make concessions in order to reach a reasonable

---

[1] Mercadier, 'l'ami des Anglais', forged letters from Shaaban to Louis, &c. His *exequatur* was revoked at special session of Divan, Plantet, i. 174–7, &c.

[2] Ibid., p. 137, 6 Jan. 1687.

[3] Ibid., pp. 141 n.–158 n.; Masson, pp. 230–1.

settlement, though at Algiers opposition was still encountered from the privateering interest, whose gains had more than compensated for their losses. In September 1689 a treaty differing little from that of 1684 was arranged with Mezzomorto, but it was not acceptable to the soldiers, whose suspicions of French good faith were probably stimulated by foreign intrigues and who, on their return from the unsuccessful siege of Oran, drove him and Ibrahim Khoja[1] into exile and elected Hadji Shaaban to be their new Dey.

His accession may be said to have inaugurated a new era in the history of Algiers, which practically ceased to be a maritime state. The supreme power had been placed in the hands of a strong man, who was essentially a soldier, and the attention of his government was directed almost entirely to pressing military problems. While French writers refer to Shaaban as a 'warrior prince' and pay tribute to the intrepidity displayed in all his enterprises, and his long and detailed letters to Louis XIV—there is unfortunately no copy extant of the one which he wrote to the pope—contain evidence of administrative and statesmanlike qualities, our consul described him as 'joyous in demeanour but prompt and decisive in character'. Morgan had a very high opinion of him, and he was undoubtedly a remarkable person, who steered his country safely through six very critical years.[2]

He realized the essential role of Algiers as the corner-stone of Turkish rule in North Africa—'dont notre état est le boulevard'[3]—and apparently envisaged a situation under which its leadership would be acknowledged in a practical manner, not only by the sister states of Tripoli and Tunis, over which he had apparently received some measure of authority from the sultan, but even by the empire of Morocco, with which, following the accession of the powerful and ambitious Ismail and our evacuation of Tangier, a decisive clash was imminent.

Although the exhausted condition of the country and, perhaps, the persistent intrigues, not only by the bashaws but by the French and English agents, of which the respective

---

[1] Plantet, i. 166–74. He ridicules, without understanding, separation of their departments, ibid., p. 136 n. Khoja meant General of Native Horse.
[2] Playfair, p. 159; de Grammont, pp. 261 and 266; Morgan, p. vi.
[3] Plantet, i. 433 and 417; IND. 13397, 20 Jan. 1694.

consular dispatches are full, prevented him from carrying out his plans in their entirety, he was able to stand up to the pressure exercised by Louis, even when our fortunes were very low, and avoid being entangled in the Anglo-French war. The treaty which he concluded with France, after reading its government a lecture on the correct method of negotiation,[1] did in fact last for the prescribed hundred years and was eagerly renewed by the French on its expiration in 1790, with the emendations for which Algiers had so long contended.[2] His policy of friendly neutrality with both France and Britain, in their prolonged struggle for supremacy in the Mediterranean, may be said to have been consistently maintained up to Napoleon's invasion of Egypt. On land, too, he laid the foundations of that state of equilibrium which was to last as long as the regency itself.

Both William and Louis had evidently been impressed by the recent demonstration of Algiers' naval power, when its cruisers had carried the war against France and Holland into the channel and the North Sea. This proceeding, though described by Pepys in a moment of irritation and embarrassment as 'headstrong and perfidious', was actually in accordance with treaty stipulations,[3] as Pepys's own subsequent actions, as well as contemporary comment, clearly demonstrate. Louis showed his appreciation of the new situation, first by offering the Algiers cruisers the use of Brest as a base for attacking our shipping,[4] and then by purchasing the consulship at Algiers, which had previously been private property, and vesting it in the crown. William simultaneously displayed equally keen interest in English representation there by his appointment, on special terms, of Thomas Baker,[5] a former consul at Tripoli and apparently an old friend of Shaaban, to fill the vacancy caused by the death of John Erlisman. The question was rendered the more urgent because the only valid treaty was with James II, whose passes were still recognized by the Algiers cruisers as the

---

[1] Plantet, i. 219 and 459–60; IND. 13397, 3 Mar. and 1 May 1690.

[2] Plantet, ii. 359–90.

[3] Herbert's treaty prevented blockade of *Tangier* by ships 'remaining cruising' outside and seizing Spanish supplies. See also Downshire MSS., i. 244–60.

[4] Promising 'des prises si considérables que tous ceux qui y auront part s'enrichiront'; and attack on English as 'les ennemis communs de la France et de la Régence', Plantet, i. 178–9.

[5] Finch, ii. 304, &c.

legal ones. Both the Dey and the Emperor of Morocco corresponded officially with James after he had taken up residence in France. The emperor even offered to help to restore him to his throne if he would turn Protestant.[1] It became the custom to refer to Herbert's treaty as that of 1698, the date of a second ratification by William's government.

While it is true that Charles II was responsible for the new precedent which placed the consulates at Algiers and Tripoli on a quasi-diplomatic basis, no ruler perhaps, in our own or any other country, displayed quite the same realization of the importance and urgency of a consular appointment as King William, despite his many other pressing cares, did on this occasion. The interest subsequently taken, even in minor matters, by such personages as the Duke of Shrewsbury and the Lords Justices seems extremely significant.

Baker was dispatched with all convenient speed on a warship with appropriate presents for the Dey and personal emoluments such as had never been contemplated before. His post as Clerk of the Cheque at Deptford was apparently kept open for him during his service abroad. Shortly afterwards he was instructed to pay heavy compensation for the illegal capture of an Algerine prize, while a sum of ten thousand dollars was also transmitted to him through Leghorn for the purpose of winning Algiers over to an offensive alliance. In spite of a stream of French allegations this appears to have been the only occasion on which we resorted to such a measure with that regency, and it is not clear whether the money was in fact actually expended. If it was, it certainly did not effect its purpose.[2]

Another interesting proof of the importance of relations with Algiers was the inauguration of official dispatch boats—by the French in 1690, to provide a regular service with Marseilles, and by our government some time before 1694, to facilitate communication between Algiers and Leghorn or other neutral ports and also with the fleet, when it finally reached the Mediterranean.[3]

On the whole our policy proved successful. Though neither

---

[1] H. de Castries, *Moulay Ismaïl et Jacques II*, Paris, 1903.
[2] S.P. 71. 3, ff. 461, 496, and 509–10.
[3] Tartan *Velocità*, S.P. 71. 3 and 98. 18.

side succeeded in enlisting the active support of Algiers, we must have been greatly relieved that it did not throw in its lot with France, when that country clearly appeared to be the victor. Even after the battle of La Hogue had helped to restore our naval prestige and a fleet was somewhat tardily stationed in the Mediterranean, the goodwill of the Barbary States continued to be regarded as a matter of very considerable importance. In 1693 our one ally, Tripoli,[1] had been forced into a state of neutrality—actually for about a year into one of nominal hostility—and in January 1696 Rooke, who had just paid a very timely courtesy visit to Algiers, reported such a deterioration in our naval position that 'from seeking and blocking up the enemy in their ports we shall be exposed to the disgrace of suffering the blockade ourselves or skulking from the enemy at sea'.[2]

Still later, when we had acquired bases at Gibraltar and Minorca or, more temporarily, on the mainland of Spain, he and other admirals found that supplies from Barbary ports were essential for the maintenance of our ships and soldiers. From this point of view Lisbon, the former alternative, now proved all too often a broken reed—its storehouses 'as bare as a beggar's bowl'[3]—while our influence in Tunis at this time was uncertain, and in Morocco, unlike the French and Dutch, we had no official representation at all. The south of France, too, had always been partially dependent on supplies of foodstuffs and raw materials from North Africa and the Levant, and its needs were greatly increased by the very lean years which ushered in the eighteenth century.

Baker's stay in Algiers was cut short by bad health, but during his four years of residence he appears to have enjoyed the friendship and confidence of the Dey, thereby, according to Morgan, laying the foundations of our influence and prestige in the area. Quite apart from the obvious difficulties of the tense international situation, he was faced with the very unnecessary problem of the large number of English captives who

---

[1] Declared war 1 Apr. 1692 but, receiving no aid, made 'very advantageous' peace, May 1693, S.P. 71. 22, ff. 459–533. Masson, p. 233, and de la Roncière, vi. 135, appear ill-informed.

[2] H.M.C. Buccleuch MSS. ii. 299.

[3] S. Martin-Leake, *The Life of Sir John Leake*, ed. G. Callender, 2 vols. (N.R.S.), London, 1920, i, p. xci.

had not yet been redeemed and were, not unnaturally, becoming very unruly. In addition, he would appear to have entered into Shaaban's scheme for some kind of union of the regencies under the leadership of Algiers, probably with a view to a grand alliance against France or French aggression.[1] At all events, when in 1694 he handed the consulate over to Robert Cole, he was instructed to proceed to Tripoli to conclude a treaty, and took the opportunity of trying to supersede with his own nominees the consuls there and at Tunis, which Shaaban had temporarily captured, in spite, it was alleged, of French intervention.

Presumably he was acting under some general instruction from King William and to a certain extent in concert with the Dey, though the French agents, who were acutely worried at this intrigue, which they did their best to counteract by bribes, presents, and threats, reported that Shaaban flatly rejected his advances. Certainly nothing came of them, perhaps because the Dey was too concerned with his military commitments. These were to lead soon afterwards to his assassination by the soldiers, whose discontent and suspicions were said to have been stimulated by the bashaw.[2]

While Baker's intervention probably damaged our relations with Tunis and did us little good at Tripoli, Shaaban's attitude towards him and his country continued to be extremely friendly. Not only was an Algerine cruiser placed at his disposal for the transportation of himself and his family, since none of our warships were available, but the Dey in an official letter paid testimony to his good services and expressed the hope that the king 'would not forget so good and faithful a servant', who 'since his coming has gained the love of all our people'.[3] Before he left, Baker had the great satisfaction of being able to report that no Briton taken under His Majesty's colours remained in slavery in any of the regencies,[4] and this question ceased to arise from that time in connexion with persons who were

---

[1] IND. 13396, 20 Jan. 1694; Burchett, p. 510; Treaty signed 11 Oct. 1694. Plantet, i. 414 n., 428 n., and 453 n.

[2] IND. 13397, 8 Aug. 1695.

[3] S.P. 102, f. 98. It also contained charges against consuls at Tunis and Tripoli, who claimed it was forged. Rooke was ordered to investigate, Buccleuch, ii. 274.

[4] S.P. 102, f. 98. The *Betton Trust* was never used for this in the Regencies, *Piratical States*, p. 141; H.O. Papers, iii. 548; Blaquiere, ii. 207 n.; *A.R.* 1816, p. 335.

definitely recognized as British subjects. An announcement to a similar effect was made almost simultaneously by the French.

Even greater progress in the task of cementing friendly relations was made during the consulship of Robert Cole, which lasted up to the virtual end of the war with France. As a member of a prominent family of London merchants, long connected with the Barbary trade, he had been resident in Algiers most of his life, and had apparently played a considerable part in Herbert's peace negotiations.[1] During the interval between Erlisman's death and Baker's arrival he had administered the consulate at the request of Shaaban, who described him at the time as 'a very just and careful merchant, a man very diligent and willing to do any service to his King and country and to give me content and my subjects'.[2]

Joseph Morgan, who during part of Queen Anne's reign was his vice-consul and chancelier, had a very high opinion of him as a 'high-spirited gentleman' and 'a great favourite of the Algerines'.[3] Indeed, all the Deys appear to have spoken well of him. His intimate knowledge of the people, their language and customs, proved of great advantage to us during an exceptionally difficult period, both internally and externally, and by his hospitality and mode of life he set an unusually high standard for his French colleagues to live up to. He and Baker were evidently old and close friends—it is quite likely that each owed his appointment to the other's recommendation—and the ability of Baker to act in London, both as his personal agent and as an official adviser on Barbary affairs, proved extremely helpful.

Special qualities were obviously required, since in his consulship of eighteen years he had to deal with no fewer than nine Deys. In Shaaban's successor he found a man of very different type, a gentle character who had no desire for a position which is said to have terrified him. Cole enjoyed very pleasant and profitable relations with him at first,[4] but soon reported 'since the Dey has growne apprehensive, not without reason, of being cut off, he is become so very waspish that I have not been able

---

[1] F.O. 355. 2, Bu. 2, July 1681.   [2] Playfair, p. 161.
[3] *Several Voyages*, ii. 134.
[4] Discussing French and Dutch intrigues over Dey's morning coffee and opium-pill, S.P. 71. 3, f. 679. The next Dey was an old friend, S.P. 102. 1, ff. 102–3.

to make any further steps in a peace with Holland and this Kingdom and a war with France which I will procicute as a fare occasion offers'. He attributed the failure in part (as other consuls did on other occasions) to 'lack of His Majesty's ships coming to impress the people and *strengthen the Dey's hand'*. Ahmed had, however, no desire to engage in war on anyone's account, and would even have made peace with Spain but for French opposition.

On his death Hassan Chaouch (1698–1700) paved the way for a closer understanding with England by showing an unusual appreciation of our difficulties at the time. Although he encouraged privateering and is described by Morgan as an 'indolent miser', he imposed strict discipline on the ship's captains and was praised by the French for his honesty, moderation, and goodwill. After pointing out to King William that 'our ships have a large scope to cruize in' and the consequent risk of meeting British vessels in 'remote parts of the world' unprovided with passes, he expressed, in his anxiety to avoid misunderstandings, the hope that His Majesty would 'find out wayes that may preserve your Subjects'. He then announced his intention, in view of our difficulties, to dispense with the production of passes by British ships coming from the East Indies and American colonies.[1] The question was eventually regulated by the provisions of the Cole–Munden treaty of 1700[2] and Byng's renewal of the peace in 1703.

When Hassan, who found the soldiers quite unmanageable, resigned soon afterwards and retired to Tripoli, to the unusual accompaniment of official compensation and salutes from all the forts, his successor Mustapha (1700–5), whom the French describe as 'généreux', 'très honnête homme et de beaucoup d'esprit', showed himself no less friendly and considerate, as the above treaties and the colonial state papers of the time clearly indicate—too liberal and accommodating, in fact, to suit the London merchants and the privy council.

He, too, found the military problems too absorbing to allow of any foreign entanglements, and resisted increasing pressure

---

[1] Buccleuch MSS., ii. 337.
[2] The exemption from condemnation of ships and crews lacking proper passes was cancelled at merchants' request, Vernon to Cole, Hampton Court, 12 May 1701; S.P. 71. 5, f. 135, 23 Nov. 1713, and ff. 275-9, 1714.

from both sides for an active alliance. In 1702 Cole was instructed to reward the chief secretary for having disclosed to him 'diverse secret practices of the King of France aimed at destroying our peace with Algiers', but his own efforts were equally unsuccessful. Admiral Byng, who arrived the following year to renew the peace on the accession of Queen Anne, failed to extract any promise of an alliance from the Dey, who, however, showed his goodwill—towards Cole at any rate—by making some voluntary concessions in regard to customs duties and ship's passes. Byng, indeed, proved an indifferent and uncongenial negotiator.[1] He compared very unfavourably with Aylmer, whose squadron some four years previously had, according to French accounts, scored a distinct success by a demonstration of friendliness and liberal entertainment on board for the ship's captains of Algiers.[2]

The soldiers now seem to have got thoroughly out of hand, as a result partly, perhaps, of restrictions on normal trade imposed by the Anglo-French struggle but mainly of a long period of continuous warfare against Tunis, Morocco, and the Spaniards at Oran, without any adequate remuneration out of military or maritime spoils. Privateering is said to have come to a standstill, intrigues by the bashaw, consuls, and other foreigners tended still further to weaken the authority of the Deys, and, although descriptions of the resultant anarchy and bloodshed have obviously been often greatly exaggerated, no fewer than four were elected during the five years which followed the murder in 1705 of Mustapha by his disgusted soldiers.[3]

Cole was fortunately able to extract considerable advantage from what were apparently very unfavourable conditions. Both his ingenuity and resources were subjected to a severe strain by the constant demands for supplies from our warships and forces employed in Gibraltar, Minorca, and Catalonia. In spite, however, of exceptionally hard times, due partly to scar-

---

[1] *Memoirs relating to Lord Torrington*, ed. (Sir) J. K. Laughton (Camden Society), London, 1899; *Byng Papers*, ed. B. Tunstall (N.R.S.), 3 vols., London, 1930–2, i. 16–24; S.P. 71. 4, ff. 113–14.

[2] Aylmer's 'very civil reception' worried France, Plantet, i. 559 n. Compare Treasury Papers, iii. 250–1, with Luttrell, *Brief Historical Relation of State Affairs*, iv. 518.

[3] Parallel of 1805–17 illustrates deterioration of Algiers economy through prolonged Anglo-French war.

city and partly to financial difficulties, which actually entailed borrowing from the Public Treasure for an expedition against Oran, Mustapha's successor Hussein (1705–7) managed to be very helpful without incurring the ill will of the French, who expressed a high opinion of him.

Cole describes the arrival of warships, transports, and merchant vessels, sometimes without funds and 'in a starving condition', and their supply with provisions of all sorts, in spite of the famine, through the 'Dey's kind intervention'. The gentlemen on the transports, mainly officers returning from Catalonia in search of recruits, were among the principal bene-ficiaries, for 'never were men more courteously treated'. It is sad to record that Cole's report ends with the statement that 'Captain Cook in defiance of treaty carried off a Grecian slave', another charge presumably on the consul's usually long overdue emoluments.[1]

In 1708 Cole's 'Fidelity, Resolution and Vigilance in that most hazardous and troublesome station'[2] were rewarded and his difficulties somewhat eased by the capture of Oran, which had so long been a running sore in Algerine territory, a lawless and disreputable centre from which sedition had been fomented among the neighbouring tribes, crops damaged, and a profitable traffic in kidnapped Moors steadily maintained. Queen Anne had already declined an invitation to occupy it with the assis-tance of Algiers on the ground that she was an ally of Charles III of Spain, but the activities of a blockading squadron act-ing in the name of that monarch must have seriously weakened its defence, a result for which Cole is said to have been given considerable credit. Morgan, who witnessed part of the siege operations, makes the interesting statement that the Spanish commandant, when summoned by the commander of our squadron to surrender the place to Charles III, replied that he would rather do so to Mohammedans than to Protestants.[3]

Oran was of peculiar importance at this time, since it pro-vided a new and very convenient outlet for the export of Algiers grain. The French claimed a monopoly of trade in the eastern section of the regency, where their concessions were situated,

---

[1] S.P. 71. 4, f. 167. For Tetuan, see Stephen Martin-Leake, *Life of Sir John Leake*, i. 229 and 224, and Algiers, ii. 250 and 276.
[2] Treasury Papers, iv. 290.   [3] *Several Voyages*, ii. 134.

and the Deys were determined that it should not be extended to the west. The British consequently were given the sole right to establish a vice-consulate and factory there. Shaw tells us that during the Algerine occupation of Oran the British exported an average of 7,000 to 8,000 tons of wheat yearly, and another report says that it gave annual employment to fifty British ships.[1]

This facility was most opportune, since the Battle of the Grain in the Mediterranean was in full swing. In the very next year the commander of our naval forces was instructed that the greatest service he could render his country would be to secure the grain of Algiers and Tunis for the use of our own forces and deny it to the French.[2] Various entries in Luttrell's *Relation* for that year show the interest taken in London in the interception of supplies destined for the south of France, where great scarcity existed.

In fact the last years of Cole's consulship, which ended on 13 November 1712, when the negotiations at Utrecht were well under way, were occupied mainly with the prosaic question of supply, in which he did not apparently receive the maximum of co-operation from our own officials. Impatient admirals, in suggesting that the consul should be 'roundly dealt with' or complaining of his action in monopolizing supplies, probably had no conception of the difficulties involved, especially in a country where the export of foodstuffs was popularly regarded with the greatest suspicion and dislike, as the Dey's oath of office showed.

Baker, on the other hand, pointed to Cole's 'commendable and dextrous' cornering of grain to defeat French intrigue, his 'seventeen years unparalleled services performed in the most perplexing and hazardous station in the world', and the urgent need for remitting more promptly his allowances, 'as he was reduced to great perplexities by his supply of corn to Barcelona for her Majesty and the King of Spain's forces'.[3] It does not

---

[1] Pinkerton, xv. 598; S.P. 71. 7, f. 565.

[2] *Byng Papers*, ii. 346. Sunderland called it 'a service of the utmost importance', ibid., p. 348. See also Taubman.

[3] Treasury Papers iv, 11 July 1711. France tried to corner grain and 'cut off that important relief of her Majesty's garrisons of Port Mahon and Gibraltar, as also for her forces in Ca alonia'. Charles III also owed Cole for supplies, Treasury Books 1712, p. 101.

seem to have occurred to the authorities at home that ready money was essential for the provision of grain, which was not only in great demand but could only be exported by very special licence. They might, even, have made comparisons between Cole's presumably disadvantageous position as an individual in a neutral country and the relatively elaborate organizations which had so much difficulty in obtaining any satisfaction from our allies in Portugal and Spain. As it was, Cole's inability to settle his accounts promptly led eventually to recurrent difficulties with Ali Pasha, an old friend of his, who from 1710 set a new precedent by combining the offices of Dey and bashaw.[1] The settlement of his debts after his death became the subject of a series of official representations.

His path was not smoothed, either, by various incidents at sea, such as difficulties connected with ships of Gibraltar and Minorca, which were still officially regarded as enemy, the illegal action of the Governor of Gibraltar in issuing ship's passes, which were worthless, and the wanton attack on an Algiers cruiser by an English privateer, which is said to have endangered his life and certainly greatly incensed the queen,[2] the more perhaps because at the time we found that 'corn was scarce and dear'.

His success in establishing friendly relations is corroborated alike by a letter sent through him—though it actually arrived after his death—to the Dey by Admiral Jennings from Minorca, recording his 'grateful sense of your kind promise to afford a supply of provisions, at a more favourable season, for her Majesties' Forces in Garrison'; by a tribute paid to him a few months earlier in a letter from the Dey to Queen Anne, expressing the hope that he would be continued in office as he is 'Counsellor both for you and for us, one that understands the affairs of the place' and has always acted properly; and by the report that on his death the 'Pasha and Dey' not only took trouble in securing his property but 'shewed the family the utmost civility that can be expected'.[3] It was, however, necessary to maintain a watch at night over the Christian cemetery to ensure that his body was not carried off by Spanish slaves.

---

[1] S.P. 71. 4, f. 389, June 1712.
[2] Ibid., f. 359; H.M.C. Portland MSS. x. 246. It killed seven Turks.
[3] S.P. 71. 4, f. 429, 10 Nov. 1712.

EPILOGUE

THE peace of Utrecht coincided with a very definite land-mark in the development of the regencies, each of which about that time adopted a new and permanent form of administration, and also of the Mediterranean area in close proximity to them. Unlike the situation which followed the Elizabethan era or the collapse of the first empire, relations between Christians and Turks after the death of Queen Anne were on the whole friendly and sympathetic. Practical proof of the wisdom of the recent change of policy by the later Stuarts and Louis XIV was soon forthcoming in the long peace which both countries enjoyed with Algiers, until the ambitions, passions, and new ideals emanating from the French Revolution wrought such radical changes in southern Europe. Relations were almost equally stable with the other regencies, apart from French designs on Tabarca, whose undisturbed occupation during two centuries by the Genoese furnished such a re-markable refutation of charges of Moslem intolerance and aggression.[1]

Dynastic changes in Spain and southern Italy had by no means been beneficial to us, and it would appear that under the Georges our interest in the Mediterranean was at most intermittent. The bases that we acquired there, more or less accidentally—Gibraltar, Minorca, and, later, Malta—appear to have been esteemed at first for their bargaining value in other fields, and our treatment of Morocco, on which Gibraltar was at times dependent for the barest necessities, was inexplicably cavalier.[2]

France, on the other hand, sought compensation for its losses in remoter areas—as it did again after the Seven Years War—through the extension of its commercial and political influence in North Africa and the Levant, putting into execution the projects of Colbert and his successors. To the east Malta, and·in course of time Tunis as well, served as a forward base,

---

[1] Driault, *Recueil des instructions données aux ambassadeurs de France*, vol. xix, pp. 184–99; Du Cane MSS., pp. 248–342; *G.M.* 1742, p. 446; S.P. 71. 29, f. 403.
[2] App. I; Jackson, pp. 258–65.

while we were increasingly dependent on the goodwill of Leghorn and Algiers. For the first time, perhaps, France really became an oriental power, regarding the Levant trade as a monopoly and the regencies as commercial colonies.[1]

The steady decay of the famous Levant Company, despite periodical assertions of naval supremacy in the Mediterranean, contrasted with the prosperity of its East Indian and Royal African rivals. Traffic in negro slaves and slave-grown products became increasingly the backbone of our oversea trade. It would be hard to find any evidence to support a conventional belief that we tolerated or curried favour with the regencies in order to obtain privileged treatment for our Mediterranean traffic.[2] The continuation of corrupt military governments in Gibraltar and Minorca, long after the strategy of King William and Marlborough had become obsolete, might figure among the arguments to the contrary.

It was these two somewhat involuntary acquisitions which furnished almost our sole connexion with the North African coast, and the deficiencies of their administration provided a fertile source of friction and suspicion. The problem was more acute than in the days of Tangier, since their ships were of a type long associated with enemy activities and manned by the dreaded Balearic islanders or those Genoese residents of Gibraltar whose national status was admittedly doubtful. The Algerines suspected, not without reason, that they were owned by enemies and engaged in carrying to Spain foodstuffs which were only allowed to be exported as a special concession to satisfy the needs of our garrison. It was constantly urged that great care should be exercised in the issue to such ships of Mediterranean passes, as provided by the treaty of 1716, and that at least one Englishman should be included in the crew. Unfortunately, the competent officials were by no means averse to the illegal issue of passes, mostly to Genoese vessels, or of privateering commissions or to participation in the resale of grain to Spain, and their vice-admiralty courts acquired a very bad reputation. Further problems arose from the vague definitions of their territorial

---

[1] Driault, p. lxxvi; Masson, _18e siècle_, pp. 246–66.

[2] Cal. H.O. ii. 504; Sir N. H. Nicolas, _Dispatches and Letters of . . . Viscount Nelson_, 7 vols., London, 1844–6, iv. 125–6; T. Smollett, _Travels through France and Italy_, London, 1907, pp. 127–8; App. J.

waters. Similar difficulties were caused later by our occupations of Corsica and Malta.

The resulting situation called for delicate handling, especially at Algiers, where the Deys, in spite of their investiture by the sultan, were little more than the chief executives of a Turkish military colony. They were not 'ignorant common soldiers' and only conformed to a type in that they were regular soldiers and natural-born Turks, chosen by the unanimous vote of the army on account of their experience and special qualifications to fill a position, whether they wished it or not, which rendered them in effect for the rest of their lives the slaves of the state. Most of them, indeed, succeeded almost automatically from one of the principal posts of the administration and were already familiar with the consuls and their affairs.[1]

While they exercised complete control over the civil administration the army acted as a sort of opposition, jealously watching over what it believed to be not only its rights under treaty or local law or the Dey's oath of office, but also the interests of the empire, to which Algiers retained a special responsibility. Practically all of them were at some time the subject of commendation in reports from our consuls—even from some who had been expelled for hostile or obstructive behaviour—and not infrequently from their French rivals as well.

Most of the friction came from external causes. The position of the Deys, like that of our consuls, was always rendered more difficult by the European wars, and when these became unduly prolonged, as at the beginning of the eighteenth and nineteenth centuries, the strain was apt to become too great. Between the conclusion of the peace of Utrecht, however, and the rupture of the treaty of Amiens only two Deys were assassinated, although it was customary to walk abroad unarmed and unattended. In spite of recurrent plague epidemics, earthquakes, and droughts it was a period of steady progress. Trouble on the high seas was infrequent. So far from being the 'terror of the Mediterranean' and 'scouring the Atlantic' the regencies had practically ceased to have any navy worthy of the name. In about 1780 the total marine force of Algiers, much the most powerful of the regencies, was said to be no match for two good frigates, and this might at any time be required for the sultan's

[1] e.g. Wilberforce to Dundas and Wickham, F.O. 3. 8, 26 Sept. 1798.

service, even as far away as the Black Sea. By about 1700 the
reputed orgies of triumphant privateers had become only a
memory.

The general attitude of the Deys appears to have been
reasonable. They had no desire to break with either Britain or
France, though they had developed a preference for the former,
who had apparently earned the reputation, alike in Morocco,
Turkey, and the regencies, of being more trustworthy. The
rulers of Algiers probably appreciated the value of Gibraltar
and Minorca as protection against aggression from France or
Spain and also, perhaps, of the traffic we carried on with those
garrisons. The sale of our prizes in the port was by no means
unwelcome, provided it was not accompanied by violations of
territorial waters or similar illegalities. The chief beneficiaries
seem to have been the British and French merchants. The
situation was, however, often delicate owing to the suspicions
of the army or at times the complaints of merchants and sea-
captains, both of which might be fomented by foreign intrigue.
It became essential for the Dey's hand to be strengthened, as
Baker had formerly put it, by the countenance of our warships
and the co-operation of our consuls.

It is evident that at first relations were satisfactorily maintained. Morgan relates that 'our business with the Algerines
had for forty years only been as friends and allies . . . thanks to
Shaaban Haji's Friendship and Gratitude to Consul Baker and
very prudent management on our side ever since'.[1] Similarly,
a French writer in 1730 attributed the remarkable prosperity
of our merchants in Portugal partly to 'the constant peace
which they take great care to maintain with the Kings of
Africa'.[2] Considerable support of a more negative character
comes from a number of sources.

In Tunis Richard Lawrence managed to carry on the consulate with credit, though mainly at his own expense, for nearly
forty years till his death in 1750. Admiral Baker paid a very
warm tribute to his services in 1716, and Shaw, who was very

---

[1] Morgan, vi. See also Pinkerton, xv. 679–80; S.P. 71. 8, f. 188 (1745); *Piratical
States*, p. 141.

[2] *Description de la ville de Lisbonne*, Paris, 1730. For Dutch testimony see *Journal
of the Board of Trade*, 1718–22, p. 380. Note absence of complaint in official documents, travels, &c., e.g. L. S. Sutherland, *A London Merchant (William Braund) 1695–
1774*, Oxford Hist. Series, London, 1933.

favourably impressed with what he saw of Tunisia about 1730, wrote 'all affairs with the Regency were transacted in such a friendly complaisant manner that it was no small pleasure to attend Mr. Consul Lawrence at his audiences'.[1] Our government, however, gave him little support and for some reason treated the bey, the extremely able founder of the present dynasty, with studied discourtesy. From being the country where the British enjoyed the greatest friendship and advantages, it gradually drifted into the arms of France. By the end of the seventeenth century it no longer had any ships fit to go to sea. Its chief troubles were on land, where the Bey of Constantine was only too ready to intervene in dynastic dissensions. At the capture of the city by the Algerine and insurgent forces in 1754 all the Christians and their households, amounting to some hundreds,[2] were given shelter in our consulate, which, unlike the others, was well respected.

At Tripoli conditions can hardly have been unsatisfactory, as the brothers Lodington administered the consulate for over forty years, until in December 1729 the younger retired 'after an absence of forty-five years, nearly thirty as consul'. It had always been, and continued to be until Napoleon's invasion of Egypt, a state in which we had no direct interest beyond the 'maintenance of a good correspondence'. As this entailed the payment of a salary, the post tended to develop into a mere sinecure and was, from 1733 to about 1765, the scene of very curious and at times scandalous conditions, to which the home government normally displayed complete indifference. Lord Halifax expressed horror at his discovery that the consulate had for two years been managed by a woman, the widow of the previous consul, who, however, seems to have got on exceptionally well with the bashaw and his ministers.

Tripoli was the poorest and worst governed of the regencies, but in some respects the friendliest. The spectacle of Captain Vanbrugh and the bashaw embracing each other after a very pleasant visit was by no means unusual, and was indeed typical of the experiences of French and British consuls during that

---

[1] S.P. 71. 27, ff. 237–8; Pinkerton, xv. 565.

[2] 500, Masson, *Établissements*, p. 589, but see J. P. Bonnafont, *Réflexions sur l'Algérie*, Paris, 1846, p. 43. Tunis did not become vassal of Algiers before or after 1754 or 'independent of the Turkish yoke' in 1782–1814.

century.[1] Masson's picture of the decrepit condition of the state after 1692 rests on the flimsiest of evidence, which was almost immediately contradicted by the course of events and his own admissions. In 1700 de la Faye found the new quarter of the city a *paradis terrestre* and we know that it had over several years an exceptionally good ruler. De Tassy pays a special tribute to its good observance of treaties, which was confirmed by our consul a century later.[2] Keppel's visit in 1751 was probably providential, as he found the consulate in great confusion and no reliable evidence as to what our treaties really were. The report of James Bruce, who incidentally had left the consulate at Algiers in a very similar condition, must be regarded with some suspicion, as the regency was at the time suffering from internal disturbances, and he was also obviously misled by the consul's malice.

While Tripoli and Tunis under their hereditary systems of government turned increasingly to renegades and emancipated slaves—mainly Italian—and ex-ambassadors for the conduct of Christian affairs, the Turkish rulers of Algiers were always dependent on the advice and assistance of foreign elements—successively Spanish captives, Jewish agents, French priests, English merchants, various foreigners consular and mercantile, and finally those Jewish financiers whom the French conquerors were to find so useful.[3]

From Herbert's peace until the end of the Seven Years War, perhaps the happiest and most successful period in our relations with the regency, the English merchants, despite the small volume of English trade, exercised a preponderant influence in its external affairs, more especially when the consul himself was one of the merchants or received their support. William and Anne both contributed to the local prestige of the consulate and factory, although there were no more than two English houses and their value to British commerce at least correspondingly small. French consuls complained bitterly of the impossibility of maintaining the standard set by their English colleagues, and attributed their influence and prestige to the lavish expenditure of official funds, instead of to the real cause—better under-

[1] S.P. 42. 79, ff. 729–32, 1729; Lucas, *La Grèce*, ii. 81–82.
[2] See also laudatory letter from George III and Pitt, F.O. 76. 1, 10 Aug. 1761.
[3] Campbell, ii. 206–9; Esquer, pp. 16–21.

standing and goodwill. Indeed, consuls of either side during the century were apt to boast that they enjoyed greater credit in the regency than their colleagues in spite of the fact that they gave smaller presents or none at all. In the same way it happened at times that preferential treatment was accorded to what appeared to be the losing side in the long Mediterranean struggle.[1]

After Cole's death the Dey's principal adviser appears to have been Edward Holden, whom the French accused of being a secret agent and *homme de paille* of the British government. The position of his partner Charles Hudson (1720–8) is, however, fairly described by a French colleague: 'The emoluments of the English Consul are very large, being the only merchant of that nation. In exchange for the Military and Naval stores with which he supplies the Government he receives oil, corn and other commodities, the exportation of which is allowed only to him.'[2] At this time his firm also operated an exclusive and very valuable agency for the export of wheat at Oran under the management of John Ford, the vice-consul, who became the Deys' principal confidant before and during the Seven Years War. It was principally owing to the experience and local influence of such men that the problems of the Deys and the correct diplomatic procedure and interpretation of treaties were explained to ministers of the Hanoverian régime, and that the negotiations and official visits of naval commanders were made easy and successful.

Unfortunately, the attitude of that régime was detrimental to the system that had been so successfully built up under the Stuarts. Interest in the Mediterranean declined, and the previous close cohesion between the government, the London merchants, the factories, and the consulates steadily diminished during the peaceful years before the resumption of war on a large scale in the Mediterranean. The effect was noticeable at even the most important posts nearer home—at Lisbon, Cadiz, Seville, and Leghorn, where the historic factories became largely independent of control.

---

[1] England in 1689–96 and 1756–9. Algiers was *seule et fidèle* ally and 'sole and constant support' of France following Revolution, S.P. 95. 1, 11 July 1793; Plantet, ii. 439–40, &c.

[2] *Piratical States*, pp. 239–40.

Consular appointments were increasingly made to suit departmental convenience, to 'make provision' for a consul displaced elsewhere, possibly on account of his own shortcomings, or, in the interests of official patronage, to find employment for someone who had no qualification and might prove wholly unsuitable. In 1726 Pope[1] heralded this unfortunate development in the case of two political pamphleteers with the couplet:

> Like are their merits; like rewards they share.
> That shines a consul; this commissioner.

A century after the death of Queen Anne a consulate had come to be regarded as a 'refuge of the destitute'.[2]

In 1729 established tradition was broken in the regencies by the appointment, not of Holden as urged by the London merchants and the Dey himself, but of Charles Black, who, in spite of his undoubted ability, had been recalled from Cadiz at the factory's request because of his 'pride and ill-nature', and was later described as a 'drunken brute'. The Dey refused to receive him owing to the discourteous informality of his arrival, and he was brought back the following year by Admiral Cavendish, together with the customary credentials and royal tokens of goodwill. Although in 1733 he wrote 'We live in Peace and find a good inclination in the Dey and People towards every thing belonging to our King and Country', he was recalled in 1739 on further complaint, and made a somewhat humiliating departure on a French vessel.

Holden was promptly appointed, reference being made in a royal letter to his special suitability through knowledge of the language and local customs and his favour with the Dey,[3] but he died the same year. John Ford was recommended as his successor, partly on the ground that, while vice-consul at Oran, he had 'by his courage and conduct protected the English House from being plundered by the Moors' during the confusion of the Spanish attack. Provision had, however, again to be made for a consul from Spain whom the outbreak of war had reduced to financial straits. Captain Pocock had some difficulty in reconciling the Dey to irregularities in the manner of the new

---

[1] *D.N.B.* vii. 410, Thomas Burnet.
[2] R. H. Gronow, *Last Recollections*, London, 1934, p. 110. Compare C. Redding, *Fifty Years' Recollections*, 3 vols., London, 1858.
[3] S.P. 71. 7, 11 Nov. 1738.

consul's arrival, apparently with the grudging assistance of Ford.

During the thirty years between the peace of Utrecht and the outbreak of another Anglo-French war the Mediterranean was an unusually peaceful scene. While the naval strength and activities of Algiers and Tunis dwindled into insignificance,[1] increased importance was attached by the various maritime states to trade with them and the use of their ports. The Dutch, Hamburgers, Swedes, Danes, Austrians, Neapolitans, and Sicilians were among those who tried to obtain a share of the advantages enjoyed in the regencies by the British and French, and have the satisfaction and material benefit of trading in the Levant under their own flag. Such a development was, however, not in the interest of either France or Britain. The former is credited with preventing peace between the regencies and Spain in 1700 and Naples in 1740. About the same time it opposed Swedish trade aspirations in Turkey, and presumably was responsible for instructions from Constantinople to break off relations between the regencies and Austria. French naval operations against Tunis were primarily designed to obtain commercial concessions at the expense of British and Genoese rivals. However little Britain was interested in the development of commerce in that area, the ability of Neapolitan or other Italian vessels to undercut freights from London to the Mediterranean[2] can hardly have been more welcome than attempts to inaugurate direct trade from the plantations.[3]

Among curious instances of the changing attitude in the Mediterranean and adjacent waters may be cited the petition of the Royal African Company in December 1715 for the protection of a warship, with the interesting explanation that the 'cause is not piracy', so prevalent at that time in various other areas.[4] Others can be found in the fact that passengers, if furnished with a passport from a friendly consul, preferred to travel between Italian ports by sea rather than land; in the gratitude

---

[1] Masson, *18ᵉ siècle*, pp. 356–61, confirmed by Taubman, Shaw, American State Papers, Blaquiere, &c. In 1803 Algiers had thirteen sea-going ships, two commanded by Americans, reinforced since 1774 by numerous defence boats.

[2] Masson, *18ᵉ siècle*, p. 357 n. For peaceful progress in Algeria, see Peysonnel, Shaw, a later chaplain, S.P. 71. 8, ff. 301 sqq., and *Piratical States*, ch. xxi.

[3] Cal. S.P. (Col.) 1724–5, p. 121.

[4] A.P.C. (Col.) vi. 107.

expressed by the Grand Master at Malta in 1742 to the Bashaw of Tripoli for timely aid during a famine in Sicily; and in a later request from Tripoli for Maltese assistance in arresting a naval officer who had gone off with some ships and might take to piracy.[1] Spain's interest in remaining on good terms with its Algerine enemies, once it had regained possession of Oran, is illustrated by its action in allowing Algiers cruisers to pass 'civilly' and without interference during their subsequent hostilities with Portugal.[2]

Perhaps the most remarkable feature of the century was the growth of the 'caravan' trade, i.e. the transport of goods between ports of the Ottoman empire, in which almost all maritime nations were anxious to participate. The coast-wise traffic of Barbary, which even in 1742 was described as 'the principal Nursery for Seamen the French have, employing about 1,200 vessels great and small', was probably as important to the marine of France as its produce was to the inhabitants and factories of Provence.[3]

A matter of very considerable importance to Britain and France, which evidently was not unnoticed by Spain, was the internal development of Barbary. Of this we have interesting evidence in the experiences of Peysonnel, Shaw, and Bruce in Algiers and Tunis; in the remarkable era of peace and prosperity in the province of Constantine between 1710 and 1790 as recorded by Dr. Bonnafont;[4] and in the very considerable profit that the Compagnie Royale d'Afrique managed to extract from its concessions in Eastern Algeria and Tunisia before its suppression by the French Assembly in 1794.[5] After the Spanish recapture of Oran and Mers-el-kebir the port of Arzew was developed to export the produce of the West. In course of time we had occasion to realize the importance of the coral fisheries of Algiers and Tunis to the economy of Corsica, Sicily, and Naples.[6]

[1] Knox, *A New Collection of Voyages, Discoveries and Travels*, iv. 411; G. B. Henderson, *Crimean War Diplomacy*, &c., Glasgow, 1947, p. 302; Add. MS. 32840, ff. 66–69, 8 Sept. 1752. See also Mifsud, p. 265; Tully, p. 67.

[2] S.P. 71. 9, f. 71, 24 June 1751.

[3] Considerations on the Barbary Trade, 2 Mar. 1742, S.P. 71. 11, ff. 246–7; S.P. 71. 10, ff. 180–3, Feb. 1757; Masson, *18ᵉ siècle*, pp. 401–5.

[4] *Réflexions*, pp. 42–44.

[5] Garrot, pp. 589–92.

[6] F.O. 3. 8, 3 Jan. 1796; 3. 18, 11 July 1816.

The history of Britain's relations with Barbary from 1739 onwards is mainly one of increasing indifference and lost opportunity. Prior to the revolutionary war our interest in Tunis and Tripoli was confined to the payment of consular salaries and allowances and the dispatch of an occasional warship or royal present. At Algiers Ambrose Stanyford's consulship (1741–52) brought little profit to the government or himself. The former paid no heed to his projects for concessions, which the Deys were anxious to grant at the expense of the Spaniards and French at Oran or near Bona, and on his death had to pay his very considerable debts. British relations with the Dey were carried on mainly by John Ford and a Scottish merchant, George Logie, who was also consul for Sweden. Thanks to their assistance and still more to the reasonable and conciliatory attitude of Keppel and the Dey the affair of the *Prince Frederick* was satisfactorily settled.[1]

The appointment of Stanhope Aspinwall (1754–61), after a good record in the backwater of Constantinople, proved more disastrous.[2] Whereas Stanyford only quarrelled with the soldiers when the worse for liquor, his successor set an unfortunate precedent by quarrelling with everybody—first, with the vice-consul and the merchants, who accused him of despising commerce, while he called the sale of prizes, to which we officially attached great importance, no better than piracy. He quarrelled with the secretary of Gibraltar and took no steps to facilitate food supplies. He quarrelled with the Dey, though he was our warm friend even in the darkest days of the war and was the subject of appreciative tributes from a series of consuls and naval commanders. The spectacle of our consul attending an official ceremony alone, while his countrymen appeared in the train of an enemy colleague, must be rare in our annals.

Alarm at the growing hostility of Spain, however, put a temporary stop to the casual insouciance with which our relations with Barbary had been conducted.[3] Aspinwall was recalled in an almost brutally inconsiderate fashion; his enemy Ford was appointed in his stead; and Captain Clevland was

---

[1] *Mariner's Mirror*, May 1953.   [2] S.P. 71. 10 and F.O. 3. 1.

[3] Lawlessness of British privateers, Fortunatus Wright, &c., aroused complaints of consuls and Dey. See Cal. H.O. i. 212, &c. Pitt dismissed as 'void of foundation' complaints of *Diana*, despite loss of seventy-one Moslem passengers, S.P. 71. 10, ff. 553–4; F.O. 3. 1, 29 June 1760.

sent, rather belatedly, on a tour of conciliatory visits, which
paved the way for better understanding.[1]

Unfortunately the interest was not maintained. Ford died
in England before he could take up the appointment, and the
consulate at Algiers was left vacant until in May 1762 Clevland,
at the Dey's desire, appointed Ford's partner, Simon Peter
Cruise, 'the only British merchant established there', to act
pending the arrival of the new consul. With Cruise, whom Clevland found very helpful but our histories hand down as a man
of 'infamous character', the traditional connexion of British
merchants and the Deys came to an end. It was replaced to a
considerable extent by the friendship displayed by a succession
of Deys with Joseph Meifrund, a French merchant whose residence in Algiers coincided roughly with the second half of the
century.[2]

Official indifference at home, complicated doubtless by
naval wars, corrupt practices at Gibraltar and Minorca, and
the active hostility at Algiers of Aspinwall and James Bruce
(1763–5), contributed to the extinction of British interests,
commercial and maritime, along the southern shore of the
Mediterranean. The Barbary States, with the possible exception of Tripoli, then of minor importance, slowly drifted into
the arms of the Bourbons. By 1768 alarming signs of a *rap-
prochement* with Spain were reported from Algiers and Morocco.
By 1786 the long feud between Spain and the regencies, which
other Christian powers had done so much to foster, was brought
to an end, and peace restored to the Mediterranean.[3]

The triumphant conclusion of the Seven Years War helped
to divert our attention to opportunities in other fields and
obscure the essentially precarious character of our position
inside the straits. A regular feature of English relations with
Algiers over a period of 230 years was the alternation of cordiality and even deference, when danger threatened from
Mediterranean powers, with indifference and sometimes hostility when it had been successfully surmounted. This was fairly

[1] For instructions, 'most gracious reception at Algiers', 1762, and 'amicable
adjustment', 1765, see S.P. 42. 101.

[2] 1752 to 1802.

[3] Cal. H.O. ii, esp. 391–2; S.P. 71. 10, 3 Oct. and 20 Nov. 1765. In 1785, 313
French deserters from Oran, mostly undesirable, were repatriated, de Grammont,
pp. 331–2; Campbell, i. 82–85, &c.

consistently reflected in the character of consular appointments, and was, perhaps, never so clearly demonstrated as by our irresponsible action in this regard once the last critical stage of that war was over.

The consulate was conferred on James Bruce solely to study antiquities in North Africa, and he was sent through France under a safe-conduct to examine classical remains in Italy before reaching Algiers after the war. In spite of some likeable qualities, he was arrogant and irascible and, judging by his letters, there may be some reason to question his mental stability. While he frantically summoned warships to his aid, he speaks in high terms of the Dey's treatment of him. He even boasts in his memoirs of having been 'on good terms with the whole Regency, as well with the common soldiers as with the merchants', and reported elsewhere that the Algerines 'never fail in all possible good faith and friendship to the King's subjects'.[1] His successor complained that he had left 'everything relative to Publick Affairs in much confusion and strangely neglected'.

A most unfortunate development, resulting in part from the absence of English merchants and in part from our naval triumphs, was the changed relationship with the navy. Bruce evidently quarrelled violently with Clevland on his second visit and, without producing any proof, accused him of corruption, while Clevland regarded Bruce's complaints against Algiers as ill-founded or irrelevant. Spry and Harrison apparently behaved with unnecessary rudeness to Kirke[2] and Sampson,[3] both of whom were recalled after very short periods in spite of the Dey's protests. 'Provision' had to be made for Campbell Fraser, the heir to the Lovat barony and nephew of a duke, who after a very brief stay had been summarily recalled from Tripoli and sent to Algiers with strict instructions to behave as became the king's representative.

Able, ambitious, and arrogant, his views coincided only too well with the changing attitude of naval commanders, which, in addition to the natural effect of resounding triumphs, appears

---

[1] The *courageux et généreux* Dey, Venture, p. 101, turned to France in 1764. Regretted as a 'man of Generous Disposition and Lover of the English', F.O. 3. 1, 9 Oct. 1767.   [2] Cal. H.O. ii. 37, 53, and 60; S.P. 71. 10, ff. 697 and 718.
[3] Playfair, p. 205.

to have been influenced by a new conception of the liberty automatically extended to all fugitives by the British flag. Though this was expressly disapproved by our government, and a vast and uncontrolled system of slavery was recognized as the foundation of our national prosperity, the Mahometan system came to be regarded as peculiarly evil, and public opinion was inclined to commend those commanders who were prepared to see Europe 'swim in blood' in order to facilitate the escape of one Algerine captive.[1]

The period was also marked by a striking reversal of the traditional attitudes of England and France towards the Turks. While we began to cultivate the friendship of Naples and Sicily, we abetted, or allowed ourselves to be identified with, Russian and Austrian hostilities against our Turkish allies and the development of rebellion and piracy in Greece. France, on the other hand, tried to strengthen its position and find compensation for its losses elsewhere by the occupation of Corsica and the consolidation of its political and economic ties with the Ottoman empire.

Thus developed the curious phenomenon that, in proportion as internal conditions in Algeria improved, and France displayed increasing anxiety to fall in with long-standing Algerine objections to the expiring treaty, and notwithstanding our concern at the increasing interest of Spain and our growing dependence on Algerine supplies, the tendency was for relations to be conducted in a spirit of greater arrogance with it than with the other regencies or Morocco.

From the conclusion of the Seven Years War may be said to date a new and apparently special relationship with Algiers, which, to adopt Consul Falcon's expression, would not allow the Dey to be 'king in his own country'. The interpretation of treaties and even of international law underwent a sudden change. Consuls and captains insisted, without reference to the home government, that a slave became free if he merely touched a warship's boat at a wharf; that our ships could buy whatever foodstuffs they wished, anchor where they chose, and capture prizes wherever they liked. Disregard for local neutrality was

---

[1] Tucker, i. 446 and ii. 338; Cal. H.O. ii. 506. St. Vincent believed he had visited Algiers and Tunis, Conn, *Gibraltar in British Diplomacy*, p. 259 n.; E. P. Brenton, *Life and Correspondence of John, Earl of St. Vincent*, 2 vols., London, 1838, ii. 354.

developed to the point of maintaining, in the end successfully, that Britain alone had the right to condemn and sell prizes in Algiers, and, in a matter affecting the rights of American seamen, our consul told the Dey that King George was not in the least interested in the rules and regulations of the port. Piracy, in the view of Blaquiere and Mahan, consisted of 'unpardonable effrontery in continuing to be at war' with states which had become our allies.

Our consular history at Algiers during the reign of George III must surely appear a unique record of incompetence, insubordination, insolvency, quarrels, and unauthorized intrigue, interspersed with expulsions or recalls, official admonitions and payments of debts from Treasury funds. It was also marked by a complete transformation of the local atmosphere. The English merchant disappeared, and the area came to be regarded as the special preserve of adventurous spirits from the Hebrides and Highlands of Scotland.[1] While our consuls, sometimes with the support of their government, showed a new solicitude for personal dignity and privilege, they did not disdain to borrow large sums from Jewish brokers or a Dey's wife or to let the control of consular affairs pass into the hands of such dubious characters as John Woulfe, Isaac Bensamon, and Juan Escudero.[2] During a century every consul but two was either expelled or recalled or insolvent, and the two exceptions merely serve to point the moral.[3]

It would be interesting to know how far the position of our navy in the Mediterranean or its dependence on Barbary goodwill and supply was reflected in the vicissitudes of our relations with Algiers and our consular arrangements. In February 1783 Nathaniel Davison left his post ostensibly because he was insulted by Britain's loss of prestige, but mainly because during most of his three years stay he had received no instructions or remuneration. At the great administrative reorganization follow-

---

[1] G.M. 1811, pp. 79–82.

[2] Our government paid Woulfe's debts. Bensamon's unauthorized connexion lasted fifty years to 1829. 'Le misérable Escudero', agent at Bona, wrote conflicting reports of the 'massacre'.

[3] Holden and Charles Logie (1785–94) alone understood local language and customs. Logie, born in Algiers, suffered from ill-health and resigned against the wishes of king and Dey. In London he represented Algiers interests, especially claims against Britain.

ing that calamitous war the Barbary States were separated from
the rest of the foreign field, including other parts of the Ottoman
empire, and placed under the colonial section of the Home
Office. At Keppel's suggestion a consul born and bred in Algiers
was sent and furnished with suitable instructions. Contributions
to the defences of Algiers and Mogador implemented in 1787
the new policy designed to safeguard Gibraltar and equilibrium
in the Mediterranean.[1]

The last phase of the legend began and practically ended with
notable fiascos. No evidence is cited for the characteristic claim
that Spain in 1786 'finally extorted a treaty with Algiers which
put a stop to piratical raids on the Spanish coast',[2] or for assertions that in 1815 'the suppression of African piracy was
universally felt to be a necessity' and the 'suppression of the
slave trade which the Barbary States practised on a large scale
and at the expense of Europe' was an object of the Congress of
Vienna. The number of prizes and captives made between 1786
and the collapse of the Napoleonic system was in fact negligible.[3]
Those 'chronic problems' were probably suggested at Vienna
by Sidney Smith and Alexander to Castlereagh, whose very
questionable representations in 1819 had a most humiliating
ending in a very pertinent lecture on piracy from the Bey of
Tunis.[4]

The convenient assumption that Barbary consisted of savages
whose institutions and past history, including traditional and
beneficial alliances, were of no interest to us[5] was apparently a
Victorian development of Scottish and American interpretations

[1] Compare present of cannon, &c. to Algiers, F.O. 3. 6, 25 May 1787, and Plantet, ii. 359–83, with menaces elsewhere: Russia, G.M. 1786, pp. 517 and 895;
Portugal, F.O. 3. 6, 7 Oct. 1788; Venice, Tuscany, &c., G.M. 1787, p. 261; American war, 1785–93. Algiers tried to become 'inexpugnable' through 'subsidies',
voluntary or enforced.

[2] E.B. xxv. 533. Compare de Grammont, pp. 337–9 and 346; A.R. 1785, p. 24;
G.M. 1786, p. 799.

[3] African Slave Trade did not concern Barbary, Parliamentary Debates, A.R.
1815. In June 1814, there were perhaps 600 captives in Barbary. Early 1816
Italian coral-boats flocked to Algeria. Compare Gilbert's libretto with Algiers
'piracy', Pananti, pp. 34–66.

[4] Plantet, Tunis, iii. 570–4 n., mentioning French and American claims for
fourteen British prizes in Tunis waters; F.O. 8. 3, 11 Sept. 1819. Collingwood to
Castlereagh, 4 July 1807, Correspondence, pp. 255–6, and F.O. 77. 8, 6 Oct. 1817.
A.R. 1815, pp. [154] and [157–60].

[5] C. N. Parkinson, Edward Pellew, Viscount Exmouth, London, 1934, pp. 420–1.
Compare Sonia E. Howe, The Drama of Madagascar, London, 1938, p. 154.

of Spanish history. Prescott's tribute to the universal recognition of international law 'founded on the immutable basis of morality and justice' ignored the constant disregard of human rights, consular duties and immunities, treaties, and historic autonomies between the French Revolution and the Reform Bill. Mutual recriminations of Frenchmen, Spaniards, Americans, and Britons following the clash between British naval and French military power in the Mediterranean were reinforced by our frank admissions of official violation of neutrality and 'British piracy in Barbary waters'.

St. Vincent's attitude, when forced out of the Mediterranean, was a significant tribute to the relations that he, together with Minto and Hawkesbury, had developed, especially with the Dey. 'We at present stand on high ground with Tripoli, Tunis and Algiers, and the occasion should not be lost to obtain supplies from the Rock in the hour of trial.'[1] Very different, however, was the attitude adopted during the anxious period (1799–1804) towards Algiers, as distinct from Tunis and Tripoli, and the new Dey (1798–1805) from whose special goodwill and experience so much had been hoped.[2]

Directed mainly from Turkey, Sicily, and Malta, British policy seemed designed to browbeat and humiliate the 'tiger dey', nullify 'the letter and spirit of the Treaties with Algiers and the uniform practice under them', and terminate 'the long and uninterrupted harmony' between Great Britain and the regency. Inconsistent with the attitude of St. Vincent, Warren, and Collingwood, it was severely criticized by Logie, Falcon, and Abbott.[3] Nelson's attempt to 'rouse up strong resentment at home' in December 1799 and his (repeated) threat to sink the Dey's fleet at sea without giving 'the scoundrel an idea of my intentions'[4] did not result in compliance with his unalterable demands, but did help to undermine the Dey's authority. In March Falcon's successor reported a murderous attack on

[1] Brenton, i. 206.

[2] F.O. 3. 8, 26 Sept. 1798; Nicolas, iii. 26–27. For attitude of Bonaparte and Talleyrand, see Plantet, ii. 479–96.

[3] P. Abbott, merchant of London and Algiers, F.O. 3. 10, 20 July 1804.
     ʿcolas, iv. 125–6 and vi. 281. Neapolitan crews of *Ape*, &c., were apparently
     ᵉd in 1816 and returned voluntarily to Africa, Colletta, ii. 202–3. See also
         59, 113, 146–7, 209, &c. and F.O. 3. 10 of 29 Jan. 1803 and 18 Jan.
             ᵗ surely Italian, even in name.

'the poor man'; in June, the 'enormities' of Maltese privateers; and, in July, an unprecedented *pogrom*, described as a severe blow to the French interest, sure to be attributed to English guineas. In August the assassination of the Dey and his principal minister synchronized with Napoleon's denunciations of the regencies as a menace to Italian liberty and with the disquieting emergence of Arab fanaticism in the interior.[1]

The sudden cordiality of Nelson's last letters,[2] written in ignorance of his old opponent's death, clearly reflect revived interest in Algerine co-operation. Even more significant is the concern demonstrated after Trafalgar had made Britain supreme at sea—in the correspondence of Collingwood[3] and Windham, in the missions of Exmouth[4] and Heytesbury,[5] and in conciliatory or apologetic letters from George III and the Prince Regent.

During the ensuing peace sea-communications must have been strangely defective. An Algiers dispatch of 1 June 1814 arrived in London the following February. A praiseworthy attempt to improve consular organization by placing the regencies under the direct supervision of the Governor of Malta revealed the fact that it had no communication with Algiers, from which after long delays correspondence had to be sent through London. A 'pithy' protest from the governor to the Bashaw of Tripoli on 16 March 1815 and subsequent discussions about an American privateer bringing in two British prizes suggest complete ignorance of the peace of Ghent. In 1823 the governor, for want of a ship to suspend the consul at Algiers for his 'most indecent and insubordinate' conduct, died of apoplexy while dictating a demand to the War Office for his removal.[6] Naval strength in the Mediterranean at the time might have prevented the growth of Greek disorders or the sailing in 1830 of the French expedition, as Nelson claimed was done during the consulate.[7]

[1] F.O. 3. 10 and *G.M.* and *A.R.* 1805.

[2] Nicolas, vii. 47, 78–79, and 98 n.

[3] Compare Lane-Poole, p. 292, with interest in Algiers shown by *Correspondence* and F.O. 3. 11, 26 Mar. 1806.

[4] 'Cultivating the Dey's friendship', Pellew to Croker, F.O. 3. 14, 17 Apr. 1812.

[5] To facilitate supplies for Portugal.

[6] W. F. Lord, *Life of Sir Thomas Maitland*, London, 1897, pp. 161–3 and 278–9.

[7] Nicolas, vi. 303, while Falcon threatened Algiers with joint Anglo-French attack.

If Britain had felt that its destiny lay in those waters, the story of its relations with Barbary was surely one of lost opportunities. We might so easily have acquired, no less legally than Gibraltar, Minorca, or Malta, the ports of Ceuta or Oran (or even, perhaps, Bona) with the advantage of friendly and productive surroundings. Exmouth's proceedings destroyed the commercial and strategic advantages which we then enjoyed in Algeria, without bringing any lasting compensation in gratitude or prestige. Little practical effect was given to subsequent projects for peaceful penetration from Britain or Malta. Even in 1830 friendly diplomacy might have obtained from France the long-coveted port of Arzew.[1] The long and unprecedented peace with old rivals may well have accounted for our slowness to appreciate the value of permanent naval strength in that area which William and Marlborough had formerly recognized as the 'keyboard of Europe', and merchants and statesmen of France had so long regarded as the highway to the treasures of the East.[2]

---

[1] Esquer, p. 410.

[2] Austrian criticisms early in 1830 of British inconsistencies and French 'prevarications' suggest that neither country had then a definite Mediterranean policy. See also, G. Lacour-Fayet, *Talleyrand*, 4 vols., Paris, 1930–2, iv. 38, 223, 444; and A. Debidour, *Histoire diplomatique de l'Europe*, 1814–78, 2 vols., Paris, 1891, i. 105–6, 272.

APPENDIX A

List of Consuls, 1585–1714

Algiers

1585–? JOHN TIPTON, whose jurisdiction nominally included Tunis and Tripoli. Murdered in the Adriatic.

1598–?1605. JOHN AUDELEY, perhaps never formally appointed but called the 'Queen's Consul' and 'Publique Minister for the English Nation'.

1606–9. RICHARD ALLEN, departed clandestinely.

?1611–18. JAMES FRIZELL, apparently acted informally.

1620–?1622. Richard Forde, appointed temporarily by Sir Robert Mansel.

1624–?1638. JAMES FRIZELL, ? died in Algiers.

1648–53. HUMPHREY ONEBY, died of plague.

1653–4. EDMUND CASON, died of plague.

1655–64. ROBERT BROWNE, provisionally appointed by Admiral Blake. Appointed in 1656 'His Highness' Consul'. Confirmed by Charles II. Died of a flux.

1664–6. CAPTAIN NICHOLAS PARKER, appointed by Captain Allin. Recalled to naval service.

1666–73. JOHN WARD, replaced by

1673–?1679. SAMUEL MARTIN, dead by 1680.

1682–3. CAPTAIN JOHN NEVILL, temporarily appointed by Admiral Herbert. Returned to naval duty.

1683–4. PHILIP RYCAUT, agent and consul general, recalled.

1684–90. JOHN ERLISMAN, agent and consul general. Died at his post.

1690–1. ROBERT COLE, temporarily appointed by Dey.

1691–4. THOMAS BAKER, agent and consul general, retired for ill-health.

1694–1712. ROBERT COLE, agent and consul general. Died at his post.

1712–13. THOMAS THOMSON, temporarily appointed by Dey.

1713–20. SAMUEL THOMSON, agent and consul general. Resigned or dismissed.

Tunis

Under protection of French consul until 1618.

1622–? WILLIAM COOKE, appointed provisionally by Sir Thomas Roe. Confirmed 1623 by Levant Company, which promptly severed connexion with Tunis.

1638–50.   WILLIAM WOODHOUSE, appointed by royal commission. Replaced by

1650–63.   THOMAS BROWNE, appointed through Levant Company at request of Admiralty. Superseded temporarily by SAM BOOTHOUSE (? 1651). Left with Blake's fleet 1655 and returned 1658, THOMAS CAMPION acting in interval. Removed in 1663 for having been 'for the usurper'.

1663–?   JOHN ERLISMAN, agent and consul. Royal commission. Later H.M.'s Controller of Revenue at Tangier. See Algiers.

?–1683.   FRANCIS BAKER. Royal commission in 1677 but acting previously. Relinquished post to his deputy.

1683–?1697. THOMAS GOODWIN, ? died.

?1697–?1700. JOHN CHETWOOD, acting.

1700–?1711. JOHN GODDARD, agent and consul general. Died.

?1711.   JOHN WALDECK, chancelier of consulate, acting.

1711–50.   RICHARD LAWRENCE, agent and consul general. Died.

(Apparently all the consuls from 1663 to 1750 were partners in the same firm.)

Tripoli

No definite reference is available to consuls of any kind, English or foreign, functioning there until

1658–67.   SAMUEL TUCKER, provisionally appointed by Admirals Stokes and Lawson (1662). Left for London and refused to return on terms offered.

1671–5.   NATHANIEL BRADLEY. Royal commission. Left with Admiral Narborough on outbreak of war.

1676–86.   THOMAS BAKER, agent and consul general. Resigned to become Clerk of Cheque at Deptford. See Algiers.

1686–1700. NICHOLAS LODINGTON, do., formerly trading to Sallee. Compelled to leave post during nominal hostilities 1692–4, his brother and partner Benjamin remaining in charge. Returned to business in London.

1700–29.   BENJAMIN LODINGTON, do. Resigned after 'absence of 45 years, nearly 30 as consul'.

Sallee

1637–8.   GILES PENN. Royal commission. Returned to sea service.

1638–53.   ROBERT PICKFORD, delegated by Robert Blake, agent
            of Charles I and Barbary Company. ? Left for
            Madeira.
1654–6.   Two well-known London merchants, THOMAS WARREN
            and ROBERT STARR, acted as navy agents at Sallee.
1657–64.   NATHANIEL LUKE, suggested 1656 for consul at Sallee.
            Appointed March 1657 consul for Tetuan and Sallee,
            residing for naval reasons at Tetuan. Royal com-
            mission 1663. Secretary to Lord Teviot at Tangier
            and probably killed in same ambush.
1665–9.   THOMAS WARREN, agent for Charles II. Brother of
            Sir William and friend of Pepys. Accompanied
            Lord Howard's mission.
1669–?   THOMAS ONEBY, consul for Tetuan and Sallee.
            Corresponded on political matters with secretary of
            state and Governor of Tangier up to 1683.

There is no official record of consuls in Morocco between 1683
and 1728. From 1667 all permanent appointments to the regencies
were by royal commission addressed directly to the local rulers. All
consuls belonged to families long established in the Mediterranean
and Levant trades, and usually closely connected by family and
business ties with consuls at other places and with the principal
merchants of London.

APPENDIX B

Barbary and Barbaresques

THE English use of both terms is open to question. The connotation of 'Barbary' varied with the angle of approach. To the normal Englishman, arriving from the Atlantic, it meant Morocco, alike in the days of Drake and Bodenham and Jackson. The King of Fez was called the King of Barbary, and that kingdom is described in the 'Polity and Religion of Barbary' (Macaulay's Essay on Addison). The consul described by Jackson in 1806 was officially called 'Consul General of Great Britain in Barbary', actually resident at Tangier, and treaties then in force used the word Barbary for Morocco. For Monson and John Smith, and also East Indiamen two centuries later, the 'Barbary Shore' was on the Atlantic.

Coming from the Levant, Britons spoke of Barbary to distinguish Tripoli in Africa from Tripoli in Syria. At Constantinople diplomats, &c., might describe the auxiliary navies of the regencies as the Barbary fleet, but usually Christians spoke of the galleys of 'Algiers and Tunis', even when acting together. Burchett (1720) says 'the Governments of Algier, Tunis and Tripoli have for a long time had their ships of War'. His statement that the Turkish fleet in the Venetian war was increased by 'auxiliaries from Tripoli, Tunis and Algier' may be compared with his exceptional mention of 'corsairs of Barbary' and 'rovers of Barbary' taken apparently from a Venetian report of 1656. Ordinarily Venice and Algiers belonged to quite separate spheres. The 'Barbary pirates' at the beginning and end of the seventeenth century operated from Atlantic ports of Morocco respectively as Christian adventurers and the emperor's navy. The Barbary Company had no connexion with the Mediterranean, but the Levant Company had some claim on Tetuan. In *American State Papers* particulars are given of the Algiers navy, but a 'Barbary cruiser' belonged to Morocco.

Barbary, in its wider sense, was from a maritime and political standpoint an even vaguer 'geographical expression' than Italy. It had no common official language or religious head. It consisted of four separate states, with which Christian powers made distinct treaties. Dutch ships in William's fleet co-operated with Morocco against Algiers, while ours did the reverse. Holland apparently included North Africa in its Levant service; Austria insisted the regencies were Turkish dependencies; Britain created in 1782 the administrative unit called Barbary States, but by 1812 enforced different neutrality regulations for each regency. In 1815 London reported war by the Barbary States against Spain.

The 'European' congresses of 1815–18, while affecting to regard Barbary as a unit for problems of piracy and slavery, applied the term in practice only to the Turkish part. The modern concept of the Barbary pirates dates apparently from a book hastily published in 1816 to make capital out of Exmouth's exploit, which concerned Algiers alone and expressly disclaimed any suggestion of piracy. The more recent concept of Barbary corsairs presumably had its origin in Byron's poem and activities of Christian corsairs in Greek waters. Lane-Poole in his *Barbary Corsairs* says Morocco is not 'strictly' one of the Barbary States, and in his *Turkey* has great difficulty in explaining what a corsair is supposed to be. In 1752 a French traveller calls Fez the capital and commercial centre of 'Berberie'. In 1838 Brenton speaks of the various 'Barbary Powers' and their navies as separate units. In 1928 a diplomatist carefully defines Algiers as 'the capital of the Barbary States and a centre of piracy'.

The use of the word 'Barbaresque' has apparently no sanction in our official records. At first such clumsy phrases were used as 'Turks and Moors' or 'those of Algiers'. At one time the generic term 'Turkish' covered even the ships of Sallee. Pepys called Algiers cruisers 'Turkish privateers', though the distinctive epithets 'Algerine' and 'Tunisian' were being generally adopted.

About 1700 Lucas explains 'Barbaresques' as people inhabiting the *coast* of Africa west of Egypt, a novel and erroneous concept, since the word 'berberisco' or 'barbaresco' was applied only to Berbers, who, unlike the Turks and Moors, were essentially non-maritime. Duro is normally careful to avoid its application to ships or seamen. Europeans generally drew a sharp distinction between the dusky Moors of the country and the 'light' Moors of the coastal cities, who, according to Foss, were like Americans, only taller.

The idea that 'the Barbaresques', i.e. the people of the regencies, were too bestial to be used in Christian galleys resulted from mis-interpretation of a phrase in Pantero Pantera, *Armata Navale*, Rome, 1614. It merely meant that Arab villagers, as distinct from Turks and Moors, were too stupid for service as oarsmen, because they were unaccustomed to life at sea. 'Barbarian' was frequently used as equivalent to Moroccan.

APPENDIX C

Giulia Gonzaga at Fondi

THE contrast between the exceptional publicity given to an apparently trivial incident of no political consequence and the customary indifference to Kheir-ed-din's urgent mission to Savona must arouse curiosity as to how far its popular appeal resulted from elaboration of an unauthorized and piquant character and even as to the authenticity of the original report, which may have emanated solely from Jovius' anti-Turkish malice.

At the time Barbarossa was travelling north along the Italian coast in great haste and treated the wife and niece of the Governor of Spelunca with 'rare courtesy'. Three contemporary reports mention his taking prisoners at Fondi, without reference to kidnapping or massacre. Probably they only indicate that it was attacked by some of his forces.

If the episode is not legendary, it is strange that King Henry's active agents at Rome and Venice passed over this tit-bit. Spanish clerics, like Gomara and Haedo, who were interested in Italy and the career of Kheir-ed-din, would surely have referred to the adventure of a lady celebrated in her own right and sister of a famous beauty in Spain. Still more remarkable is the silence of Isabella d'Este and her chronicler, Julia Cartwright, about something most distressing to that affectionate and illustrious family.

Knolles supplies a possible explanation. The expedition was conducted, 'as was thought', by certain Neapolitan renegades, or exiles, in Barbarossa's fleet. The 'suddenness of the coming' might have been connected with designs on that 'paragon of Italy and the chief prize they sought after'. The only ground for assuming Kheir-ed-din's complicity was that he 'seemed not to deny it'. No evidence is produced that he ever heard of the lady. The story is incompatible with statements by Gomara and Montluc that he and his fellow Turks were noted for strict adherence to the business of war. Doria and Charles, who make no allusion to the incident, certainly found this true of his return voyage along that coast.

APPENDIX D

Kheir-ed-din and Tunis

THE imposing Turkish armament left Gallipoli early in June 1534 to install Raschid at Tunis. By 8 August, after stoppages in Greece to land artillery and at Savona for negotiations with France, the operation was complete. Official Spanish documents, Gomara, pp. 509–27, supported by dispatches from Casale in Rome and contemporary items from Charrière, refute contentions that Kheir-ed-din forcibly occupied Tunisia, pillaged the capital, suppressed Raschid, or took the kingdom for Suleiman or himself. No such suggestions appear in the Spanish report which, from its date, 13 October 1535, may have been a belated attempt to present the Spanish case.

Conclusive evidence comes from one of Doria's letters to Charles from Rome, where he sought papal support. After pointing out that Barbarossa would not lack troops or friendly assistance, he continued: 'not only does he find himself unhampered in Tunis affairs, but in peaceful possession (*mas pacífico possesor*), taking as great care of the expedition and the rest [of the country] as if his own property. Those who say the opposite are ill-informed.' Henry received similar advice through a French ambassador at Tunis.

Despite its length the Spanish report throws little light on the actual operations. The Turkish fleet was evidently laid up, except for galleys under Sinan and Cachidiablo. The Christian oarsmen, who numbered only 1710, including Serbians and Bulgarians, probably remained on board, while the soldiers maintained order or penetrated inland, where Charles urged Hassan to stir up revolt.

Possibly Kheir-ed-din was caught unawares there by the formidable expedition which left Cagliari on 3 June 1535, and after brief assaults captured La Goletta and Tunis on 14 and 21 July. On 10 August Charles embarked, and on the 17th sailed for Sicily. Apart from occupying Bona, no attempt was made to profit by naval supremacy. Failure to act against Algiers was excused by the late season, sickness, and Barbarossa's inability to attack. Projected captures of Constantinople, Greece, and Mahdia were forgotten. The net result was Hassan's reinstatement as vassal of Spain, the retention of La Goletta and Bona in strengthened form, and relief from imminent danger to Sicily. The chief beneficiaries were Genoese.

Reliable information is lacking about the liberation of Christians —their number, origin, past history, and ultimate disposal. The

Spanish report only mentions that there were 20,000, including seventy-one Frenchmen who had been there several years. If this, apparently vague, estimate is to be added to even more Tunisian captives and the 80,000 soldiers, 25,000 horses, and 4,000 *enamoradas* originally embarked, some comment on scenes at ports of arrival might have been expected.

Marmol, a Spanish soldier and, apparently, eye-witness, presumably reports objectively the 'liberation' of Tunis. His statement that the emperor ordered the sack is corroborated by Virginio Orsini and, seemingly, by Charles himself, though denied later in the Spanish report, perhaps in reply to foreign criticisms. Knolles probably relied on some Italian account. Marmol attributed the slaughter to Spanish cavalry (not infantry or German seamen) who scoured the country round Tunis. He estimated the dead at 70,000, and the captives at 40,000! Rotalier gives details of libraries, mosques, and works of art looted or destroyed. Whatever the exact facts they were evidently regarded as exceptional.

How far the occupation represented a political or religious triumph for the emperor may be gauged by Spanish evidence, criticisms of papal commanders, and the course of events. In December Chapuys answered Henry's scoffing disparagement by pointing out that Charles's opponent was 'captain general of the most powerful prince in the world', an opinion almost textually echoed by Gomara, who dates Kheir-ed-din's naval pre-eminence from his success at Minorca. Four years later Charles was offering him dominion over Tunis.

APPENDIX E
Morat Reis, 1603–8

MORAT's career during these years is of special interest because it coincided with an important period, of which very conflicting accounts are given. Not mentioned by Corbett or Playfair, Duro singles him out in 1601–2 as 'excelling all' corsairs.

Since the prestige of Algiers and Morat was high early in 1603 it is surprising to find Knolles's *History*, p. 825, describing the defeat of the galley fleet of 'Amurat Rais, an old Pyrat, the Turks Admiral for the West Part of the Mediterranean' by, first, a Flemish ship and then by the Grand Duke's galleys, 'accounted the best in the world and such as now at this present much troubled the Turks' design'. His losses 'so broke the credit of this old and renowned Pyrat as that for a great while after he was little by the Christians feared upon that coast'. This claim does not tally with Henri's complaints or the Salisbury MSS. (1603–5).

In 1603, owing to violations of the concession, especially in exporting grain and causing famine, Morat, described by Henri as 'chef des gallères et brigantinas d'Algier', dismantled the *Bastion de France* on the divan's orders. This, added to activities by English corsairs at Tunis, involved France and the regencies in war. The 'infinity of English depredations' evidently embarrassed Moslems and Christians alike.

They evoked a letter of 4 October 1603, n.s., from Captain Murad Bey in Italian, probably to Staper. It contained a gratifying reply to a letter sent to the bashaw and Morat by Frederick Clase, 'your ambassador', and announced a practical reconciliation after outrages by some English ships. The fact that Clase was given a safe-conduct for all the sultan's dominions and messages too confidential to put on paper may indicate proposals for granting concessions at French expense.

The squire of Salignac, the French ambassador who replaced de Brèves at Constantinople, relates that in 1604 his party met the Ottoman fleet returning from Alexandretta, and received news of events there from Morat, who had signally distinguished himself. Evidently the occurrences concerned the 'belliqueux Druses' (de Brèves), the 'rebellious Pasha of Aleppo' (*C.M.H.* iii. 398), and the knights (Hubac, p. 165). Certainly Morat, arriving at Tunis in 1605, enjoyed great prestige.

He found the French mission frustrated by the divan's refusal to accept the Sultan's commands, conveyed by the envoy Mustapha. Both sides welcomed Morat as arbitrator. A very satisfactory settlement was nullified by Henri's intransigence.

A member of the mission describes Morat as a most renowned corsair, who during sixty years had successfully captured galleys from all Christian opponents possessing them. He was small, aged 80, with very pimpled face, 'brave et courageux au possible'. His two 'excellent' galleys were specially built for speed. His corps of galley-slaves was 'bien gaillarde et en bon point', and his soldiery 'tout brave robuste et bien délibérée.' He appeared simply dressed, sur-rounded by old corsairs. He received de Brèves 'fort humainement', while Ward, who, like other foreign adventurers, was on a lower plane, kissed the admiral's hand respectfully.

Mustapha waited seven months in Algiers, while de Brèves was at Paris. Though he forwarded eighty French captives, no Moslems were returned from Marseilles. Henri refused him an audience, but sent a money present, which was declined. His mission to London, facilitated by Carew, brought Staper a letter from Morat dated *pridie Calendas novembri*.

This acknowledged Staper's letter of thanks for restoring free commerce, 12 August 1606, and promised to discuss the matter later. For the moment he requested assistance with Mustapha's mission, directed against 'raids and piracies (*latrociniis*) by the Queen's subjects in the seas of my Emperor', adding 'if you have any kindness for me please look after him and see him well received'.

Staper passing on the request to Sir Edward Hoby paid tribute to both. Mustapha was 'a man of goodly presence and gallant spirit, sociable, affable and full of entertainment to all comers'. An experienced and much-travelled diplomat, he also favourably im-pressed The Hague, where he spoke freely of English piracies and Henri's iniquity in intercepting for his galleys Moslems repatriated from Sluys under cover of his passports.

Morat had probably left for Constantinople on appointment as Beglerbey of the Morea before the Tuscan attack on Bona of July 1607. About that time Algerines brought into Constantinople a large ship owned by the Grand Duke. Over 500 French were killed or captured, including several Knights of Malta. Morat's triumphant visit is described by Salignac elsewhere.

Naturally Venice objected to his residence in Greece, but Dutch shipping prospered in the Adriatic, and so, apparently, did our consulate at Patras. Substantial evidence comes in 1612 from a memorial for establishing a consulate in the Morea for the French nation, following the 'pacification' of the Peloponnesus 'par ce fameux corsaire Morat rays, lequel ha dix galères entretenues pour la deffense des places fortes'—an unusual tribute in an area notorious for piratical activity.

APPENDIX F

Ochiali and the Administration of the Regencies

THE theory that a complete and most unfortunate alteration followed the death of Ochiali, or more properly Ali, the last Beglerbey of Barbary, and resulted in the substitution of inferior rulers known as 'triennial pashas' seems quite untenable. Correspondence in Charrière, especially iv. 516–17, leaves no doubt that there never was a Beglerbey of Barbary. In his old age the 'restless schemer' Ochiali desired the position but the suggestion was immediately rejected as an impossible novelty. Haedo's ignorance of Ottoman affairs and the extraordinary absence of French records about Algiers involved Père Dan in unwarranted assumptions.

The appointment of Sala as Beglerbey of 'Africa' before that region was formally organized as the regency of Tripoli has led to confusion, augmented by the application of the title beglerbey to various Ottoman officials—political, military, and naval. Ochiali was called nineteenth Beglerbey of Algiers in 1568. His removal was reported in 1571 (Cal. S.P.F. 1569–71, p. 563) and became definite in 1572 when he was appointed Capudan pasha and, as such, Fourth Bassa or Beglerbey at Constantinople. In his time Hakluyt says 'Beglierbei signifieth lord Admirall'. From 1574 to 1830 the post of beglerbey continued in each of the three regencies, though the title pasha, or bashaw, became more usual. Perhaps the full title was Bassa Beglerbeg (Charrière, iv. 654 n.).

A beglerbey was usually a governor-general commanding military governors called beys. Haedo, who erroneously describes the Viceroy of Algiers as pasha and his military subordinate as beglerbey, correctly speaks of Ochiali as general of the sea with jurisdiction in the waters of Barbary. This he exercised through Captains of the Sea, assigned like other beys at strategic naval centres to Algiers, Tunis, and Tripoli. He was 'Bassa de mer' or maritime Beglerbey of the Empire. Fermanel writes about 1631 that in official processions at Constantinople the 'Général de Mer' was attended by about a hundred 'Beys ou Capitaines de Gallères', mounted on horseback.

When in 1581 Djafer and Ochiali combined to invade Morocco, they are called 'les seig^{rs} le beglierbey d'Algers et [le] capitaine général de nostre heureuse armée' (Charrière, iv. 61). The latter was expressly sent to achieve something on the sea. Djafer was evidently supreme on land and managed to block Ochiali's ambitious plans. Hassan, Djafer's successor, is called 'le beglierbey ou vice-roy d'Algier' (ibid., p. 272 n.). Ochiali was not employed again in the Mediterranean.

Ramadan, like Hassan Veneziano, is definitely described as successively Beglerbey of Algiers, Tunis, and Tripoli. Hassan Barbarossa, another soldier, was three times appointed Beglerbey of Algiers. Haedo describes the normal tenure, after Kheir-ed-din's death, as roughly three years, but his figures show no regularity. Presumably it was determined by political exigences at Constantinople.

When in 1586 Ochiali suspected Hassan of intriguing for his post of Capudan pasha he retaliated by trying to supersede Hassan in his governorship of Tripoli (Charrière, iv. 524 n.). Cicala, who did not, as Haedo supposes, eliminate Ochiali and Hassan by poison, was successively Beglerbey of Tauris, Capudan pasha, and again Beglerbey of Tauris. Clearly such positions could not be held simultaneously.

The regencies continued in the seventeenth century to rank with the great Pashaliks of Tauris, Cairo, and the Morea. Their rulers are described as beglerbeys in our records. The latest reference to the correct title that I have found is at Tripoli ?1741 in official mention of 'our Beler Bey's Ambassador' (S.P. 71. 23, f. 213). Probably later instances will be found in Turkish texts of formal letters. In 1813 a ruler is described as 'His Highness Ali, Dey of Algiers, Patron Grandee and Bashaw of Three Tails'.

APPENDIX G

The Turkish Capitulations

RYCAUT points out that relations between the sultan and his great land neighbours were political and reciprocal. Representatives, however, of princes in remoter lands, mainly interested in commerce, like England, France, and Holland, presented on arrival gifts which the Turk regarded as a right, 'esteeming his Capitulations and the Articles he makes with those Princes, Privileges and immunities granted their subjects'. Our capitulations began with statements that the ambassador first presented credentials and gifts. The documents were kept in the ambassador's personal custody. We had no *treaty* with Turkey until 1809.

The regencies made treaties on more or less reciprocal terms with maritime powers. Presents were normally sent to rulers of France and England on their accession and renewal of treaties. Relations between England and Algiers were from 1683 to 1806 maintained on a strictly diplomatic, though unusual, basis.

Masson's claim that capitulations of 1535 and 1569 gave France commercial preponderance in the Ottoman empire arose from confusion between political aspirations, emanating from the court, and Provençal economy, which those policies definitely hampered. Undoubtedly Venice and Genoa were more influential commercially in the Levant up to about 1565. So, probably, was England. Jenkinson's arrival in Syria was presumably facilitated by Venetians in Crete and Cyprus.

The negotiations of 1535, according to Charrière, produced simply a *traité d'amitié*, in which Francis proposed that his 'brother and perpetual ally', the King of England, should participate, together with the King of Scotland and the pope. It provided for the appointment of a *bailo* at Constantinople, like the one in Egypt, but mentioned no commercial concessions. Reports from Rincon in 1539 indicate that he had nothing further in writing, and that France had not profited by the Turco-Venetian war, a fact clearly demonstrated by Harvel.

French relations with Turkey proper and Algeria remained essentially political owing to the Spanish menace. Commercial concessions first figure at Constantinople through a dispute in 1578 about privileges granted in 1568 by the Bashaw Ochiali to the brothers Lenche (really Lincio) at La Cala di Massacarrara. The beneficiaries throughout that area, especially the coral-fisheries, were Italian.

The efforts of Catherine de' Medici to profit by the difficulties of Genoa, Florence, and, eventually, Venice during 1564–74 are reflected in du Bourg's activities at Alexandria, Constantinople, and Paris. His proposed capitulations were ridiculed by the ambassador, and resulted only in the appointment of a Florentine, Cristoforo Vento, as French consul in Egypt.

In 1577 the French ambassador claimed that under the Egyptian capitulations the king had from very ancient times enjoyed the right of protecting with his flag foreign vessels trading to Alexandria, but was told by the Grand Vizier that those capitulations contained no such provision and were only a *commandement favorable et volontaire.* They were not a treaty concluded between princes, entailing reciprocal obligations. Early privileges, however, permitted Ragusans to serve all nations, at the charterers' risk. Different arrangements could only be negotiated through a special ambassador.

At Constantinople the position changed radically after 1574. Venice had made peace. Envoys from Genoa, Florence, Lucca, and Milan were competing for concessions and negotiating peace for Spain. Only France, the ambassador said, had nothing to offer. In 1581 de Germigny, after vainly searching Turkish archives from 1530, could only counter Harborne's novel pretensions through the aid of Ochiali, whom he had known in Algiers. He sent new capitulations to Paris with a letter from the sultan requiring Elizabeth to apply through Henri for any treaty of friendship. More important, he succeeded in arranging that Foster's ship should be released under the French flag, and convincing Ochiali that the English were engaged solely in piracy.

Our ambassador requested Catherine to ensure that the 'agent for the English merchants trading into the Levant . . . might on all occasions be recommended by his [the King's] ambassador resident in the Great Turk's court, so good amity might appear to other princes, which kind of princely offices would greatly increase this amity'. Catherine, however, preferred the furtherance of French interests, to the detriment of a joint alliance with Turkey against Spain. A secret conference in March 1583 between Catherine and the consul for 'Frenchmen who trade to Algiers' was probably connected with Tipton's arrival there. By 1585 it was definitely recognized that Harborne was equal in status to any other resident agent, and at Algiers the bashaw emphasized the privileges conferred on England by the recognition of Tipton. Soon after Henri waived claim to higher rank than *bailo.*

In 1593 de Brèves claimed to have obtained new and very favourable capitulations, but much later a French ambassador knew of none before 1604. England certainly had from 1593 the right (but not exclusively) to protect foreign vessels trading to Ottoman ports. Though Henri IV had by 1598 given Dutch vessels general authority to trade there under the French flag, the English consul actually collected the consulage (Braudel, p. 501 n.). Difficulty often arises, especially when studying correspondence with Constantinople, in distinguishing ratified agreements from proposals or assertions.

Our ambassadors obviously profited by the possession of continuous documentary evidence from 1593. The English text, however unsatisfactory, leaves no doubt about its real intent. The Turks wished Christian rivals to settle details between themselves. The most important question for French and English up to 1798, the revenue (consulage) that could be extracted from other parties, was apparently amicably adjusted.

APPENDIX H

Turks and Moors in British Waters

THERE is no reliable evidence of Moslem aggression before 1624, and much to disprove it. Late in 1621, just before open hostilities ceased, such reprisal was regarded as a dread possibility. The letters of Calvert and Chamberlain, and Monson's memorial of 1623 (*Tracts*, iii. 355) about the Lizard Light, clearly indicate that none had taken place.

Positive information comes from a complaint of the privy council to Frizell, 10 June 1625, that two 'Turkish ships of Algiers *have never presumed to come so near his Majesty's coast*'. They were, however, ships of Sallee, which in 1624 came with Dutch allies, masquerading perhaps as Turks, to retaliate for the misconduct of Captain Madox, who seized a Sallee vessel and sold all on board to Spain. They operated near the Severn, a notorious resort of piracy. Captain Court reported that one ship, which returned that year, behaved correctly. Others wintered in Holland, and, according to the Drapers Company, were 'plentifully supplied'. Dutch privateers probably did the chief damage. Flushing was called a 'young Algier'.

In 1627 Harrison, the royal agent, conveyed Moors and guns to Sallee in exchange for 190 English captives (S.P. 71. 12, f. 248). In 1626 an Algiers merchant ship visited Plymouth. In 1629 Charles ordered the Bristol customs to treat Salletines like Englishmen.

The raid on Baltimore, which occurred in June 1631, about eighteen months after notice of a rupture, was a small affair by two ships in an area where our warships were curbing piracies by Nutt and others. Concern was mainly expressed at this exposure of naval weakness. Oppenheim and Lane-Poole accept Dan's hearsay estimate of 237 captives. Frizell's report of 109 agrees substantially with Admiral Button and Smith's *History of Cork*. This work does not substantiate claims that the raid—unrecorded by Birch, Knolles, and Knight—ruined a peaceful, thriving port.

After infractions by English ships, including a second 'mad act' by Madox and Wye, Salleemen appeared in 1635. Damage was disproportionate to the alarm, only 302 Englishmen being liberated from Sallee in 1637.

Evidently occasional Algiers ships approached the channel during the next years since Okeley, d'Aranda, and Spratt were taken by them.

The last visit of which there is definite record before 1675 occurred in Penzance Bay in 1640. While two county histories mention no foreign raid at all, except a much earlier Spanish one, also at Mousehole, the Domestic State Papers contain three conflicting reports of it. Among numerous excuses for official negligence the Deputy Lieutenants of Cornwall cited the damage *said* to have been done on the coast by Turkish pirates, 'reported to be at least 60 men of war'. Though they still had no particulars of actual damage, this version is accepted by Oppenheim. Nine days earlier the mayor and aldermen of Exeter reported that four large Turkish warships had taken nine small craft 'in open view' of Penzance. Another report, apparently from London, said 'those roguish Turkish pirates' had taken from the shore near Penzance '60 men, women and children; this was in the night, for in the day these rogues keep out of sight for fear of the King's ships'. This may be accurate, for a Plymouth report mentioned a combat shortly before, near the Lizard, in which three Turkish cruisers were worsted by a Virginia trader.

The next thirty-five years contain no reliable record of Moslem aggression—certainly none by Algiers. From 1641 parliament in-augurated a policy of peaceful co-operation with Barbary.

The presence of Algiers privateers during strained relations and open war between 1676 and 1681 is usually ignored, though it caused alarm in Ireland, Newfoundland, and New England. At first attention was focused, very curiously, rather on their civil behaviour than on their questionable right of search in the area vaguely described as 'waters belonging to the King of Great Britain' and sometimes as 'the Channel'. During the hostilities France granted Algiers cruisers facilities at Brest. In 1686–7 and 1817 Algiers and Tunis privateers passed through the channel, but without hostility to Britain.

APPENDIX I

Morocco

MOROCCO was the first non-European country with which we had permanent relations. During Elizabeth's reign its value as a market for English cloth was officially recognized, as also the strategic importance of Tetuan and El Arisch.

The statement in *E.B.* xviii. 857 that 'France was the first to appoint a consul to Morocco in 1577, Great Britain only doing so a century later' is most misleading. Our State Papers contain a nearly complete list of accredited agents from 1577 to 1640, much superior to rival nations in authority and continuity. The ship which in 1629 brought our agent to Sallee was named *Consull*.

Budgett Meakin's *Moorish Empire* (London, 1899) states 'when at last England appeared on the scene (in 1585) it was only to obtain an edict from Ahmed V that English subjects should not be molested or enslaved'. English ships traded with Morocco under Portuguese authority more than a century earlier, and directly before the recapture of Agadir in 1541. In 1575 Morocco was more profitable than Portugal to the London customs. In 1585, when the Barbary Company was founded to combine the concessions of the Earl of Leicester and his rivals, it provided 'a royall trade for the vente of the commodities of this land'.

After 1640 England was represented only fitfully by consuls at Tetuan or Sallee. Between the abandonment of Tangier and 1728 formal representation ceased entirely.

Sallee was normally the principal port of Morocco, serving both Fez and Mequinez, and much used by English and Dutch ships. Clearly its people were not 'savages', as stated by Oppenheim. Commercial relations were satisfactory, apart from the small wars of 1624–5 and 1635–7. In the interval Sallee, as our ally against Spain, furnished the fleet with supplies.

The appearance of Rainsborough's squadron in 1637 followed another political understanding, aimed at the 'rebels' of New Sallee. The *Casbah* adjoining was not susceptible to naval blockade or bombardment (e.g. Dapper, p. 179). Operations were conducted mainly on land by the chief of Old Sallee in conjunction with Rainsborough and the emperor. Penn claimed, and received, a small reward for devising the plan which perhaps resulted in a negotiated peace. Oppenheim was evidently unacquainted with Carteret's dispatches, Penn's report, the geographical situation and local history. The French, who inadvertently destroyed a Sallee fleet in 1636, generally ignore Rainsborough's action.

English relations with Morocco after the Civil War are hard to understand, especially as goodwill was essential to the maintenance of Tangier and Gibraltar. Muley Ismail preferred us to other Europeans, and we generally appreciated Moroccan ambassadors. Rooke cultivated cordial relations, and once presented Salletines with a small warship to replace one burned in error.[1] Unfortunately after our lasting peace with Algiers began Muley made war on it, and King William was represented in Algiers and Morocco by English and Dutch consuls with incompatible policies.

Though Tetuan was friendly and supplied Gibraltar with necessaries, including drinking-water for fleets, permanent peace was only established in 1728 after a curious little war. Owing to irresponsible consular arrangements the position was very unsatisfactory up to the Spanish crisis of 1760. The first consul general, John Russell, actually worked at the Admiralty, and his ultimate successor is said to have turned Mohammedan. One emperor complained of our incompatible attitudes—of friendship with the north coast and indifference or hostility to the rest of the country. Only after a short but serious breach towards the end of the great siege did relations definitely improve.

After the time of Charles I England had no post at the imperial court. Under the Georges official headquarters were at Tetuan or Tangier, while France established a consulate-general at the, diplomatically, more convenient sites of Sallee or Mogador. When peace was made and a vice-consul appointed in 1729 English merchants were already peaceably settled at Sallee.

While Morocco might be called Barbary both officially and colloquially a tendency developed in diplomatic circles towards the end of the eighteenth century to regard the Barbary States as synonymous with the Turkish regencies. As our consuls at Tangier were ignorant of the language and national affairs Morocco came to be considered as little more than an appendage of Gibraltar.

---

[1] I am indebted for this information to the *Journal* of the Rev. Thomas Pocock, Chaplain of H.M.S. *Ranelagh* in 1704, generously lent me by Captain E. L. Cardale, R.N. retd.

APPENDIX J

Mediterranean Passes

THIS system successfully solved the vexed question of right of search, then particularly acute in the Mediterranean owing to the novel claim that capitulations granted free passage at sea to an Ottoman port. Actually, they only authorized ships to trade freely *at*, not *to*, such port through the appropriate consul. Ships originally received safe-conducts from the sultan or his representative. Their inspection at sea provided a guarantee of ships' destinations and cargoes. Even a pope might recognize the sultan's pass (Hakluyt, v. 218). In 1628 Digby procured a pass from Algiers before leaving England for Syria.

The procedure finally evolved in 1682 did credit to both parties. Objections by Pepys and Nottingham concerned form rather than substance. Subsequent changes envisaged extension and liberalization. A Dey's desire to facilitate direct trade between the plantations and Mediterranean was frustrated by vested interests. The system was quickly adopted by Tunis, Tripoli, Morocco, and Turkey.

Its practical value was demonstrated by its permanence. McCulloch's statement that it continued into Victorian times is corroborated by Brenton in 1838 and Keppel in 1842. France adopted the system more liberally, and complained in 1826 that two vessels carrying its mails had not been visited in the manner originally agreed in its Algiers treaty of 1666.

In 1663 'these instruments were engraved upon parchment and were ornamented with the picture of a ship or otherwise decorated with marine deities. Through the engraving scolloped indentures were made and the scolloped tops were sent to the Barbary cruisers, who were instructed to allow all vessels producing passes that fitted these tops to pass unmolested.' T. Keppel, *Life of Augustus Viscount Keppel*, 2 vols. 1842, i. 158–9. Other passes were invalid. They must bear the official seal of the Admiralty and signature of the lord high admiral or three commissioners. In 1827 they were issued by the heir-apparent. From 1682 they might be signed by the Lord High Admiral of Scotland.

Issue occasioned no great expense or inconvenience. The official fee was 25*s*., reduced to 20*s*. in 1682. In 1700 blank forms were issued to consuls in southern Europe—but not Africa—with a shilling stamp impressed. Changes in the perforation were notified through proclamations and customs officers. Though periodical issue of new passes, to prevent misuse, was in our interest, obstruction came from some ministers, who even suggested a *quid pro quo* for such 'condescension' or 'concession'. The conventional account of difficulties caused by the capture of Minorca is entirely incompatible with dates, corresponding irregularities at Gibraltar, &c., and the evidence of Bruce himself. The government issued new passes with surprising alacrity in 1776 and 1782. Failure to furnish Malta with passes and the irregular practices of Nelson and Ball, despite consular warnings, have resulted in the Algerines being labelled 'pirates'.

Our treaties up to 1816 required little modification. The principle of the passes was never in doubt. Consular reports throughout the eighteenth century show that infractions by Algiers captains were rare and promptly punished. The views of Collingwood, who carefully studied such matters, are also important because the whole character of our relations with the regencies depended on the system and manner of its operation.

In 1755 our consul reported the issue of 500 passes to the Genoese and complaint by our friend, the Dey, that the governors of Minorca and Gibraltar were 'devils' who sold passes, not least to Majorcans. In 1773, some years after prohibition of these corrupt practices, Campbell Fraser, an exceptionally arrogant and hostile consul, wrote: 'the bringing to light the Iniquity Practised with regard to Mediterranean Passes had been as disagreeable as necessary a Branch of my Duty . . . an unwearied application'. He had one day the 'mortification' to observe eight vessels with British colours anchored at Algiers, and wonder how many were genuine. In 1796 Jervis, writing to the new consul about the Dey's grievances, continues: 'The history of passports, both at Algiers and at most of the consulates on the African and European side of the Mediterranean, is disgraceful to the British character.'

In 1813 another naval commander, Blaquiere, publicly complained from Malta of 'the extreme facility with which foreigners of every description have been enabled to procure Mediterranean passes'. Of 800 privateers registered as British he reckoned that 90 per cent. were owned and operated by Genoese, Italians, Greeks, and Albanians. He complains of the 'innumerable outrages and daring piracies' of these privateers, especially Greeks, of prejudice to national interests through trading with the enemy, and of practices 'particularly hurtful to the commerce of Malta'. Nothing could be more scathing than Maitland's criticism in 1814 of 'the most troublesome dunghill of corruption that I ever met with'.

In 1815 our consul at Tripoli complained of the sale of 500 British passes by the consul at Genoa for 30 dollars apiece. The bashaw agreed to recognize them, if assured that they had official sanction.

APPENDIX K

Blake at Tunis

VARIOUS statements tending to magnify the importance of the celebrated voyage or obscure its purpose may be dismissed as obvious inaccuracies. They ignore such vital considerations as dates, which apparently still range between 1650 and 1665, conditions in Barbary, and our relations with the Mediterranean. The voyage did not coincide with an attack on Rupert's ships or the arrival of the first English fleet in the Mediterranean 'since the Plantagenets'. It did not result from hostility to the regencies or violations of Lawson's treaty with Tunis of 1662 (Broadley, i. 53). It was not dispatched to 'exact compensation from the duke of Tuscany, the knights of Malta, and the piratical states of North Africa, for wrongs done to English merchants' (*E.B.* iv. 36 and vii. 494). That mission was not 'executed with complete success', nor, judging by contemporary evidence, English and foreign, did it contribute to national prestige or imperial expansion. The claim that it 'taught a wholesome moral lesson to the world' is the final development of Clarendon's legend.

The voyage began at a time of unusual peace, ruffled only by 'pirateries réciproques' of England and France and by the desire of Venice to involve its new English friends with its Turkish enemies. Cromwell had no antipathy to Islam (Carlyle, iv. 231), while our merchants hoped to expand trade with it. Liberation of English prisoners was certainly not a pressing issue or imposed by force. The primary object of Cromwell's 'bewildering changes of front' was probably peace in the Mediterranean (Corbett, i. 271–93).

The suggestion that Blake's action in Tunis waters represented a landmark in naval history originated partly in journalistic reports, but mainly from Clarendon's imaginary account of Blake's triumph over the ships of Algiers, 'where he anchored in their very mole'. He expressly states that the harbour at Tunis was entered by ships' boats. This has been elaborated into Callender's 'ignominious destruction of the Tunisian navy' in 'land-locked waters... protected by a strong castle and armed moles', manned by 'witless pirates'. There was, in fact, no harbour for ships between Bizerta and Cape Bon—only a roadstead notoriously open to attack. The 'mauvais fort' (Masson) or 'slight old building' (Holsteyn) of La Goletta was connected with a tower at Porto Farina by improvised works, armed with ships' guns and designed, as in 1535, to prevent landings (see also Coxere, Weale, Dapper, d'Arvieux, Uring, &c.).

The destruction of the 'two fortresses by English guns' is refuted by accounts of Weale and the *George*. The warships and castles were surely never within effective range. In 1640 Coppin says Porto Farina Bay was very shallow and 'big ships stay far off'. In 1710 Taubman writes 'men of war ride in the road happily distant from any castle's reach'. Experience of three centuries along the Barbary coast from Sallee to Tripoli emphasized the vital difference between control of its waters and successful naval bombardment. Little improvement in armament of forts took place, or was required, for centuries after the time of Charles V and Kheir-ed-din. Indifference to the use of artillery on land or sea was notorious.

Development of the legend is seen in Burchett's destruction of '60 great guns' on the Castle of Porto Farina; Yonge's 'most formidable forts, bristling with cannons and strengthened with walls of enormous thickness'; and Playfair's 'whole artillery of Porto Farina, not less than 120 guns of large calibre'. The description of Blake's bombardment by a contemporary (unfortunately untraceable) writer as 'only smoke and noise' is partially confirmed by Blake and Crapnell.

Reasonably precise information is available about the Barbary States. Taubman scoffs at the 'impregnable castle' of La Goletta with its 15 guns manned by renegades. The narrow entrance of the new harbour of Porto Farina (completed about 1660) was defended by 2 stone-guns and a chain. The only other protection was the old tower with 9 six-pounders. Paul (1660) and Uring (1713) thought the harbour very vulnerable. The equally important fort at Bona was armed with 5 small rusty guns and was useless against shipping (Taubman). In 1785 Hérault found only 2 large cannons at Tripoli—one Turkish, the other inscribed England, 1519. Even as late Algiers and Tunis used nothing larger than a twelve-pounder.

I have only seen two foreign references. An English vessel reported at Zante the destruction of thirty-five Tunis ships of 'high board'. Clarendon's papers record Dutch rumour of Blake's total defeat.[1] Neither Blake nor the Tunis action is mentioned by Rycaut, who in 1663 met the Dey at Tunis; by Paul, who sneered at a republican navy; by Jal, apart from earlier disparagement of Blake; or by Duro, who considered the voyage a failure. The action is ignored by Burnet and James's Introduction.

[1] By Algiers, 1657, Cal. Clarendon iii. 287.

APPENDIX L

The Algiers Army

CONTEMPORARY accounts illustrate the peculiar character and continuity of the regency during three centuries. During the 'obscure' period of the 'corsair state' detailed studies of its military, administrative, and economic systems contrast sharply with brief, conflicting references to its marine. Criticisms of 'organized' privateering indicate that its ships existed for imperial purposes rather than private enterprise. The regency's traditional responsibilities included maintenance of expeditionary forces and accumulation of public treasure from the sultan's dues on prizes, slaves, and concessions. In Algiers, the sultan's official 'Garrison of the West', all government activities were concentrated, including the control and equipment of its ships, usually operated in regular fleets or squadrons. Effective co-operation between Porte and regency was continuous. The sultan repaired damage by Exmouth's bombardment. Algiers' small navy disappeared in the Greek war.

Christians were bewildered by a provincial administration under a Dey elected for life by his fellow soldiers as, simultaneously, autocrat and slave of the state. He was likened by d'Arvieux to a King of Poland, by Shaw to a stadtholder, and by Le Marchand to a temporal pope. The chief cog in the state machine, he could in the public interest be quietly eliminated. His death, as Peysonnel remarked, was no great matter. Our records show how little disturbance it caused. A Dey, who was necessarily a native Turk, regular soldier, and Mecca pilgrim, was almost invariably succeeded without delay by one of his principal officials—the Treasurer, Minister of War (Aga), or Khoja (adjutant general) of Native Horse. The army differed little in character or composition from that of Mahomet II. In 1621 it consisted of 15,000 janissaries, recruited from natives of Anatolia or renegade Christians, 14,000 Zouaves, later described as 'sepoys', and 30,000 Moorish horse (Des Hayes de Courmesnin). The last were unpaid and only used in war-time against other Moors. Gradually the proportion and functions of Moorish soldiers increased, and the three great provinces were governed by native beys with native troops. Renegade Christians ceased to be actively employed in the late seventeenth century.

The reputation of these Turkish soldiers has suffered from the ignorance and rancour of Rycaut, who eulogized the 'supereminent' qualities of the Ottoman army, and Shaw's immature essay (1729), which is inconsistent with later observations. Of the first Turks in Algiers Pellissier writes: 'the dignity of their manners, the regularity of their conduct impressed all minds with so profound a feeling of their superiority that everyone thought them born to command'. Somewhat similar sentiments were expressed by Pananti (1814) and the French at the surrender. Knight depicts their world-wide fame as the bravest and most desperate of all Turks (1638), and Decatur proclaimed them second only to Americans (1815). Their 'excellent discipline' was praised by Foss (1793) and, in very unusual circumstances, by French officers at Bona in 1833.

Playfair and Plantet produce no evidence that they were recruited or kidnapped from 'dregs' or criminals. They were more often disparaged as tradesmen or 'taken straight from the plough'. Peysonnel (1725) mentions the soldiers' democratic spirit and his great surprise at their good sense, moderation, and industry. 'Leur amour pour l'État va au-delà du croyable.' 'Have the Romans been more valiant than the Algerines? Have they kept 200 leagues in good order with 100 men?' Venture (1788) reported the country so quiet that military tours from Algiers had ceased, and that the people of Djidjelli still retained the same privileges as Turkish soldiers. At the conquest that right still existed among the Zouaves round Bougie, and the town was 'free from every impost'. Such concessions apparently dated from the Barbarossas.

The Turks, normally docile and patient, were liable to violent explosions of rage when suspicious of treachery or fraud. Popular conceptions of Deys as 'ferocious monsters' are not supported by contemporary records. Some of those most abused in history gave practical proof, at personal risk, of restraint, consideration, and friendship. Able British and French consuls liked and respected Sidi Hassan (1791–8), whose outbursts might impress distant admirals. 'Naturally gentle and kind', still endowed after long official experience with 'mildness and patience', he found himself, as a prominent neutral, subjected to an intolerable strain, but left a pleasing memory behind. In order to do justice to the military character more detailed study is essential of less fortunate victims of external policies—Mustapha, the 'tiger' Dey (1798–1805), Omar, eulogized by Pananti, Playfair, and de Grammont (1815–17), and Hussein (1818–30).

SELECT BIBLIOGRAPHY

A comprehensive bibliography of works which throw direct or incidental light on our relations with the Barbary States would be so enormous as to defeat its purpose, especially as the most convincing evidence may at times be of a purely negative character. The object of the general bibliography of printed books is simplification through concentration on standard publications, which should be easily available to a student. References to other works, usually of a more particular nature, will be found in footnotes to the appropriate chapters. The most valuable source for such a study will obviously be our own contemporary records and narratives. They cover a very extensive but largely neglected field. The elaborate and erudite bibliographies of foreign historians, such as Fernand Braudel and Roger Le Tourneau (Ch.-André Julien II) mentioned below, provide wider scope for investigation into Barbary history. Some attempt has been made, through the medium of short appendices, to clear up certain points of special interest to British readers.

HISTORICAL MANUSCRIPTS

The only such documents that I have been able to examine for this purpose are contained in two repositories:

(*a*) The State Papers preserved at the Public Record Office, of which the most important series for the Barbary States is listed under S.P. 71. Useful information for the same period is also available from corresponding series for Spain, various Italian states, and the Levant Company.

(*b*) Various collections of manuscripts in the possession of the British Museum contain information of the greatest importance for this phase of our history. Those of which particular use has been made in this work are listed under the titles of Additional, Sloane, Cotton, &c.

The Rawlinson and Tanner collections of manuscripts are in the Bodleian Library.

PRINTED ARCHIVES AND OTHER DOCUMENTS, ETC., OF NATIONAL INTEREST

The most important, naturally, are those published by the Public Record Office. Of these special interest attaches, because of continuity, to:

(*a*) Rymer's '*Foedera*', 1066–1654, 3 vols., 1869–85, a very valuable collection of public acts, which is continued by the series of Royal Proclamations available also in the British Museum. The *Registers of the Acts of the Privy Council of England*, 1542–1628, and their *Colonial Series*, 1613–1783, should be read in conjunction with them.

(*b*) The *Calendars of Domestic State Papers*, which are almost continuous from 1509 to 1704 and contain a surprising amount of information about foreign events.

(*c*) The *Calendars of Colonial State Papers*, 1574–1736; and

(*d*) The *Calendars of State Papers*, &c., relating to English affairs drawn mainly from Venetian archives, 1202–1675.

Other calendars containing less complete series of *Foreign State Papers, Irish State Papers, Journals of the Board of Trade and Plantations, Treasury Books, Treasury Papers*, &c., are exceedingly helpful at various times.

The very valuable historical information provided in the past by numerous private collectors and editors, especially in reproducing official correspondence, has been supplemented in more recent times by the enterprise of various learned societies. An even more comprehensive continuation is provided by the *Historical Manuscripts Commission* through its publication of extracts and reports from collections of family archives and other privately owned manuscripts.

OTHER CATEGORIES OF PRINTED BOOKS

(*a*) *General Works of Reference*

The Cambridge Modern History, 14 vols., Cambridge, 1907–12. It unfortunately contains no special study of Turkish affairs later than the sixteenth century.

Dictionary of National Biography, 73 vols., 1885–1940.

Encyclopaedia Britannica, 11th ed., Cambridge, 1910–11. This has been selected partly because it has been a constant companion for over forty years, and partly because it represents so well the general point of view during the late nineteenth and early twentieth centuries.

The Historians' History of the World, 24 vols., London–New York, reprint 1926.

A History of England, ed. Sir C. OMAN (1904), 7 vols., London (Methuen), reprint 1924–7.

D. MACPHERSON, *Annals of Commerce*, 4 vols., London, 1805.

The Oxford English Dictionary on Historical Principles, 10 vols., Oxford, 1888–1928.

Oxford History of England, ed. Sir G. N. CLARK, 11 vols., Oxford, from early times to 1870.

L. F. A. VON PASTOR, *The History of the Popes from the end of the Middle Ages*, trans. F. J. Antrobus, 14 vols., London, 1891–1924.

Political History of England, ed. W. HUNT and R. POOLE, 12 vols., London, 1905–7.

L. VON RANKE, *History of the Popes during the 16th and 17th Centuries*, trans. E. Foster, 3 vols., London, 1847–8.

The Shorter Oxford English Dictionary on Historical Principles, 2 vols., Oxford, 1933.

(b) International Law, Treaties, &c.

Antonio de Capmany y Montpalau, *Memorias históricas sobre la marina, commercio y artes de la antigua ciudad de Barcelona*, 4 vols., 1779–92.

George Chalmers, *Collection of Treaties between Great Britain and other Powers*, 2 vols., London, 1790, contains texts for the Barbary States from 1662 to 1783.

G. B. Depping, *Histoire du Commerce entre le Levant et l'Europe depuis les Croisades jusqu'à la fondation des colonies d'Amérique*, 2 vols., Paris, 1830.

Sir Edward Hertslet, *A Complete Collection of the Treaties etc. between Great Britain and Foreign Powers*, 24 vols., 1820–1907. It omits even more of the early treaties in vol. i.

J. M. Pardessus, *Collection des lois maritimes antérieures au XVIIIe siècle*, 6 vols., Paris, 1828–47.

E. Rouet de Card, *Traités de la France avec les pays de l'Afrique du nord: Algérie, Tunisie, Tripolitaine, Maroc*, Paris, 1906. It contains some very illuminating information, but is apparently not entirely complete.

Sir Travers Twiss, *Black Book of the Admiralty*, 4 vols., London, 1874.

(c) French Publications of Archives and other Contemporary Documents

H. de Castries, *Les Sources inédites de l'histoire du Maroc de 1530 à 1845*. The compilation of this monumental work from the archives and libraries of a number of nations is still in progress. There are separate series for France, Portugal, the Netherlands, England, and Spain.

E. Charrière, *Négociations de la France dans le Levant*, 4 vols., Paris, 1848–60.

P. Grandchamp, *La France en Tunisie, 1582–1620*, 3 vols., Tunis, 1920–5. Unfortunately, I have not been able to obtain any of the later volumes of this extremely valuable record of notarial documents in the French consulate.

Pierre Heinrich, *L'Alliance franco-algérienne au XVIe siècle*, Paris, 1898.

E. Plantet, *Correspondance des Deys d'Alger avec la Cour de France, 1579–1830*, 2 vols., Paris, 1889. In the reference notes this is cited as 'Plantet' without any qualification.

E. Plantet, *Correspondances des Beys de Tunis et des Consuls de France, 1577–1830*, 3 vols., Paris, 1893. The texts of both works are invaluable as a guide to the attitude of those rulers, but the notes and introduction in the Tunis work are much more reliable and informative.

(d) Naval and Maritime

R. C. Anderson, *Naval Wars in the Levant*, Liverpool, 1952.

J. Burchett, *A Complete History of the most Remarkable Transactions at Sea*, London, 1720.

(Sir) J. S. Corbett, *England in the Mediterranean, 1603–1713*, 2 vols., London, 1904.

Cesareo Fernández Duro, *Armada Española desde la unión de los reinos de Castilla y de Aragón, 1476–1664*, 4 vols., Madrid, 1895. It is very valuable for its early history of Spanish relations with North Africa, but much less reliable in connexion with the eastern Mediterranean. The work after completion in 1903 by the addition of 5 volumes, which are of surprisingly little interest for this purpose, is described as *Armada Española desde la unión de los reinos de Castilla y de León*, 9 vols., Madrid, 1895–1903.

F. LÓPEZ DE GÓMARA, *Crónica de los muy nombrados Omiche y Haradin Barbarroja*, ?1545 (Memorial Histórico Español vi, Real Academia de la Historia). It is clearly intended to be primarily a naval work and may be merely an alternative title of his *Las Batallas de Mar de Nuestros Tiempos*. His account of events in Algeria is based on hearsay of a very dubious character. His chief interest evidently was the career of Kheir-ed-din as Admiralissimo of the sultan's navy. A number of Spanish documents are reproduced as an appendix to the narrative.

F. LÓPEZ DE GÓMARA, *Annales del Emperador Carlos Quinto*, ?1566, reproduced with an English translation, introduction, and footnotes by R. B. Merriman as *Annals of the Emperor Charles V*, Oxford, 1912. This very factual chronicle makes no reference to the Barbarossas as seamen or to their naval exploits at any time. Cited as *Annales*.

A. JAL, *Abraham du Quesne et la marine de son temps*, 2 vols., Paris, 1873.

G. LACOUR-GAYET, *La Marine militaire de la France, 1624–61*, Paris, 1911, covering the administration of Cardinals Richelieu and Mazarin.

G. LACOUR-GAYET, *La Marine militaire de la France sous Louis XV*, Paris, 1902.

G. LACOUR-GAYET, *La Marine militaire de la France sous Louis XVI*, Paris, 1905.

T. LEDIARD, *The Naval History of England*, 2 vols., London, 1735. Described by Laughton (*D.N.B.* xxxii. 339) as 'both comprehensive and accurate' for its time, it seems to have served as the main basis for traditional accounts in Barbary waters.

NARCISSUS LUTTRELL, *Brief Historical Relation of State Affairs*, 6 vols., London, 1678–1714. They contain a number of news-items about Algiers and the Mediterranean generally, some of them purely imaginary.

Memoirs of the English Affairs, Chiefly Naval, From the Year 1660 to 1673 written by His Royal Highness, James Duke of York, London, 1729.

Naval Tracts of Sir William Monson, ed. by M. OPPENHEIM, *with a commentary drawn from the State Papers and other original sources* (N.R.S.), 5 vols., London, 1913.

M. OPPENHEIM, *History of the Administration of the Royal Navy and of Merchant Shipping in relation to the Navy, 1509–1660*, London, 1896.

CHARLES BOUREL DE LA RONCIÈRE, *Histoire de la Marine française*, 6 vols., Paris, 1932.

JOHN SMITH, *Life, Journals, and Correspondence of Pepys*, 2 vols., London, 1841. This includes the *Tangier Journal*.

M. J. E. SUE, *Correspondance de H. d'Escoubleau de Sourdis*, 3 vols., Paris, 1839. It contains very interesting information about the naval activities of Cardinal Richelieu in the Mediterranean and especially about relations with Algiers and Tunis in the period 1637–41.

M. J. E. SUE, *Histoire de la Marine française*, 3 vols., Paris, 1855–6. The narrative only covers the period 1658–79 and was presumably terminated by his sudden death. The only direct references to the Regencies are found in an Appendix on the *Principes de M. Colbert sur la Marine, 1669–85*, which contains some brief suggestions entitled *Guerre avec les Barbaresques*, i. 529–30. The date suggests they were continued by Colbert's son.

The very valuable contributions of J. R. TANNER:

Pepys' Memoires of the Royal Navy, Oxford, 1906.

Descriptive Catalogue of the Naval MSS. in the Pepysian Library at Magdalene College, Cambridge (N.R.S.), 4 vols., London, 1903–25, referred to else-where as 'Tanner'.

Pepys' Naval Minutes (N.R.S.), London, 1926.

Thurloe's State Papers, compiled by THOMAS BIRCH, 7 vols., London, 1742.

(e) *Voyages and Travels*

AWNSHAM and JOHN CHURCHILL, *A Collection of Voyages and Travels*, 6 vols., London, 1742.

(Sir) C. R. BEAZLEY, *Voyages and Travels*, 2 vols., London, 1902, relating to the sixteenth and seventeenth centuries.

RICHARD HAKLUYT, *The Principal Navigations, Voyages, Traffiques and Dis-coveries of the English Nation*, 12 vols., Glasgow, 1906.

JOHN HARRIS, *Navigantium atque Itinerantium Bibliotheca, or a Compleat Collec-tion of Voyages and Travels*, 2 vols., London, 1705.

J. KNOX, *A New Collection of Voyages, Discoveries and Travels*, 7 vols., London, 1767.

THOMAS OSBORNE, *A Collection of Voyages and Travels*, 2 vols., London, 1745 (also known as the *Harleian Collection of Voyages*).

JOHN PINKERTON, *General Collection of Voyages and Travels*, 17 vols., London, 1808–14.

SAMUEL PURCHAS, *Hakluytus Posthumus or Purchas His Pilgrimes*, 20 vols., Glasgow, 1905.

(f) *Turkish or Levantine History*

FERNAND BRAUDEL, *La Méditerranée et le monde méditerranéen à l'époque de Philippe II*, Paris, 1949, an extremely informative work, which, un-fortunately, only deals slightly with English relations.

SIR E. S. CREASEY, *History of the Ottoman Turks*, London, 1878.

M. EPSTEIN, *Early History of the Levant Company*, London, 1908.

LORD EVERSLEY, *The Turkish Empire*, London, 1924. The chief interest lies in the Preface, pp. 5–7, which describes his sources of information and resultant conviction about Ottoman policy and practices. He gives no bibliography and, with one erroneous exception, cites no authority for statements about the Turkish Regencies.

GEORGE FINLAY, *History of Greece*, new edition by the author and revised by H. F. TOZER, 7 vols., Oxford, 1877.

G. E. HUBBARD, *Day of the Crescent*, Cambridge, 1920.

RICHARD KNOLLES, *Generall Historie of the Turkes*, 1603, a useful work, un-fortunately described as 'now entirely superseded' (*E.B.* xv. 869). Continued by successive authors, of whom SIR PAUL RYCAUT contributed the latest and largest portion. This, like his *Maxims of Turkish Polity*, is paged separately. The best edition is *The Turkish History*, 3 vols., London, 1687–1700. Another edition entitled *The Turkis History . . . with a new continuation from 1629 to 1638 by T. Nabbes*, London, 1638, contains special information which is referred to as Nabbes's work. Rycaut's contributions should be examined with great care. His omissions of important events in Algeria, with which he must have been personally familiar, are very curious.

PAUL MASSON, *Histoire du commerce français dans le Levant au 17ᵉ siècle*, Paris, 1896, and its sequel, . . . *au 18ᵉ siècle*, Paris, 1911, are valuable, painstaking, and conscientious studies. They are not very helpful, however, for Barbary and throw little light on English interests. In the reference notes the earlier work is cited as Masson without further qualification. Its bibliography contains a useful list of contemporary French works.

R. B. MERRIMAN, *Suleiman the Magnificent, 1520–1566*, Cambridge, Mass., 1944.

Relation des Voyages de Monsieur de Brèves etc., Paris, 1628. It includes much information of interest about diplomacy, &c., in the Levant and the Kingdoms of Tunis and Algiers in 1604–6.

Sir Thomas Roe's Negotiations with the Grand Signior, 1621–1628, ed. S. RICHARDSON, London, 1740.

A. C. WOOD, *The History of the Levant Company*, Oxford, 1935.

(g) Special Works on the Barbary States

ABEL BOUTIN, *Anciennes relations commerciales et diplomatiques de la France avec la Barbarie*, Paris, 1902. It is, as its title suggests, deserving of study.

A. M. BROADLEY, *Tunis Past and Present*, 2 vols., Edinburgh, 1882, is the only work in English on the general subject that has come to my knowledge. Though frequently quoted, it is very unsatisfactory from the historical point of view.

F. CHARLES-ROUX, *France et Afrique du Nord avant 1830*, Paris, 1932, a very interesting and comprehensive history of French projects for penetration into that region.

HENRI GARROT, *Histoire Générale d'Algérie*, Algiers, 1910, contains useful additional information.

H. DE GRAMMONT, *Histoire d'Alger sous la domination turque (1516–1830)*, Paris, 1887. Usually regarded as the standard history of the Regency, it is inclined to be chauvinist and anglophobe. He makes no use of English or Dutch sources, and some of his statements are clearly very exaggerated and, not infrequently, contradictory.

PIERRE HUBAC, *Les Barbaresques*, Paris, 1949 (kindly lent me by Sir George Clark). This is the first attempt that I have seen to study the history of those people from their own point of view.

CH.-ANDRÉ JULIEN, *Histoire de l'Afrique du Nord, Tunisie-Algérie-Maroc*, Paris, 1931. As less than a tenth of this comprehensive and erudite work is represented in the extremely important period of history, described as Turkish rule in Algeria and Tunisia (1516–1830), it will be realized that it throws little light on English relations or problems in that area. Its massive bibliography, unfortunately, contains few English works on the Regencies.

S. LANE-POOLE, *The Barbary Corsairs*, Story of the Nations Series, London, 1890. It only contains information of value for the period prior to the inauguration of English official relations with the area.

PAUL MASSON, *Histoire des établissements et du commerce français dans l'Afrique barbaresque, 1560–1793*, Paris, 1903. As in his other works, e.g. *Les Compagnies du Corail*, 1908, and *Les Galères de France, 1481–1781*, 1938, interest is centred principally in the commerce and marine of Marseilles, and English sources of information are ignored.

R. MICACCHI, *La Tripolitania sotto il dominio dei Caramanli*, Rome, 1936.

JOSEPH MORGAN, *A Complete History of Algiers*, 2nd ed., London, 1731, is of little interest apart from the fact that it was utilized by various later writers. He is called an 'unflagging plagiarist' by Playfair, who, according to Lane-Poole, borrowed extensively from him without acknowledgement. It is cited simply as 'Morgan' in the reference notes.

JOSEPH MORGAN, *Several Voyages to Barbary*, London, 1736. The title is misleading, as the book consists mainly of an account of the mission of Père Commelin to redeem French captives, in an English version. The chief value lies in the editorial notes and historical appendix.

JOSEPH MORGAN, *A Compleat History of the Piratical States of Barbary*, London, 1750. It is actually a translation, with some additional matter, of the very valuable work of his French consular colleague, Laugier de Tassy, *Histoire du royaume d'Alger*, Amsterdam, 1727. This latter work was translated into Italian. Morgan's ironical change of title is noteworthy but regrettable. Morgan's book was translated in 1757 as *Histoire des États Barbaresques*.

A. F. NETTEMENT, *Histoire de la conquête d'Alger*, Paris, 1856. It is very misleading in regard to the period of the Turkish occupation.

A. PELLEGRIN, *Histoire de la Tunisie depuis les origines jusqu'à nos jours*, Paris, 1938.

E. PELLISSIER DE REYNAUD, *Annales algériennes*, 3 vols., Paris, 1854. His early history is often weak. It is valuable as a sympathetic study of the contemporary character of the inhabitants and their problems by a highly intelligent administrative official.

SIR R. L. PLAYFAIR, *Scourge of Christendom, annals of British relations with Algiers prior to the French conquest*, London, 1884. It claims to be an historical account of the English consulate at Algiers and our relations with the Regency, but actually throws little light on the essential features of either. It is based largely on extracts from our state archives provided by a painstaking agent in London, but subsequently too often misinterpreted or ignored. These are contained in 4 volumes of MSS. at the P.R.O., Index 13395–8.

S. RANG and J. F. DENIS, *Fondation de la Régence d'Alger, histoire des Barbe-*

rousse, Paris, 1837. The editorial notes appear to me to be more interesting than this native chronicle.

A. RIGGIO, *Tabarca e il riscatto degli schiavi a Tunisia. Da Kara Othman Dey a Kara Moustafa Dey, 1593–1702*, Genoa, 1938.

CH. DE ROTALIER, *Histoire d'Alger et de la piraterie des Turcs dans la Méditerranée*, 2 vols., Paris, 1841.

ALPHONSE ROUSSEAU, *Annales tunisiennes*, Algiers, 1864, is likewise of little historical value.

JANE SOAMES, *The Coast of Barbary*, London, 1938.

R. LE TOURNEUR, *Histoire de l'Afrique du Nord, Tunisie-Algérie-Maroc, de la conquête arabe à 1830* (Ch.-André Julien II), Paris, 1952. A revision of part of Julien's work.

(*h*) *Descriptive works dealing mainly with contemporary history, economy, and administration*

LEO (JOANNES) AFRICANUS, *Historie of Africa*, trans. J. Pory (1600), ed. R. Brown (Hakluyt Society), 3 vols., London, 1896. Originally published in Italian (? from Arabic original), Rome, 1526. It covers the period between the conquest of Granada and the foundation of the Turkish state of Algeria.

EMANUEL d'ARANDA, *Relation de la Captivité et Liberté du Sieur d'Aranda*, Brussels, 1662, 3rd ed. Translated by J. Davies, London, 1666, as *The History of Algiers and its Slavery*. The historical part is unfortunately very poor.

E. BLAQUIERE, *Letters from the Mediterranean*, 2 vols., London, 1813. He commanded a small unit of the Royal Navy and described visits to Tunis, Tripoli, Sicily, and Malta.

JAMES BRUCE, *Travels*, ed. A. Murray, 8 vols., London, 1805.

THOMAS CAMPBELL, *Letters from the South*, 2 vols. (1834), London, 1837.

PIERRE DAN, *Histoire de Barbarie et de ses Corsaires* (1637), Paris, 1649, a very superficial, prejudiced, and apparently confused work by a Redemptionist Father, based on a visit to redeem captives in 1634. As it creates the illusion that Barbary was composed of maritime states it should be compared with Sue's *Escoubleau de Sourdis* (above).

OLFERT DAPPER, *Africa*, trans. J. Ogilby, London, 1670. It contains a very full description of Barbary, and more especially Algeria, based apparently on a number of nearly contemporary narratives, particularly that of Gramaye.

J. B. DE LA FAYE, *État des Régences de Barbarie, Tripoly, Tunis et Alger*, The Hague, 1704, a narrative of an official voyage during the Peace of Ryswick. Together with the works of Paul Lucas and Nathaniel Taubman it throws interesting light on a period generally regarded as obscure and uneventful.

J. Foss, *A Journal of the Captivity and Sufferings of J. Foss; several years a Prisoner at Algiers*, Newburyport, 1798. An American seaman, captured on a United States ship in 1793, he gives a frank and interesting account of Algiers at that time.

J. B. GRAMAYE, *Africae illustratae libri decem in quibus Barbaria gentesque ejus ut olim et nunc describuntur etc.*, Tournoi, 1622, a sort of sequel to the works of Leo and Haedo. He travelled through Barbary after six months' captivity in Algiers. A portion is reproduced by Purchas, vol. ix, who alone is responsible for the introductory abuse.

DIEGO HAEDO, *Topographía e Historia General de Argel*, Valladolid, 1612. A new edition, in much more legible print, by Ignacio Bauer y Landauer, 3 vols., Madrid, 1927, has only come to my notice very recently. Most modern historians quote from English or French translations. It consists of two main works—the *Topography* or general description of Algiers and its people, which is immensely valuable but generally neglected, and the better-known *Epitome de los Reyes de Argel*. The latter, though acclaimed by de Grammont and Lane-Poole as the most trustworthy account of the early history of the Regency, is not even mentioned by some historians. The remainder of Haedo's book, which contains references to Cervantes, was evidently a later work, written apparently in the interests of religious propaganda and, perhaps, to secure eventual royal approval.

L. HÉRAULT, *Voyages dans les États barbaresques de Maroc, Alger etc.*, Paris, 1785.

Histoires des dernières révolutions du Royaume de Tunis et des mouvemens du royaume d'Alger, Paris, 1689 (?Anon. B.M. 279 b. 34).

FRANCIS KNIGHT, *Relation of Seven Years Slavery under the Turks of Algier* (1631–8), in Osborne, ii. He gives a very different account of Dan's mission and of Algerine history. The second part, entitled 'A Description of Algier with its Original Manner of Government, Increase and present flourishing State', contains very valuable material, which has been much neglected. It should be compared with the works of Dapper, A. Roberts, de Tassy, Peysonnel, and Morgan, who may not have known it.

P. B. LORD, *Algiers with notices of the neighbouring States of Barbary*, 2 vols., London, 1835.

P. LUCAS, *Voyage dans la Turquie etc.*, 2 vols., Amsterdam, 1720.

P. LUCAS, *Voyage dans la Grèce etc.*, 2 vols., Amsterdam, 1714.

THOMAS MACGILL, *An account of Tunis, its government etc.*, Glasgow, 1811.

M. DUREAU DE LA MALLE, *Peysonnel et Desfontaines, Voyages dans les régences de Tunis et d'Alger*, Paris, 1838, a reproduction of the recorded experiences of two French scientists. The former by Charles Peysonnel relates to Algeria and Tunisia in 1724–5 and gives a much more thorough, sympathetic, and, probably, reliable account of the city and government of Algiers than Shaw. Unfortunately it was not published until after the Conquest. Desfontaines only describes Tunisia in 1783–6. His general picture of the people, &c., tallies with that of contemporary visitors such as Poiret, 1785–6, and Hérault, 1785.

Mémoires du Chevalier d'Arvieux (?1702), ed. J.-B. LABAT, 6 vols., Paris, 1736. Prototype of the professional consul and diplomat, he was consul at Sidon, Tunis, Algiers, and Aleppo; took part in an important mission to Constantinople; and was a well-known figure at Versailles.

F. PANANTI, *Narrative of a Residence in Algiers*, trans. and adapted by E. Blaquiere, London, 1818, from the original *Avventure e Osservazioni sopra le Coste di Berberia*, 2 vols., Florence, 1817.

A. J. PARÈS, *Un Toulonnais à Alger au XVIIIᵉ siècle ; Meifrund, Pierre Joseph 1723–1814*, Paris, 1931, a unique picture of the residence at Algiers from 1752 to 1802 of a prosperous and influential French merchant.

J. L. M. POIRET, *Voyage en Barbarie*, 2 vols., Paris, 1789. Contains interesting information about Eastern Algeria and Tunisia during 1785–6.

A. ROBERTS, *The Adventures of Mr. T— S—, an English merchant taken prisoner by the Turks of Argiers*, ? London, 1670. It gives a very unusual and, in many respects, informative picture of Algeria during the Commonwealth.

THOMAS SHAW, *Travels . . . relating to Several Parts of Barbary*, Oxford, 1738. References are quoted from the reproduction in Pinkerton, vol. xv. His descriptions of the interior of Algeria and Tunis are of genuine interest. It is regrettable that so much importance has been attached to his earlier and clearly ill-considered account of the government of Algiers.

R. TULLY, *Narrative of Ten Years Residence at Tripoli in Africa* (1783–93), London, 1816.

J. M. VENTURE DE PARADIS, *Alger au XVIIIᵉ siècle* (?1788), ed. E. Fagnan, Algiers, 1898, notes by an able and experienced official at an interesting and important point in Mediterranean history.

(i) Incidental works relating to Mediterranean history and foreign relations

R. BUSQUET, *Histoire de Marseille*, Paris, 1945.

STETSON CONN, *Gibraltar in British Diplomacy*, Yale, 1942.

G. T. GARRATT, *Gibraltar and the Mediterranean*, London, 1939.

Canon Mgr. A. MIFSUD, *Knights Hospitallers of the Venerable Tongue of England in Malta*, Malta, 1914.

H. E. NAPIER, *Florentine History*, 6 vols., London, 1846–7.

Recueil des Instructions données aux Ambassadeurs de France, from the Treaty of Westphalia, 1648. Of the volumes directly connected with the Mediterranean I have found only the following three of more than negative interest:

Vol. VI, *Rome*, ed. G. HANOTAUX, Paris, 1888.

Vol. X, *Naples et Parme*, ed. JOSEPH REINACH, Paris, 1893, contains a most informative historical introduction.

Vol. XIX, *Florence, Modène, Gênes*, ed. ÉDOUARD DRIAULT, Paris, 1912, chiefly interesting for the problems of Corsica and Tabarca.

E. M. G. ROUTH, *Tangier, England's Lost Atlantic Outpost, 1661–84*, London, 1912.

F. SAYER, *History of Gibraltar*, London, 1862.

E. G. SCHAMERHORN, *Malta of the Knights*, London, 1929.

VITO VITALE, *Diplomatici e Consoli della Repubblica di Genova*, 1904–12 (Atti della Società Ligure di Storia Patria, vol. lxiii).

For Dutch sources I have relied mainly on:

P. BLOK, *Life of Admiral (Michiel) de Ruyter*, London, 1933.

I. BLOOM, *The Economic Activities of the Jews of Amsterdam in the 17th and 18th centuries*, Williamsport, 1937.

G. GRINNELL MILNE, *Life of Lieutenant Admiral de Ruyter*, London, 1896.

La Vie de Corneille Tromp, ? Leyden, 1694.

Life of Cornelius van Tromp . . . from 1650, London, 1697 (apparently anonymous translations from the Dutch. References are to the English text).

The best source for Morocco in particular is always the compilation of de Castries (Pays-Bas) up to the Restoration.

INDEX

Names and titles are given in their simplest and commonest form. Owing to diversity of English practice names of Spaniards are accented only in the Bibliography. Only contemporary, i.e. pre-Victorian, authors are normally included.

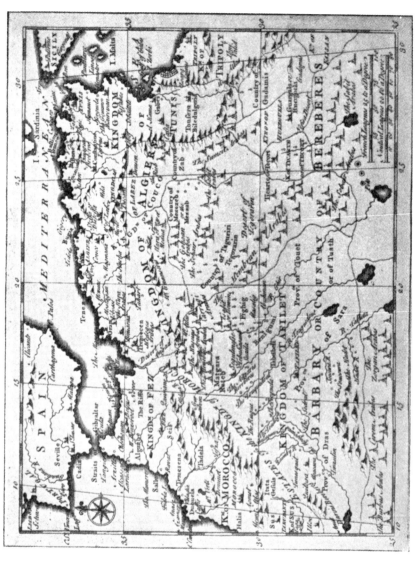

Map of Barbary.   From J. Morgan, *A Compleat History of the Piratical States of Barbary*, 1750